The Politics of Evil

In *The Politics of Evil*, Clifton Crais provides a new interpretation of South African history, and a fresh approach to the study of power, culture, and resistance in the modern world. Encompassing all of South Africa's history in his analysis, Crais examines the formation of an authoritarian political order and the complex ways people understood and resisted the colonial state. He explores state formation as a cultural and political process as well as a moral problem, and he looks at indigenous concepts of power, authority, and evil, analyzing how they shaped cross-cultural encounters and the making of a colonial order. Apartheid represented one of the great evils of the twentieth century. This book reveals how the victims of apartheid understood the triumph of this evil in their lives as they elaborated rich and at times violent visions of a world free of colonial oppression and white supremacy. Professor Crais concludes by looking at the contemporary political transition, the challenges to creating a durable democracy, and the persistence of evil in South Africa.

CLIFTON CRAIS is Professor of History at Kenyon College, Ohio. He is a member of the editorial board of the *Journal of Social History* and the *International Journal of African Historical Studies* and the author of *White Supremacy and Black Resistance in Pre-Industrial South Africa* (Cambridge, 1992), co-editor with Nigel Worden of *Breaking the Chains*, and editor of *The Culture of Power in Southern Africa*. He is also the author of a forthcoming book on the history of poverty, *A Century of Sadness: Power and Poverty in South Africa*.

African Studies Series 103

A list of books in this series will be found at the end of this volume

The Politics of Evil

Magic, State Power, and the Political Imagination in South Africa

Clifton Crais

Kenyon College, Ohio

CAMBRIDGE
UNIVERSITY PRESS

#488 37938

PUBLISHED BY THE PRESS SYNDICATE OF THE UNIVERSITY OF CAMBRIDGE
The Pitt Building, Trumpington Street, Cambridge, United Kingdom

CAMBRIDGE UNIVERSITY PRESS
The Edinburgh Building, Cambridge CB2 2RU, UK
40 West 20th Street, New York, NY 10011-4211, USA
477 Williamstown Road, Port Melbourne, VIC 3207, Australia
Ruiz de Alarcón 13, 28014 Madrid, Spain
Dock House, The Waterfront, Cape Town 8001, South Africa

http://www.cambridge.org

First published 2002

Printed in the United Kingdom at the University Press, Cambridge

Typeface Times 10/12 pt   *System* LATEX 2$_\varepsilon$ [TB]

A catalogue record for this book is available from the British Library

Library of Congress Cataloguing in Publication data

Crais, Clifton C.
The politics of evil: magic, state power, and the political imagination in
South Africa / by Clifton Crais.
    p.   cm. – (African studies series; 103)
Includes bibliographical references (p. 280) and index.
ISBN 0 521 81721 8
1. South Africa – Politics and government.   2. Political culture – South Africa –
History.   I. Title.   II. Series.
DT1798 .C73   2002
968 – dc21   2002017402

ISBN 0 521 81721 8 hardback
African edition ISBN 0 521 53393 7

For Benjamin and Christine

It is worth listening to those who scorn all human things in comparison with wealth and do not think there is any place for great honor and virtue except where riches flow lavishly.

Titus Livy, quoted in Niccolò Machiavelli, *Discourses on Livy*, trans. Harvey C. Mansfield and Nathan Tarcov (Chicago, 1996), 271

Contents

Illustrations

Maps

Acknowledgments

Books have a way of not getting written. This one is no different. During a sabbatical year in 1995 at the Stanford Humanities Center I began writing a project on poverty and the political imagination. That project proved to be far too lengthy and now has grown into two books, of which the present volume is one. The administrative duties that beset the newly tenured created further postponements although, in a way, they provided some perspective on power and how modern bureaucracies function and fail.

More gloriously, the births of Benjamin and Christine redirected energies away from writing and towards fatherhood and the miracle of watching children grow. In elusive yet powerful ways they have helped me see the world more complexly and more wondrously. Parenthood creates its own hustling and bustling, the madness of rushing to and fro, but it also creates pauses and possibility and moments of exquisite silence and sensibility. Reading and discussing *Alice and her Adventures in Wonderland*, especially the monstrous delights of the Queen of Hearts, and the adventures and perils that Harry Potter has faced, helped me consider more carefully the problem of good and evil and magic. Most of all Benjamin and Christine reminded me of the relationship between history and wonderment.

The academic world is one so filled with gifts. I have certainly received my fair share, for which I am very thankful. Fellowships from the Centre for African Studies, University of Cape Town, and the Institute for Social and Economic Research, Rhodes University, helped support some of my preliminary research. Generous funding from the National Endowment of the Humanities and the American Council for Learned Societies permitted additional research. From the beginning to the end institutional support from Kenyon College has been invaluable. A fellowship from the Stanford Humanities Center financed a year of writing and reflection among a group of remarkable and generous scholars. Richard Roberts made my stay at Stanford all the more enjoyable. I thank him for his support and friendship.

I am forever indebted to librarians and archivists working and living on three continents. In South Africa I conducted research at the following institutions: Cape Archives; South African Library; South African Museum; African

Studies Library, University of Cape Town; Mayibuye Centre, University of the Western Cape; Stellenbosch University; Cory Library, Rhodes University; Natal Archives, Pietermaritzburg; University of Natal Library, Pietermaritzburg; Central Archives, Pretoria; Transkei Archives, Umtata; Barlow Rand Archives; Supreme Court, Bloemfontein; Supreme Court, Grahamstown; and the African Studies Library, University of the Witwatersrand. In England librarians and archivists were most helpful at the British Museum; the School of Oriental and African Studies; the Public Records Office; and Rhodes House, Oxford University. Librarians at Stanford and at Kenyon College have been exceptionally helpful and patient. Graham Goddard of the University of the Western Cape Robben Island Mayibuye Archives and Celia Blight at the Cory Library helped me track down photographs. I am also very thankful for the assistance I was afforded by clerks at the Supreme Court, Grahamstown, who very kindly photocopied crucial legal documents concerning the early years of the armed struggle. Mrs. Elaine Heath kindly responded to my queries and provided me with a copy of documents relating to the death of Hamilton Hope.

I have had the opportunity of presenting my thoughts to various seminars around the world: Rutgers Center for Historical Analysis, at a conference on religion and colonialism; Centre for African Studies, University of Cape Town; Institute for Historical Research, University of the Western Cape; Institute for Social and Economic Research, Rhodes University; a conference entitled "Ethnicity, Identity, and Nationalism in South Africa: Comparative Perspectives," Grahamstown; Stanford Humanities Center and the Symposium on Law, Colonialism and Property in Africa, Stanford University; the Kenyon Seminar, Kenyon College; Canterbury University, New Zealand; University of Nairobi; the Global Studies Seminar, Denison University; at the University of Michigan, Ann Arbor, at a conference on reimagining South Africa; and meetings of the African Studies Association and the Northeast Workshop for Southern African Studies. I am thankful for the opportunity to present my work in many places and for the helpful comments of colleagues. I am especially indebted to the History Department at the University of Natal, Durban, for inviting me to share my work with them and with their colleagues at the University of Natal, Pietermaritzburg.

I cannot begin to thank all the people who have helped me these past few years. Here is but a partial list: Richard Abel, Michael Adas, William Beinart, Colin Bundy, Keith Breckenridge, Cathy Burns, Alison Drew, Bob Edgar, George Fredrickson, Gail Gerhart, Donald Goldberg, Jeff Guy, Lewis Hyde, Allen Isaacman, Stephanie Jedd, Jim Lance, Tim Lane, Phyllis Mack, Govan Mbeki, Pat McAllister, Thom McClendon, Meredith McKittrick, Laura Mitchell, Don Moore, Vivek Narayanan, Thembeka Orie, Colin Palmer, Ciraj Rasool, Sean Redding, Richard Roberts, Christopher Saunders, Andre du Toit, Robert Thornton, Leslie Witz, Kerry Ward, Diana Wylie, Nigel Worden,

Dan Younger, and, inspiringly, Davis' "Flamenco Sketches." Jeff Bowman, Reed Browning, Joan Cadden, Ellen Furlough, and Roy Wortman have been most supportive colleagues at Kenyon College. Benjamin Schumacher provided astronomical data. I am also indebted to the administrative assistance of Jean Demaree. Larry and Christine Scully provided a home away from home, one filled with love and art and food and good drink. Special thanks to Mr. and Mrs. Mali, the Pickering family, the congregation of the Church of the Prophetess Nonthetha, and W. M. and the other men who spoke to me in Qumbu in the context of great violence and personal insecurity. I have provided only the initials of interviewees, many of whom requested anonymity. Interviews were conducted in two separate trips, in 1992 and 1993.

I am very indebted to Jessica Kuper, who expertly steered this project through the publication process. Jessica has helped make the African Studies series what it is today. I hope she is proud of this book, one of her final projects before retiring from the Press. Two anonymous readers for the Press offered clear and wise criticisms and suggestions. Their reports helped me clarify many of my arguments. Mary Starkey, copy-editor par excellence, went through the manuscript with a fine-toothed comb, correcting mistakes and suggesting more felicitous phrasing. Elizabeth Gutting also helped with the copy-editing. Jean Demaree was always there to lend a helping hand. The University of Wisconsin Cartographic Laboratory prepared the maps.

Conversations with Govan Mbeki helped me think through many of the issues explored here, especially the rural political struggles he knew so intimately. Govan passed away as this book neared completion. In the middle of my research I was able to speak with Chris Hani, who was born and raised in the Eastern Cape. Our discussion ranged over a number of topics, from Shakespeare to state formation. Mainly we spoke of the historical drama of the Eastern Cape, the lessons its history offered, the many challenges that would face a democratic South Africa. Six months later Chris Hani died at the hands of white extremists.

Over the past fifteen years I have been blessed with teaching some remarkable undergraduate students at Kenyon College. Students in my seminars on cross-cultural encounters and on South African history endured my fascinations, helped me refine many of my ideas, and took some chances. Many helpful comments and recommendations were made by students at a seminar in Spring 2002, who read the entire manuscript. I am very grateful to them. A seminar on the consequences of modernity helped me explore in greater detail the character of global processes and how they have unfolded locally over the past two centuries. An honors seminar on history and theory encouraged me to look beyond the narrow confines of so much historical writing and to remember anew the responsibilities when studying the past, particularly the problems of inequality, sadness, and evil. A number of my Kenyon students are now pursuing advanced degrees. I am especially indebted to Grace Davie, once a student, now friend, and soon to be colleague, who made helpful comments on this project.

Pamela Scully read many of the chapters and made numerous suggestions for revision. More than anyone Pam has helped me write this book, by just being who she is. Together we have raised our two children, negotiated our way through the inevitable challenges facing a dual-career academic couple, and shared ideas and readings in between diapers and the utterly exhilarating exhaustion of parenthood. These have been the best delays of one's life.

Chronology

1780s–1880s	The hundred years of colonial war
1853	Cape Colony receives representative rule
1865	Discovery of diamonds in Griqualand West
	Annexation of British Kaffraria (later Ciskei homeland)
1870s	Series of colonial wars and raids in the Transkei
1872	Cape Colony receives responsible government
	Creation of the Department of Native Affairs
1878	Peace Preservation Act
1880–1	Widespread rebellion and conflict in Transkei and Basutoland
1886	Discovery of gold on the Witwatersrand
1894	Annexation of Pondoland, completion of the colonial conquest of the Transkei, Glen Grey Act
1899–1902	South African War
1910	Act of Union
1913	Natives Land Act
1920s	Increasing segregation
1920	Native Affairs Act
1927	Native Administration Act
1939	Betterment Act
1948	National Party victory
1950s	Beginning of apartheid
1951	Bantu Authorities Act, introduced into Transkei in 1956
1952	Native Laws Amendment Act
1960s	Triumph of apartheid
1960	Pondoland Revolt, widespread resistance and repression
1994	First democratic elections

Introduction

Voters waited patiently in queues that circled around city blocks or twisted a mile or more across the countryside. People who had never before been allowed to vote entered the polling stations and marked their ballots. "Now I am a human being," a black man said, as South Africa held its first democratic elections in 1994. Nelson Mandela declared that "never again shall it be that this beautiful land will again suffer the oppression of one by another." So ended one of the great disgraces of the twentieth century, the collapse of apartheid and the withering of white supremacy at the southern tip of Africa.[1]

A decade earlier, at the beginning of a wave of protest and violent repression that led to apartheid's dissolution, few people had believed that democracy would arrive without a violent and prolonged revolution. Massive popular resistance and horrible state violence did occur. The security forces arrested some 30,000 people in the ten years between the outbreak of widespread resistance in 1984 and the elections. Tens of thousands of people died in political violence, far more than the bloody conflicts in Northern Ireland or Israel. By the late 1980s many areas of the country had fallen to military occupation. In the final years of apartheid torture had become a ubiquitous feature of police interrogation. So also had clandestine "third force" operations that carried out numerous murders and massacres. In the famous Boipatong massacre of July 1992 some thirty-eight people died while, quite literally on the other side of town, politicians struggled to design a democratic future for the country.[2]

But the armies of the liberation movements never marched triumphantly down the streets of Pretoria. By the early 1990s Nelson Mandela had been released from his many years in prison and the apartheid government had unbanned the African National Congress (ANC) and other political organizations, many of whose leaders languished in prisons or had lived for decades in exile in Africa, Europe and the Americas. Politicians set out on the difficult and all too frequently bloody road from the authoritarianism and racial oppression of apartheid to democracy and the political reconstruction of South Africa. Again in 1999 South Africans went to the polls, cast their ballots, and delivered an overwhelming victory to the ANC.

The challenges the country faces are daunting. Democracy has arrived, at least in terms of formal political institutions, but South Africa remains a place of horrific inequality and chilling violence, the most visible legacies of colonialism, apartheid, and hatred. Measured in terms of the distribution of household income, South Africa has had, and continues to have, among the greatest disparity between wealthy and poor anywhere in the contemporary world.[3] Among black South Africans the unemployment rate averages more than 40 percent; in many rural areas the rate tops 70 percent. The violence and tyranny of everyday poverty remain a pervasive feature of the social landscape: grossly inadequate housing, water, and sanitation; disease, malnutrition, and infant death; alcoholism, broken families, sexual violence, the jealousies and hatreds born of desperation, and the continued bloody persecution of the innocent and the suspected whose bodies are beaten and set alight. Three-quarters of the poor live in rural areas; the Eastern Cape Province alone accounts for approximately 25 percent of South Africa's poor. Most recently South Africa faces one of the world's worst HIV/AIDS crises, with infection rates in parts of Natal and the Eastern Cape reaching as high as 30 percent of the rural population.[4]

At the same time the local state has all but collapsed in parts of the country, especially in the former sham "homeland" of the Transkei in the Eastern Cape, one of the putatively self-governing states created under South Africa's policy of grand apartheid or "separate development." The few, largely inadequate services that once had been available have largely disappeared. Corruption is rife. Illegal weapons have flooded into the area. Since 1993 hundreds of people have met violent deaths in conflicts over livestock and other resources and over the economic largesse of the "new" South Africa. In 1996, to take but one example, seven men massacred thirteen people, burnt their huts and destroyed their property. The violence has been so bad that the ANC government appointed a commission to look into stock theft, violence, and political corruption; there was even talk of calling in the military, a surreal prospect given South Africa's recent history of state violence. According to one reporter "the situation" has "degenerated into endless violence. Men, women and children fled their homes, while others were killed . . . Those who managed to flee went to 'nowhere'." "We want to sleep in our houses," one resident pleaded. "It's a long time that we have been sleeping in the mountains with our children."[5]

During the day struggles arise over access to and control over political power. At night different conflicts unfold. There are battles between thieves and their enemies. Men are shot down. Thieves are captured. In a hidden place men suspend a suspected robber over a fire and demand confession. The man screams, flesh burns, the suspect dies. The night is filled with mysterious, dangerous movement, the motion of witches and the terrible, seemingly relentless violence of men. At the top of a cliff a woman has been accused of witchcraft. The belly of a live horse is slit open. The animal is disemboweled. The witch is murdered. The men force her warm body into the wet cavity of the horse, the gash is sutured, the horse's anus sewn closed, and horse and witch pushed over the side of the cliff.[6]

Witchcraft is not confined to rural areas, to "backward" peasants, or simply to the poor and the uneducated. In the sprawling suburb of Soweto, for example, "people . . . understand the powers spoken of as 'witchcraft' as palpable realities that are utterly commonplace and yet shrouded in the utmost secrecy." For "every aspect of social life, including politics, is permeated by these powers."[7] In parts of the country witchcraft, and its very often brutal eradication, became intertwined with the transition from apartheid to democracy, including the 1994 elections.[8] As elsewhere in Africa, "political innovation confronts the narrow link between power and the occult."[9] The end of apartheid's authoritarianism created new tensions, jealousies, and hatreds, and revealed historic, if usually whispered, conversations people have had about power, politics, and the location of evil in their lives. This understanding of evil and its relationship to power and the human emotions that can unleash such terrible horror, this politics of evil, has shaped people's actions as it has shaped their understanding of themselves and the dangerous world they inhabit.

Arguments and predicaments, questions and speculations

It is common to list the many injustices committed in the eras of colonialism and apartheid – particularly among those who may see present-day South Africa as something of a political miracle, a bright spot in a contemporary world of disorder and tragedy, a "rainbow nation," the beginning of an "African renaissance." In less than three decades, for example, the apartheid government forcibly "resettled" over three million people, almost a fifth of its 1960 population, destroying lives and livelihoods in an unrelenting pursuit of a racist political dream.[10] (Put another way, this would be equivalent to 57 million people in the United States today.) "I have seen," wrote Desmond in 1969, "the bewilderment of simple rural people when they are told that they must leave their homes where they have lived for generations and go to a strange place . . . their cries of helplessness and resignation . . . the sufferings of whole families," and "children sick with typhoid, or their bodies emaciated with malnutrition and even dying of starvation . . . in the richest, most advanced and most rapidly growing economy on the continent of Africa."[11] In language darkly reminiscent of Nazi Germany, the government quite literally defined such people as "redundant." They were superfluous, unneeded and unwanted in a society in which the color of one's skin quite literally could mean the difference between life and death, poverty and plenty. So-called "resettlement" camps, and in fact the homelands themselves, became places of extraordinary destitution, want, and ever-present death. The United Nations condemned apartheid as a crime against humanity, a "crime against the conscience and dignity of mankind," one of the great evils of the modern era.[12]

Evil certainly; but traditionally evil has had a different, if ultimately related, meaning among many of those who have been subjected to the everyday violence of the state. Evil is not simply a synonym for injustice, unfairness, or even the oppression committed by individuals acting as "bad" people, as in the Christian Pietist tradition that reminds us of our inherent sinfulness, our banishment from God's bounteous Garden of Eden. Rather, evil is the intentional or instrumental use of occult forces, to use Western parlance, to cause harm and to bring disorder. Evil stands in opposition to life and, especially, to the ways life should be lived. Certainly people are capable of being bad. Evil, however, attacks individuals secretly and mysteriously, hurting or even destroying the innocent who are unblemished by original sin. Moreover, evil attacks the wider community, like some ravenous animal, sowing chaos and discord where there should be order and harmony.[13] Evil is the very opposite of *ubuntu*, of hospitality and sharing and of those virtues that make one human and good and life worth living.

Historically these occult forces could be used to create a life worth living, for example by bringing nourishing rains and ensuring bounteous crops. Magic is still used to ensure or to restore harmony and health. Witches use magic selfishly to hurt, even to destroy. Their perfidy stems in part from the triumph of our baser emotions: jealousy; greed; arrogance; naked ambition; hate. Witches are especially evil because they use some intimate knowledge of their victims to sow tragedy, as if those who know us best are most capable of doing harm.[14] In an 1856 case of witchcraft, for example, the witch-finder discovered small amounts of fat in the hut of the accused witch, perhaps the fat of the *impundulu*, the magical lightning bird that serves witches in their evil work. The fat contained hair thought to be from two of the accursed victims, one of whom, a chief and relative of the alleged witch, was dying from the evil magic. The accused witch also had close connections with whites. He appeared to the magistrate as "courageous and a straightforward man," but also "overly ambitious."[15]

Witchcraft beliefs were, and are, wonderfully malleable, if frighteningly and very often tragically so. They have, for example, fused with Christian ideas of sin and evil and purity and goodness, creating visions of terrible malevolence and nourishing dreams of an apocalypse that would set the world aright and return the downtrodden to a land of harmony and plenty. Belief in occult forces have at times shaped people's perceptions of whites and the state. In the 1970s, for instance, bulldozers destroyed the homes of some ten thousand people near Cape Town as part of the state's program of forced resettlement. As elsewhere in South Africa during this time, the police had conducted surprise night raids, checking passes and subjecting Africans to the state's ever more detailed control, arresting people, dividing families. In the end they attempted to bleach a "black spot" from white South Africa. The people who suffered the indignities of dispossession "believed that the whites who had pushed them off the land and hunted them in the bush," that is, employees of the state, "were either under evil influences or were possibly witches themselves."[16] Four decades earlier, people in the Eastern Cape called the poll tax, first introduced in 1925, the *impundulu*.[17] More generally some people in this region believed Europeans had access to powerful bewitching substances. Rumor had it that "unscrupulous Europeans" sold "what they claim to be the fat" of witchcraft familiars such as the *impundulu*.[18]

Where there is power and all the emotions it unleashes, there is the occult. "Witchcraft, this terribly diffuse notion so highly current in Africa, continues to be a key element in discourses on power."[19] The moral discourse of magic has been a central and historical feature of the African political imagination, a way of understanding the iniquities of the world, the tyranny of hatred, but also the way the world should be. And yet, paradoxically, witchcraft is at once "an everyday reality" and "an enormous public secret."[20] The pervasiveness of magic in people's daily lives speaks of a world and a past that is rarely disclosed, a history of deadly important whispers that concern the most basic of issues: life and death; jealousy, hatred and selfishness; agriculture and the rains; the persecutions of the state; the exploits of the powerful and the exploitation of the powerless.[21]

South Africa, and especially the Eastern Cape, offers an exemplary, if sad, history of the politics of evil in the colonial and postcolonial world, particularly the ways common people have conceived of, experienced, and shaped their political world in the face of hardship and persecution. Historical developments that unfolded elsewhere in the world over the course of centuries appeared in this distant corner rapidly, and very often violently. States and bureaucracies emerged in the space of just a few decades. Towards the end of the nineteenth century South Africa underwent a breathtakingly fast industrial capitalist revolution. And within this maelstrom of change new ways of apprehending the world surfaced as people struggled to make sense of their lives.

This work is an exploratory venture into this extraordinary and exemplary past; exemplary not only because of its richness, but also because in the tragedy and pathos of this past may lie the imaginative possibilities for exploring how to "experience difference in equality."[22] The book is concerned less with policies and institutions than with an intimate history of the emergence and transformation of power's exercise and of people's experience of subjugation. It is concerned with understanding the play of power and the politics of evil in the everyday lives of people from the nineteenth-century colonial conquests to the collapse of apartheid and the contemporary challenges of building a durable democracy at the southern tip of Africa. Ultimately also, this book is about the creative imagination of people as well as their capacity to hate and to engage in terroristic violence to end a world they see as profoundly evil.

The period covered in this investigation engages with three basic themes in African history and modern world history: cross-cultural contact; the rise of a colonial order, especially the emergence and development of a state; and the ways people understood and fashioned their world. How, for example, do we write of the "contact zone" between African and Western conceptions, perceptions, and practices of power and authority?[23] This is in many respects a practical question. But it also raises the more fundamental issues of communication, translation, and understanding, the possibilities of people speaking across their differences, even in situations of great inequality.[24] For the historian of power and politics this means analyzing the everyday relationships of ruler and ruled, the ways in which colonial rule came to be accomplished and transformed, and how people understood the triumph of authoritarianism in South Africa that confounded the lives of so many people. How did Africans shape the process of state formation, expose it to critique and, at times, organize resistance to it? And, finally, what is the relationship between state formation and the rise of new sensibilities among the colonized, especially the colonized poor, the creation and recreation of political identities within the contact zone of conquest, rule and the white supremacy of an authoritarian state? How, in short, do people construct meaning in the face of power?

"Between conscious and unconscious," two anthropologists have written, "lies the most critical domain of all for historical anthropology and especially for the analysis of colonialism and resistance. It is," they continue, "the realm of partial recognition, of inchoate awareness, of ambiguous perception," where "individuals and groups know that something is happening to them but find it difficult to put their fingers on quite what it is."[25] This ambiguity, this intractable problem of history and understanding, arises not simply from the complexity of cross-cultural encounters, but also because of the *a priori* assumptions that silently yet powerfully shape culture and experience. Cross-cultural encounters are neither simply situations in which two cultures collide, and in their collision are transformed, nor are they situations of perfect translation in which historical actors share a universal practical rationality.[26] There is speech and communication and translation across culture, but there is also, and very often simultaneously, misapprehension and misunderstanding.

Herein lay a predicament. Historical evidence rarely speaks directly to the ways people conceptualize their world, particularly in the early colonial context where the scholar largely relies on records produced by Europeans who were translating the African world according to their own culturally bound ways of understanding themselves and others. The very fact that colonial authorities declared witchcraft illegal, for example, drove it from archival record, so that state policies and practices powerfully shaped the production of written evidence. One analyzes actions, particularly those that shed light on perception, and draw on linguistic, ethnographic, and comparative data, to reconstruct the conceptual world of people and the ways in which those concepts shaped their perception and actions. Those concepts were of great importance in the colonial encounter, and yet they remained largely unspoken. For example, magic was, and continues to be, a ubiquitous feature of the way many Africans understood and understand the world, reaffirming the everyday assumption of the importance of people's connectedness to others and, indeed, to the natural world around them. Ideas about occult forces shaped African understandings of Europeans and their relations with them, yet these ideas for the most part remained implicit in people's actions. As such they remain mostly hidden in the historical evidence, especially since European rulers with their ideas of the truthfulness of the empirical world had trouble empathizing with, let alone understanding, a social reality not their own. We are left reconstructing the past along a border between reasonable likeliness and "probable truths" and mere plausibility and unwarranted speculation.[27]

Scholars for the most part have been unaccustomed to seeing conquest and rule as forms of cross-cultural contact, a contact zone involving an astoundingly complex interplay of African and European modes and models of power and political practice. Recent work on cross-cultural encounters has evinced surprisingly little interest in the state, though this literature has significantly called attention to the importance of explaining "the politically constructed dichotomy of colonizer and colonized . . . as a historical shifting pair of social categories."[28] In general the state enters later, after the colonization of consciousness, after the damage has been done, a political *deus ex machina* to order the African world in the name of commerce, civilization, and, ultimately, white supremacy.[29]

A number of writers have raised new questions about state formation and rule. For Abrams, whose work was influenced by Africanist political anthropology, the central issue is how the state "comes into being."[30] Other scholars have emphasized the importance of understanding the "profoundly cultural content of state institutions and activities" as well as "the nature and extent of state regulation of cultural forms."[31] "States," after all, "*state*; the arcane rituals of a court of law . . . visits of school inspectors, are all statements. They define, in great detail, acceptable forms and images of social activity; they regulate, in empirically specifiable ways, much – very much, by the twentieth century – of social life."[32] Colonial state formation represented part of a more global, and today with advances in cybernetics and in genetic knowledge a continuing, historical process. As Minogue has argued more generally, state formation "has been one of continuous growth, both in their claim to regulate the lives and property of their subjects, and in their physical capacity to enforce such claims."[33]

In the Eastern Cape, and indeed elsewhere in South Africa, this process of growing state power began with colonial conquest and culminated in the authoritarian order that was apartheid, especially state controls over labor and parate development. State formation and rule thus began in "dialogue of cultures"[34] that is cross-cultural contact. Even t conquest was quintessentially a cross-cultural encounter d peoples with often radically different ways of conceiving the ether and struggling to make sense of what was happening to others. The Transkei was conquered largely by employees of a cy of a modern state, the Department of Native Affairs (DNA, later NAD). An important charge of those employees was the transformation of African society in such a way as to render the African world the object of bureaucratic rule. This required, among other things, the existence of clear and stable categories, jurisdictional boundaries, and, indeed, an ethnographic model of colonized society. Put another way, an integral feature of state formation was a "desire to know,"[35] to attempt to define in greater and greater detail the subjects of state control, in short to create a taxonomy through which rule could be accomplished.

Viewed this way conquest entailed the attempts by bureaucrats and others to render African territory and society legible to the modern state. This involved increasing simplification and standardization. The Eastern Cape, for example, would become perhaps the best-mapped "native area" in South Africa, perhaps in all of Southern Africa. In the 1920s and 1930s alone the state passed more laws relating to Africans than in the previous century of colonial rule. Between 1910 and 1961 the state appointed no less than forty-two commissions concerned with "native affairs." Over the course of the nineteenth and twentieth centuries the state's vision narrowed considerably, bureaucrats focusing increasingly on issues of land, labor, and "tribal" political structures. These developments centered on the definition of the African as the subject of a colonial political order, not in the case of whites as citizens participating in the political process.[36] Bureaucrats, moreover, did not necessarily know their colonial subjects any better, nor were they interested in knowledge for its own sake. The opposite was more likely to be the case. Information and understanding could be very distant cousins, at times seemingly not on speaking terms. Very often the more officials looked the less they saw.

Legibility, "a central problem in statecraft," and the narrowing of vision that inevitably accompanies it, "provides the capacity for large-scale social engineering."[37] At the same time "the political capacity to generate consent through the institutional spaces of civil society," which was afforded to whites in South Africa, was "notably absent"[38] in the colonial context. South Africa in the twentieth century saw an extraordinary growth in the state: in the complexity of its institutions; in the rising prominence of social science; and, importantly, in its coercive capacity, including the taking of life. Legislation passed in this era was preoccupied with rendering the colonized a simplified category ever more legible to state rule. At the same time legislation introduced policies that reworked the rural economy and the structures of colonial rule and provided the mandated force to help ensure their implementation. The years between 1910 and 1956 especially – between the Act of Union and the introduction into the Transkei of the 1951 Bantu Authorities Act – saw not simply the rise of segregation and then of apartheid but also the emergence of an increasingly authoritarian and racially oppressive state that was willing to deploy its coercive might in pursuit of social engineering on a population that was increasingly denied the capacity to confront it.[39]

The South African state was thus a modern state, informed by the most advanced technologies of the day. Its modernist roots lay deep in European history. Modernity, and in many respects apartheid was modernity gone mad, has been the subject of a voluminous literature.[40] Beginning in the nineteenth century, the industrialization of the state permitted the ascendency, both conceptually and practically, of a new kind of power. The intellectual revolution of Enlightenment rationality came to reside at the center of statecraft, specifically the importance of empirical information to the formation of bureaucracies. These agencies of government were often staffed by officials imbued with an optimism that social problems could be solved using the appropriate political technologies and human history thereby advanced. There emerged an administrative perfectionism that had an insatiable appetite for information on and about the population it managed, a "governmental state" limited only by its dreams for changing the world.[41]

There were always critics of rhapsodic political optimism, such as Edmund Burke and Thomas Malthus. And in the twentieth century Nietzsche and Weber advanced powerful if different critiques of the Enlightenment and its legacy. Weber, for example, believed that bureaucratic rationality would end in instrumental rationality, that is in a rationality unencumbered by moral or ethical considerations. Rationality, and its drive for greater and greater empirical and seemingly value-free information, would thus create an "iron cage" from which there would be no escape, ultimately producing the very opposite of human freedom. The very technical and seemingly neutral language of apartheid ("redundant" people who were "endorsed" out of areas, "resettlement" sites, and so on) demonstrates precisely Weber's dread of the possible terrors of rationality. Later writers such as Adorno and Horkheimer continued this theme, most famously arguing that the European Holocaust was a consequence of, and not a deviation from, the Enlightenment.[42] More recently Foucault argued that "for the first time in history . . . biological existence was reflected in political existence; the fact of living was no longer an inaccessible substrate that only emerged from time to time . . . part of it passed into knowledge's field of control and power's sphere of intervention." "Power," he continued, "would no longer be dealing simply with legal subjects . . . but with living beings, and the mastery it would be able to exercise over them would have to be applied at the level of life itself," thus giving "power its access even to the body."[43] This new form of power, what Foucault termed "biopower," helped create disciplines such as demography and shaped issues relating to labor power, and led to redefinition of political subjects and the focus of various disciplinary practices on them.[44]

"Biopower may have been a uniquely bourgeois form of modern power," a recent observer has noted, "but it was also an inherently imperial one."[45] Apartheid represented the authoritarian culmination of the modernity of the colonial state, the endpoint of its social engineering that began with the violence of conquest and the making of colonial rule.[46] A distinctive feature of the apartheid state lay not simply in its authoritarianism, the triumph of instrumental rationality in which the ends increasingly justified the means. Rather, officials within the apartheid state became obsessed with controlling labor and bodies, part of a complex "linking of bureaucracy to surveillance"[47] most obviously seen in the pass system and "influx control." Between 1952 and 1962 – the decisive decade in the creation of apartheid – over three million Africans were convicted under the pass laws; "an enormous proportion of the urban African population had been caught by the courts in the net of the influx control laws."[48] These arrests formed part of a web of laws whereby the state redefined human beings as mere objects of state policy, forcibly resettled "redundant" people, refined the migrant labor system, and reorganized the entire system of rule in the homelands to solve, once and for all, the "native question."

The story of state formation is thus the story of the rise of authoritarianism in South Africa, the colonial realization of the fears evinced by scholars such as Weber who warned of the dark side of rationality once it had become untethered from ethics and morality in the pursuit of "technical" problems. This process of rising instrumental rationality became especially pronounced in the 1920s and culminated in the advent of apartheid some three decades later. It entailed not simply the promulgation of laws and a considerable expansion in the state's coercive might but, also, the increasing bureaucraticization of rule as the state's social engineering penetrated ever more deeply into the lives of its subjects.

Yet both state formation and colonial rule unfolded in ways that were frequently disorderly, fragmented, at times even inchoate. This is especially so in the colonial context, in the cacophonies of translation that comprise cross-cultural encounters. For Africans translated into indigenous concepts – and in so doing blurred and complicated – the colonial state. And at times Europeans wittingly and unwittingly donned the political masks of the people they were busily subjugating and, ostensibly at least, bringing into the clear light of Western civilization and its battery of political technologies. Colonial rule emerged out of the complex interplay of structures, practices, discourses, violence, identification and indistinction, that together created, very often confused, and always complicated the lived categories of ruler and subject, colonizer and colonized.[49]

Preoccupied with discourse, some recent post-modernist approaches to colonialism and the state have run the risk of neglecting the history of the magistrates and other officials, the men with guns, the prisons, and the many instruments of rule – some banal, others grotesque – that were so integral to colonial domination.[50] Yet being dispossessed or shot is never a discursive act. Nor is torture. South Africa attained a certain infamy for all three of these acts of state. Rule takes us from the realm of discourse and the politics of knowledge to the messiness of history and the confusions of cross-cultural encounters. Because rule emerged from the contact zone of African and European interaction, its study forces us to integrate a history from "above" with one from "below." How, precisely, did rule come to be "accomplished"[51] and transformed over the course of the nineteenth and twentieth centuries? Who were these men with guns and telegraphs and books and their often grand plans for reforming African society? And how did Africans understand, shape, and contest colonial rule? More precisely, how did the colonized comprehend bureaucracy and, particularly in the twentieth century, the dominance of instrumental rationality within the authoritarian state?[52]

Focusing on rule brings a concern with politics and power to this book's third and final major issue: how Africans understood and acted within the brave new world of colonialism. But first a definition and a caveat. This work is not principally concerned with elite politics or with the history of organizations such as the African National Congress. Nor is it a study of the reaction and resistance of a particular socioeconomic class.[53] I am interested primarily in those people who did not occupy the more fortunate positions within colonial society, who did not lead but who sometimes participated in organized oppositional politics or formed local social movements of their own that contested the state and its functionaries. Put another way, a central concern is with the history of those who came to be the principal focus of the state's instrumental power, the very people who would come to represent a "technical" problem for the state, for example those defined as "redundant." These were the people who hovered on the edge of landlessness and poverty as officials introduced policies of rural economic reform, or the poor the authorities hounded as they struggled to make ends meet. "Subaltern" is used as a convenient shorthand, as long as we remember that the subaltern and their politics developed as part of an engagement with colonialism and, ultimately, with the problems of power and authority that transcended the colonial order itself.[54]

A concern with engagement shifts attention beyond an emphasis on the state as a structure of foreign imposition mitigated only by the presence of indigenous collaborators. We are interested here in the ways in which people became intrigued by the forces that sustained European visitors, intruders, and, particularly in the nineteenth century, conquerors. The power of the modern bureaucratic state especially captivated Africans, even when its actual control remained very weak, the effectiveness of its policies uneven, and its intervention more erratic and disruptive than clear and conclusive. This fascination included the "commonplace rituals"[55] of rule. Africans became fascinated with and at times appropriated the embodiments of state power: books and paper, telegraph machines and telegraph wires, land beacons, even the bodies and clothes of rulers and the spaces they inhabited and struggled to rule from.[56]

Colonial rule was foreign... but precisely how so? Wherein lay its foreignness, the hidden abode of the modern state's power? How did people – whether colonial subjects or postcolonial citizens – understand, shape, and expose state formation to critique? How, for example, did the colonized make sense of the state's attempt to render their communities, ultimately their very bodies, legible to state power? On the one hand Africans translated the brave new world of colonialism into their own concepts and precepts. On the other hand modern power differed significantly from the precolonial world, with its porous and shifting boundaries and a mental map in which power was unevenly distributed across space and time. What were the indigenous grammars of power and authority with which the colonized comprehended and critiqued the state? How did these grammars change over time, as people engaged with new institutions and systems of belief such as Christianity? To what extent was resistance, even rebellion, more than rejection of the state's policies, but also part of wider and ongoing conversations among the colonized about power and authority? How do we understand the location of state artefacts and procedures, for example passes and trials, in subaltern social movements? And what does it mean when the colonized represented the modern state as evil, its officials as purveyors of magic that destroyed?[57]

The importance of witchcraft in South Africa's recent political transition, in what is also the continent's most advanced state, speaks to many of these same questions.[58] As in the past, state formation and political transition have raised anew the relationship between politics and the occult, the issue of authority and legitimacy, and the problems of suffering and evil. People have probed the state and their contemporary predicaments using a grammar of magic, and especially of witchcraft, that formed part of a historic and continuing discourse about the rule of tragedy and sadness in world. The suggestion explored in this work links the instrumental rationality of the authoritarian state, which in its amoral pursuit of technical problems stands resolutely opposed to the good life, with African witchcraft beliefs that spoke to questions of hatred, jealousy, and misfortune. The politics of evil thus refer both to the injustices perpetrated by the state and to the political imagination of the state's subjects and victims that transcends a given political moment.

In the politics of evil, then, lay a complex intertwining of culture, consciousness, and power, of concept, percept, and action, that allowed for a critique of the state using indigenous grammars relating to magic and misfortune. These grammars could lead to the elaboration of ideas and actions committed to a social justice tied to conceptions of social health. But these grammars could just as easily lead to an all-consuming hatred and to unspeakable acts of violence in the name of eradicating evil from the world. In both cases magic and misfortune, and especially witchcraft, created the connective cultural tissue linking perception to action. Much of a witch's insidious power stems from the panoptic surveillance of their victims. Unencumbered by ethical or moral obligations, their cool calculating behavior has as its goal the attainment of a singular goal – selfish appropriation at another's tragic expense. Witches, and the modern state, depend on the accumulation of detailed and often intimate information. Herzfeld has written that "bureaucrats work on the categories of social existence in much the same was as sorcerers are supposed to work on the hair or nail clippings of their intended victims." Both are faceless, at least until revealed, operate in secret, are in a sense cold, and perpetrate evil.[59]

Cross-cultural contact, state formation, understanding and action – these are the major themes explored in this work. Yet the issue of magic is particularly difficult to analyze historically. One speaks of the occult obliquely and in whispers, so that people rarely volunteered information that might enter the written record or become part of detailed oral traditions reaching deep into the past. Witchcraft was illegal under colonial law, and indeed remains illegal today. This has had the effect of marginalizing witchcraft in the official archive compiled by Europeans who believed magic did not exist. And yet we know that belief in witchcraft is extraordinarily common and did not, as it were, emerge out of thin air. We are left with a historical puzzle missing many of its most important pieces, pieces whose shape we can describe only indirectly and by inference and at times by conjecture, as so many "probable truths" of an elusive past.[60]

Event history

Because this work covers a large geographical region and over a century of extraordinarily rapid historical change, a brief history of conquest and the state is apposite. The conquest of the Eastern Cape began in the last quarter of the eighteenth century and ended, well over a century later, with the 1894 annexation of Pondoland.[61] The hundred years of war and colonial conquest falls into two phases, the first ending in the 1850s. White settler expansion, first by Dutch speakers and then by British colonists, culminating in the creation of a rural capitalist economy, was a powerful motor of early colonial expansion. This motor was created locally, not imperially; officials based in London were reluctant conquerors of African territory. Poor communications and a muddled vision of empire contributed to the disorder, lawlessness, and violence of this period. London officials continually complained of the high costs of conflict and conquest in a colony that was more an imperial headache than a gem in the

1 Southern Africa

colonial crown. In general preferring not to expand its colonial possession, the British government typically reacted to conflict by irresolutely annexing new territory and then either reversing conquest or extending only nominal rule over African communities.

Despite decades of conflict in British Kaffraria, what under apartheid would become the Ciskei homeland, the creation and extension of a system of colonial rule began only after the Cape Colony received representative rule in 1853. This process of colonial state building culminated in the 1865 annexation of the territory. Colonial expansion in the second half of the nineteenth century differed significantly from the earlier era of conquest. In contrast to the often reluctant imperialism of the earlier epoch, the 1865 discovery of diamonds in Griqualand West, and the rush that immediately followed it, helped create an environment for more spirited colonial expansion; so also did the discovery of gold in the South African Republic some two decades later. More generally the second half of the century saw important ideological shifts, particularly the rise of scientific racism and increasingly negative European stereotypes of

non-European peoples. The years after the 1856 Indian Rebellion, and Jamaica's
Morant Bay Rebellion nine years later, witnessed a marked rise in European
cultural arrogance and, ultimately, the eclipse of universalist Enlightenment
ideas that had informed the movement to end the Atlantic slave trade.

The permissive factors of cultural arrogance, racial superiority, and economic
greed helped spur colonial expansion in South Africa and in many other areas
of the non-Western world. There were other factors. Two of the most important
features of the second era of conquest lay in the increasing industrialization and
bureaucratization of the state. Together they represented a radical strengthening
in Europe's ability to intervene, and to sustain that intervention, in the affairs
of other societies. The state's coercive capacity, its capacity to do violence,
increased steadily in this period. In the last quarter of the century "the cost of
crude steel dropped by three quarters or more."[62] More accurate weapons became cheap and plentiful. The Snider-Enfield rifles used in the Transkei during
the 1870s, for example, tripled the range of the earlier muzzle-loaders. The
state, moreover, attempted to monopolize control over advanced armaments.
Act 13 of 1878, the "Peace Preservation Act," for instance, extended state control over weapons and attempted to disarm Africans who possessed arms and
ammunition without proper license. The act would also become the catalyst for
the outbreak of widespread African revolt beginning in 1880.

The first trains began to be built in the Cape in the 1860s. The pace of railroad
construction quickened in the next three decades. By the end of the 1870s one
could travel from East London to Queenstown, in other words through the entire
Ciskei region. In the 1880s and 1890s most train construction took place in the
interior, connecting the diamond mines of Kimberley and the gold mines of
the Rand with the coast. Only in 1919 did the railroad finally reach Umtata, at
a time when the state and mining capitalists had turned their attention to the
Transkei as a labor reservoir.[63] In the meantime steam-powered ships brought
distant areas of the Transkei in closer connection to Cape Town. But one of
the most important outcomes of the industrial revolution, and one that would
become very important to colonial rule, was the telegraph. Invented in 1838,
the first telegraphic message went out six years later. By the beginning of
the twentieth century tens of thousands of miles of cable had created a web
of telegraphy across much of the British Empire. Conquest and the telegraph
very often moved hand-in-hand. By 1877 the telegraph had reached Qumbu,
Maclear, Mount Frere, and Kokstad, the most remote areas of colonial expansion
in the Eastern Cape (see map 3, p. 54). It was, one magistrate wrote, an
indispensable technology in addressing that "great question of the government
of the Natives."[64]

These changes radically reduced the costs of colonial expansion and greatly
improved the responsiveness and coordination of European colonialists. The
costs of administration also declined steadily in the second half of the nineteenth

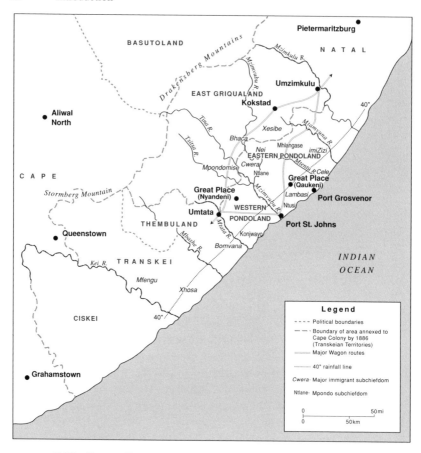

2 The Eastern Cape region

century, while bureaucratic efficiency rose markedly.[65] The costs of paper and printing plummeted, new technologies such as typewriters (invented in 1868 and a common instrument in the offices of magistrates in South Africa by the turn of the century) appeared, and postal services improved. By the end of the century the Eastern Cape was awash with the printed word, the technology, and the administrative practices and procedures of a modern industrialized state.

In 1872, seven years after the Ciskeian annexation and nineteen years after representative rule, further power devolved to the Cape with the granting of responsible government. That same year the Cape government created a bureaucratic agency specifically concerned with conquest and rule, the Department of Native Affairs (with the 1910 Act of Union renamed the Native Affairs

Department and then, under apartheid, the Department of Bantu Affairs and Development).[66] The period from the late 1860s saw a flurry of colonial expansion, beginning with the annexation of Basutoland and Griqualand West, the latter incorporated into the Cape Colony in 1880. In the space of just ten years most of what became the Transkei fell under colonial rule.[67] The only exception was Pondoland, annexed in 1894. A crucial feature that distinguished the Transkei from its western neighbor was that the Cape administered it as "an autonomous native area."[68] In general officials in the Transkei were employees of the Department of Native Affairs, accountable to the chief magistrate based in Umtata. (The Ciskei received a chief magistrate in the early 1920s, as part of the introduction of the new policies of segregation to that region.) This allowed the colony to annex territory without actually incorporating it; importantly, among other things the state was able to control the extension of the Cape franchise to the Transkeian areas.[69]

Sir George Grey, governor of the Cape Colony in the 1850s, had proposed a system of direct rule for the area that would become the Ciskei. This system entailed the drawing of boundaries, gathering statistical data, collecting hut and other taxes, forcing Africans into villages or locations, appointing European resident magistrates, and destroying chiefship by elevating the importance of headmen and converting chiefs as employees of the state. "Under such a plan," Grey wrote, "the worst part of the Kaffir polity is broken down."[70] Ultimately many of Grey's ideas would be put into practice east of the Kei River. The road to rule in the Transkei, however, was most circuitous, leading eventually not to Grey's mission of "civilizing" (and with it the possibilities of Africans gaining the vote), but to indirect rule under a system of internal colonialism wherein Africans remained colonial subjects. On paper at least, by 1877 and the beginning of the so-called Ninth Frontier War much of the Transkei had fallen to colonial rule.[71] Conquest, however, was the source of much confusion and, eventually, even more conflict. Chiefs saw many of the agreements they entered into as so many alliances, not the recognition of subordinate status. As we shall see, they were in fact quite correct.

Indeed, under these early agreements colonial territory fell only "under the general jurisdiction of European Magistrates but subordinate to their Chiefs, who continued to exercise their powers." Here magistrates had an "appellate jurisdiction"; they were in some sense passive actors serving as intermediaries between African and colonial territories. Africans, in short, were "assured of their own internal government under Native custom." Chief Matanzima, a descendant of whom would become the first head of the Transkei homeland, thus could argue before the 1883 Native Laws and Customs Commission that in the early years of colonial rule his people remained "completely under my control." The magistrate simply "assisted in cases from the colony."[72] Internal official documents substantiated Matanzima's claim. Officials soon realized that since magistrates had "no jurisdiction in Civil Cases" they could hardly enforce hut taxes and administer fines.[73] At first, then, magistrates governed "principally through their own Chiefs and in accordance with Kaffir laws and customs, when not opposed to justice or humanity."[74] Chiefs could "exercise authority and settle law suits except cases of murder, crimes arising out of witchcraft, serious assaults and thefts from other tribes and from the Colony."[75]

Early magistrates not surprisingly evinced "uncertainty as to the law" they were "administering."[76] As the report of the Native Laws and Customs Commission, held in 1881 following widespread rebellion throughout much of the Transkei, made clear:

We find no uniformity in the criminal law or procedure, which until lately has been administered beyond the Kei. Some magistrates inform us that they administer the Kafir law; others that they administer the Colonial law; some that they adopt our Colonial mode of procedure some that they apply Kafir law and procedure in some cases, and the Colonial law and its procedure in others. All are agreed that a Criminal Code is desirable in order to give certainty to the law that they are called upon to administer, and to enable those subject to the laws to know them. And this knowledge can best be secured by means of a code translated into the Kafir language, which, even if not read by the vast majority of natives, will in substance be learnt by them from missionaries, educated natives, and others, who, from the code itself, will be able to acquire a knowledge of law at present unattainable. Added to this, the laws administered in Tembuland and Gcalekaland have, until recently, had no legislative sanction or authority.[77]

Formal annexation ultimately resolved this "very unsatisfactory state of affairs,"[78] but not before the outbreak of serious violence. In the final years of the 1870s the state reneged on earlier agreements by which Transkeian peoples originally came under colonial tutelage. This was a crucial period of state formation in the Transkei. The "days when native chiefs still exercised a large measure of power and conducted affairs with a due sense of their rank and dignity" were quickly coming to an end.[79] With the drawing of administrative boundaries the state restricted the jurisdiction of paramount chiefs to the magisterial districts in which they lived. Magistrates deposed and arrested chiefs and paramounts, threatened them with flogging, and appointed others in their stead. The state deposed and attempted to arrest the Thembu paramount in 1876 only to reinstall him a few months later. As had happened in the Ciskei, the state "degraded" chiefs into "petty" headmen, often with "barely a hundred followers."[80] In selecting headmen officials created a new class of intermediaries.[81] Headmen, and not the chief, represented the "first court in a village," holding "powers under their own laws."[82] On top of these interventions the state prohibited witchcraft and other seemingly barbarous African customs.[83] It shifted fines from chief to magistrate, so that, for example, "when cattle are part of the judgement in a case they will be first driven to the Magistrate's office."[84]

By 1879 the colonial accumulation of power had become unmistakable. Late in that year magistrates and chief magistrates began reading to and distributing among their subjects the state's more unified laws of administration set out in the high commissioner Sir Bartle Frere's proclamation of 15 September. This was shortly followed by the disastrous implementation of the 1878 Disarmament Act. Both the Act and Frere's proclamation definitively shifted power to the colonial state; among other things the proclamation clarified the colonial division of law and procedure. By 1880 the colonial legal system was far clearer, and colonial rule far firmer, than it had been just a few years earlier. The state continued its division of civil and criminal law. While Africans could bring civil cases to headmen, they also had the right to go directly to the magistrate or, later, to appeal the headman's decision. Criminal acts fell squarely under the magistrate's control. These developments, this bringing into being of a colonial state, led directly to the outbreak of war, engulfing most of the Transkei, including Griqualand East and Lesotho. Almost a century would pass before the region would again, in the 1950s with the introduction of apartheid, see such widespread conflict.

The conquest of the Eastern Cape formally ended with the 1894 annexation of Pondoland. That year also saw the promulgation of the Glen Grey Act, shepherded into the Cape parliament by prime minister and minister for native affairs Cecil Rhodes. Rhodes considered the act as nothing less than a "Native Bill for Africa."[85] The same year that colonial conquest ended a new period of political innovation and transformation began. For the Act "sought to restructure social relations . . . to accelerate the process of proletarianisation; to redefine the terms of access to . . . land; to reduce the participation of Africans in the Cape electoral system; and, finally, to create a new level of local administration."[86] The Act, for example, sought to reorganize space in the native reserves on the basis of individual tenure. It also introduced a labor-tax provision that began forcing people to take up migrant-labor contracts. The new structure of governance would consist of a series of local district councils and a Transkei General Council; reintroduced in the twentieth century, the council system would transform earlier patterns of colonial rule and begin an era of segregationist political engineering.

The Glen Grey Act is more important in terms of what it stood for than for what the legislation accomplished, which at first was very little indeed. Controversial from the beginning and the subject of interminable discussion, the Act ultimately proved unworkable. In 1905, for example, the state rescinded the labor-tax provision. The council system was stillborn. And one of the most basic intents of the legislation, the creation of a more orderly system of landholding based on individual tenure, failed miserably. The Act nonetheless illustrates an important shift in the political history of South Africa in the immediate aftermath of colonial conquest. One of the functions of the councils, for example, was to oversee economic development: the control of stock; the building of roads and other infrastructure; agricultural improvement; and public health. The Glen Grey Act thus represented not only the beginnings of segregation and the state's intervention and regulation of the economy, but also the expanding importance of information to the bureaucratic state. Indeed, one of the striking features of the archival material surrounding the Act is its concern with information and, more generally, the attempt to combine scientific principles with colonial rule.[87]

Officials introduced the Glen Grey Act within the broader context of a phenomenally rapid industrial revolution in South Africa that had a seemingly insatiable appetite for cheap African labor. The post-1890 period would see the rise of both an authoritarian state and a capitalist state singularly, indeed obsessively, concerned with marshaling and controlling African labor. The emergence of a "labor-repressive" economy became an ineluctable feature of authoritarian rule.[88] The vast bulk of African labor lay in the very areas the state had just conquered. Controlling labor involved transforming people's relationship to the land and, thus, inevitably entailed colonial rule. This coalescing of rule and economic management can be seen in legislation such as the 1894 Glen Grey Act, the 1920 Native Affairs Act, the 1927 Native Administration Act, and, during the 1950s, in the legislation that introduced apartheid. By that time the Native Affairs Department had become directly, indeed crucially, involved in the recruitment of African labor.[89] Under the 1952 Native Laws Amendment Act that established a labor bureaux system, for example, NAD officials "were expected to coordinate their activities in order to subject the circulation of labor into, within, and out of their areas to vigilant control."[90]

During this period spiraling poverty, landlessness, and reliance on long-distance labor migration became conspicuous features of life in the Eastern Cape. So also did the ecological degradation of agricultural and pastoral lands. Systemic poverty had its origin in the nineteenth-century political subjugation of African communities: economic poverty had distinctly non-economic foundations.[91] Put another way, it was as much the transformation of systems of domination unleashed by conquest as the incorporation of the region into a world capitalist economy that shaped the patterns of rural economic change. These transformations led to almost continuous conflict over access to productive resources. As elsewhere on the continent, conquest, and then in the early part of the twentieth century the introduction of indirect rule, created a layer of debate (reaffirming in the minds of officials their assumptions of the irrational nature of African society) over the meaning of custom and authority that had an important impact on how people gained and maintained access to economic resources such as land.[92] Economic stratification kindled envies and ignited hatreds. Throughout much of the Ciskei there were "constant quarrels among the people about land, and many of them have gardens on such poor soil that the returns are not good." A very few prospered but "the mass of people" were "entirely destitute and . . . have nothing but their grain for subsistence and the payment of taxes."[93] As early as the late 1850s, in the Ciskei state officials burnt out of newly established locations people who were not registered to be there or who had failed to pay their taxes.[94] The poor lived in "wretched huts patched up with pieces of tin and old sacks, dirty squalid occupants, many of them suffering from terrible and loathsome diseases."[95]

The colonial reorganization of space had important economic, political, ecological, and epidemiological consequences. Villagization, the formation of locations begun in some areas as early as the late 1850s and continuing into the twentieth century with legislation such as the 1939 Betterment Act and, ultimately, into the apartheid era, created enormous conflict over custom and over access to land and other property. In the twentieth century it vastly inflated the power of headmen and chiefs and created a dense and ongoing sociology of dispute around access to land; this conflict in turn helped determine crop selection but also created a situation in which people had little commitment to preventing ecological damage. In most areas there were "tremendous complaint[s] amongst the people for having no lands."[96] The locations created by the colonial state in the nineteenth century were "very congested and many married men are without land."[97] Land consolidation by headmen left many "completely hemmed in."[98] People complained "that our lands are being taken away by the headman."[99] "About the allotments of lands there is tremendous complaint amongst the people for having no lands allotted to them. When good and fertile lands are obtainable at the time when there are people in need of them," the headman "chooses of these those of his relation in blood he does this even to old men so long as they are of his consanguineous relations."[100] More generally people's access to land became increasingly precarious,[101] and "land matters" were very often in a state of quite considerable "confusion."[102]

Africans invariably associated villagization with ill-health. Among other things it permitted the contamination of water supplies and allowed for a far more rapid transmission of diseases – particularly tuberculosis, whooping cough, influenza, and smallpox – than was possible in the older patterns of dispersed settlement.[103] Certainly airborne diseases became an important feature of social life for Africans living in locations, especially for children. "Very large numbers of children," wrote a Thembuland official in 1894, "chiefly those of very tender years, were carried off by . . . influenza, measles and whooping cough." "Many thousands died." A few years later, in 1898, many children died when an influenza epidemic struck the area.[104]

Villagization tended to reduce the rate at which people allowed once-cultivated land to return to fallow. The very widespread adoption of maize was especially hard on soils, particularly when people were unable to plant nitrogen-fixing legumes alongside the plants. With the formation of locations and the expansion of maize production soil fertility declined rapidly, so that by the early part of the twentieth century increasing areas of once-arable land had been largely denuded of their topsoil. Villagization did nothing to alleviate the insecurity that conquest produced. Quite the opposite, particularly given the fact that continued access to land required payment of taxes in addition to other stipulations. Colonial land policies invariably ushered in a new wave of contestation and instability over access to land. As a result of these colonial practices people had as early as the 1850s "been subjected to many and oft-repeated removals,"[105] a phrase ominously similar to the forced removals of the apartheid era. Yet the more conflict and confusion over access to land the more tempted officials were to create yet a new barrage of policies aimed at solving problems they had helped create in the first place.

The drawing of colonial borders also had important ecological repercussions. The demarcation of crown forests deprived many people of access to wood. Before colonial rule, in times of drought or depleted pasturage people living in lowland areas moved their stock into more mountainous terrain. In many instances under colonial rule this would have entailed traversing district boundaries. Theoretically this was possible once people were granted passes to move from one district to another. In practice, however, magistrates refused African requests to bring animals into upland areas. Stock, not surprisingly, "suffered very severely."[106] So also did pastures, which soon became overgrazed. As with human illnesses, the formation of locations quickened the spread of livestock diseases. The first great cattle pandemic – lungsickness or bovine pneumonia – occurred in the 1850s in the context of colonial war and conquest. It spread throughout virtually all of the Eastern Cape and into Lesotho. The disease, however, remained largely endemic to the herds and continued to afflict cattle well into the twentieth century. In 1896–7 rinderpest attacked cattle herds, in many places sweeping off hundreds of thousands of cattle. For well over a century the death of cattle from diseases has exceeded their birth, so that the Eastern Cape has been a net cattle importer.[107] The stock that did not die was typically so poorly nourished that it failed to produce significant amounts of milk. In the 1940s, even "families owning fairly large herds of cattle . . . nevertheless have no milk for domestic usage."[108]

With the exception of large parts of Pondoland, poverty had by the end of the nineteenth century become a common fixture of life for Africans living throughout the Eastern Cape. Africans were "unable to purchase grain for seed." Some, especially women and injured men, were "actually starving."[109] In 1885, drought meant "starvation to the poorer class."[110] In one district that year some 30,000 cattle perished, and unless they received help "old men, women and invalids . . . must die of starvation."[111] In 1902 "a great many people" in the area were "in a starving condition."[112] Droughts hit large parts of the region six times between 1885 and 1927, catapulting the poor into destitution and, very often, the destitute into premature death. In the last two decades of the nineteenth century infant mortality rates, a good if sad indicator of social health, for the Ciskei ranged around 50 percent. Even in areas near to markets and with a seemingly "plentiful food supply," infant deaths were "so great . . . that the native mind at once began to attribute it to supernatural causes."[113] In the 1930s infant mortality rates exceeded 50 percent. Another report based on data collected during "an exceptionally favourable [agricultural] year" noted that, in some areas, from 60 to 75 percent would perish in their first year.[114] In the next decade a report estimated that "only about 1/3 of all children born in the Transkei will reach the age of 16."[115]

Official concern with labor thus unfolded in the context of spiraling poverty. The labor-tax provision of the Glen Grey Act, which required that people work outside the district, had the immediate effect of forcing more men to the mines where wages were relatively good. In 1895 one official wrote from Glen Grey that of the 662 passes he had issued, roughly half were for people migrating to the mines.[116] "Many of the young men who I know personally and to whom I spoke at the beginning of this year," another wrote the same year, "have recently returned with certificates of having been at work outside of the Dist for 5 and 6 months. They asked for exemptions and when told that their work would exempt them for 1895, but that they must pay for 1894, they said 'How could we go to work in 1894, when we only heard of the law in 1895'."[117] In 1897 men were "returning daily from Johannesburg and elsewhere whence they have been to work purposely to gain money required to pay for their land." On returning, however, many found they were unable to secure the land to which they believed they were entitled.[118]

In the past men often had been "unwilling to go to work at the [diamond] Fields," mainly because they were so far away and "also because they can earn as good as wages . . . at Port Elizabeth and East London."[119] From the early part of the twentieth century, however, there was "a tendency towards going further a field [sic] for work." The "local labour market" no longer was capable of "absorbing what is now available and I am inclined," one official wrote, "to believe this tendency is likely to grow."[120] By around 1908 from four to six thousand men left Pondoland alone, many of them heading first to Queenstown for the train ride north.[121] By 1910–11 over seven thousand left from the Bizana and Flagstaff areas of Pondoland; from other places, for example Lusikisiki and Libode, a "large number" went to work on the gold mines.[122] Most first went to Queenstown, and thence north to the Transvaal. Others traveled not to the mines but to Cape Town and as far away as German South West Africa.[123] Men from places such as Alice and Keiskammahoek in the Ciskei walked the roughly three hundred miles north to the Natal coal mines; many never returned from the dangerous work underground.[124]

The general pattern, however, was for migrants to head north to the diamond and gold mines. By the end of 1909, for example, over forty-eight thousand people from the Cape worked on the gold mines of the Witwatersrand, a huge increase in just a few years.[125] By this time perhaps as much as 20 percent of the male workforce was migrating to the Transvaal, and wages earned on the mines had become a "principal" source of money in a rural economy that was "miserable" and "depressed."[126] Labor recruiters fanned out over the Eastern Cape, typically offering migrants cattle and cash advances for their labor. Many Africans walked from their rural homes to railway termini such as Queenstown, Indwe, or Aliwal North where "several Labour Agents" were "recruiting . . . on a large scale."[127] By 1908, for example, a recruiter might be able to send north upwards of one thousand migrants.[128] The men

are brought in from the Transkei, and are . . . generally engaged by the Labour Agent offering the highest price; the Agent then usually communicates with Johannesburg with the view of securing the best market available, the Natives being delayed at Queenstown as long as three or four days while negotiations are proceeding, during which time they are brought to the Railway Station each morning and marched back each evening.[129]

By the 1920s large swaths of the Eastern Cape had collapsed into a wrenching rural poverty. In many areas a "vast majority of labourers" headed to the mines of the Transvaal; their wages prevented starvation and widespread famine.[130] "Under present conditions," a magistrate wrote in 1926, "it is necessary for the solvency of the district that a large proportion of the able-bodied men should go out into European areas in search of work . . . The supply of Native labour overwhelmingly exceeds the needs of the male population. The surplus available may be taken as 75% of the able-bodied male population." Indeed, the "scarcity of arable land . . . is one of the main influences in forcing Natives to seek work in mining centres and the larger towns." "It is clear," the official stated plainly, "that failing greatly improved methods of production" the native reserves "could not reabsorb and maintain all its absentees who are at present in European areas."[131]

The depression of the 1930s ravaged the Eastern Cape. At a 1932 meeting in Queenstown, for example, "the cry was insistent: 'We are starving. We cannot pay our debts or taxes'." At least a third of the population relied "entirely on labor." And indebtedness was so deep that "very soon it will be beyond their capacity to meet."[132] "Famine conditions" were "acute" in Herschel.[133] "The accumulated effect of the depression," the native commissioner wrote, "only made itself really felt towards the end of 1932 and during 1933. During these two years and also in the previous season the crops were a total failure and then to cap it all a terrific drought." "By this time," he continued, "the people were actually starving; the stock was depleted by 75% . . . [and] many had nothing to put in, others had no cattle with which to plough."[134]

These patterns – increasingly landlessness and indebtedness, reliance on long-distance labor migration, and dependence on maize production – worsened in the 1940s and 1950s. They became the subject of intense state scrutiny culminating in the introduction of Hendrik Verwoerd's policies of "Stabilisation, Reclamation and Rehabilitation" and of the apartheid policies of separate development. In the 1950s, for example, the state issued a seventeen-volume report entitled the *Report of the Commission for the Socio-Economic Development of the Bantu Areas within the Union of South Africa*, which later became known as the Tomlinson Commission report. By this time poverty in the reserves had reached quite extraordinary levels, and dependence on long-distance labor migration was ubiquitous. In some locations over half the population might be landless, many of them "squatting" on the commonage; as in the past, these people were subjected to removals by the state.[135] The vast majority of men migrated to the mines, to Cape Town, and to the port cities of East London and Port Elizabeth. These were the people who would starve if not for migrant labor. They had been fast "becoming poorer and . . . hopelessly in debt." Even the lucky few who held "land outside the scheduled areas" were "bonded up to the hilt and in many cases are in arrear with their interest . . . the people as a whole are gradually being drained of their resources and . . . their economic condition is steadily becoming worse."[136]

These economic conditions and industrial South Africa's reliance on migrant labor invariably raised acute political problems, the hoary "native question." Segregation and then apartheid were so many answers to the vexing issue of how to rule the masses of Africans living in the reserves. Cape politicians began using the word "segregation" around the turn of the century, especially with regard to the control of labor and the "native reserves." By the late 1920s segregation had become a "key word" in the state's political discourse.[137] At the center of this political discourse lay an administrative agency, the Native Affairs Department (NAD), created to direct and oversee the administration of the state's African subjects. The NAD had been created in 1910, the same year the Act of Union had formed a single state from what had been four independent colonies. The NAD grew to be the single largest bureaucratic institution in the country, a veritable "state within the state." That prescient and ominous phrase first surfaced in the 1903 South African Native Affairs Commission that was "appointed to recommend an African policy" for the new union.[138]

In the 1920s and 1930s the state promulgated a web of segregationist policies throughout the country and, importantly, intervened directly and powerfully in colonial rule and in organizing and regulating the economy. This era witnessed the meteoric rise of a capitalist bureaucratic order in which economic intervention became a matter of state action and Africans increasingly came to be seen as colonial subjects, defined racially and ethnically as members of tribes, and as units of labor. The year after political union, for example, the Mining and Works Act segregated employment. Laws such as the 1911 Native Labour Regulation Act and the 1932 Native Service Contract Act mark the state's increasing role in creating an industrial capitalist order. Three years after union the state passed the Native Lands Act. That act racially organized space, extended the state's control over labor, and, in later years, dispossessed tens of thousands of Africans and confined them to the 7 percent of the land that comprised the "native reserves." By 1914, in parts of the Eastern Cape the Act was

being so stringently enforced . . . that the Natives . . . have no place to go with their stock and families. The owners of farms are compelled, owing to the provisions of the Act to drive all Natives, who are not bona fide servants, from their properties, with the result that a large number of these unfortunate Natives have no place to go to, and are simply driven from pillar to post.[139]

The 1925 Native Taxation and Development Act, in force from 1926, reworked the system of taxation in the native reserves, adding to a lengthy regime of taxation the hated labor tax and the poll tax and, importantly, requiring that all taxes be paid in cash.

One of the Glen Grey Act's distinctive features had been its concern with managing African land and agricultural production, from the regulation of commonages to the "enclosing of arable lands."[140] The 1913 Land Act forms part of a lineage of state action concerned with the definition and demarcation of space, and the political definition and location of the state's subjects. The Act continued the state's fascination with, and concern over, space and territory that had begun with the creation of administrative districts in the early years of colonial conquest. But this period marked more than simply the extension of earlier practices and ideas regarding space. There was a quantitative increase in the state's concern with space, but also an important qualitative shift as officials sought far more technical and more detailed reorganization of productive space, the scientific management of African agriculture, and, ultimately, the control of African migrant labor. Anti-soil-erosion schemes, ridging, and contour farming – all of which required detailed mapping – comprised the most obvious examples of these developments. This state surveillance of space continued into the twentieth century; rising poverty and landlessness forced the state's attention. By the early 1920s the state had become obsessed with the land issue, and especially with arable land which bureaucrats assiduously attempted, if not always successfully, to measure. As one official asserted, "nothing but Legislation will put Land Matters on a satisfactory basis."[141]

Legislation indeed followed, culminating in the 1939 Betterment Act. Reworked in the apartheid era in what came to be known as "rehabilitation schemes," the Betterment Act represented the state's concern with labor and production. It also marked the ascendency of social engineering and the newly minted coercive powers of the state. The Act pursued a reworked policy of villagization "to separate migrants from full-time farmers and to herd the former into rural dormitory villages while keeping the latter on farms."[142] It also sought to conserve natural resources, especially forests, soils, and pasturage, from overcutting and from erosion and overgrazing.

The state represented the colonized racially, economically, and ethnically: as "non-whites"; as laborers; and as members of "tribes." The 1920s and 1930s witnessed a retribalization of the "native reserves" on the basis of the principles of indirect rule, what Mamdani has rightly termed "decentralized despotism."[143] The 1920 Native Affairs Act rationalized native administration, further bureaucratized colonial rule, and refined and expanded upon policies first set out in the Glen Grey Act. In addition to implementing the council system, the legislation took up the issue of rural development later addressed in a range of betterment and rehabilitation policies. These and other changes culminated in the 1927 Native Administration Act and marked the decisive shift towards territorial segregation. The act created a new system of Native Civil Courts using "native law and custom," and, importantly, embarked on a process of retribalization by introducing a system of indirect rule that strengthened the authority of chiefs. The state now reconstituted chiefs as functionaries of a vastly larger bureaucratic and segregationist state and, at the same time, reworked the duties of resident magistrates who now labored under the title of "native commissioners."

The 1927 Native Administration Act introduced a new system of colonial domination, based on the principles of indirect rule, to the Ciskei and Transkei. The Act reorganized the political map of the Transkei.[144] It thus reversed, profoundly so, the nineteenth-century goal of destroying chiefly power. The 1927 Act marked the "emergence of a more authoritative and centralized state armed with significant powers to dominate the relationship between state, capital, and labor."[145] As Evans has argued, "the 1927 act promoted a new discourse centered around greater efficiency, centralization, and internal coordination."[146] It was also unmistakably coercive: one section permitted the arrest of people "promoting feelings of hostility between natives and Europeans"; and authoritarian: under the Act the governor-general "as supreme chief" ruled Africans "by decree."[147] Using these powers he could "divide" or "amalgamate" or even "constitute a new tribe."[148]

A striking feature of the twentieth-century state was not simply its explosive growth and its increasingly authoritarian nature, but also the centrality of social engineering. Both reached a massive scale in the 1950s with the rise of apartheid. If nothing else apartheid represented the culmination of colonial social engineering and bureaucratic authoritarianism, a unique political marriage of undemocratic rule with ideas of scientific management and technical control.[149] With legislation such as 1952 Bantu Laws Amendment Act and the 1951 Bantu Authorities Act, the state completed its transformation of rule, at the center of which were chiefs and tribes. Apartheid was retribalization writ large. Officials pursued retribalization with abandon and, if necessary, through the barrel of the gun. In the late 1950s, and especially in the early 1960s, coercion and state violence became ubiquitous features of the South African political land-scape. These sad developments emerged in the context of widespread African resistance and a kind of bureaucratic madness that possessed officials and drove them to make their political and administrative fantasies the lived nightmare of the great majority of South Africa's people.

Ways forward

This brief chronicle of conquest and the state in South Africa is thus, ultimately, the story of the rise of a racist and authoritarian political order that pursued policies of social engineering scarcely exceeded anywhere in the modern world. The roots of authoritarianism, however, lay deep in the soil of conquest even if early officials barely knew what their mission was and the state remained too weak to enforce its often muddled policies. In the formation of bureaucracies, in the drawing of administrative boundaries, in the colonial state's tribalism, and in the state's will to know lay the beginnings of a political system of racial oppression that quite literally ruined the lives of millions of people. Rule required clear and stable categories, unchanging jurisdictional boundaries, and, indeed, an ethnographic/tribal model of colonized society. Bureaucratic growth entailed greater and greater delineation, and at the same time greater simplification, of colonial categories and the space the colonized inhabited. The gathering of colonial information in the pursuit of enhanced control demanded an unusual "narrowing of vision" that "brings into sharp focus certain limited aspects of an otherwise far more complex and unwieldy reality."[150] The very ambiguity of the colonial situation, the very fact that Europeans knew so little, created a situation in which the demarcation of political space and the definition of the political subject became matters of acute importance to colonial state formation and the daily practices of rule.

The roots of subaltern culture and consciousness lay still deeper, in the ancient conversations Africans have had – and continue to have – about power and land, authority and the rains, heroes and healing, virtue and wickedness. These ancient, lively, and ongoing conversations have been a central feature of South Africa's political history, just as important as the laws decreed by officials in a state that would become the epitome of modern evil. The first chapter explores the African political world in the context of colonial conquest, in a story of ritual, death, and rebellion at the edge of the British Empire. Here I examine how Africans conceived of the political world, and the ways these conceptions shaped interactions with their European conquerors. A central issue concerns the dramatic and heroic relationship between political authority and agriculture, chiefship and the rains. The making of the early colonial order entered this theater of politics, both changing and creating the semantic ground on which the newly colonized imbued the colonial world with meaning. Colonialism was not simply the colonization of consciousness.[151] It entailed rather the ongoing, creative, and open-ended productions of meaning and sensibility in a context of uneven power and exploitation, certainly, but also a growing repertoire of symbols by which people understood themselves and others. Culture is neither unchanging, a hermetically sealed repertoire of symbols, nor simply a reflection of somehow more fundamental historical processes. Culture is the complex production of meaning as people give voice – and in turn shape – to experience and action.

Chapters 2 and 3 offer an ethnography of state formation, especially the reasons why and the ways in which Europeans struggled to accumulate information on and about their African subjects. The focus here is more on the stratagems of state formation, less their actual success, and the ways people reacted to them and, at times, made them their own. I am especially interested in understanding how the colonial state sought to "create, under its control, a human landscape of perfect visibility; the condition of this visibility was that everyone, everything, had (as it were) a serial number."[152] The explosion of poverty in the native reserves and the colonial redefinition of the African as a unit of labor powerfully shaped colonial information gathering and control. This search for order, more properly this ever-increasing *demand* for order, can be seen in practices ranging from mapping and censuses to agricultural planning and ethnographic reporting. It is within this context of accumulating information, especially in the twentieth century, that rule became more bureaucratized and state rationality became increasingly instrumental, culminating in the triumph of authoritarianism within the tragedy of apartheid.

Part 2 shifts attention to an analysis of popular culture and resistance, building on a generation of innovative scholarship first produced in works such as Beinart and Bundy's *Hidden Struggles in Rural South Africa*. Chapter 4 analyzes the ideological work of the subaltern in the twentieth century. The chapter sets out three basic arguments developed in greater detail in the remainder of the book. First, the twentieth century saw continuing engagement with, and appropriation of, the colonial state. Second, evil became an acute problem for the subaltern in this period, as poverty insinuated itself ever more deeply in their lives and as the state persecuted them more consistently and more effectively. Third, as both a moral and a political problem, ideas about evil helped fashion new definitions of person and community and influenced how people confronted an increasingly intolerant political order. Christianity played an important role in these developments, particularly ideas about the devil, original sin, and the never-ending battle of good and evil. Christianity offered people the possibility of drawing a much more severe picture of the world, combining with earlier ideas of magic and witchcraft to form a kind of subaltern Manichaeanism, a social reality of terrible darkness and apocalyptic salvation.

Chapter 5 sets out this political order, the government legislation that created segregation and apartheid. Apartheid, especially the Bantu Authorities system and various development policies, created a wave of resistance that coursed over the region. Chapter 6 explores the 1940s and, especially, the 1950s. Here I am mainly interested in the continued appropriation and, ultimately, the reproduction of the state within social movements in the context of apartheid's introduction and continued economic collapse. In many respects twentieth-century struggles culminated in the early 1960s. Chapter 7 analyzes South Africa's single most important modern rural insurrection, the Pondoland Revolt, within the broader context of poverty, labor migration, and state formation. By the end of the revolt nationalist organizations such as the ANC and the Pan Africanist Congress (PAC) had realized the futility of non-violence before the tyranny of the apartheid state. At the same time the state abandoned any pretense to democracy or respect for the most basic human rights, bullying its African subjects, wantonly destroying livelihoods and lives, and pursuing with abandon policies roundly condemned by the international community and utterly reviled by the vast majority of South Africans. The book concludes with the beginning of the armed struggle. Here I focus on the attacks by Poqo (which means purity or a state of standing alone), the armed wing of the PAC, on African collaborators with an evil regime that produced one of the great injustices in modern world history.

The stories told and the issues examined in this exploration of an exemplary past – the meaning and exercise of power, the tragedies of poverty, the forces of jealousy and hatred, how people produce meaning in the face of power – together form a cautionary tale of sorts for understanding contemporary South Africa. What is the future of power and politics? Will the country achieve a durable democracy? Or will it succumb to the selfishness of those who brandish power and seek it for its own sake? Are today's problems, from poverty and hopelessness to the conviction that witches continue their evil work, the "morbid symptoms" of a society caught between its past and a world not yet fully born?[153]

Certainly the leaders of the African National Congress are now faced with a host of difficult and perhaps intractable problems; many of these problems they have inherited from the apartheid regime. They also have inherited the apartheid state itself: its many bureaucratic agencies; its administrative procedures; even its buildings. These artifacts of apartheid are important reminders of the ubiquitousness of the state, the fact that the state's presence has been hegemonic even if its rule seldom was. It also raises a pragmatic challenge. "The immediate task facing the democratic state, and a task upon which the fate of democracy . . . may yet turn," one writer has argued, "is to fuse the legitimacy of the democratic regime to a bureaucratic framework" of an unmistakably authoritarian political order detested by its recalcitrant subjects.[154]

This task is particularly complicated in the former homelands such as the Transkei. Here, in one of the twentieth century's most monstrous exercises in social engineering, policymakers combined their vision of traditional government, on the basis of the principles of indirect rule, with a modern authoritarian political order centrally concerned with marshaling and minutely controlling African labor. The results were a perversion of African political principles and practices, an economic system based on male migrant labor, an explosion of poverty, and widespread ecological collapse, to list but a few. In the minds of many people the politics of apartheid were, quite understandably, also the politics of evil.

What to do with the former homelands – particularly given crises ranging from HIV/AIDS to terrible poverty to institutional involution and the collapse of what few basic services there are – has been a pressing issue for South Africa's newly elected officials.[155] In contrast to revolutionary regimes elsewhere on the continent, including neighboring Mozambique, the ANC government has pursued a conservative policy. It has not sought a dismantling of rural political structures. Indeed, it is preserving structures that scarcely ever had any formal legitimacy in the eyes of black South Africans, who exposed them to critique and organized social movements that contested the state's claim to rule their lives. Most recently the government has embarked on a comprehensive program of developing "a vision which will harmonise the indigenous institutions of traditional leadership with our evolving system of democratic governance."[156] But will this compromise erode democracy and encourage the kinds of patrimonialism that has so afflicted much of the rest of the continent?

The authoritarian political order that a democratizing South Africa has inherited and seems to be replicating has its historical roots in the country's colonial past. The "colonial state" certainly constituted "the basic form of the apartheid state,"[157] both in terms of discrete policies and in the seemingly most mundane ways. Administrative boundaries created in the nineteenth century during the formative era of colonial state building have remained surprisingly stable. These boundaries were centrally important to the creation of a segregationist political order in the early twentieth century and, later, to the creation of apartheid itself. They remain largely in place today, not simply as vestiges of the *ancien régime* of authoritarianism but as enduring features of the post-apartheid political order.[158]

Part 1

Cultures of conquest

1   The death of Hope

He is the grain of the people,
We are all given life's grain,
We are all given life's grain
He gives it to the favored ones!

Mdukiswa Tyabashe[1]

Fury said to a mouse, That he met in the house, "Let us both go to law: I will
prosecute you.–Come, I'll take no denial; We must have a trial. For really this
morning I've nothing to do." Said the mouse to the cur, "Such a trial, dear
sir, With no jury or judge would be wasting our breath." "I'll be judge, I'll be
jury," said cunning old Fury: "I'll try the whole cause, and condemn you to
death."

Lewis Carroll, *Alice's Adventures in Wonderland* (New York, 1989), 47

He held Hope in his hand. "Go on I will follow," the Mpondomise paramount
chief told the British magistrate Hamilton Hope in the early days of October
1880. And "where you die I will die." As Mhlontlo spoke these words of unwavering loyalty the chief's wife lay ill not too far away, slowly perishing from a
long disease. Mhlontlo looked up and out to the hills cascading down from the
high mountains of Lesotho from whence the clouds and rains descended and
turned the wintered landscape into green pastures and waving fields of sorghum.
But the skies still refused to give up their rains. Drought, the worst to hit the
region in almost a century, held the land hostage. The crops had failed. Cattle
scrounged on brown scrub. In the north war had broken out. More was to come.

Mhlontlo had been busily organizing his warriors as the moon reached its
fullness and showered the land with shadows, and then began to wane, and
falling stars showered the night skies. Ritual specialists ministered magic to
make the warriors strong, to protect them in battle, to vanquish their enemies.
Hope expected the ritually strengthened warriors to be British allies in the colonial war against rebel Basotho. The white magistrate also had been preparing
himself: forging alliances with African chiefs; amassing a considerable arsenal
of modern weapons; and asserting in ways both banal and ritualized the political
supremacy of the British Empire.

As October wore on and spring ripened and began looking to summer, however, Hope became increasingly apprehensive. The magistrate had been warned that he "was plunging blindfold into a trap laid for me by" the Mpondomise paramount chief. "I shall be rather amused," Hope wrote, if the chief, "true to his reputation disappoints everybody's expectations; if he does not I shall no doubt have convincing proof that everybody is right. My own opinion," he concluded, aware both of the moment's drama and contingency, "is that as in a game of cards, having led my King of Trumps if anybody in the game holds the Ace I lose the trick, if not my King wins."[2]

Hamilton Hope departed from his offices in Qumbu, in the Transkei, on Wednesday 20 October 1880, for Mhlontlo's location and the seat of the Mpondomise paramountcy at Sulenkama. The day before Hope had written that "I meet Umhlonhlo and his Impi tomorrow at Sulenkama, and take as many as I can with me from here [sic]; but though I go without hesitation, it is as well to provide for contingencies." "I go strengthened," he continued, "by the feeling that I am doing right, and that the Almighty will guide me . . . I have done my utmost to steer a straight and proper course in these matters, and if I fail, and have been deceived, I shall have shown that I backed my opinion."[3]

Hope took with him three white officials, four African policemen, and a Khoikhoi servant. The nine men proceeded on horseback and on two scotch carts along the wagon road that stretched north to Natal and south to Umtata, the colonial capital of the Transkei. Just over 5 kilometers out from Qumbu the men turned left and on to the narrow path that led north into foothills and to Mhlontlo's residence.

The men, carts, and horses lumbered up the path. The 30-odd-kilometer trip was going very slowly. The path they traveled was broken and uneven. Rain further complicated their journey. By now the great drought was finally coming to an end, replaced not by light rains but by furious downpours that turned rivulets into rushing streams and made the track on which the men were traveling slippery and unstable. They stopped and made camp for the night. Rain was not the only complication hindering their progress. For the men brought with them 51 Snyder rifles, 7,000 cartridges, percussion caps and gunpowder, in addition to a substantial provision of food. This was not an inconsiderable supply of weaponry. All told the men were transporting more than 1,000 pounds of weapons and supplies. A far larger quantity of weapons was in transit to Qumbu and arrived there by early Saturday morning.[4] Mhlontlo had requested the arms in return for agreeing to fight as allies of the British against the Basotho rebels in what became known as the Gun War of 1880–1. In return Mhlontlo assured Hope that he would assemble his warriors at Sulenkama, where chief and magistrate, ruler and subject, would gather in preparation for war.

Hope arrived in Sulenkama on the morning of 21 October. He was anxious to press on north to Matatiele. He was, after all, a conqueror in the great age of British imperial expansion in South Africa and around the world.[5] Not to press on immediately to battle was for Hope to acquiesce to barbarism. But delays ensued. Hope suspected treachery. Were the warnings correct? Mhlontlo assured Hope that his army would gather on Friday. On Thursday evening the chief dined with the magistrate and spent the night sleeping under the scotch cart filled with ammunition.[6]

By Friday morning only some 400 men-at-arms had arrived. Hope "addressed a few words to them," explaining his intention and his desire "to make as much haste as possible." The chief intervened. "All his men were not present," he told the magistrate. Mhlontlo suggested, and Hope agreed, reluctantly, to wait until the following day, Saturday, 23 October. On Friday evening the chief again dined with Hope, along with his brother and four other men. Chief and magistrate "had a long conversation." Hope again explained to Mhlontlo the urgency of departing from Sulenkama on Saturday to make war on the rebel Basotho.

By Saturday morning the number of armed men had nearly doubled. The rains had stopped. The army, including the "principal men of the various clans," formed a "great curve a short distance" from Hope's encampment.[7] Warriors continued arriving during the day. In the early afternoon Mhlontlo "came to Mr. Hope and sat down in the Marquee with us all, and after partaking of a friendly glass of Brandy and water, asked us all to go up to the 'Umguyo'" ritual celebrations that fused agricultural fertility and chiefship and "where he said it would be decided upon what number of men would be enrolled" to fight in the colonial war.[8]

Hope saw the event as affirming the political supremacy and power of the magistrate, another moment when Africans recognized the power and legitimacy of the British Empire. To garner so many warriors would unequivocally demonstrate the magistrate's mastery over a chief who had too long resisted acknowledging the fact of colonial subjugation. Yet Hope could not overcome all the suspicions that swirled in his head. Might subversion be lurking behind this moment of ostensible submission? Might Hope's apogee suddenly become his nadir?

The chief asked the magistrate to address the warriors, many of whom were then performing a war dance. Hope agreed. The men – chief, magistrate, Hope's clerk and two other white men – entered the great curve. Hope and another official "seated" themselves "upon the rug" of Hope's favorite horse. Another man stood behind them, while the last was "a short distance away watching the men as they danced and sang their war songs," the warriors with weapons in hand pretending to stab their victims.[9]

Suddenly a great piercing whistle followed by a loud shout rang through the air. Everyone "stood still."[10] "Pondomise there is no word from me," Chief Mhlontlo told his people, "the words you will hear [are] from your Magistrate." "We are Government people in the true sense of the word," the chief continued.

"Government is our rock and shade." If Hope found these words comforting, what the chief now said mystified the magistrate, reversing in his mind the very semantic logic of the chief's declaration. "I am going to inform Sunduza [Davis, one of the white men]," Mhlontlo declared, "the words which *I wish* Mr. Hope to say."[11]

The chief led Davis away from the magistrate, out of the great curve of assembled men. Some 30 feet from where Hope and the other whites sat the chief stopped and turned around. He pointed to Hamilton Hope, and cried out, "You Pondomise! There are your chiefs!"[12]

Six men, all ritual specialists, rushed upon Hope and the two other white men. Mhlangeni, who also served as one of the chief's councillors, "seized" the magistrate by his long white beard and, "so drawing upwards his head, stabbed him in the breast." Within minutes all three men were dead. The remaining white man, Davis, survived; Mhlontlo saved him because Davis's father and now his brother served as missionary to the Mpondomise.[13] Mhlontlo, Davis reported, "was fighting only against the Government."[14] "The English government," Mhlontlo said,

has either entirely changed from what it was doing a few years ago, or it must be ignorant of what its Magistrates are doing. We are harshly treated. We came under the Government in order to gain peace and quietude, instead of which we have been in a continual state of unrest from the treatment we have received. Faith has been broken with us over and over again . . . Our cattle are to be branded; our arms are to be taken away; and after that our children are to be seized and carried across the water.

"I shall not be taken alive," Mhlontlo ended, "and a man can only die once."[15]

The chief later refused requests by Davis and his brother to bury the mutilated bodies. They were to remain there as fallen enemies, as carrion for birds and scavenging animals, their bones scattered to the winds; "the bodies must be eaten by birds, or their medicines would not act."[16] That Saturday Mhlontlo organized an escort to bring Davis back to the Qumbu magistracy. There he packed his bags and fled to Shawbury mission station. The telegraph wire had been cut, a few poles destroyed, the telegraph stolen; rebels would destroy most of the telegraph wires that webbed themselves across the Transkei. Mhlontlo had confiscated the munitions that had arrived the day of Hope's murder: 265 Snyder rifles and 15,750 rounds of ammunition. By 29 October 1880 the magistrate's offices and jail had been destroyed by fire.

Before the destruction of the buildings Chief Mhlontlo briefly occupied the magistracy. He sat in Hope's "great chair," before the law of the man and empire that had ruled over him. The "great table from the house of trials (court-room)" lay before the chief. On it sat "that great book, the book of causes (criminal record book)." A man "turned over the leaves of the book and read aloud from it: 'So-and-so charged with the crime of so-and-so; found guilty; sentenced to so-and-so'." "And then there would arise a great shout, and the armed warriors would rush upon the book and stab it with their spears, the while they shouted the death shout . . . the warriors exulted and laughed aloud and made mock of the Government, who, they said, was now dead."[17]

Hope was not the only magistrate whose power was mocked in the great rebellion of 1880–1. In Thembuland to the west warriors looted and burned to the ground the magistracy of Walter Stanford, who later became chief magistrate for Griqualand East, a central member of the 1881 Native Laws and Customs Commission, under secretary for Native Affairs, and chief magistrate of the Transkei – in short, a man of exceptional status, to African and European alike. But first there was a "high festival in my office" overseen by the rebel chief Dalasile.

A blanketed warrior representing Ndabeni (myself) occupied the judicial bench. Another on a chair below was addressed as Lufele (Daniel). Then a mock prisoner was placed in the dock and the form of a criminal trial was mimicked with keen humour. Nor was Webb (Umquwu) the chief constable left out of the piece. At the conclusion of the dramatic entertainment, the offices, our houses, and the police huts, were set on fire.[18]

And, in a quite different spectacle of ritual, representation, and revolt, but still a reversal of power, in Tsolo magistrate Welsh and ten other trembling whites locked themselves up in the jail. Chief Mditshwa offered to escort them to safety, but they refused.

"I'm here Welsh! Come out, I'll go with you to Mthatha [Umtata]." "No, I'm afraid of you! You must come in!" "No, come out! I'll go with you! But I won't come in there!"[19]

Power, ritual, and representation on the edge of empire

Structures and symbols of political process

Hamilton Hope died a ritual death, doubly so. Exalted yet destroyed, feared, and hated, the white magistrate and tempestuous colonial overlord became a central actor in the ritual reiteration of African political society and in the exploration of the colonial state's power. Only somewhat conscious of his role in a larger African drama of power and polity on the edge of empire, Hope was less aware that he was participating in his own ritual, a liturgy of Logos, his own attempt to construct a colonial political order through symbol and speech, myth and mimesis, ontology and action, to create the subaltern by bringing them under Western modes of discourse, action, control. Here, then, was a collision and a conjoining of political rituals, the making of empire, the remaking of African polity.

And Hamilton Hope has been apotheosized not once but twice. In late 1891 the British "had a suitable monument erected over the grave." Ceremonies ensued, attended by a few whites, but mainly by Africans. The assembled formed a great arch around the monument, reproducing the great arch of people that witnessed his ritual slaughter. During the ceremonies a group of Africans and their horses stood some distance from the event, in the precise place where chief Mhlontlo had sat that late spring morning in 1880.[20] Sir Walter Stanford, then chief magistrate of Griqualand East, presided over the ceremonies. In yet another strange twist Stanford, pointing to the European magistrates who now ruled over the region, borrowed Mhlontlo's words spoken at the moment of Hope's death: "Pondomise, there are your chiefs!"[21]

Memorialized, Hope remains in the hills around Sulenkama. In his death he became ever present and, in a sense, eternally exalted. This is the second apotheosis, the second elevation of the white magistrate within people's' understanding of past and present. "The Government still holds Hope against us,"[22] people recalled in the 1950s and still today, explaining both their poverty and their oppression at the hands of whites. Go to Qumbu and people will want to show you Hope's memorial. His death marks their poverty. Hope's death also marks a central point in their historical consciousness of colonialism, ritual creating memory. For in the ritual death of a white man an act of resistance became also the moment of colonial subjugation, "the assumption of subaltern status."[23] As A. C. Jordan composed the past in his *The Wrath of the Ancestors* (*Ingqumbo Yeminyanya*), the Mpondomise homeland, according to the fictional character Zwelinzima,

was no longer the land of heroes whose exploits used to fill him with pride and exultation. Today, alas, it was a land whose sun was dark, its light grown dim with the shadow of death. In this land the murmuring of bees he had so often heard with the ears of childhood had become the moaning of affliction, and the abundance of milk had become the bitterness of the *mhlontlo* juice. These legendary heroes whom he had so often seen in the dreams of childhood, armed with spears and shields, today became shadows in a strange wilderness, and their war-songs became the wailings of men in agony.[24]

I have lingered in the hills of Qumbu, where today there is so much violence and death, because in Hope's murder lay an exemplary story of encounter, conquest and culture – and the creation of boundaries, physical and mental, how they come to be marked with "sensible things,"[25] and the ways they can be safely crossed and dangerously violated. The death of Hope awakens a number of evidentiary and theoretical problems in writing about the edge of nineteenth-century empire. We know, for example, that Hope's was a ritual murder, and that parts of his body were used in making magical substances. The record, however, is silent on how these substances were made, or even precisely how people might have perceived the relation between Hope and occult forces, though we do know that people often imbued Western technology and technique with magical forces. Hope the colonial conqueror died at a ritual celebrating

the paramount chief and agricultural fertility, a ritual that both entailed threats
to the leader and a re-expression of his legitimacy. What we do not know for
certain is whether or not people may have understood him within the same
discourse of power, production, and magic.[26]

These are only some of the most important evidentiary issues. They are
compounded by theoretical and, ultimately, by interpretive challenges. Cross-
cultural encounters entail the "misreadings of meanings, the transformation
of meanings, and the recognition of meanings" as "native and intruding cultures are conjoined."[27] Understanding this conjoining in the context of ritual
moments is doubly difficult. As "signifying practice," ritual both "defines and
authorizes,"[28] and thus is central to the making and remaking of the world,
the drawing-up of boundaries both mental and physical.[29] But ritual, as in the
mguya Hope attended, is more than making sense of the world. Interpretive
moments, rituals, are ways of exploring and of exerting control over a world
in motion, a world of contingency, conjuncture, contradiction. On the edge of
empire people "resolved into indigenous concepts" the Europeans who came
among them, including colonial officials.[30] But just how deep did this resolution
go? To what extent were people able to speak across their differences?

Hope's death at the *mguya*, a celebration of authority and fertility among
Mpondomise that in this instance was timed with the arrival of spring, calls
attention to a deep history and common tradition of political symbol and process. The association of power and production, authority and fertility, is an
ancient one in Southern Africa, as it is elsewhere on the continent. In the
precolonial period rituals and sacred emblems of authority – for example the
mguya and leopard skins – manifested this association. Colonial conquest, however, ended a common tradition of political society begun over a millennium
ago in epic and in small localized migrations of Bantu-speaking agriculturists who farmed sorghum and herded cattle. This early history has disappeared
into the soils and into the languages people have used to describe and to give
meaning to their world. From time to time archaeologists discover sites of
early settlement, providing rare, crucial data, and pushing back in time the
arrival of the first agriculturists. We know, for example, that small numbers
of farmers lived in the Transkei at least by the end of the fifth century A.D.
A thousand years later their numbers had increased dramatically, and farmers
had pressed inland from the coast up into the hills and mountains leading to
Lesotho.[31]

Language aids in this reconstruction; like the soil itself language can be
unearthed to reveal core concepts in the mental world of people.[32] For if the
way people have felt and have understood their world is shaped by yet prior
understandings, if "objective perceptions are ordered by a priori conceptions,"[33]
the words for the "sensible things" that created boundaries and established
meanings help us discern a distant yet formative past. This is important because

colonialism was all about the creation of and contestation over new boundaries, and the meaning of the material objects that signified them: roads, district maps, censuses, even the "house of trials" and "that great book, the book of causes (criminal record book)."[34]

Two of the most powerful and quintessential emblems of precolonial political authority were the lion and the leopard.[35] European travelers observed the skins of both animals on the persons and at the homes of chiefs and paramounts.[36] The missionary van der Kemp described the Xhosa chief Ngqika, for example, as "covered with a long robe of [a] panther's skin."[37] Leopard and lion skin indicated "royalty or superiority," a later missionary noted.[38] Warriors might eat lion or leopard, and ritual specialists made potions from the animals which they sprinkled on warriors before a battle.[39]

Europeans also knew of rituals associated with those who slew these mighty animals. To kill them was revered yet associated with a great "impurity" that, to cleanse, required "a special festivity." For the vanquishing of these great animals re-enacted mytho-historical relationships between people and the land and the beginnings of the social order as people knew it. "When the hunting party has returned to the neighbourhood of its village," Alberti wrote in the early nineteenth century, "the one who inflicted the first wound on the Lion that was killed, is hidden from view by shields held in front of him."

At the same time one of the hunters leaves the troop and praises the courage of the slayer with a screaming voice, accompanied by a variety of leaps, and then returns again, when another one repeats the performance, during which the others incessantly shout hi! hi! hi! and beat their shields with knobkirries at the same time. This is continued until one has really reached the village. Now an inferior hut is constructed not far from it, in which the lion slayer has to remain for four days, separated from any association with the rest of the horde, because he is impure. Here he colours his whole body with white ochre, and youths who have not yet been circumcized, and who moreover are in the same position of moral impurity, bring a calf for sustenance and perform the necessary services for him. When the four days have passed, the impure person washes himself, colours himself again as usual with red ochre, and is conducted back to the horde by an official of the chief. Finally a second calf is slaughtered, which everyone may eat with him, as the impurity now no longer exists.[40]

The lion skins ended up at the kraal of the chief, the gathering of people and the circulation of the hide marking the authority and the political boundaries of a chiefdom.[41]

The ancient origin of the word for chief, *inkosi*, means "lion," though most Xhosa speakers today would not be aware of this linguistic connection of animal and ruler. The widespread dispersal of *inkosi* suggests that the first agriculturists arrived with complex institutions of political authority centering on the elevated status of big men, the founders of chiefdoms whose status was adorned by

1 Xhosa chief Kreli (Sarhili), wearing a leopard skin (reproduced with permission, Cory Library, Rhodes University)

sacred animals.[42] This hypothesis is confirmed in the second emblem of political authority. The word for leopard scarcely differs in places as far away as Angola and Burundi; there are still more distant roots in West–Central Africa in the heartlands of proto-Bantu some five thousand years ago. In the Eastern Cape the root for leopard is shared by two other words: the authority or mandate of a political leader, and to celebrate that leader's jurisdiction.[43]

Hope's murder was a premeditated act. He died, indeed was ritually murdered, by the paramount's "witchdoctor," at a celebration that had roots in a distant past and which reaffirmed in ritual practice some of the most basic concepts of political authority and its relationship to agricultural fertility.[44] September and October are crucial months in the agricultural cycle. With the hoped-for rains people cleared lands, planted seeds, and anxiously awaited the appearance of green sprouts reaching skyward from their roots in the African soil. This period is marked astronomically. Indeed, 20 October, the day Hope left his offices for Sulenkama, came exactly twenty-nine days after the southern hemisphere's vernal equinox, the precise equivalent of one lunar month. By the time Hope arrived in Sulenkama people would have noticed that the days were growing longer and the sun was rising and setting further to the north. Venus would have appeared low and bright and crystalline in the western sky; in the east, and opposite Venus, Jupiter and Saturn would have sat in an unusually close configuration. The annual spring Orionid meteor showers, one of the easiest to observe, had dazzled the evening skies for about a week. The celestial display peaked on 20 October. Two days earlier, 18 October, the moon had sat full and ripe in the spring sky.[45]

October was an especially auspicious, and in times of drought downright anxious, period for farmers. It is easy to forget just how fragile agriculture can be, especially in the Eastern Cape. People worried about the appearance of locusts and grasshoppers, whether animals such as baboons might ravage crops in the dark of night, or if the cattle of an inattentive herder might stray into the fields. We know that rainfall has been, and continues to be, variable and often extremely localized, so much so that one can see rain falling in one area while, literally next door, another area remains bone dry. While the Eastern Cape is not nearly as dry as regions to the north and west, it is prone to recurrent drought. We can imagine people in times of drought looking up into the sky at the showers of the Orionid meteors and lamenting an earth unquenched by the spring rains.

People have long fretted over the arrival of nourishing rains but also the possibility of destructive downpours. With the change of seasons, and especially with the arrival of the spring rains, lightning struck violently and capriciously as thunderstorms bolted down from the Lesotho highlands, creating fires, destroying homesteads and crops, occasionally killing the innocent. As one nineteenth-century writer described it, when the appearance of the sky indicates the approach of a storm, magicians . . . shout and yell in the most frantic manner to divert the storm from its course. Such storms frequently diverge from the straight line, and occasionally part into two or more sections in their course. This is attributed to the power of magicians. He who has the highest skill diverts the storm from his own locality, and should he fail it is because one more powerful than he was working against him, and sent the storm on the course it took.[46]

The spring was thus particularly a time of destruction as well as creation, of promise and of portent, of glittering skies and warmer days, an uneasy moment in the making and remaking of the world. Hope's final days were lived out in precisely this grand drama about which he knew very little.

In short, people faced the problem of contingency and order, the expected and the unforeseen. Not surprisingly fertility and the fabulous were closely intertwined. A pioneer missionary, van der Kemp, described how, during "great thunder-storms," people said they saw "a man dressed in green . . . leaning against the stump of a tree, having his eyes fixed towards the ground; when they offer him corn, meat, or milk, or invite him to come into their houses, as they commonly do, he never accepts the invitation, and seldom speaks." But "once in a tremendous storm he has been heard to say, 'Do not be afraid, I only play with this country!'"[47] Storms quite literally brought out sorcerers who worked their magic in competition with others to avoid destructive cloudbursts and to bring nourishing rains to the crops.

Where contingency plays with the country, authority brings order. Politically powerful individuals tamed forces that could destroy and, in so doing, brought fertility to the world. The connections between farming and authority, between chaos and order, between destruction and production, had roots in the origins of political society and in the expansion of agriculture. Agriculture created a dramatically different landscape, but only after newcomers had become well established in the area. This could take many, many decades. Trees needed to be cut down, land broken with stick or hoe, animals that might compete with or kill cattle or destroy crops controlled. Leopards and early agriculturists shared the same environment, wooded areas near sources of running water. Chiefs, "owners of the land," descended from these pioneer lineages and heroic founders who made peace with the land and the animals and original inhabitants living on it. People imbued them "with a special ritual relationship to the land and its spirits."[48] They wore rings of elephant ivory, the skins of leopards and lions, and bracelets of copper and iron, representing chiefs as hunters and the possessors of metals. Chiefs were, in short, the "sons of those who wear ivory arm-rings," the "Sons of heroes."[49]

Migration is a central feature of the common tradition of agriculturists, and, with it, a consciousness that they are intruders whose relation to the land is powerful precisely because it was once so fragile. Agriculturists first settled near the coast. Over many centuries they began moving inland, into the hills

2 Xhosa homestead: *View of a Kaffir Village*, 1803, painting by Alberti (Africana Museum, Johannesburg)

and valleys that led in precisely the same direction whence came the rains and lightning and thunder. These Bantu speakers, with their cattle, sorghum and iron, did not enter a vacant land. In the far west of the Eastern Cape there were pastoralists, the Khoikhoi. But especially and ubiquitously there were the people of the eland, the hunting and gathering Thwa (San) whom the agriculturists recognized as the original inhabitants of the land. The newcomers had to make peace with those who came before them, those who knew the land best and who had the most elemental connections to it. The people of the eland lived in the mountains where rain clouds formed. Agriculturists saw these original inhabitants as the "producers" of rain.[50]

This relationship of autochthon and newcomer was paradoxical, as it is elsewhere in Africa.[51] In the Eastern Cape agriculturists at once despised and revered Thwa. Many they married and brought into their world of agriculture. Others they vanquished. But in all cases, as one scholar has written in a very different context, "mastery of the land had to involve the legitimizing presence of a quintessential autochthon."[52] Chiefs recognized this presence by inviting rain doctors to their residence to produce showers that succored the land. These hunter-gatherers, these "authors of the rains," came to the chief's enclosure and performed ceremonies that would bring agricultural fertility. When rains still did not appear the autochthon would say that the rains had been bewitched, their magic defeated by someone more powerful and devious. "Did you not see" how "the heavens gathered blackness, the clouds enveloped the sun, the lightening spread through the land and the thunders roared?" "Now that was *my* rain. I made it and intended it to fall on this land, but there is a power wielded by some person . . . which paralyzes my efforts and blasts your expectations."[53]

The association of chiefship with rain, autochthons and, especially, with magic, are ubiquitous features of political society, a central part of the common tradition of the Eastern Cape.[54] Bhaca, for example, locate the celebration of rain and fertility with a distant and revered chief who had exceptional control of the magical world. Chiefs' elevated status,[55] their symbolic power and control of powerful magic, stemmed from their origin as founding heroes. They opened new areas to agriculture and herding, defeated the animals of forest and grassland, vanquished enemies, made their peace with the original occupants of the land. Their magic, with its connections to the founding of society, could help ensure nourishing rains and bountiful crops.

Fertility and, especially, rain thus formed an ineluctable part of this notion of ownership and of the founding of new communities by heroes. One observer wrote in the early part of the nineteenth century that "they fancy the influence of their departed chiefs," whose spirits could bring drought and famine.[56] Chiefs were responsible for the rain because of their descendants' relations with autochthonous hunter-gatherers. Xhosa chiefs enlisted Thwa (San) rainmakers, in a sense reproducing founding mytho-historical relationships between agriculturists and hunter-gatherers as the former migrated some one thousand years ago towards the land of the rains.[57] Such "rain-doctors . . . are supported for their imaginary services by their respective Chiefs" who "institute a grand feast . . . which is often continued for several days, while" the rainmaker deploys "his magic charms."[58] "Procuring rain in time of drought," Hunter wrote in her classic 1936 ethnography of the Mpondo, "is normally the business of the chief. Where the district chief is powerful he is appealed to for rain."[59] Bhaca chiefs "acted as the tribal rainmaker."[60] Once they had performed their magic "even if the sky was clear it would rain before you reached home."[61] In 1913, for example, a colonial official wrote that the Bhaca chief Rolobile had "a great name as a 'rain maker'." Rolobile "had 'doctored' the hills and caused a heavy rain so that the Kinira river should be impassable . . . It is also widely believed that the recent drought was caused by Rolobile refusing to make rain, as he had been suspended" by the British.[62]

"It was an ancient custom" among Thembu "to hold meetings in times of drought at the graves" of paramount chiefs "and 'cry' for rain."[63] Mpondomise chiefs descended from heroic men and autochthonous women who brought rain to the land and thus made agriculture possible. Malangana is remembered among Mpondomise as being a pioneer who led people from Natal into the Transkei. An accomplished hunter, Malangana "was a master of magic" who defeated the many leopards that prowled virgin forests. His grandson Ngcwina married a Thwa woman, whose son, after an epic struggle with his brother from another wife, became chief. A "big rain" followed. "The rain came, and thus was originated a practice among the Mpondomise: when there is a drought, they go to the Thwa to plead for rain. That custom was born on that day" of marriage.[64]

Rites associated with the agricultural cycle, such as the *mguya* Hope attended, reiterated the elevated status of chiefs. At the beginning of spring chiefs blessed the seed and brought the rain, typically around late September or October after the vernal equinox, when the Orionid meteors might be showering the sky and rain clouds began descending from the Lesotho highlands. At first harvest households delivered a portion of the grains to the chief, in the offering of first fruits that took place when the green maize became available in late December or January. In some parts of the Eastern Cape harvesting required "permission from the Great [paramount] Chief."[65] "It is accounted a very great crime," a European explorer wrote in the early nineteenth century, "for any person to partake of the first fruits of the harvest before this ceremony has been celebrated."[66] These rites, as we shall see later, rearticulated the chief's status as hero/founder and controller of magic.[67] Importantly, rituals associated with rain and fertility were intimately connected to the political system. Chiefs ensured the fertility of the land at the same time that they strengthened their warriors.[68] In so doing they affirmed their elevated status and created, recreated, and clarified the boundaries of their rule.

But precisely because they were so important to social health and to the drawing of social and political boundaries, these rites were not without danger. Subordinates might not proffer their offerings, declaring their independence and reworking the local map of power. Within the rites themselves, political process and structure could be probed, interrogated, and ultimately reworked. Among the Bhaca, for example, chiefs were both praised and insulted, a "ritual rebellion" central to the reconstitution of the political order. At the *mguya* Hope attended warriors brandished their spears, weapons that could have been turned against the chief himself.[69]

A central feature of chiefs' elevated status, then, was their access to, and control over, magic.[70] The historical record, oral tradition, and ethnographic reporting is replete with the association of magic and chiefship, as it is in other areas of Africa.[71] Magic formed an important part of the eighteenth-century Xhosa paramount chief Gcaleka's attempt to centralize power. Maqoma and others did the same in the first half of the nineteenth century.[72] The Mpondomise founder chief Malangana "was a master of magic – yes, a king having exceptional magical ability."[73] The Bhaca chief Rolobile deployed powerful magic is his conflict with chief Mngcisana. Not only did he create destructive downpours and drought, Rolobile bewitched Mngcisana with an *isidliso*, a magical creature that enters into the stomach or esophagus and kills its victim unless the person can attain powerful medicines to counteract the witch's animal. Mngcisana "became very ill" and "was suddenly seized with violent fits of vomiting and purging." He said "he was bewitched and that his own Native doctors extracted two large toads from his body!"[74]

These concepts carried over into early relationships between Africans and Europeans. Chiefs, for example, believed that early missionaries had access to rain magic; not surprisingly they tried to control them. "Where [was] the rain," a chief asked van der Kemp, "alluding to the dryness of the season; and desired that I would pray to Thiko [God] for rain." Ngqika also requested the missionaries to "make it rain." Since the chief's "magicians could make no rain, I should give rain to the country." The missionary said he could not "procure rain." But he later "prayed for rain in subordination to the glory of God." Heavy rains followed. The Africans "of this country all knew what had been transacted between Gika and me with respect to the rain."[75]

Historians have written of the paradoxical nature of authority and its relation to magic. We have noted the importance of precedence, that chiefs were descended from pioneers, and thus were considered to have a special relationship to the land and to the forces that protect and make it bountiful.[76] Access to and control over magic was connected to their pioneer status. Vansina has written that leaders "had extraordinary powers, identical with and often superior to those of witches . . . A battery of charms helped him to repel the attacks of witches, and his own witchcraft killed competitors or subjects."[77] And yet, paradoxically, witchcraft was both "an ideology of equality and cooperation" and central to political competition and the centralization of power.[78] Equally paradoxically, the chief embodied collective identity and was simultaneously the most individualistic of figures, capable of behavior that could extend well beyond ethical norms. They both made and unmade the world.

Magic was central to a chief's accumulation of power, especially in what has been glossed in the historical record as "eating up" through witchcraft accusations, inevitably one of the first practices the British prohibited. Rapacious and individualistic, they aggressively "ate up" others to concentrate power within themselves. Ritual specialists allied with chiefs accused others of witchcraft, confiscated their stock and, typically, redistributed a portion in the creation of new political alliances. Such eating up was especially pronounced in periods when chiefs attempted to expand their power or when that power came to be contested. Sickness and death inevitably involved suspicions of witchcraft; Ngqika suspected the rain doctor van der Kemp of poisoning him.[79] Magic, thus, resided at the center of competitive politics, a politics that brought conflict and disorder as well as stability and abundance.

Power lay as much in chiefs' and the heads of agnatic lineages' capacity to control material resources as in the command of symbol and ritual, reflecting a conceptual map of power and producing a distinctive geography of rule. Like the display of metal filings arranged by the force of a magnet, power was concentrated at the center but dispersed at the periphery. Chiefs' magic both repelled and attracted, by bringing rain and through "eating up," as did the more mundane but no less important processes of strategic marriages, the resolution of disputes, tribute, cattle loans, and death dues. In return for nourishing rains commoners gave up stock and produce to chiefs at crucial moments in the agricultural cycle. In so doing people participated in the drawing and redrawing of political domains, the location of power and the identification of its boundaries.[80]

Drought substantially imperiled the power of chiefs. With drought political boundaries blurred. Competition flared into open hostility and conflict, and misfortune befell the world. In times of drought people looked to new centers of political authority within an always contested world of chiefly rivalries – or they sought alternative bases of social health. For chiefs, and especially paramount chiefs, never totally controlled the ritual and magic necessary to bring rains. Autochthons, representatives of an original world, lived nearby in the foothills and mountains rising from the agricultural lowlands. Relationships with autochthons made possible a restaging of the mytho-historical contacts that first brought agriculture and rainfall. There were other ritual specialists with powerful magic. There were also one's own ancestors, whose spirits scrutinized the living.[81]

The environment, then, fashioned and refashioned political domains. Political boundaries also expanded and contracted with the careers of individual chiefs, whose character helped determine the extent of their rule. The early reign of a chief was an especially important time when political boundaries might be redrawn or more clearly defined, and new frontiers created. With the waxing of power, however, came its waning. Chiefs' deaths always gave rise to suspicion. Their illnesses or deaths inflamed agnatic tensions and rivalries; sons might even be accused of bewitching fathers.[82] Succession invariably became a time of considerable instability and conflict in which political domains might be substantially reworked, especially in the relationships among chiefs and between chiefs and lineage heads.[83] Each of these variables, and for ruler and ruled they were intimately interrelated, meant that the many hundreds of political boundaries were constantly expanding or contracting, coming into resolution or fading into ambiguity. Frontier zones or unsupervised areas formed at the edges of domains. These in turn had an important impact on life at the center, at the homesteads of chiefs and paramounts.[84]

A central feature of political process were the attempts, whether successes and failures, of chiefs to centralize power, and to extend that power over bordering chiefdoms. To do so required the stimulus created by the unequal distribution of powerful symbols and magic, economic goods, trade, or population. Such disequilibrium seldom existed until the late eighteenth century, and when it did exist it was fleeting. Moreover, because of the alternative bases of social health that existed at the level of individual homesteads, chiefs never monopolized control over those symbols necessary to ensure agricultural fertility. Magic's ubiquitousness defeated its centralization.

European observers noted how chiefs seemed to be the "absolute Lord, and Master of his own *clan*."[85] Yet there were no kings, for paramount chiefs seldom wielded "an authority over the *whole* nation." People may have called themselves, for example, the Xhosa, "yet each horde or the subjects of what may be termed independent chiefs, have separate [*sic*] and particular appellations by which they are distinguished from those of the other rulers."[86] As Alberti described the Xhosa in the early years of the nineteenth century, they

are divided into hordes. Each of these hordes has its chief, whose power and standing in respect of other chiefs is related to the respective number of households. At times a horde does not live together, but has settled in different places and has divided itself into two or three sections. In that case the sections in which the chiefs does not live are governed by persons appointed by him ... depending upon the number of such chiefs occupying a certain stretch of country with their hordes, they fall under a Principal Chief, who regards this area as his domain over which he exercised his sovereign powers.[87]

At best there were unstable principalities[88] in which one chief effectively exerted power over a number of others. Typically the attempt to create a principality failed, as in the case of the late eighteenth- and early nineteenth-century Xhosa chief Ngqika. Ngqika's sub-chiefs "jointly decided to leave the unjust one, together with their hordes, and to take up their abodes in another region, whereby he was compelled to withdraw his new law."[89] The most effective strategy to frustrate attempts at political centralization was simply for households or larger groups to move to new areas. People left "by gradual emigration," van der Kemp wrote. "Some kraals break up, and march towards the borders of the country, and there they stay."[90]

"When the people or chiefs get annoyed with him they speak out freely and if it be not arranged they more seldom rebel than show their displeasure by gradually leaving him." The leaders of petty chiefdoms might be "attached to some more powerful chief," but the "authority of these chiefs is however extremely limited." In short, the "great chiefs" could not "control the subordinate ones," nor did a "subordinate one [have] any efficient check upon the individual members of their respective kraals."[91] Because rule was exceedingly personal power dissipated rapidly with distance from the chief's kraal. The pilfering of cattle from the chief's more distant kraals, whereby "herders" and others "contrive to impose upon the Chief,"[92] demonstrated both the extent and the fragile limit of a chief's political domain.

In short, until the nineteenth century African polities, anywhere in the Eastern Cape, cannot be described as states.[93] Paramount chiefs were invariably weak; people most often followed their local chief over that of the paramount.[94] Political society was as highly competitive as it was localized. Chiefs and other big men attempted to consolidate and to extend their control, but their successes were at best limited and usually fleeting. The deaths of chiefs began the process anew, so that political boundaries were more or less permanently in flux and the existence of numerous, often overlapping, frontier areas characterized the political geography of the region.[95]

This complex political landscape, formed by the environment and fashioned by the lives of people who sought authority or who fled the pretensions of the powerful, began to change in the second half of the eighteenth century, and then rapidly and irrevocably in the nineteenth century. The pace of change also quickened radically. New symbols and sources of magic appeared, typically first in the guise of European missionaries and then the representatives of the colonial state. New sources and networks of trade appeared, and in a few areas there were changes in population density and distribution. All of these factors became part of the field of political competition and process.

These changes did not inevitably lead to state formation; indeed, virtually all of the Eastern Cape remained stateless. In the early part of the nineteenth century, however, states began emerging in the wider region. By 1818 the Zulu kingdom had arisen north of the Mzimkhulu River. The kingdom's consolidation and expansion, particularly in the 1820s, powerfully reshaped politics in the greater Eastern Cape region as groups of people moved south. One such group was the Bhaca under chief Madikane who settled in the area just north of what is today Mount Frere and near territories claimed by the Mpondomise. Other groups moved further south, in some cases across the Kei River. These complex migrations generally created a more competitive and more anxious political world that, in some areas, accelerated the process of political centralization as chiefs, and especially paramounts, sought strategic alliances and attempted to extend and strengthen their control over regions. The most notable examples of these processes are the rise of the Sotho kingdom high in the Drakensberg mountains and political centralization among the Mpondo under Faku.

Colonial conquest followed closely on the heels of this competition, centralization, and rising disequilibrium. Indeed, the colonial state should be counted as the fourth example of political centralization unfolding in the wider region, a state with a wholly different set of symbols, processes, and conventions that sometimes destroyed and often distorted what had been a common tradition of political process and society. The conquest of the Eastern Cape began in the last quarter of the eighteenth century and ended, well over a century later, with the 1894 annexation of Pondoland. In the Transkei conquest generally proceeded in two waves. The first wave, roughly period between the 1850s and the 1870s, depending on the areas, entailed a series of political agreements in which African rulers accepted British rule. In so doing the British expected them to end political conflicts, glossed in the archive as "tribal wars." The second wave involved transforming conquest into rule: the collection of taxes, the greater elaboration of administrative boundaries, and, importantly, a decisive shift in power away from chiefs and to magistrates.

Much of the political conflict in the nineteenth century coincided with, or immediately followed, drought. The colonial conquest of the Transkei unfolded during a particularly unstable climatic period. Periodic droughts had long characterized the area. Generally speaking, however, the second half of the nineteenth century saw more frequent and more punishing droughts as a consequence of world climate changes rooted in disturbed Pacific Ocean air masses.[96] The drought that began in the closing years of the 1870s was especially long and punishing, perhaps the worst in the living memories of people. We know, further, that drought created anxiety among people who relied on rainfall for their agriculture, heightened fears of the malevolent use of magic, and produced political instability. Colonial conquest thus unfolded at precisely a time of exceptional apprehension and insecurity.

Until the late 1870s the British were not always clear how they intended to rule these new possessions. In some respects their early rule in areas such as Thembuland and further to the east was similar to that over their protectorates. Chiefs retained much of their power. Few in number and their control nominal, resident magistrates ruled "principally through their own Chiefs and in accordance with Kaffir laws and customs, when not opposed to justice or humanity."[97] In many areas chiefs used the first magistrates in their attempts to consolidate

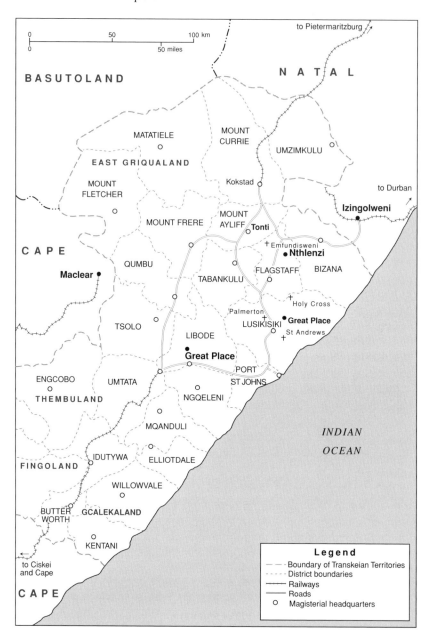

3 The Transkei

and extend their power. Weak magistrates evinced "an unwillingness to mea-sure" their "power and authority with that of the Chief" under them.[98] In the early 1870s, for example, the Thembu paramount chief Gangelizwe used colo-nial officials in his attempt to extend his control in the region south of the town of Umtata, in a border area occupied by people who defined themselves as Bomvana but whose chiefs at times recognized the Xhosa paramount Kreli. Gangelizwe's visit heightened political competition with Kreli, which ended in war in 1872.[99]

The early "position of affairs" in Thembuland, one official wrote in a confi-dential report, was such that the chief magistrate and individual resident mag-istrates ruling over chiefs "exercise[d] judicial functions by the grace of the Paramount Chief, the Colonial Government tacitly agreeing to support their action." Where "the duties and powers of our officers should be of a character well defined, abiding, and indisputable," they were in fact "vague, ephemeral, and subject to the caprice of a barbarian."[100] One legal opinion held that "deriving their authority to exercise judicial functions over the chiefs," resident magistrates had "no legal right to exercise jurisdiction... as *British Officials*" because the territory did not yet fall "within the jurisdiction of any civilised government."[101] In short, magistrates were there on sufferance of the paramount chief.

Conquest was achieved mainly through a series of agreements between chiefs and officials. Violence typically took place after, not before, colonial rule had been extended over a given area. Chiefs initially agreed to have their people "placed... under the protection" of the Cape government. They saw these agreements as alliances and, importantly, not recognition of subaltern status. Indeed, technically Africans were not colonial subjects, even if "the colonial government had been exercising de facto jurisdiction."[102] And magistrates, including the chief magistrate, "had no legal status independently of the will of the Chiefs."[103]

This muddled situation, in which the British were not exactly sure what they were doing, changed towards the end of the 1870s. In 1877 the colony annexed Griqualand East and the region between the Kei and Bashee Rivers. Griqualand East had received its first magistrate six years earlier; annexation formalized a prior process of colonial conquest, making *de jure* what was in many respects already *de facto*. In 1884 Mqikela, the Mpondo paramount and son of Faku, who had led Pondoland on the road to political centralization, quite literally sold Port St. Johns in return for a yearly subsidy. In 1885 the colony annexed Thembuland, Emigrant Thembuland, Gcalekaland, and Bomvanaland. The following year saw the incorporation of what became the Mount Ayliff district and the so-called Rode Valley near Mount Ayliff and Mount Frere.[104] All that remained was Pondoland, annexed to the colony in 1894.

By 1877 and the beginning of the so-called Ninth Frontier War resident magistrates, employees of the Cape Colony's Department of Native Affairs, had spread out over much of the Transkei. Two years later the colonial state proclaimed a set of rules and regulations for the Transkei that helped clear up, at least in their minds, the increasingly confusing situation on the ground.[105] The laws both continued and radically expanded the colonial accumulation of power. Much of this centered on the relationship of chief and magistrate, and specifically around legal issues. The rules mandated a police force for each magistrate. These employees of the state, instead of the chief's attendants, became the "messengers of the court." Fines chiefs had once levied for "blood crimes" such as assault now became the property of the colonial government. More generally the magistrate became responsible for the prosecution of criminal offenses. In civil cases heard before the chief, Africans had the right of appeal to the magistrate's court.

In addition to these legal rules there were other regulations. Only the magistrate, for example, could sound the "war cry" that had been the privilege of the chiefs alone. A colonial decorum was instituted in Africans' behavior on public roads and, especially, in the magistrates' offices; this in effect helped ritualize people's face-to-face relations with magistrates. There were also controls on movement: "The pass system will be rigidly adhered to, no one will be permitted to leave his district without having a pass signed by his magistrate." Finally, the government required magistrates to keep a record book of criminal and civil proceedings, a census book, and a book setting out and describing his district boundaries and the boundaries of individual locations.[106]

These laws and regulations built upon previous legislation, especially the prohibition of witchcraft and the practice of "eating up," and the creation of hut taxes. Together they represented not simply a frontal assault on the institution of chiefship but an attack on the common tradition of political process and structure. A series of land commissions in the 1870s reduced what had been literally hundreds of shifting political units to less than thirty magisterial districts based on rigid boundaries. This redrawing and simplification of the political map had profound implications. Many lesser chiefs who had enjoyed authority over others now found themselves effectively deposed and transformed into headmen and functionaries of the colonial state. Their domains were incorporated into the various magisterial districts in which a colonial official might rule over just one or a few chiefs. In Engcobo in Thembuland some thirty chiefdoms were reduced to just four; only two received subsidies so that, in reality, the other two chiefs had been utterly emasculated. The nineteen chiefs under the putative control of Dalasile were reduced to seven; these in turn became headmen.[107]

Conquest also ended paramount chiefs' historic attempts to expand their control over outlying domains. Their status was in effect reduced to that of other chiefs, and thus the domain of their rule shrank considerably. Gangelizwe might be the Thembu paramount, but his authority roughly paralleled that of Dalasile. He might "exercise authority and settle law suits except cases of murder, crimes arising out of witchcraft, serious assaults, and thefts from other tribes" in his "own section," but the chief's "authority should not extend beyond" that "section."[108] The Mpondomise polity was split into two, creating the districts of Tsolo and Qumbu. People may have recognized Mhlontlo as having higher status than Chief Mditshwa, but under colonial rule his control remained largely confined to Qumbu district. To these examples one can add others, from the Xhosa paramountcy in the west to Pondoland, the last region to be annexed by the British, in the east.

The redrawing of the political map immediately created great anxiety, heightened political competition, and led, ultimately, to open conflict. At first political boundaries blurred very considerably. For example, in part on the basis of his dealings with officials early in the 1870s the Thembu paramount Gangelizwe considered his control to extend south just over the line separating the Mqanduli and Elliotdale districts.[109] This area was a classic borderland, which appears in the archival record as multi-ethnic, that had been contested earlier by the chief and the Xhosa paramount Kreli. Gangelizwe especially disliked the fact that the magistrate was permitting "people to reside . . . without the procuring the opinion of the Chiefs."[110]

From the 1870s the officials considered such apparently blurred boundaries as unacceptable; the British would not tolerate the existence of borderlands that appeared to them to epitomize African irrationality and barbarism. This shift formed part of a broader trend. What had become increasingly clear by the late 1870s – to both colonizer and colonized – is that magistrates no longer ruled on sufferance of the chief. This became abundantly clear with the collection of hut taxes and the prosecution of defaulters, the drawing up of censuses that concretized new political boundaries, and the increasing intervention by magistrates in areas once controlled by chiefs. As the power of magistrates waxed, that of chiefs waned. Magistrates were busily "eating up" others, chiefs and commoners alike. No wonder that conflict and misfortune, especially drought, followed.

Killing Hope, making rain

Hamilton Hope was the third magistrate to rule over the Mpondomise. In the early 1870s, following a period of political expansion and contraction, Mhlontlo and a number of other chiefs in the East Griqualand area accepted British suzerainty. Hut tax first became payable in 1875. In a long report written at the end of 1877 the second magistrate confidently asserted that "Magistrates now occupy the *position* formerly held by the Chiefs."[111] The official exaggerated; the situation was far more complex. Mhlontlo was not so compliant; indeed, he remained very much committed to enlarging other areas of political authority.

In a witchcraft case Mhlontlo had eaten up one of his subjects. The magistrate had intervened, fining the chief fifteen head of cattle. While "he has not refused to pay the demand," Mhlontlo "greatly embarrassed me by his passive opposition and non-compliance."[112] In other respects the chief seemed cooperative; officials often had difficulty understanding why a chief might appear pliant in one instance and intractable in another. The chief, for example, "personally afforded" the magistrate's "clerk every assistance in making" a census of his people "as accurate as possible, and in which he evidently took considerable interest."[113] In this and in other instances the chief was attempting to use the British in such a way as to enlarge his political domain, even as colonial officials were concluding that the chief was submitting to their control.

Hope became magistrate in 1878. He had previously served in southern Basutoland where he ruled as the first magistrate over the Basotho chief Moorosi. Frequently flogging his subjects Hope earned the dubious "reputation for being cruel and vindictive."[114] He was, in short, explosive and tyrannical. The next magistrate inherited a discontented people who rebelled shortly after his arrival and then, again, in the great Gun War of 1880–1.[115] In the first rebellion Moorosi lost his life to colonial gunfire; his severed head became a war trophy for the colonial troops.

Hope's reputation, as well as the death and mutilation of Moorosi, would surely have reached Mhlontlo. Hope had bragged in 1878, before moving to Qumbu, that "it has lately (for some reason unknown to me) become the fashion for native[s] to give utterance to absurd threats about me. At a meeting of Mooirosi's army, where there were about 700 wretches armed to the teeth, which took place within rifle-shot of my house a few weeks ago, it was actually proposed to open the ball by cutting my throat!" "I can't but be flattered," Hope boasted, "that even at Kimberley the natives do not forget me."[116]

His arrival among the Mpondomise created some considerable concern. It also offered an opportunity to roll back some of the previous magistrate's efforts to erode chiefly rule. In late August 1878 Mhlontlo called a meeting with the new magistrate. This itself was important. Colonial rituals of subordination usually entailed a new magistrate first calling a meeting of his subjects. Equally importantly, Mhlontlo attended the meeting, instead of sending his chief councillors and ritual specialists.

The Mpondomise leaders wasted no time. "We are here today about the letter sent by Government appointing you as our Magistrate," said Tyali. "We have not come for anything else." Next the recently appointed headman Zenzo raised the central issue of the jurisdiction of chiefs and headmen.

Bebeza
We thank Government, our Father today . . . Our first complaint we made to the first Magistrate [Orpen, and related to Hope by marriage] who said your ground is your

inheritanace. Well I don't see the ground today. Again, I was once a chief, but when Government came I had to give up my chieftainship. I was a chief under Umhlonhlo I am now no longer able to get any fines.[117]

Others continued in much the same vein. When headman Mtoninzi criticized the rule of Shaw, who served as the second magistrate over the Mpondomise, Hope chastized him. Mtoninzi, however, was not deterred: "We want all cases to be taken first to Umhlonhlo." Then Noranga added: "Why do you stop us when we talk about Shaw? He ruled us wrong – he beat us with the 'cats' without the word from the Chief."

Hope was unimpressed:

Some of you have spoken very well, but you are all making one mistake – it is this: That although you admit you are under the Government you seem to expect Government to come down to your level and adopt your customs and let you dictate to the Magistrate . . .

You want me always to consult Umhlonhlo – who is the leader – but I will not when it is necessary . . . So long as he behaves well and is willing to assist me, I will consult him . . . he and the other headmen may act as arbitrators in civil cases, but not must use force to carry out their decisions, and every man may appeal to me before he complies with the judgements of chiefs and headmen – but you must not expect me to send cases to the Chief.

The magistrate ended by saying "that the Government is first and the chief second."[118]

Finally Mhlontlo spoke. "I asked Mr. Shaw to show me the first letters from Government, those that refer to our being taken over so that we could discuss them, but he declined to go into old matters . . . We want you in the presence of the Minister to take those first letters and read them to us so that we can understand the law. The letters are still here, let them be read – they are not dead."

Hope ended the meeting. "You were only trying a new horse, to see if you could tease him, and whether he was likely to buck if you were not careful – each [speaker] has had a little ride on him to try, and now that you have seen what sort of horse you have got, I hope you are all satisfied."

Laughter followed. The people dispersed.

The meeting in fact had settled little. A November 1878 case of "smelling out" again raised the division of power. The case began near the homestead of headman Mtoninzi who, three months earlier, had publicly criticized Shaw's rule only to receive the magistrate's sharp admonition. A "man of some importance" had fallen ill. Accusations of witchcraft followed. Hope rescued the accused, who had been "very much injured from the tortures" inflicted by the witchdoctor and others, and arrested all the men with the exception of the "wizard" Cekeso. Hope alleged that Mtoninzi "encouraged" the men "to torture her till she produced the charms," and thus had contravened colonial law.[119]

Hope demanded that Mhlontlo attend the trial. The accused "admitted their guilt but said that Mtoninzi had said that I had given him authority to torture any one who might be 'smelt out' provided he stopped short of killing them." Unimpressed by this argument, Hope fined the men and sentenced them to hard labor, including Mtoninzi, once the chief, then colonial headman, now a convict "breaking stones and wheeling a barrow."[120]

Hope's efforts to accumulate power for himself and for the empire proceeded. In January 1879 he spoke to Mhlontlo concerning the *mguya* that had just been performed at the chief's home in celebration of the first fruits. The chief explained to Hope that J. A. Orpen, the first magistrate, had allowed his people to conduct *mguya*, the celebrations of authority and fertility that reaffirmed the heroic status of chiefs as the descendants of men who slew leopards. He further explained that "besides Doctoring the people to strengthen them in case of war," *mguya* offered the opportunity for the chief to discuss pressing matters with his people. Nonetheless, Mhlontlo assured Hope "that the ceremony . . . had no political significance."[121] The magistrate's concern lay with what he considered to be the political implications of doctoring the army. In short, Hope feared conflict. Nonetheless, he left the interview reassured of Mhlontlo's fealty.

The situation, however, scarcely improved. Hope busied himself with the collection of hut taxes and the increasingly serious boundary and other land disputes emerging from colonial conquest,[122] as well as discussion of the Moorosi rebellion taking place in nearby Basutoland. Hope began a campaign of assiduous collection of taxes, including arrears dating back to 1875. Mhlontlo complained in February. In May 1879 the issue had become serious enough for Hope to call for a meeting with the chief, accompanied by about four hundred men.[123]

Hope began the meeting by demanding the payment of "all arrears." Mhlontlo immediately countered by demanding "to know where is the record of any meeting called by Mr. Orpen or Mr. Shaw to pay the Hut Tax for 1875." From here the meeting became rancorous. The government "has not shewn us anything," pronounced one clearly intoxicated man,

or any reason why we should pay the Hut Tax, we have not obtained ground yet to shew we have come under Government . . . I have only paid Hut Tax once. I do not see the truth of the Government in not giving us the ground we wanted. This ground has been given to other chiefs. We would like to get some of our ground back. We must grumble, we always do grumble. I will pay Hut Tax when Mhlonhlo pays. Government has him round the neck and is strangling [*sic*] him.[124]

Others continued in much the same vein. "We will never hear the truth of our words," Zenzo asserted. "How will people accept a law that has never been proclaimed?" At this point Hope read an extract from an 1874 meeting between Orpen and the Mpondomise concerning hut taxes as a condition of British colonial supremacy. Zenzo mysteriously fainted.[125]

Following a short recess, Mhlontlo spoke. "You have enemies all around you," he told his people. "We can't fight Government as he masters all tribes, even those we were afraid of." The chief agreed to pay the taxes, including arrears, though he asked the Hope for his patience as his people were poor. Few had money. Many were in debt to traders. As one man put it – and his choice of words is important – the shops were "eating us up."[126]

Hope began collecting taxes in July, beginning, significantly, with the chief to show that the white man clearly ruled over Mhlontlo. The chief and his people paid Hope £157 in two days, a considerable sum. "Since then the people generally have come freely to the office" to pay their taxes. Hope "received every assistance from the Chief Umhlonhlo in the collecting of the Tax and the discovery of defaulters."[127]

In about September 1879, one year after becoming magistrate, Hamilton Hope and his clerk attended the spring *mguya*. Coinciding with the vernal equinox and the beginning of spring, the *mguya* was to bring rain and fertility to the land. Hope not only authorized the ceremony but participated in it, on the chief's invitation. By attending the ceremony the magistrate began to enter the most intimate domain of Mpondomise power and ritual, though he seemed unaware of the relationship between the *mguya* and agricultural fertility. About four to five hundred people attended the *mguya*, most arriving by horse. In the morning they "gathered in front of the cattle Kraal," in a space people deemed ritually and symbolically important, and there "had a dance." In the afternoon, Hope asked the chief "to put his men through some military manoeuvres which he did with considerable skill and precision."[128]

After a few men of influence spoke, the chief began his speech. He had called "these sons of the great English Bull" to the ceremony. "We are thankful," Mhlontlo said,

that the Magistrate has had sufficient confidence in us to allow us to stretch our legs in a dance, for although our enemies are still saying that we wish to fight against the Government, we are not such fools, and our Mguyo is a time honored custom amongst us and we guyn [celebrate] in times of peace, and for our harvests.

Mhlontlo then instructed his people to pay their taxes. "This is the chief thing that ensures you the protection of Government."[129]

Hamilton Hope was now approaching the zenith of his power. It was clear to him that his efforts to establish the British Empire in the distant Transkei was finally bearing fruit. Hope saw the *mguya* as a moment of submission, as affirming the political supremacy and power of the magistrate.

But the situation was far more complex. The spring *mguya* represented perhaps the most critical and most symbolically significant moment in the Mpondomise ritual calendar, tied as it is to the changing heavens and seasons and to the highly charged relationship between power and the production of rain. The suggestion here is that Hope scarcely understood that Africans were attempting to appropriate his power so as to bring rain. In doing so they were placing an important burden on the white official, and potentially exposing Hope to new kinds of critique. His zenith of power and control could easily become also a moment of subversion and decline; for the spring *mguya*, the ceremony Hope himself had participated in, failed to bring nourishing rains. By the end of the year large parts of the Transkei were experiencing a severe drought.[130] Drought laid bare the always fraught relationship between magistrate and chief. In December Mhlontlo complained of Hope's conduct in criminal proceedings, especially his generous use of the whip. Again the chief returned to the earliest years of colonial rule. Mhlontlo asked "that Mr. Orpen should be here, and we wish to talk to him ... as our first Magistrate and Governor. We wish to speak to him before our good Magistrate," Hope.

Crisis loomed by March 1880, when green mealies should have been eaten and Africans throughout the Transkei would have celebrated the first fruits ceremonies. The crops, as Hope later wrote, were an "entire failure."[131] He had taken part in a ceremony meant to bring rain after the dry winter months. Instead, the land lay bleached by drought. Nor was this all. Mhlontlo's chief wife had fallen ill early in the spring, and was "slowly dying of a lingering disease."[132] Hope was also unwell; he had been sick for some time and was finding his work "very exhausting."[133]

In March, as drought gripped the land and the chief's wife lay sick of a disease that lingered like the dry days, chief and magistrate again locked horns, again around the resolution of disputes. One of the chief's sisters had been slighted "on her way down to her husband," an important moment in the marriage ceremony. Moreover, "a lot of young men ... attacked and rather maltreated her [bridal] escort."[134]

Mhlontlo leapt into action, fining the attackers and sending a leopard's tail to a man who had made insulting remarks to the bridal party. The brouhaha constituted a "blood case" and thus involved fines. Not surprisingly, the magistrate learned of the conflict and, especially, that the chief had acted "with his usual impetuosity."[135] Hope informed the local headman that no one "but myself had the power to enforce any fines" and was soon threatening people with humiliating flogging. But he went one step further. Not only did he order his chief constable to confiscate the leopard's tail, he had it returned to Mhlontlo.

Sending the leopard's tail back to the chief was a great insult and an outrage. The chief "had flown at" the policeman "in a great rage, refused to hear any message and ordered him off the premises with the tiger tail, which he was to take back to where he got it." But the policeman refused, leaving the leopard's tail at the chief's residence. Only after some of the chief's men threatened him with death did the functionary take the tail away.[136]

The affair of the leopard's tail involved complex and highly charged meanings. For Hope the chief's sending back the leopard's tail meant that, once again, Mhlontlo was refusing to recognize British rule. For the chief, as for other Africans, the tail meant much more, particularly in the context of the punishing drought. It symbolized not simply chiefship but also, and most importantly, the mytho-historical relationship between authority and the land. Not surprisingly, and indeed seemingly inexorably, the fracas of the leopard's tail led to a large meeting between the magistrate and his subjects, which about nine hundred people attended, roughly twice the size of Hope's previous meetings with the Mpondomise. Chief Mhlontlo did not attend, though his principal praise singer and war doctor did. Both spoke. So, of course, did Hamilton Hope, who reiterated that only the magistrate could levy fines. He also took possession of the leopard's tail, the use of which he declared was illegal. Hope admonished the chief and ordered all assembled that they "must look to the Magistrate for your orders." "Coming armed as you did the other day. My Police have been insulted. The people have come here armed. No one must insult or come armed. I will tell you when to come armed . . . There are some things I wish attended to. You must pay up your Hut Tax."[137] The tax, Hope argued, was the "grease of the wagon" of rule. The magistrate ended his disquisition by banning Sunday beer drinks.

The chief's praise singer saw things somewhat differently. He pointed out the relative impotence of headmen. Soon the meeting began unraveling; Hope's threats to flog people did not help matters. The men in effect began arguing the case and, at the same time, protesting against the position of headmen and the banning of Sunday beer drinks. Jara pointed out how Hope and Mhlontlo "were friends and they now seem at variance." "Speak you wizards who did this." Jara uttered what had been implicit: the use of magic in the creation of political conflict. The drought, Mhlontlo's wife's illness, and the rising political temperature all indicated the use of powerful and malevolent magic.

Hope of course did not believe in the use, or abuse, of occult power. Magic had long since lost its earlier dominance within the British cultural imagination.[138] For Hope, belief in magic represented so much poppycock swirling in the confused, unscientific, and irrational heads of barbarians who responded best to the whip, not the rules of logic. He was certainly unwilling to enter the semantic ground of magic beyond the prosaic issue of property and its confiscation, "smelling out" and "eating up." Hope concluded the meeting, returning to the issue of the powers of headmen. "The Headmen wanting more power is an old tale," he began. "All they want is to be able to 'eat up' people's cattle. You Headmen have power to settle garden disputes, to bring people to the office who have delayed in paying their Hut Tax, that is enough power for you to have, and that is all you will get. I am over the Headmen, and not they over me," he reminded them. "Smelling out" [witchcraft accusations] I hear is in existence, if I find out such a thing I will inflict a very severe punishment." Hope then announced he was going away, and that his clerk would be collecting hut taxes. He would return to his death.

In the meantime, drought continued ravaging the area; the specter of starvation loomed. Even Mhlontlo's crops failed. The chief was forced to sell a considerable number of his cattle to purchase £200 worth of grain. His wife's illness progressed. But August is usually one of the driest months, the leanest part of the year, but also a time of expectation. Would the spring rains come?

Mhlontlo's wife died in early October 1880. By this time war had broken out in Basutoland and in neighboring Griqualand East, what has become known as the Gun War of 1880. Soon virtually all of Basutoland and much of the Transkei was in open rebellion, the largest conflict ever to have engulfed the region. By the middle of the month the chief was busily "organising his tribe and Doctoring them." Hope reported seeing "armed parties . . . hovering round on the hills." The question for the magistrate was whether the Mpondomise would rebel or would ally themselves with the British.[139] Heavy spring rains were falling. Hamilton Hope still felt unwell.

On 19 October Hope received a letter from a missionary, Stephen Adonis, warning him that Mhlontlo "meant treachery" and that "mutiny had been along intended and on a certain day [would be] carried out."[140] Three days later the magistrate at nearby Maclear had "grave reasons from reliable information" of "an intended plot."[141] Yet Hope pressed on to Sulenkama through a rain that, to him, seemed "incessant."[142] Clearly Chief Mhlontlo was rebuilding his power. Hope may not have fully known it, but by the end of the second week of October the magistrate was "now dancing to" the chief's "fiddle in every possible manner." The chief was "delighted to wait a little bit."[143]

It was in a setting of quenching rains and incipient rebellion that Hope met his death before the largest assembly of Mpondomise the magistrate had ever witnessed. The spring *mguya* represented perhaps the most crucial ritual moment in the agricultural year, for it was tied to the bringing of rains and the blessing of the seed. The vernal equinox, the Orionid meteor showers, the glittering of Venus, Jupiter, and Saturn in the night skies marked a time of hope after the lean and dry winter months. The people must have been especially desperate because of the widespread crop failures the drought had delivered to the region. Would the change of seasons augur the promise of good crops, or would misfortune tighten its grip on the land? *Mguya*, celebrations of the leopard, were also moments when the institution of chiefship was exposed and potentially opened to criticism as well as reaffirmed and at times even expanded. Hope's authority was overthrown so that Mhlontlo's chieftaincy could be revalidated. The morning before Hope's death Mhlontlo had sat apart, the once vanquished, now exalted chief participating in and surveying the reconstitution of the chiefship and the return of social health before a grand and extremely charged political ceremony.

In movements of exaggerated deference, messengers crawled between the army and the chief.

Hope's murder, then, destroyed at least temporarily the colonial accumulation of power and the attempt to build legitimacy on the edge of empire. His demise, already foreshadowed by his ill health, rebuilt the chiefship, strengthened the Mpondomise army in their coming war with the British, and brought rain. Hope was not only killed, he was ritually murdered – or better sacrificed – a "great bull" offered to renew society and polity.[144]

The complex choreography of his entrance into the great arch of the Mpondomise army and his murder there all point to Hope's death as ritual sacrifice. But this was not all. He was not simply murdered – his person was mutilated. We know very little about this mutilation, but this much is clear: Mhlangeni, one of chief's ritual specialists, stabbed Hope, the great bull, to death; Mandondo mutilated the body "for war purposes";[145] Hope's long beard was cut off, and his clothes stripped off. Mhlangeni then wore Hope's trousers and donned his long white beard. He subsequently led attacks on colonial troops.[146] A few years later he was arrested, but miraculously managed to escape from the Kokstad jail. Another ritual specialist took the magistrate's coat. On 24 October this man led an attack on the Maclear magistracy, where a colonial official shot him dead. He was wearing the great bull's coat.[147]

Denouement

By December 1880 colonial troops had regained control over most rebel areas. "The rebels ... appear to have become almost completely disorganised and demoralised, and split up into small parties, which bolt at the approach of any of our smallest patrols, so that all real fighting may be said to be over."[148] Troops confiscated crops "at pleasure"; thousands of cattle were also taken. A number of rebels had fled up into the mountains and sought refuge in caves. Commandant Jenner, however, was "trying to get some dynamite, that he may worry up some of those fellows who have still a weakness for the mountains."[149]

Mhlontlo fled into the mountains of Basutoland, where he lived for some two decades in exile and as a fugitive. In 1903, however, the colonial authorities apprehended him. In a long trial ending in May 1904, he faced charges for the murders of Hope and the other white men. The case received widespread attention. Yet after deliberating for only twenty-five minutes the jury returned a verdict of not guilty. The jury found the chief innocent precisely because he had not personally murdered the men. The court thus viewed the chief as an individual subject who stood before the law, scarcely aware of an African world that stressed the interconnectedness of people and the world they inhabited.

According to one account, the "verdict was received with breathless interest and elicited shouts from the natives in Court, which were immediately suppressed." Mhlontlo thanked the judge and, outside the court, received "many congratulatory remarks and offerings from natives. So ended a trial," the local newspaper concluded, "which has evoked no small interest on account of the revival of a tragedy which at the time of its occurrence thrilled both Europeans and natives."[150] In 1906 Mhlontlo returned to his home, not as a chief but as a simple commoner. He died in 1912, living on barren land, "poor, in debt, and having to purchase grain for his family."[151]

The death of Hope and the memory of Mhlontlo continue to breathe life into public discourse on the past and present. Mpondomise tribal leaders have called for the "restoration of its lost kingdom,"[152] in effect a return to imagined precolonial borders and a heroic history. Increasingly people have spoken publicly of a Mpondomise past, of valorous chiefs, and, especially, the loss of land at the hands of British conquerors. In August 2000 plans were being made to honor Mhlontlo, to correct "those historical imbalances and restore back to the community what is truly theirs . . . His only crime was to resist oppression and the death of the then Qumbu magistrate, Mr. Hamilton Hope."[153] Hope's monument remains standing at Sulenkama, protected by a wrought-iron fence and tall trees shading the African sun.

What is not remembered today, and is only obliquely suggested in the archival record, is the issue of magic and how people may have envisioned Hamilton Hope's relationship to the use and abuse of occult power. We know that people saw, and indeed many continue to see, power and magic as inseparable. Magic has been a crucially important way of understanding the world, particularly the problems of power and evil.[154] In the secular West magic has been consigned to the very margins of our apprehension of reality, the antithesis of rational cognition, as indeed was the case with Hamilton Hope himself, who explained away witchcraft as a misguided mark of the barbarism he intended to correct, with the whip if necessary. In places such as the Eastern Cape, however, magic was at the center of people's imagination, the way they made sense of the world.

We know further that Hope attended two *mguyas*, both associated with the coming of spring, with the rains, and with the reaffirmation of chiefship. Indeed, in the first *mguya* Hope had unwittingly mimicked the chiefship by having the warriors parade before him.[155] Rains, however, did not follow this ritual celebration. Instead drought, hunger, and sickness had prevailed. At the second *mguya* the rains arrived – and Hope met his death before the warriors who a year earlier had participated in a "ritual rebellion," where "warriors of the tribe made feints at stabbing,"[156] and recognized the authority of the chiefship and, perhaps, Hamilton Hope as well. We know, finally, that Hope's body became "medicine" (*muti*) to ritually strengthen the warriors. The medicines did not bring victory against the better armed colonial forces. Following one famous battle it was said that "Umhlonhlo's witch-doctor has it that the failure was due to the fact that Mr Thompson's 'medicines'" were "more powerful than his (Umhlonhlo's) own."[157]

The evidence powerfully suggests, though does not unequivocally demonstrate, that magic was an important feature of the colonial encounter, including the violence of conquest itself. Because magic was so pervasive a force, especially in issues relating to agriculture and to political authority and particularly in times of drought, we can speculate that most Mpondomise believed that Hope had access to and control over occult powers. These are "probable truths,"[158] not absolute ones. They raise acutely the problem of understanding how Africans appropriated and translated the European world into their own. For translation is both about identification and difference. Hamilton Hope was killed in an act of premeditated murder, vanquished as a colonial invader. Might he also have been seen as a chief, however illegitimate in the end? Just who was this long-bearded white man, this "great bull" who lived and died at Africa's southern tip?

2 Ethnographies of state

> Despotism is a legitimate mode of government in dealing with barbarians,
> provided the end be their improvement.
>
> John Stuart Mill, *On Liberty*, ed. G. Himmelfarb (London, 185), 69

Hamilton Hope was a bureaucrat. Like many other officials in the Eastern
Cape, Hope organized the collection of taxes, conducted censuses, amassed
and processed statistical data, and established and monitored his jurisdictional
boundaries. He was an employee of the Cape's Department of Native Affairs
(DNA), created in 1872 at the beginning of a new wave of colonial expansion in South Africa and, indeed, across the continent. Hope's routine and
routinized activities helped create the colonial state. They also represented the
imperial manifestation of the continuing bureaucratization of power and the rise
of administrative sciences rooted, most immediately, in the early nineteenth-
century political revolutions of the British state. Science and empiricism came
to statecraft in ways never before imagined; in activities as banal as training
administrators there developed a "science of government."[1] Like the surveillant
state those revolutions created, a state increasingly interested in the minutiae
of its subjects, a guiding principle of officials such as Hamilton Hope was, as
he put it in 1879, "to take cognizance of everything that goes on."[2]

Hope's words are particularly demonstrative. For "cognizance" refers not
simply to knowledge gained through observation but also, and importantly, to
"official observation of or authority over something."[3] Cognizance combines the
ostensibly neutral claims to objectivity by which science legitimates itself with
the jurisdictional power of the state to administer the law. The legal definition of
"cognizance" is the "right and power to try and determine cases," in other words,
jurisdiction. To be "cognizable" is to be "capable of being identified as a group
because of a common characteristic or interest" and "of being judicially tried
or examined before a designated tribunal."[4] Much of Hope's daily activities
centered precisely around attempting to make the African world cognizable to
the rule of a modern state.

For Hamilton Hope to rule was to know, and to know was to rule. He sought
mastery over Africans through the collection of knowledge about them and

the world they inhabited. Knowledge and rule came together most forcefully in the law, in Hope's "house of trials" where Mhlontlo's warriors had stabbed the book of law before setting the building on fire. But there was much more. In addition to administering colonial law, He explored African "custom." He produced what amounted to ethnographic reports of Mpondomise society. He employed a clerk and African policemen to help in his day-to-day duties, from prosecuting offenders to collecting statistical data. He had his own spies. He mapped and demarcated territory. He discussed issues with headmen and chiefs, especially concerning that domain of human action Europeans so neatly bracketed as "the law." And in between he did what bureaucrats do . . . he pushed a lot of paper. Hope wrote letters, drafted memos, issued passes, responded to requests, followed directives, and sent telegrams to colleagues and superiors.

This white-bearded man, bringing civilization to the Dark Continent, was an avatar of bureaucratic modernity. Africans in the Transkei, and indeed elsewhere in Africa and in the nineteenth-century colonial world, were conquered as much by European institutions, procedures, techniques, and Enlightenment rationality as by guns. Hope mapped African land, counted its people and redacted their culture as part of the creation of a veritable science of government that, like science itself, had a capacity to predict; and he helped create a double definition of the conquered, as individual and as tribesman, as essential cognizable subjects of the state. To know was not to understand empathically as much as to dominate belligerently, to submit Africa to increasingly technical forms of rationalization, and to deduce the future on the basis of information that could fit into categories.

Hamilton Hope was a ruler. He was also certainly a conqueror, perhaps in some respects even a chief.[5] He subdued people whom he considered to be "barbarians," amassed power, extended his control over a number of chiefdoms, created a new political domain centered most immediately on the Qumbu magistracy. He was a young, ambitious, intensely competitive and tempestuous man, a ruler attracted to "high-handed proceedings,"[6] a master if ultimately also a victim of colonial theatricality. He controlled fiery instruments of death. Attracted to violence, Hope came to Qumbu with a reputation for flogging people, including chiefs, unmercifully.

If the hypothesis presented in the last chapter is correct – that people considered occult forces to be operating especially powerfully during important political moments, and that this concept shaped their perception of Hope's actions and thus was transferred to perceptions of the colonial state – it is probable that the Mpondomise believed Hope had access to magic and control over powerful symbols and rituals. We know that conquest unfolded during a time of acute drought – indeed one of the worst to hit the region in living memory. The misfortunes that accompany droughts inflamed the human emotions of suspicion and apprehension and shook the foundations of political society generally. We know that Hope participated in two important ritual moments at the center of Mpondomise culture and society, both occurring shortly after the vernal equinox and involving agricultural fertility and political authority. In addition, parts of his body ended up as African *muti*; this fact alone demonstrates the belief that the white man's body contained supernatural powers that could be harnessed – and, as we have noted, at least one important ritual specialist believed that Europeans had their own magic "medicines."[7] It would be most surprising if people had believed Europeans had no connection to magic. Data, however, suggest quite the opposite.[8] (To the north, in 1877 the Zulu paramount Cetshwayo had said: "I feel the English Chiefs have stopped the rain, and the land is being destroyed . . . [I] want the Great [English] Chiefs to send me the rain.")[9] We may presume, therefore, that people may have believed that Hope's magic did battle with that of Mhlontlo, a chief "renowned for his power of magic."[10] Did Hope in effect "eat up" rivals to his authority, strengthened by a magic whose origins lay ultimately in the technology of an industrial capitalist revolution and an empire ruled by a queen residing at the end of the earth? Certainly he took control of the skins of leopards, a quintessential mark of chiefship and the mytho-historical founding of political society. But did Hope, that "great bull," withhold the rain?

Herein lay an important paradox of state formation and rule arising, initially, out of the Janus face of modernity but ultimately played out in colonialism's daily practice where the problems of translation, identification, difference, and meaning remained so acute. The creation of colonial categories, so central to state formation in South Africa and throughout the colonial world, entailed also their substantial blurring. The inchoateness of colonial expansion and the not inconsiderable "uncertainty" as to what magistrates were in fact supposed to be doing – in short the very weakness of the early colonial state – helped make this blurring possible.[11] So also did the fact that both Africans and Europeans translated each other's political practices into their own indigenous concepts.

The ambiguities of conquest and rule return us to one of this work's central problems: how we understand the history of state formation in South Africa in the period from colonial conquest to the authoritarianism of the apartheid order. This chapter introduces three major lines of argumentation concerned with tracing the principal stratagems of state formation and the ways these worked themselves out (or failed to) at the local level. Much recent work on knowledge and colonialism typically has been more concerned with ideology than with practice;[12] one goal here is to bridge intellectual, cultural, and social history as conventionally envisioned. The Transkei in the late nineteenth century is distinctive because it was conquered by a fledgling bureaucratic agency created to administer native affairs. Moreover, throughout the colonial period the region was administered separately from the rest of the Cape. The region's history presents an acute case of the complex history of state formation and rule in Africa.

The first argument is that colonial state formation required, at least epistemo-logically, the creation of a map and a model of society upon which bureaucrats could act. "To take cognizance of everything that goes on" entailed creating such a model of society and then, in subjecting it to the state's surveillance, attempting to make that model real.[13] This Western form of cognition, more-over, had an important spatial component that, at a minimum, required the existence of stable political boundaries or jurisdictional units. Second, despite the modernity of the early colonial state, it nonetheless remained quite weak; that is, it lacked the power to bring together model and reality. Third, the acts of cultural translation that comprised cross-cultural encounters complicated the making of colonial rule; it was in part out of the often messy and ambiguous daily interactions of Africans and Europeans that the colonial state came into being and the categories of ruler and ruled, colonizer and colonized, came to be experienced.[14]

To know and to rule

The modernity of conquest and rule

In the Eastern Cape, as elsewhere in the colonial world, space, numeracy, and culture represented the three primary modes around which the state emerged and through which it made legible the subjects of its control.[15] Each was im-portant in transforming African bodies and the communities they inhabited so that they could be intelligible to the state, rendering Africa cognizable, creating a model upon which bureaucrats could act. Beginning in the nine-teenth century and continuing through to apartheid, space and numeracy came together in the state's tribalism; in other words, in the hands of bureaucrats a basic feature of culture centered on its spatiality and its reducibility to numbers. Culture could be bounded geographically and counted (as, for example, in the phrases "American culture" or "there are 247 million Americans"), and thus be exposed to scientific scrutiny. The colonial subject as tribal subject thus could be simultaneously counted and fixed on a map. This double rendering, perhaps best epitomized in the pass system that provided demographic infor-mation on the person and their "tribe," would be a constant feature of colonial rule in the nineteenth and twentieth centuries. It allowed, moreover, not only for a unique spatialization of culture in the form of native reserves or tribal homelands, but also for a predictive administrative practice in which a person's individual life history was immaterial to the object of policy. Indeed, over the course of the twentieth century officials evinced a near obsession with rendering Africans ever more cognizable to the state, creating with apartheid a regime of official information where moral or ethical considerations were, quite simply, irrelevant.

Map XVII.

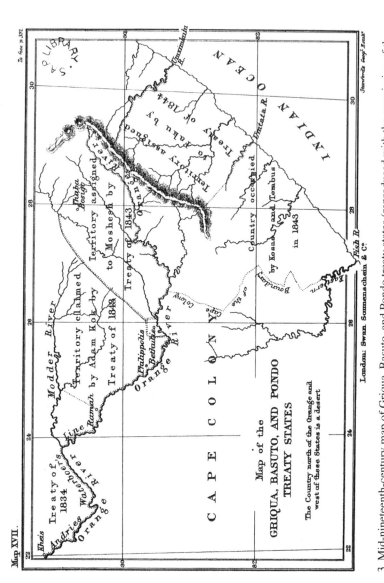

3 Mid-nineteenth-century map of Griqua, Basuto, and Pondo treaty states (reproduced with the permission of the South African Library, Cape Town)

But first, two caveats: the amount of bureaucratic energy that poured into the Eastern Cape in the late nineteenth and twentieth centuries is unmistakable; the reports, commissions, laws promulgated, debated, and passed, even the tours of DNA officials, all point to the state's interest in and concern with the region. This focus became all the more powerful in the twentieth century as the Eastern Cape came to supply ever greater numbers of migrant laborers for the mining industry. Throughout the period, however, the state's interest in collecting information remained quite narrow, focusing primarily on issues such as land and tribal governance. The state created a highly simplified base of knowledge that consisted of largely attenuated information directly related to economic management and to rule. All of the information collected and processed, therefore, did not necessarily mean that officials knew their African subjects in the conventional sense of developing a subtle and complex understanding. Empathy and empiricism could be worlds apart.

Second, intentions and executions were often distantly related. We have noted before, for example, that the Glen Grey Act in many respects failed at least partly because the state lacked the coercive power to implement the new laws. The space between policy and practice could be quite considerable, though it narrowed over the course of the twentieth century. On the ground this meant that the state very often was more disorderly than calculated and determined, more disruptive than hegemonic. The state thus could be ever-present without being especially effective. The encounters people had with it might increase dramatically without it being particularly effective in getting people to do what officials wanted.

Mapping represented an artifact from a broader Western tradition of man dominating nature. The closer Europeans deemed others to be near nature, with all its apparent disorder and irrationality, the greater the need to submit them to rational modes of organization and thought; hence Mill's advocacy of despotism "as legitimate mode of government in dealing with barbarians." The perspectivist revolution of fifteenth-century Europe augured new ways of organizing space according to a grid, more precisely dominating nature and, ostensibly, liberating man from his baser instincts. Perspectivism emphasized the "ability of the individual to represent" the "truthful" and helped lay part of "an effective material foundation for the Cartesian principles of rationality that became integrated into the Enlightenment project."[16] Perspectivism and the deployment of Euclidean geometry had important economic and political implications, creating, for example, new kinds of cartography that could be used to alienate land, bring it into capitalist production, and render it taxable. Ever more scientific maps became increasingly important to statecraft, and not simply in terms of making citizen and subject liable to taxation. They were, rather, central to the very idea of the transformative capacities of the modern state, including its expansion overseas.

The second half of the nineteenth century saw a revolution in surveying and cartography on a par with that of the early modern period.[17] To map was to know, and to know one had to map. Maps were, of course, "fantasies of possession and demarcation," and played a powerful role in shaping ideas of colonial supremacy.[18] Mapping "became a lethal instrument to concretize the projected desire" of Europeans "on the earth's surface."[19] In 1863 officials at the Cape completed an exceptionally detailed trigonometrical survey using state-of-the-art scientific equipment, despite the Cape's distance from the metropole and its relative economic unimportance. One such tool, well describing the confidence of Enlightenment rationality and the truth of empirical information, was known as the "universal instrument."[20] The mapping of frontiers, newly conquered areas, and the creation of boundaries between polities became central features of imperial expansion and the colonial accumulation of information, particularly in areas that did not have centralized states. Indeed, cartography comprised a central part of colonial rule, from the most mundane aspects of administration to destructive displays of military might. Not surprisingly many of the early Transkeian magistrates first participated in conquest as surveyors of African land. They moved across barbarous territories still free of European control, taking measurements, recording information, bringing a dark Africa into the clear light of science.[21]

Compared to earlier ones late nineteenth-century maps were extremely detailed, noting individual locations, roads and, importantly, demarcating clear and rigid administrative boundaries based on static conceptions of tribe. Maps thus plotted the domain of the state's control and, simultaneously, culture's location. In the earlier period maps quite literally contained empty spaces, with areas designated "Nomansland" or vaguely described as being occupied by "scattered clans." These spatial ambiguities had largely disappeared by the century's end. By the end of the 1880s the entire region had been surveyed, borders created, and administrative units defined, an extraordinary accomplishment when compared to elsewhere on the continent, including other regions of South Africa.[22] Maps became far more detailed. Shepstone's sketch map of Natal, prepared for the 1883 Native Laws and Customs Commission, included no less than ninety-four "tribes". What earlier maps would have noted areas of "scattered clans" Shepstone defined as "unoccupied ground" and readily subject to colonial annexation. "Nomansland" had once referred to regions that did not fall under a given polity. For Shepstone the word signified territory not yet under colonial control. What was not conquered remained ambiguous.[23]

In the years of conquest the colonial organization of space principally concerned issues of administrative jurisdiction and control – the creation of magisterial districts, the formation of locations, and so on – in short, the spatial location of power. From the early 1850s on through the 1894 Glen Grey Act and beyond, officials produced maps of African lands and struggled – and well

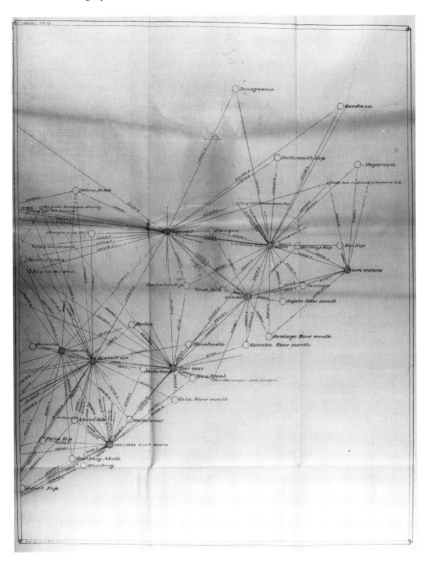

4 From the trigonometrical survey of the Cape, 1863 (reproduced with the permission of the South African Library, Cape Town)

into the twentieth century failed – to get their new subjects into "villages" where each villager was to be allocated individual property to farm as well as access to "communal" land. Surveying and maps were thus central to defining the colonial subjects but also, and importantly, to controlling them. From the beginning the issue of control was unmistakable. It was important for magistrates "to be very careful to allow no native to occupy a Hut in your District, except in one of the already established Native Villages – and to impress upon the Chief and the paid [head]men of each village that no Native can be allowed to reside in it unless he is first brought to you by the Headman and is duly registered."[24] This from the chief official in the Ciskei in 1859. The effort on the part of the state to create a "village system" would be an enduring feature of colonial rule right into the era of apartheid. It was, for example, a central feature of the 1939 Betterment Act and, in the 1940s and 1950s, the introduction of "Closer Settlement Schemes" that formed an important part of apartheid's introduction and its desire to secure "cheap Native Labour for Industrial requirements."[25]

Mapping thus became one of the most basic features of early colonial rule, one of the elementary forms of state formation. The creation of boundaries and administrative units were one and the same thing. They defined the jurisdiction of resident magistrates, chiefs, and headmen. Mapping was thus a central process by which Africans became cognizable, knowable to the state and subject to its rule. Mapping was also a prerequisite to other forms of accumulating colonial knowledge: classification, enumeration, and quantification. Benedict Anderson has drawn attention to maps and censuses as important "imaginings of the colonial state," particularly in the second half of the nineteenth century when "colonized zones entered the age of mechanical reproduction."[26] It is not surprising that the telegraph reached the most remote parts of the Transkei two years before the 1879 promulgation of the Rules and Regulations for the Government of the Transkeian Districts. That document was centrally concerned with mapping and counting.

The common precolonial tradition of political process had entailed the existence of multiple and overlapping political domains and the creation of unadministered areas on the borders of chiefdoms, a complex map of power in which boundaries more or less remained permanently in flux. This tradition operated on the basis of principles that fundamentally, indeed radically, differed from than those upon which colonial rule rested. The colonial state spoke of homogeneous space and of fixed boundaries, of lines and right angles, as a grid capable of potentially endless subdivision upon which the colonizer assigned more and more detailed information. It was also premised on prediction; colonialism's mapping always had an anticipatory logic to it. Conquest thus represented both the beginning of a "new polity and [of a new] political geography."[27] As we shall see shortly, mapping created colonial space, as a space of rule, on the basis of a rigid conception of ethnicity, a territorialization of culture.

This mapping and remapping of colonial space continued throughout the nineteenth and twentieth centuries, though in far greater detail with the increase in the state's coercive powers and its preoccupation with a more minute understanding of its subjects. For example, the 1892 Glen Grey Commission

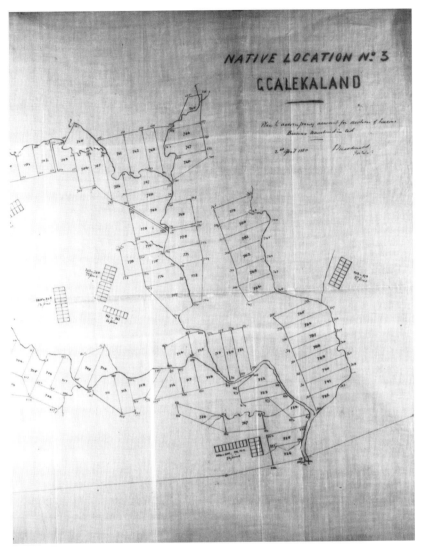

NATIVE LOCATION N° 3
GCALEKALAND

5 Native location map, 1880 (reproduced with the permission of the South
African Library, Cape Town)

that formed the basis of the Glen Grey Act, Cecil Rhodes's "Bill for Africa"
passed two years later, concerned itself with the organization of colonial space.
Indeed, the narrative of the report is also a story of a colonial political geography. Likewise, implementing so "large a scheme,"[28] especially the proposed
introduction of individual tenure, required an ever more detailed surveying of

colonial land. Following the Act's passage the state in fact undertook a trigono-metrical survey, and "proper beacons" were "erected at the corners of each lot."[29] Soon over seven thousand six hundred lots had been well surveyed, re-sulting in the dispossession of over a thousand claimants and their families but, according to the magistrate, offering the possibility of greater agricultural production.[30]

Glen Grey, however, was the exception, not the rule. Much of the greater region remained a dizzying mess created, in varying combinations, by fitful at-tempts at surveying, reversals of policies, bureaucratic indecision, and African resistance that ranged from feigned consent to active opposition. Most obvi-ously, the state simply lacked the power to translate policy into practice. This situation began to change with the new century, most immediately as a result of political consolidation and the increasing reliance of industry on laborers from within South Africa's native reserves. The post-South African War Milner gov-ernment expended enormous energy on political boundaries and on the ways in which people and information would circulate within the political territory of the Union of South Africa.[31] As part of the 1903–6 South African Native Affairs Commission, officials around the country amassed detailed information on space, particularly on native reserves and locations, including population density and labor migration statistics.

The nineteenth-century state had been primarily concerned with the map-ping of administrative districts and with submitting African lands to colonial taxation. Twentieth-century mapping, however, increasingly concerned the sci-entific management of space and, with it, the colonial subjects that occupied it. This can be seen in legislation such as the 1913 Natives Land Act and in the greater definition of territory based on race and ethnicity but also, and impor-tantly, in policies concerned with agricultural production. Part of implementing the 1913 Act, as well as later ones such as the 1936 Native Trust and Land Bill, required local officials to draw up maps of the areas occupied by Africans and the forms that occupation took. With betterment policies, that is, with the state's surveillance of and intervention in African rural economies, cartography became ever more detailed. Anti-soil-erosion schemes, ridging, and contour farming comprised the most obvious examples of these developments; all pro-duced and/or required detailed maps. Beginning especially in the 1920s, and then again in the late 1940s and 1950s, officials went out surveying and allotting arable lands, defining in greater detail commonage and forest and other lands directly under the state's supervision of what it defined as natural resources.[32]

The Cape's cartographic regime differed in some respects from the role of maps elsewhere in Africa and in other parts of the empire, for example India. Almost everywhere cartographic information generally improved. The Eastern Cape, however, lacked the centralized states and empires of South Asia, which had their own rich cartographic history and written languages Europeans could learn or appropriate for their own uses. Second, mapping in the Eastern Cape took place earlier and in general with more accuracy than many other areas of the continent, in part because the devolution of power from Britain to the Cape reduced communication problems between and among various administrative agencies. Perhaps most important was the simple issue of labor. Throughout the colonial world the labor question remained a constant and often vexing subject. However, in the Eastern Cape, particularly in the context of South Africa's spectacular industrial revolution, the problem of marshaling and controlling labor emerged decades earlier than most other areas and, moreover, unfolded roughly at the same time as conquest itself.

Cartography and transformation, mapping and large-scale social engineering, were thus closely wedded. The question was not simply the accumulation of information but the deployment of data in transforming society. Maps turned from representations (however fanciful) of the world to political fantasies of how the world might be reordered. Their predictive or anticipatory role loomed ever larger. As we shall see in a later chapter the despotic possibilities of mapping became ever more apparent in the 1950s with the introduction of apartheid, a set of policies that had space at their very epicenter. Apartheid completed what the nineteenth-century conquest had begun. The apartheid state, however, was more capable of transforming its political dreams into the wrenching nightmares of forced removals, retribalization, and, perhaps most horribly, the creation of resettlement camps for people who had been "endorsed" out of the places they lived.

To the mapping of space came the counting and classification of bodies; the two were closely associated.[33] A preoccupation of the state, its "classificatory logic,"[34] drawing lines and counting people, were among the first duties of new resident magistrates. As with maps, over the course of the late nineteenth and twentieth centuries censuses became more accurate and more detailed with the growth of the state and its coercive power. To count was to know. To do both entailed the creation of fixed categories. A renewed interest in censuses and statistics followed each of the formative moments of state formation: conquest; segregation and the reformulation of rule; and, finally, apartheid itself. "The modern colonial state," Appadurai has argued with respect to the British in India, "brings together the exoticizing vision of orientalism with the familiarizing discourse of statistics. In the process, the body of the colonial subject is made simultaneously strange and docile . . . statistics are to bodies and social types what maps are to territories: they flatten and enclose."[35] In the colonial imagination Africans always constituted a social problem, and uncolonized Africans were doubly so. Social problems were the privileged domain of statistical operations.[36]

Censuses most clearly marked the emergence of a taxonomic state, a state centrally shaped by the rise of positivism. Censuses were "statistical operations *par excellence*."[37] Lord Kelvin had said at the end of the century "that when you can measure what you are speaking about, you know something about it."[38] Statistics had begun as a science in the 1830s, and it was from the beginning concerned with identifying social problems. The century as a whole, and especially its second half, saw increasing interest in statistics and a phenomenal rise in the collection of numbers.[39]

As with mapping, increasingly detailed organization and classificatory rigidity distinguished nineteenth-century counting. "The fiction of the census is that everyone is in it, and that everyone has one – and only one – extremely clear place."[40] This place of enumerative fixity was ethnic and racial and was especially designed for the "invasive investigation" of difference.[41] To render statistical, moreover, was an important part of the civilizing mission – and a crucial marker between civilization and barbarism. Civilized societies had statistics; they also had history. Barbarous societies had neither.[42] Barbarism, moreover, represented a most serious social problem. If the reorganization and mastery of space was an intrinsic process by which man liberated himself from nature, statistics were a way to imbue barbarous human communities with historicity and thus to mark them with the sign of improvement.

To count was to know, and to know was to rule. The less colonizers knew the more they wanted to count in such a way as to create a narrative of the colonial subject that was coterminous with the interests of the state. As with mapping, statistics were a colonial operation of the margin, an exercise most pronounced where colonial control was weakest. It is thus not surprising that the British administered a census of its newly conquered territory in the Ciskei two decades *before* the first official census of the Cape Colony in 1865. Over the course of the century censuses increased in the scope of what they counted. Europeans had once grouped Africans into very broad categories – heathen, savage, barbarian, and so on – and they scarcely bothered to attempt to count them or their possessions. Resident magistrates initially categorized the population on the basis of ethnicity, and to a lesser extent according to gender and generation. Subsequently officials began amassing statistical data on property and production: livestock, wagons, ploughs, and the amount of grain produced in a given season. Then on life and death as, for example, in the promulgation of the 1896 Birth and Death Registration Act. By this time resident magistrates had begun including discussion of birth rates in their annual reports.[43]

Again, throughout the nineteenth century and well into the twentieth century a considerable gap separated official intent from the state's abilities to implement policies concerned with collecting statistical information. As state resources expanded and administrative agencies centralized their operations, however, information became more detailed and its accumulation more regularized.[44] The 1914 Statistics Act mandated the annual collection of statistical data ranging from the population to "vital social, educational, and industrial matters" to "the tenure, occupation and use of land." A striking feature of the Act was its coercive powers, a feature largely absent in the nineteenth-century state's collection of statistics. The coercive dimensions of the Act did not long remain dormant; from the 1920s in particular officials convicted Africans under the Statistics Act for providing "false" information. The Act thus marked, among other things, the centrality of the state in organizing and regulating an industrial capitalist economy. This inevitably also entailed the regulating and surveilling of bodies; the 1914 Act permitted the state to collect statistics on "any matter" it deemed important.[45] Indeed, it is roughly at this time that the state began collecting data on mobility, nutrition and health, and sexuality. In the 1920s and 1930s especially, the state began assiduously collecting data on poverty, nutrition, fertility and infant mortality; among other things it "discovered" poverty and designed welfare programs to address it.[46]

Statistical data did not so much reflect social reality as provide the basis for social transformation. Like maps, censuses brought into the colonial grammar of rule and, in quite basic ways created, subject populations.[47] Map and census simultaneously constituted colonial subjects and established the basis for controlling and disciplining their bodies and their movements. The modern pass system, born in the nineteenth century and continuously modernized in the twentieth century, embodied both map and census in a single document that at once defined and controlled the colonial subject. Dating from 1857, passes described the colonial subject by ethnicity, located that ethnicity within administrative boundaries, and explained the nature of their movement within the colonial system. It also included physical descriptions.[48] As early as the 1880s much of an official's daily work was taken up with the pass system. The state required that the "pass system will be rigidly adhered to." No person "will be permitted to leave his district without having a pass signed by his Magistrate." Moreover, the state required Africans carrying passes to "report himself at any Magistrate's office en route, and on his return will bring his pass to his Magistrate, reporting his return to his District."[49]

Condensed in a single piece of paper lay one of the most basic features of state formation. The pass system formed part of an extraordinary bureaucratic expansion in the twentieth century and consumed a remarkable portion of the state's expenditures. Passes, in a most basic way a kind of textual state terrorism that wrecked countless lives, not surprisingly became the single most powerful and hated marker and instrument of domination in South Africa. An elementary form of state formation became its quintessential instrument of oppression.[50]

The twentieth-century state especially was a state of diagrams and forms, of highly simplified and putatively objective information that elided the instrumental exercise of power. Maps, diagrams, and forms were the central ways of rendering the colonized more legible. Anti-soil-erosion schemes, ridging, and contour farming required both the mapping of space and the collection

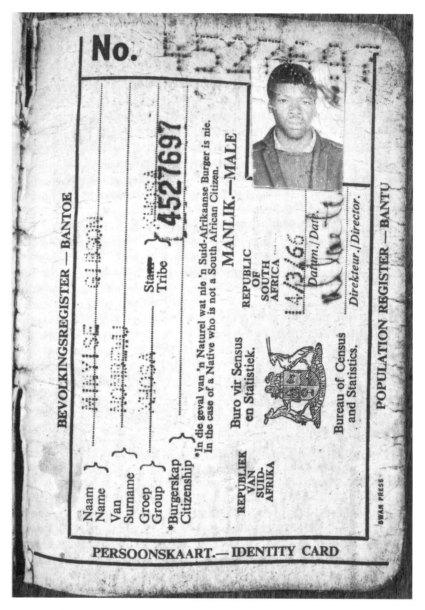

6 A pass, 1966 (reproduced with permission Cory Library, Rhodes University)

of information that could be enumerated. The combination of mapping and numbers represented the transformation of the state's subjects as objects of an emerging social science.[51] Joined with the state's coercive powers, the combination marked the rise of authoritarianism in South Africa.

Maps and censuses were thus central features of the colonial claim to power and integral parts of state formation. They were both important ethnographic productions and ethnographic instruments of the colonial state, central to exercising control over people and economic resources.[52] Apartheid represented the epitome of this process of information gathering and categorizing – and of the authoritarian possibilities inherent in it.[53] Particularly in the 1950s the state expended enormous energy in microscopically detailing colonial space and enumerating the subjects of its control. Apartheid was thus, among other things, the endpoint of the state's simplifications that began with conquest itself, the colonial culmination of rendering Africans cognizable.

Yet the more the state looked the less it saw; this is one of the great paradoxes of authoritarian bureaucratic orders, perhaps of modern state formation in general. Scott has observed how "state simplifications" increasingly have "the character of maps" and, I would add, diagrams.[54] Legibility entails not simply simplification but also stereotype. This rendering of objects and subjects "more legible and hence more susceptible to careful measurement and calculation" presumed an uncomplicated and manageable reality, even if that reality was becoming ever more complicated.[55] The more microscopic the gaze the more stereotyped the image. Officials were not interested in knowledge per se but, rather in a few, largely crude, measures they believed were necessary to maintain colonial rule. The issue was "standardization and formalization,"[56] not complexity and nuance; information and control, not knowledge and understanding.

The most stereotyped of images was that of tribal society.[57] Map and census were important instruments in the creation of a model of African society upon which the state could act. Maps and numbers, space and numeracy, made possible the creation of colonial categories that could be fixed spatially, thus allowing for a state-sponsored territorialization of culture. This concern with locating culture geographically grew inversely to the rise of migrant labor, which spread people from the reserves over the entire expanse of South Africa. As capitalism seemed to lead to the dispersion of people, raising in the twentieth century the specter of detribalization, officials redoubled their efforts to ensure that colonial subjects could not escape their tribal appellations.

The ethnographic diagram of chiefly genealogies and the maps of native reserves represent the two endpoints of the fixing of culture in space; in one sense the latter circumscribed the former. Power and control lay at the center of both. The genealogy is precisely a schematic representation, indeed an instrument, of power and jurisdiction premised on a putative "common characteristic or interest."[58] Culture was from the beginning an essential feature of colonial state formation, not something the state later "discovered" in formulating its policies of segregation and apartheid. This location of culture in space comprised an intrinsic feature of conquest and early colonial rule, of rendering Africans "cognizable," for example through sedentarization and by attempting to create ethnically pure districts. The conquest state attempted to organize space on the basis of homogeneous tribal designations demarcated by administrative boundaries; indeed, early colonial officials forcibly and violently removed Africans designated as belonging to a different "tribe." Again, however, throughout the nineteenth century the state lacked the coercive power to make its model of African culture real. This changed in the twentieth century, and especially in the 1950s with the introduction of apartheid, though ultimately even the apartheid state was unable to realize its authoritarian vision for the African "homelands."

The modernity of tribalism is now well established. The enormity of its simplifications, the audacity of its reductions of African culture and history, is at times less apparent. The earlier period of European exploration offers a useful counterpoint. In the eighteenth and early nineteenth centuries Europeans produced exceptionally rich and detailed narrative accounts of the African societies they encountered; these texts remain among the most important documents for reconstructing the African past. Authors described such details as dress and cuisine and at times also evinced uncertainty as to what they were describing. There is in some of this writing an almost playful quality, the *jouissance* of the Enlightenment naturalist expressing wonder at the world he observed. Discussions of politics and succession were also primarily narrative reconstructions. Diagrams, when they did appear, summarized or "subjoined" (Alberti's phrase) material presented in narrative form.[59] With conquest, with ethnographic description driven by the state's will to know, diagrams, maps, charts, and tables became increasingly important; words simply expanded upon, and when necessary qualified, information presented as maps, numbers, and diagrams. Genealogical diagrams, for example, became the cadastral maps of culture and power, forms of simplifications and plays of power. The products of the state's ethnography attained the quality of legal proceedings and of highly functionalist manuals of colonial rule.[60]

This change from the exuberance of discovery to the banality of administration formed one part of a wider codification of African "custom" begun with John Maclean's *Compendium of Kaffir Law and Custom* (Maclean was the chief colonial official for the Ciskei in the 1850s).[61] Chanock and others have focused on the codification of custom and the drawing up of texts on "native law" as central to the colonial creation of tribalism and to the state's policy of indirect rule.[62] The state utilized these texts in the formulation of policy and in the law's daily practice. The main thrust of nineteenth-century colonial policy in the Eastern Cape was the civilizing of the African and the destruction of tribal society, not its preservation and political reconstruction. Yet even destroying tribal society necessitated knowing something about it.

The state in effect developed a model – a tribal model – of African society upon which it could act surgically, in the nineteenth century to destroy chiefship, in the twentieth century to reconstruct it. This model building initially unfolded at two levels. The first magistrates "took cognizance" of the people over whom they were extending rule and attempted to organize administrative space on the basis of discrete tribes. The early correspondence of these magistrates took the form of extended ethnographic descriptions. Second, the state conducted numerous commissions and produced various reports, particularly in the 1870s following the creation of the DNA and its expansion into the Transkei. In addition to establishing borders and defining tribal groups, they provided detailed colonial renderings of African institutions and set out the administrative structures and procedures of colonial rule. The first years of the 1870s saw no less than three reports and one commission: on the "social and political condition of natives in the Transkeian Territory," on the "social and political condition" of the Thembu, and the Griffiths–Ayliff–Grant Commission that began drawing boundaries in the Transkei. These were followed by the 1876 Griqualand East Commission, reports on labor and on land tenure and topography, and, most importantly, the massive 1883 Native Laws and Customs Commission. That commission, more than any other before it concerned with the accumulation of information and its relationship to the problem of rule, led directly to the Cape's annexation of the Transkei.

The 1883 commission marked both the culmination of developments in the Transkei in the preceding decade and the beginning of a more fundamental codification of customary law and clarification of colonial rule. In important ways the commission became a central part of the process of state formation. In the calling of witnesses, the hearing of testimonies, and the narrative report itself the commission bore the unmistakable attributes of legal proceedings. It in fact led to the promulgation of considerable legislation, particularly the Transkeian penal code, which effectively extended laws in the Cape Colony to the conquered territory, continuing an earlier pattern in the Cape of defining the colonized as individual subjects.

One of the first acts of conquest was to locate Africans within a snare of legalities, beginning with the state's monopoly over the taking of life and including issues concerning property – for example theft, murder, and assault – and practices deemed by officials as repugnant and "barbarous." Here the state shifted rights and procedures from chiefs to the magistrate. Criminal law centered on person and property, defining the African as an individual with inalienable rights but also, and importantly, subject (at least theoretically) to the full disciplinary apparatus of the state. This creation of the colonial subject as bourgeois individual can be seen not only in legal concepts and discourse but in the quotidian

practices of the law itself: the manner by which accused were arrested by policemen, their appearance standing singly before the magistrate, their incarceration
in jail cells, flogging, and, ultimately, execution by hanging.

This approach to law and punishment differed considerably from traditional
conceptions and practices of justice. Typically infractions involved as much the
person directly involved as the community of which he or she was a member.
Thus people could be found guilty of offenses they themselves did not commit.
The "*property* of the people constitutes the great fund out of which the debts
of justice are paid." Moreover, Dugmore continued, the "law is so accommo-
dating as to give credit," so that many years later a case could, in effect, be
reopened.[63] The central issue revolved around the restoration of balance within
the community, less personal culpability or the restoration to the individual of
harm done to them.

In the legal proceedings before the magistrate's court, however, Africans rendered their lives as narratives of the individual. They quite literally stood alone
before the law. Paradoxically, the silences, the information Africans withheld,
helped contribute to the state's, and especially the law's, epistemic violence,
its constitution of the subject as individual actor. The law's violence was both
spatial and textual. Speaking alone in front of the magistrate, Africans' speech
was not only reduced to the written word but transformed into writing, into the
reproducible Western forms of the state.[64]

Before the law the colonized was rendered fully cognizable, identified as
subject to the state and entrapped in what Weber described as the "iron cage"
of bureaucratic rationality.[65] But Africans were made doubly cognizable. For
as criminal law and procedure defined them as individual subjects, civil law –
more precisely native civil law or what subsequently became customary law –
continued to be applied to the conquered.[66] There was thus a simultaneous
and doubled definition of the colonized, a definition that complicates conventional narratives of native policy that emphasize a transition from citizen to
subject, individual to tribesmen, or from direct rule to indirect rule. This dividing of legalities simultaneously located Africans in two worlds, two sides of the
modernist coin of colonialism, defining them as both individual and as "ethnic
subject,"[67]capable of participating in the essential historicity of progress but
trapped nonetheless in the timelessness of tribe.[68]

The state's production of native culture thus cut two ways. It could be used
in service of the civilizing mission just as easily as it could be deployed to
entrap Africans in a colonial tribalism. The latter triumphed in the twentieth
century. The 1920 Native Affairs Act and the 1927 Native Administration Act,
for example, marked the shift towards the centrality of tribe and the state's
commitment to territorial segregation. As in the past culture was a central
feature of bureaucratic formation. The 1927 Act created a new system of native
civil courts, using "native law and custom," and, importantly, embarked on a

process of "retribalization" by introducing a system of indirect rule that greatly strengthened the power of chiefs. With legislation such as the 1952 Bantu Laws Amendment Act and, especially, the 1951 Bantu Authorities Act, introduced in the Transkei in 1956, the state completed its transformation of rule, at the center of which were chiefs, tribes, and customary law.

By this time the discipline of anthropology had become a central feature of native administration. Anthropology shared with segregationist policy a view of culture as a bounded system of shared beliefs, practices, and customs. This system could, at least ideally, be located spatially, so that the geographical designation "Thembuland" and the category "Thembu culture" were synonymous. As early as the 1920s and 1930s anthropologists had worked for the state. This continued in the era of apartheid. Hammond-Tooke, for example, assembled genealogies and produced studies of the state on the patrilineal "rules" of the segmentary "system" and of the creation of "tribal clusters" through "segmentation."[69] Indeed, as he put it in a letter to a Bantu Affairs commissioner in 1965, his "considerable research into the tribal structures and history of the various Mfengu tribes" had "resulted in the recognition of a number of chiefs."[70]

Theory and practice

Conquest and the categorizing state

The system of resident magistrates, by 1878 in place everywhere but Pondoland, depended on demarcated and stable boundaries. The reorganization of political space that was so central to the creation of colonial administrative units formed one of the most basic, and most contested and confused, features of state formation in the 1870s, leading directly to the outbreak of widespread violence in 1880. It contradicted the earlier political landscape described in the previous chapter: the shifting borders of chiefly rule, the relationship between boundaries, the economy and ecology and migration, and the numerous unadministered areas that formed on the edges of political domains. In their place emerged stationary boundaries using roads, land beacons, natural boundaries (especially rivers) and, ultimately, based on colonial understandings of African tribes. The nineteenth-century invention of Fingoland, Thembuland, Pondoland, Bomvanaland, and the like prefigured the later tribalism of the segregation and apartheid eras.

With conquest "territory is divided into boundaries,"[71] as one African man put it. This reorganization of space typically entailed four processes, beginning with the negotiations between colonial officials and African leaders and the many proclamations that preceded or immediately followed them. Second, the magistrate, chief magistrate, and other colonial officials toured their new domain. Third, the building of magistracies created new loci of power. Finally, magistrates began the actual surveying or resurveying of the land, the planting of boundary flags, and the calculation of distances between the various seats of colonial power.[72] Here the various commissions established in the 1870s, very often headed by newly appointed resident magistrates, were especially important in the colonial mapping of conquered territory.

These processes generally produced four basic and related outcomes. Most obviously they led to a new political system, based on the magistrate assisted by headmen and chiefs. This system had potentially revolutionary implications since it shifted power away from the chief and to the magistrate. It also simplified what had been a very complex political system. The demotion of chiefs and their transformation into headmen, indeed in many areas the abolition of chiefship, indexed the colonial simplification of African politics. A second outcome was the attempt – often initially unsuccessful – by magistrates to "settle" people in villages, what in later years became locations. This was a radically new system of settlement, and one that Africans very often protested against and ultimately subverted. As the "chiefs and the leading men of the Idutywa Reserve" told their magistrate in 1864, "the system of being huddled together in villages" created "a great deal of sickness on account of the constant accumulation of filth, and they mentioned several other evils connected with the system."[73] Third, officials began forcing out of magisterial districts (usually by burning their huts) people they defined, typically on the basis of tribe, as illegal residents.

Finally, colonial borders had important economic and ecological repercussions. The demarcation of crown forests deprived many people of access to wood. In times of drought people living in lowland areas had moved their stock into mountains. In many instances under colonial rule this would have entailed crossing district boundaries. Theoretically this was possible once people received passes to move from one district to another. In practice, however, magistrates refused African requests to bring animals into upland areas. Stock not surprisingly "suffered very severely."[74] So also did pasturage, which was soon denuded. In short, the ecological degradation of the late nineteenth century was related to the colonial reorganization of space.

The colonial archive for the 1870s and 1880s is replete with discussions of boundaries, their drawing up and the anxiety and contestation they invariably caused, and the displacing of people that frequently followed the colonial organization of political space. Africans made it clear that they lived in a world in which boundaries were not "fixed" and in which political claims very frequently overlapped. People living in what became known in anthropological discourse as "maximal lineages" did not inhabit contiguous areas. "There is no fixed boundary," one chief told the chief magistrate; "our people are intermixed."[75] Some of his people were "about 18 miles from my Kraal. The space between us is filled up by" people attached to other chiefs.[76]

To Europeans African political space seemed at best confusing and at worst incomprehensible, and because it was so it was incapable of being subjected to rational modes of governance. As one official stated in 1858, African "boundaries are always exceedingly vague." People might "without the slightest hesitation" take possession of "any vacant spot." "I could," he continued, "find no Kaffir who could accurately define Kreli's boundary between the Gwali and the Tsomo" rivers. For, he summarized by way of principle, a "'direct line' was utterly unintelligible to a Kaffir."[77]

This confusion, this unholy mess of vague changing boundaries and absence of "direct lines," produced, so officials argued, equally confusing tribal intermixtures and chiefly domains. It followed, then, that to reorganize space, to create rational permanent boundaries, inevitably also meant bringing clarity to tribe and chiefdom. Put another way, officials sought to fix African political culture spatially so that, for example, chiefs would be responsible for all people inhabiting a clearly demarcated ward or district. For until then it would be "quite impossible," the chief magistrate dictated to one chief, "that either judicial or fiscal administration can be satisfactory so long as the several sections of tribes . . . remain intermixed as at present."[78]

A central goal of the state, then, was not simply to map territory but, in doing so, to reorganize the population. The one was inseparable from the other. In the late 1870s Pondoland might only just be emerging from its status as a *terra incognita*, but elsewhere the state had "finally settled and determined" political boundaries.[79] The decisive years in this early colonial boundary making were 1878 and 1879.[80] Chiefs were very often "dissatisfied" with the process and with the results.[81] In August 1878, for example, boundary issues surfaced in a key meeting between the magistrate and Chief Mditshwa of Tsolo, in which the chief agreed to accept a salary from the state in return for acknowledging his political subordination. "I am a Buffalo," Mditshwa said, "a Chief, though you have come to be a greater Chief." Most of the meeting was taken up with a discussion of boundaries. According to the chief, the result of the colonial boundary making had been that some of "my people are taken away. Today I have no ground and Govt. money is in my hands. Thomson has eaten my ground. A great many of my people are wandering about . . . I say this country is destroyed. For what country do I receive this money?"[82] The colonial drawing of borders, the chief pointed out, already had created the recent Mpondomise fracas with nearby Thembu. The magistrate's reply was that the creation of a "defined boundary" would prevent further strife. He thus missed the chief's point that the colonial drawing of boundaries fomented conflict, rather than preventing it.

The magistrate admitted that the "boundary is not clearly defined," but promised that the "boundary question" would be soon "settled" by a land commission. This is precisely what happened. A year and a half later, in December

1879, the chief magistrate, Charles Brownlee, and the resident magistrate met at Tsolo with Mditshwa. The main topic of their discussion concerned the relationship between boundaries discussed by J. A. Orpen, the first magistrate, and those later created by the Griqualand East Commission, composed of Alexander R. Welsh, J. R. Thomson, and Hamilton Hope. (Each of these men would were or would become magistrates.) Orpen, however, had set no land beacons. The commission did. The chief bristled at Brownlee's dismissive early remarks. "You must know," he began, "that we will speak. We will dispute. We will agree to the things we like, but will dispute about those we are dissatisfied about ... I went to see you at Kokstad about the boundary and am anxiously waiting to hear what the decision is. If I am satisfied I will tell you. When Government took me over I was told I would not be reduced from my Chieftainship."[83] Mditshwa then recounted his relationship with Orpen and early discussions concerning boundaries and the extent of the chief's authority.

The commission saw things differently. Their erection of a land beacon immediately raised the chief's ire, as it conflicted with his understanding of the agreement with Orpen. "I told them we were off Mr. Orpen's line," Mditshwa recalled, adding that he had called upon three men who corroborated his understanding of the boundary. The commissioners told one of them "to shut up as he was speaking nonsense." Despite Mditshwa's protests Brownlee told him the boundaries "would stand." Among other things, including the displacement of people, the result for the chief was that a number of people who had once lived under his control were now "out of my District."[84]

The developments unfolding in Tsolo during the late 1870s took place across the Transkei. Lines drawn vaguely in the early part of the decade became boundaries marked by beacons sunk into the ground. Of course the power of officials to turn principle and policy into daily practice varied enormously across the area and over time. People moved to one place might return or, in other cases, simply ignored the demands of the colonial officials who now ruled over them. Nonetheless, it seems clear that many, especially chiefs, clearly understood some of the implications of this colonial gerrymandering. Next door to Tsolo, for example, an important boundary dispute occurred between Hope, Mhlontlo, and the western Mpondo chief Nqwiliso, concerning the southern part of what was becoming the Qumbu district, in a classically border or unadministered area on the edge of the domains of the Mpondomise paramount chief Mhlontlo, and Nqwiliso. This area, just south of the vital wagon road stretching from Umtata north to Natal and near the Shawbury missionary station, was roughly equidistant from the great places of the two chiefs. Located in a relatively remote area, chiefs and people remained largely independent of the control of either Mhlontlo or Nqwiliso.[85] Hope described the situation as that of "Pondo and Pondomise Squatters who were reciprocally occupying each other's ground."[86] The magistrate's description reflected both the state's belief that boundaries and ethnicity should be coterminous and the reality that the many border areas of precolonial politics were interminably multi-ethnic.

Once boundaries had been drawn by the various commissions the state considered them inviolate. Hope was averse to any "alteration of a fixed boundary laid down by the Commission of 1872"; to do so would have "established a very troublesome and dangerous precedent." And so the state removed "squatters" to their respective ethnically defined districts. The "Pondo squatters" vacated some twenty-two "villages"; they were subsequently occupied by Mpondomise who had been living in Pondoland.[87]

These early forced removals importantly took place not after but during conquest. The state's tribalist fantasies of space organized on the basis of homogeneous tribes were thus an intrinsic, and at times violent, feature of British imperial expansion. The Tsolo and Qumbu examples were repeated elsewhere in the Transkei, as had happened decades earlier west of the Kei River. This was especially true for areas near and along the Mbashe and Umtata Rivers that, according to officials, represented various ethnic boundaries. In the former, DNA officials ultimately created an ethnically defined magisterial district for the Bomvana centered on Elliotdale. However, this was a classically ambiguous region. In addition to the Bomvana, the general area was composed of small Thembu, Mpondo, and Xhosa chiefdoms. Both the Thembu and the Gcaleka paramounts had historic ambitions to extend their control over this region; so did several western Mpondo chiefs.[88] These ambitions flared into open conflict in 1872 involving Xhosa, Thembu, and, to a lesser extent, Mpondo. Unsurprisingly, the conflict began shortly after the state commenced surveying the region.

In the early 1870s the Bomvana chiefdom acknowledged the political supremacy of the Gcaleka paramountcy. Much of the rest of the area largely remained an unadministered zone of shifting political alliances. For example, people under the control of the Bomvana chief Pali had once been under Konjwayo, a small Mpondo chiefdom. Or, as a Mpondo councillor put it, describing well a frontier zone and the ethnic ambiguities that frustrated colonial officials, the people under Pali (Bomvana) "belonged to" the Konjwayo Mpondo. They were, to make matters worse, "Bomvanas."[89] Pali's people lived on both sides of the Umtata River. They successfully resisted the attempts of Nqwiliso to extend his control over the area, indeed aligning themselves with the Thembu in the 1877 conflict.[90]

The drawing of colonial borders ultimately severed the relationship between the Bomvana and the Gcaleka, refuted Mpondo aspirations, but initially at least provided an opportunity for Gangelizwe, the Thembu paramount, to attempt to extend his control southwards. The creation of the Elliotdale district in effect thwarted these attempts because it recognized, or more accurately created, an independent Bomvana chiefdom, though only after 1880 did Bomvana chiefs begin receiving salaries from the state, thus sealing their fate in the new colonial

political geography.[91] Thus was created Bomvanaland, though some areas remained in dispute and the wider region continued to be a politically ambiguous
zone, with Gangelizwe and Mpondo chiefs at times attempting to control the
area on the border of the Elliot and Mqanduli districts as well as areas closer to
the coast.[92]

The case of the Mpondo "squatters" and the creation of Bomvanaland well
illustrate the ethnic gerrymandering that was a central feature of colonial conquest. Certainly by contemporary standards nineteenth-century borders were
often poorly or incompletely demarcated. Certainly the coercive power of the
state remained relatively weak throughout the nineteenth and well into the twentieth centuries. And certainly Africans – chiefs and commoners – subverted,
rejected, or simply ignored the state's geographic decrees. The reorganization of political space nonetheless represented a central feature of early state
formation.[93] Without it the magisterial system was impossible. The newly drawn
boundaries clearly troubled many chiefs. The new borders typically restricted
their authority and muted their attempts to extend control over outlying chiefdoms. What, after all, was "the necessity for these boundaries which appear
only to cut him [the chief] off from the other Chiefs of his tribe?"[94]

Once a region had been mapped and defined ethnically, magistrates began
counting their subjects. Following the 1877 annexation of what came to be
known as Fingoland and the Idutywa reserve, for example, Sir Bartle Frere
commanded headmen to "submit to the Chief Magistrate a list of the members of
the tribes resident within, or belonging to his subdivision, to whom he proposes a
tract of land should be allotted for occupation."[95] Censuses created considerable
apprehension, among chiefs and commoners alike. In 1877, Mhlontlo "took
considerable interest" in the tabulation of his people. Everywhere censuses
caused "considerable apprehension" and entailed an intricate political dance
between chief and colonial officials.[96] In 1879, for example, the Thembu chief
Dalasile asked Stanford "to delay the census work." Dalasile had been requested
to do so by the paramount chief Gangelizwe. The two chiefs consulted and
retracted their earlier opposition to the census.[97] However, at the end of the
month Dalasile told Stanford that while "he had no objection to the census being
proceeded with," he nonetheless wanted to "call his people together to explain
them fully the nature of it." Stanford refused the request, arguing that "the
census had already been explained to the people." Despite the chief's ostensibly
agreeing to the census, his brother refused to have his kraal enumerated.[98]
Indeed, throughout the region Africans evinced hostility at being counted. As
Stanford wrote in August 1879, "The Qwatis [a Thembu clan] have a great idea
that if I could be got rid of they would hear nothing more of Hut Tax, census or
disarmament."[99]

Like maps, censuses varied considerably in accuracy.[100] Well into the twentieth century the state generally did not have the resources to precisely count

its African subjects, who could elude or ignore the officials who wandered into their areas with pen and paper. Africans feared that censuses, despite their faultiness, formed part of the state's "ulterior designs upon themselves and their property."[101] Such fears were well founded. Typically the collection of hut taxes immediately followed map and census. Officials then generated a list of defaulters, who were subject to arrest and prosecution. The collection of hut taxes also provided one means of controlling the location of people. Those who did not appear on the tax lists were, by definition, illegally residing in the area and thus subject to having their huts burned down and themselves and their families turned out of the area.[102]

The actions of colonial officials from the mid-1870s – surveying, counting, proclaiming – ultimately contradicted the agreements they had entered into with African chiefs earlier in the decade. Those agreements had, in effect, transformed African polities into colonial protectorates. Technically magistrates were in a role subordinate to that of African chiefs. Magistrates "had no legal status" that was independent of the chief's decision to allow them to reside in his territory.[103] In the second half of the 1870s this "very unsatisfactory state of affairs"[104] became ever more apparent; 1875 saw not simply the annexation of Thembuland but the colonial dictate that paramount Gangelizwe's "authority should not extend beyond his own section."[105] The outbreak of violence in 1877–8, the so-called Ninth Frontier War, stemmed in part from the annexation of Fingoland, the creation of the Idutywa reserve, and, more generally, an attempt by the state to establish political boundaries in the classically border area around the Bashee River.[106]

In 1878, as we have noted, magistrates across the Transkei began more assiduously collecting hut taxes, in addition to administering censuses, grouping people into locations, deploying the pass system, and bringing Africans before the colonial law. In July 1878, for example, magistrate Welsh, based in Tsolo, faithfully patrolled his magisterial boundaries, issued passes, and apprehended and prosecuted offenders. He took special offense at a man who "had come into the Dist. without a pass which is contrary to the orders of the system pursued by myself and other Magistrates in this Territory," a system that "has to be as strictly as possible enforced."[107] The following month Chief Mditshwa accused the magistrate of being "eaten up."[108]

Three developments in 1879 indicated the decisive shift in and increasing volatility of the colonial relationship. First, officials began announcing and implementing Frere's 15 September proclamation that extended far greater colonial control over the region and, definitively, attacked the power of chiefs. The proclamation formalized what was already happening on the ground with the shift of power away from chiefs and to the colonial state and its African collaborators. (As one man put it in 1903, "the Chiefs are thin and hungry for the country is full of Headmen who make themselves Chiefs of the Blood."[109])

By the end of 1879 officials, and importantly very often the chief magistrate himself, quite literally began distributing the law to their subjects. "It is right that you should know the Laws," the chief magistrate told the people of Tsolo. "I am now going to read them... Government has put officers in the land to take cognizance of everything that goes on."[110]

A second development was the state's introduction of the Disarmament Act designed to prohibit Africans from owning guns. Africans clearly believed that the Act formed part of the British conquest of "their country."[111] The final development took place a considerable distance away from the Eastern Cape: the British defeat at the hands of the Zulu at the battle of Isandlwana in January 1879. Stanford, an acute observer, wrote in early February 1879 that people had heard "wonderful stories of the Zulu successes."[112] Later that year he wrote presciently that "I do not believe in startling changes in the management of natives... unless we find ourselves strong enough to face another war and keep a standing army at hand to suppress disaffection. It is the weak manner in which disarming has been attempted and the absurd efforts to curb the power of the chiefs that is the cause of so much ill-will amongst the native tribes."[113] Indeed, Stanford wrote to Elliot in July 1879, the state had "destroyed the confidence in us of every tribe from the Kei to Natal, and afforded such an opportunity as I believe has never been before for the Natives to unite in a war of races."[114]

The Disarmament Act and Frere's proclamation coalesced with issues surrounding the elementary forms of state formation. In August, for example, officials met with increasing resistance to their attempts to conduct censuses. Resistance was especially strong in Emigrant Thembuland and in the region between Tsolo and Qumbu. In the former area an official "was not allowed to take a census."[115]

Yet by early 1880 the issue of the "assumption of Sovereignty" had been decided.[116] Officials continued their creation of borders, the drawing up of censuses, the collection of hut taxes, in short the creation of a system of colonial rule. They continued with the Disarmament Act as well as actions designed to diminish the power of chiefs and to create a system centering on magistrates and headmen. In many areas taxes were only collected for the first time in 1880.[117] Following the state's establishment of boundaries using flags along the new border separating the Mpondomise and the Mpondo, people were forced from their homes.[118] The Mpondo chief Nqwiliso complained that "my people are being turned away and burnt out of my country."[119] In late July an African working for the state reported that Thembu had "received messages from the Pondo Chief Nqwiliso and Mqikela to ask them to join them should some huts that are built by the Pondos in the Pondomise country (Mr. Welshes [sic] District) be burnt by the Government."[120] "Secret meetings and doctoring at many of the Kraals of the minor chiefs" were taking place; these minor chiefs were the ones most likely to be converted into mere headmen in the new colonial state.[121]

By February 1879 rebellion had broken out in Basutoland, the so-called Moorosi Rebellion. King Letsie had petitioned the British to revoke the Disarmament Act, but to no avail. Soon Africans throughout much of that region would join together in what has come to be known as the Basuto Gun War. In fact the conflict was far wider. By the end of 1880 Africans living in a huge swath of territory were in open rebellion. From Basutoland rebellion spread through most of the Transkeian districts that bordered it, from Griqualand East to Engcobo and Xalanga, a region of some 15,000 square miles, much of it very mountainous. "Messengers continually passing" between the various regions helped relay information not simply to rebel areas but further afield as well, for example into Pondoland.[122] By the end of October 1880 Europeans had deserted the rebel areas, most fleeing to Umtata or Queenstown.

Much of the violence was directed towards magistrates, the people who in the previous years had quite literally been creating a colonial state. As Stanford wrote, the war was "simply to regain independence, and it is as much a war of the people as it is a war of the chiefs."[123] The magistrate of Xalanga district observed that "the Chiefs were trying to bring about a combination of the different Tribes with the object of throwing off European rule."[124] According to the official,

nearly all the Chiefs in Tembuland had entered into an agreement to rebel, that Umhlonhlo was the moving spirit in the plot, and was to give the signal for the commencement of hostilities ... It is very remarkable that up to the even of the rebellion there were none of the usual premonitory signs, which formerly preceded any outbreak among the natives.

People, he continued, had been "instructed to do nothing which might excite the suspicion of" colonial officials.

They thought if they could drive the white man out of their country, things would naturally fall into the old groove again, and then, what they have considered their golden age, would return, when the Chiefs and their Counsellors would possess unlimited power ... European rule tended to curtail this license: the Chiefs saw that their power was departing from them while the people imagined that all which in their eyes constituted freedom was being gradually destroyed. The people are as much interested in this war as the Chiefs and judging from appearances have entered into it heart and soul.[125]

In areas such as Engcobo and probably in other districts as well, upwards of three-fourths of the population rebelled.[126] By the end of 1881, some 12,000 people had surrendered to Stanford alone; they were "now reduced to extreme poverty."[127] Drought had returned. So also had disease. In 1882 smallpox ravaged large areas of the Transkei. Conquest had been completed. All that remained was Pondoland, annexed to the colony in 1894.

3   Rationalities and rule

No one knows who will live in this [iron] cage in the future, or whether at the end of this tremendous development entirely new prophets will arise, or there will be a great rebirth of old ideas and ideals, or, if neither, mechanized petrification, embellished with a sort of convulsive self-importance.

Max Weber, *The Protestant Ethic and the Spirit of Capitalism*, 182

With the native people as a whole at their present stage of development, the tribal system and native law, under proper administration, appears to be the most efficient machinery of government in definitely native areas.

Major J. F. Herbst, Secretary for Native Affairs, 1926[1]

The will to know, to identify, to categorize Africa according to the precepts of Western rationality formed an ineluctable part of both the politics and the practice of conquest. In contrast to much of the rest of Africa – indeed, much of the nineteenth-century colonial world – officers from an administrative agency, the Cape Department of Native Affairs, conquered much of the Transkei. That bureaucracy required, at least at first conceptually, the existence of clearly established boundaries and fixed social categories, a kind of political grid upon which officials could act. Administration, indeed statecraft itself, depended on modern conceptions of space. In the Eastern Cape, and indeed elsewhere in Africa, ideas of space joined a belief in culture as a bounded system. These elementary forms of state formation entailed so many acts of simplification to render Africa comprehensible to modern governance. They were intrinsic features of colonial expansion, not something that occurred after conquest had been completed and the problem of control presented itself to European rulers.

The resistance that shook the region in the 1880s would not be equaled until the introduction of apartheid seven decades later. Both these moments of African opposition and insurgency concerned state formation and the West's rational empiricist instruments of domination, the first as colonial conquest, the second as the triumph of authoritarianism in South Africa. In the nineteenth century the colonized began entering modernity's "iron cage." In the twentieth century they found themselves entrapped by an authoritarian bureaucratic order which defined them as "temporary sojourners" in white South Africa or, simply, as "redundant" people.[2] This very language of authoritarianism, in which people became so many technical problems, spoke to an ongoing process of making subject populations ever more identifiable to the state.

The modern state rested on stable colonial categories; this is the very nature of making the world "cognizable." Yet in the process of creating them (that is, in the process of state formation) those very categories blurred considerably. Officials had their general models of how the world should be. Making them real was altogether a different matter. Despite the censuses, commissions, reports, and attempts to map the land with beacons and surveying flags, the early colonial state simply lacked the financial resources and coercive might, not to mention the political consensus, to complete any program of social engineering.[3] This would change fitfully and unevenly in the twentieth century, first with an emerging consensus on the importance of segregation and then, in the 1950s, with the apartheid policies formulated by the National Party government.[4]

The issue here is not simply one of state power, its extent and the nature of its exercise. Administration and rule are not synonymous; the first concerns bureaucratic structures and regulations, the second the relationship of those who wield power and those who are subjected to it. Conquest and those daily activities that entailed the making of rule comprised so many cross-cultural encounters of a political kind, an interaction of peoples who shared a fascination with power, its origins and operation. At the same time they often perceived the world very differently. People, for example, believed that chiefs could bring rain, thus suggesting not only an intimate relationship between politics and fertility, but also a conception of social reality that did not separate the secular from the sacred or the animate from inanimate. Such, of course, was not the case with resident magistrates, who could not believe that chiefs controlled rain or, for that matter, that witches could secrete animals into the stomach or esophagus of their victims. Africans searching for *muti* were, quite simply, "making a fool" of themselves.[5] Officials lived in a world of ritual and symbol too, particularly in the everyday, repetitive practices that comprised their professional lives.[6] But they also saw the world in a way that joined the empirical to the epistemological, "that nothing was present to the mind that was not first present to the senses."[7] Among other things this allowed for a distinction between the real and the fictional, the objective and the untrue.

Rule entailed an interplay of rationalities and symbols, different rationalities and different symbols but not necessarily incommensurate ones. Thus far we have suggested that both Europeans and Africans "resolved" one other into their respective conceptual universes, though the imaginations of each could encompass parts of the world of the other.[8] The construction of African "barbarism" at times ironically entailed positive comparison.[9] Likewise Africans perceived agents of the colonial state within their own conceptions of political society, even as they also distinguished colonial rule from precolonial politics.

We also have argued for the modernity of the early colonial state. The ways in which the state came into being – the maps, censuses, regulations, and laws – locate early colonialism in the revolutionary changes of the Enlightenment, especially the importance of information. The suggestion here is that the authoritarian possibilities that were already present in the early colonial state came to fruition in the twentieth century. Put another way, the "decentralized despotism" of the twentieth century had its formative roots in the earlier period.[10] The rise of an authoritarian political order involved not simply an enlargement in the state's coercive capacities; it also entailed the triumph of what sociologists have called instrumental rationality, the "iron cage" Max Weber feared and the rise of a political system where the ends justified the means – even if it meant the destruction of human life itself. This shift, in turn, had important implications for the ways colonial subjects understood and critiqued the colonial order within the space of rule and rationality.

White skins, black masks?[11]

Recent work on Theophilus Shepstone, secretary for native affairs in the colony of Natal, has explored the ways he appropriated "the 'axioms and aesthetics' of the indigenous culture."[12] The official "surrounded himself with the trappings of Zulu kingship, including a praise singer and a snuff-box bearer, presided over Zulu dances, and gave African women to his loyal African henchmen." Moreover, the "annual first fruits ceremony" became a "prerogative" of the chief native affairs officer in the colony.[13] At the same time Cetshawyo, who became king in 1872, invested Shepstone not simply with "an important role in the [coronation] proceedings" but symbolically transformed the white official as Shaka Zulu, founder of the kingdom.[14] A white skin began wearing, wittingly or unwittingly, the black mask of the people he helped conquer. Zulu conceptions of time helped make this conflation possible, since "cause and effect were not chronologically determined," and "prophecy and preordination . . . functioned to explain and justify."[15] In at least some respects, Shepstone really could become Shaka Zulu.

In the Eastern Cape, magistrates participated in a similar blurring of African and European political models and processes. Take, for example, the rule of Joseph Cox Warner, who served as Thembu agent from 1852 to 1864. "On entering the offices or meeting Mr. Warner . . . the Tembu salute to chiefs was always given. The syllable 'ah' was loudly pronounced followed by the Kaffir form of Mr. Warner's name 'Wana', the right hand being uplifted. Mr. Warner followed the practice of the native chiefs and gave no salutation in return." Then "business" began "in native fashion by the question 'Whence do you come?' Then would be taken the opening to say, 'Chief, we are sent here by your son', giving the name of the chief they [the 'councilors'] represented."[16]

Africans arranged, and bureaucrats participated in, elaborate installation ceremonies for magistrates. In 1876, for instance, the state appointed Sir Walter Stanford magistrate over the Thembu chief Dalasile. His recounting of the ceremony is worthy of extended quotation. Dalasile provided seats for Stanford, another official, and "for the leading chiefs. There was a pause after we were all seated and then on a signal from the chief the people saluted me in native fashion, 'Ah Ndabeni! – my name among the natives, meaning, 'In the news'." At this point the Dalasile and his brother "came forward to 'shake hands'. Very slowly and deliberately Dalasile walked" toward Stanford.

He lifted his feet very high, and with each step there was a swing of the arms, which he held high, that brought his body half round first on one side, then on the other. Qole imitated his brother with just sufficient restraint to keep his feet a little lower in marching and the swing of his arms a little shorter, true deference to the greater man. Not a word was spoken and after the ceremonial hand grip the chiefs returned to their seats with gaits unchanged.[17]

After Stanford delivered his address, Dalasile spoke. "I have agreed," he said, "to come under the government, but I do not give myself over." Waving "his arm over the assemblage," the chief declared that "these people . . . are mine. They remain on my back." He spoke, Stanford wrote, "in a deep guttural tone, which I afterwards found was not his natural voice but assumed for the occasion."[18]

Installation ceremonies such as these took place across much of the Transkei during the 1870s. Magistrates saw them as important moments in establishing colonial rule, of defining ruler and subject. Adopting the "mantle" of the colonized culture could be a strategy of translating one political system into another.[19] A magistrate would often refer to himself as *inkosi*, a chief. In the early years of rule the day-to-day relationship between colonizer and native closely paralleled that of chief and commoner. In both cases, for example, subjects "were expected to bare their heads, clasp both hands when receiving an object" and, of course, "refrain from criticizing his actions and decisions."[20]

Magistrates reveled in their paternalism. They imagined themselves as fathers of the people they ruled, tutoring them in the civilization Africans lacked. That Africans at times referred to the magistrate as "father" and themselves as their "child" may have contributed to a paternalist ethos. While they were attracted to new technologies and spent much of their time writing letters, reports and memoranda, they guarded their paternal authority. They generally sought tactile relationships between themselves and the people they ruled, even as technology and the bureaucratic organization and practices of the state inexorably led to a more impersonal system of rule. "The facilities offered by modern telegraphic and post systems are great," the 1883 Native Laws and Customs Commission reported, "but [they] are insufficient when we come to deal personally with the Kafir. Nothing can be more unsatisfactory to his mind than a brief, cold, inanimate telegram or dispatch." "Anything," the report continued, "in the nature of an abstract idea like 'Government' is to him impossible; and he is apt to be altogether confounded by the frequent or sudden changes of Party Administration."[21]

But as in the case of Shepstone in Natal, the installation ceremonies noted above and those surrounding the brief administration of Hamilton Hope could just as easily complicate the categories of colonizer and colonized as lead to their creation. It was, in short, not always clear who was appropriating whom. In surveying the land, in censuses, and in the commonplace rituals of rule magistrates amassed power in ways that both created a new political order and, at least at times, seemed to continue an older one. Under the Cape's system of direct rule the magistrate assumed many of the functions that had been performed by the chief, especially the allocation of land, the resolution of disputes, and the collection of tribute. (Early taxation, often paid in kind, differed little from older forms of tribute.) Where the chief had once sat with his councilors, now the magistrate ruled with the assistance of headmen backed by the local police. Politically emasculated because they were not part of the formal system of colonial administration, the traditional chiefs served primarily in a consultative capacity, though they remained symbolically, and potentially politically, important within the community.[22]

There were other similarities between chiefship and the early years of colonial rule. Precisely because the early state's coercive capacity remained so limited, the magistrate's power dissipated rapidly from his office. The district may have been mapped, the people counted and their taxes collected, but many areas within his domain remained for the most part either loosely administered or still practically unconquered. Like precolonial politics early colonial rule was mainly organized around personal, face-to-face relations. Power very often remained tactile – and personalized. The character of colonialism depended much on the personality of the magistrate; the arrival or departure of a magistrate could substantially reshape the local political landscape.[23]

The early colonial state as it unfolded on the ground certainly represented a break with the past. At the same time, however, a sociology of power that had characterized African political systems since the invention of chiefship continued. This is the essence of politics as cross-cultural encounter. The transition to rule entailed early magistrates, as so many avatars of modernity, donning the political masks of the people they had just subjugated. At the same time the colonized could fold the colonial state into their own political practices and conceptions of power. This kind of understanding could become the beginning of new critiques of the colonial political order.

Ruling by decree

The rise and triumph of authoritarianism

From the 1890s, the colonial state shifted towards greater, more detailed, and more systematic intervention into the lives of its newly created subjects. At first this shift proceeded erratically at best. The continued weakness of the colonial state, and the considerable range of opinion that existed at various levels of government on the crucial subject of native policy, created an uncertain political climate and frustrated official efforts to close the gap between policy and practice. Over the course of the twentieth century, however, the state's coercive capacities increased dramatically. NAD officials and other bureaucrats still bickered over the proper answer to the all-important "native question." But shorn of the earlier preoccupation with barbarism and the civilizing mission, the tenor of many of these disagreements became increasingly technical. What should the state do about urban Africans? What was the best way to manage the migrant-labor system? How should the state address problems such as soil erosion, overstocking, and poverty in the reserves? What new bureaucratic agencies might be necessary to "rehabilitate" impoverished areas? What changes would be required to strengthen the powers of tribal authorities? Prime Minister Hertzog insisted that the "time had come for a definite native policy." The native, he argued clearly, and intolerantly, "will have to be told in the most unequivocal language that the European is fully determined that South Africa shall be governed by the white man." The challenge was thus to determine the "final solution" to the difficult, but not intractable, "native question."[24]

In large part the change towards a more interventionist state related most immediately to the crumbling economies of the reserves and to the South African economy's greater reliance on African migrant labor from within its borders. At the turn of the century Africans from the Cape's native reserves began working underground in the gold mines of the Rand in much larger numbers.[25] With this development it became absolutely "necessary" for the government "to have a thorough check on their [African] movements."[26] By 1910, the Cape provided almost one-third of the total black labor force on the gold mines, representing 60 percent of the laborers from within the newly formed Union.[27] Both figures rose steadily. By the mid-1940s the region provided the greatest proportion of laborers for the mines, three times as many as the other provinces of the Union combined.[28] As far as the gold-mining industry was concerned, wrote the 1944 Mine Natives' Wage Commission, "the migratory system of peasant labor must continue. Any other policy would bring about a catastrophic dislocation of the industry and consequent prejudice to the whole economic structure of the Union."[29]

Africans in the reserves might be colonial subjects, but they were also now at the very foundation of South Africa's industrial order. Especially after the 1910 Act of Union, local officials became far more involved in managing the black working class. By the 1920s local NAD officials had provided detailed reports on topics such as the labor supply and the flow of migrant labor, consumption patterns, and the cost of living.[30] The state, in short, had become a crucial participant in marshaling labor and observing the African working class. When, in 1936, the secretary for native affairs issued a general circular requesting native commissioners to encourage Africans to seek employment since "sufficient labour is not offering to meet the industrial position,"[31] he was simply continuing what had become a common action of government officials.

This shift from the creation of rule to the imperative of management neces-sitated increased bureaucratization and "fundamentally" entailed a system of "domination through knowledge":[32] information, that is, not necessarily under-standing. The proliferation of bureaucratic offices and agencies, the explosion in the number of commissions, surveys and reports, the greater assiduousness with which officials collected data, the fiscal resources made available to bureaucrats, the centrality of science (soil engineering, nutrition, demography, microbiology, ethnology, to name but a few) to statecraft, the massive size of the archive itself – all of this testifies to the fundamental relationship of information to bureaucra-tization and modern statecraft.[33] In this more recent period it was not enough to count or measure once the objects and subjects of the state, but rather to submit them to continual, more regularized and more precise observation. This can be seen in the very character of the colonial archive. Singularity and distinc-tiveness characterize the archive for the eighteenth and much of the nineteenth centuries. Astounding duplication and textual monotony mark the twentieth-century archive, so that the historian wearies from reading multiple copies of the same report or memorandum distributed across the bureaucratic agencies that comprised the state.[34]

To the extent that "behind Enlightenment rationality is a logic of domination and oppression," wherein an early desire to control nature inexorably led to "the domination of human beings," for those living in South Africa's native reserves that logic unfolded with the advent of an increasingly bureaucratic and authoritarian political order.[35] Bureaucratization and the ascendency of science and its relevance to rule are, of course, processes originating in the West that have spread globally. We live mostly in an empire of empiricism. The political forms these developments help usher in – dictatorship or democracy, welfarist or laissez-faire policies – are shaped by the local organization of economic and political power. The South African political order has been peculiarly bifurcated. On the one hand, the dawn of the twentieth century saw the gradual rise of a welfarist state in which whites were citizens and significantly participated in and shaped the policy-making process. At the same time, however, there arose an authoritarian order in which Africans remained colonial subjects. In the first case white electoral politics tempered state decision making and shaped the character of the state's collection of information on its citizens. In the reserves, however, where labor became the sine qua non of policy, the state was willing to deploy its considerable coercive might in pursuit of what ultimately became a vast system of colonial social engineering.

Especially in the three decades between 1920 and the introduction of apartheid in the 1950s, state rationality went from bureaucratic to instrumental, a pursuit of technical solutions based on empirical data in which decisions were largely unencumbered by ethical considerations. This shift was made possible in the conquest state's attempt to render African society legible and thus open to "large-scale social engineering."[36] These developments – rising bureaucratization, an authoritarian state, and the increasing dominance of instrumental rationality – seeped into the minutiae of rule. They ultimately transformed the structures and daily practices of colonial domination by increasing the frequency and magnitude of people's encounters with the state.

The rise of authoritarianism is revealed in the genealogy of its legislation; the 1894 Glen Grey Act is a convenient starting point. That the Glen Grey district would be the site of a grand experiment in colonial social engineering is important. On the one hand, officials considered the district one of the "most civilized of any of those [areas] reserved for natives,"[37] as if the main tenets of nineteenth-century colonial policy had borne their progressive fruit. On the other, in the years immediately following colonial conquest land issues had become especially rococo, with quite confused and frequently conflicting patterns of African landholding. One of the "most civilized" areas had become, in the eyes of the state, virtually unintelligible. As elsewhere "grants to natives" existed "in a state of chaos, and some steps must be taken to place them on a sound basis."[38] Among other things the architects of the Act hoped to bring order (through taxation and new surveys) to the possession of land – in short, to render space more legible to state practice. Indeed, in 1908 the state appointed a full-time surveyor for the district.[39]

One of the most unmistakable features of the Glen Grey Act was its tripartite concern with land, labor, and governance. Along with other legislation, such as the 1896 Birth and Death Registration Act, Glen Grey marked a definitive turning point in state formation by bringing together within a single law state legibility, rule, and capitalist development. This shift represented among other things the importance of biopower to capitalism, in which "power would no longer be dealing simply with legal subject over whom the ultimate dominion was death, but with living beings, and the mastery it would be able to exercise over them."[40] In the nineteenth century the state's will to know had lain in techniques, for example, cartography and censuses. Controlling African labor came a distant second to establishing colonial suzerainty in the great age of the scramble. That steeplechase had come to an end by the turn of the century.

The new challenge centered on labor, the control of bodies, and the extent of state regulation of the economy. The 1914 Statistics Act, for example, combined information with regulation, the counting of bodies with the accounting of wages. Perpetually colonial subjects, Africans now also became economic units. The despotism of the former well served the latter. The twentieth century thus saw not simply the rise of segregation and then of apartheid – the victory of bureaucratic authoritarianism – but the triumph of a particular kind of concern with Africans within a state that had a massively enlarged coercive capacity.[41] That capacity can be seen most obviously in the use of the police in enforcing such apparently mundane policies as fencing or the dipping of stock; behind the state's vision of rural "development," its scientific management of space and agriculture, stood the threat, and often the use, of police violence.

Rule came to be increasingly instrumental, technocratic, and, importantly, based on social science. The deluge of legislation in the 1920s and 1930s, and then again in the 1950s, marked the constant chatter of the state and its will to know. In the 1920s and 1930s alone it passed more laws relating to Africans than in the previous century of colonial rule. People's encounters with the state increased as the latter concerned itself with rule and with labor. As thirteen men put it in 1948, that the NAD "professes to be trustee to the native population seems to us to be a farce, in that it allows the operation of the 'master' and 'servant' principles by any State authority over its wards without consultation."[42] "Without consultation," indeed.

"The labor supply exists right enough, but proper legislation, together with additional taxations, is required to secure it, and until this comes about this [bad] state of affairs must remain."[43] In the first two decades particularly the labor question specifically and, more generally, the regulation of bodies became vital issues of state concern. Discussion of wage rates, for example, might be joined to consideration of food intake.[44] Information gathering and economic regulation became intertwined. Particularly from the 1920s on officials went out into rural areas surveying land, intervening in agricultural production, culling and controlling stock, and attempting to create more permanent and more clearly delineated settlement patterns, in addition to counting people and their property. Censuses became more complex and more assiduously conducted; from the 1920s native areas were submitted to censuses every five years. These entailed not simply counting people but also their distribution across each district and detailed descriptions of land and land tenure, agricultural production, stock and stock mortality, and the man-hours expended by NAD officials in civil and criminal litigation.[45] Maps became more detailed, boundaries more clearly established, and the pass system far more aggressively administered.

In the 1920s, for example, superintendents of natives "engaged in measuring the arable lands" in the areas under their control and in restricting agricultural production on lands deemed by the state to be commonage.[46] Statistics on land tenure became ever more detailed; conjoined to this material were data on population and livestock. By 1945, the state had divided space into at many as eighteen different categories; three decades earlier that number had typically ranged between three and four.[47] Clearly the state had become more interested in the minutiae of space. In the 1930s, it required officials to provide detailed information on a location-by-location basis. The information they were required to provide included the area of the location, population, livestock, water supply and distribution, topography and soil analysis, a definition of arable and residential lands, and, importantly, determining the "carrying capacity" of African land when "properly controlled." In addition, officials were required to supply various details regarding the state's betterment policies, from the establishment of "rotational grazing areas" to afforestation to the state's capacity for "future supervision and control."[48] Sometimes local officials provided their superiors with information down to individual lots. In 1938, for example, the Alice magistrate wrote how "Arable lots Nos. 85–86 should be abandoned on account of being on a very steep slope," while three other lots "are recommended for abandonment on account of extensive erosion" and two other lots required a proper "line of demarcation."[49]

Accompanying each new wave of legislation was a demand for new information, sending state employees out into the reserves measuring everything from land to nutrition to disease to mortality rates. This information-gathering process reached frenetic levels in the late 1940s, and particularly in the 1950s and early 1960s. This period saw, as the chief magistrate described it in 1955, the introduction of "vast rehabilitation programmes and other agricultural and engineering activities in these Territories,"[50] involving everything from stock culling, boundary making, and fence building to closer settlement schemes. The voluminous studies and reports in the period after 1948 indicate the government's insatiable demand for information, information that very often led to the promulgation of policies that many Africans "viewed . . . with suspicion, being of the opinion that the Government is introducing this system as a means of obtaining cheap Native Labour for Industrial requirements."[51]

In short, by the mid-1950s the reserves were being subjected to policies that required a far greater number of administrators and other state employees. (Just to destroy almost half a million animals in 1961, to take one grisly example, required considerable bureaucratic manpower. Destroying one animal every minute would require a person to labor forty hours per week for four years straight; one animal put down every fifteen minutes would take over sixty years.)[52]

7 Resettlement site, Ciskei, 1970s (reproduced with permission from the Mayibuye Centre, University of the Western Cape)

The extent of this social engineering can be seen in the chief native commissioner's annual 1955 report for the Transkei. He began by pointing out that the new policies and the state's rapid growth had created a large number of unfilled positions. The report then moved on to education, the introduction of Bantu Authorities, economic conditions, and then a lengthy discussion of labour and the functioning of the labour bureaux that organized the migrant-labor system. Then the official provided statistics on health, particularly figures on "persons inoculated, deverminised and vaccinated." Much of the rest of the report was devoted to land issues and rehabilitation. The report ended with "ethnological matters."

In 1955 a member of the staff for the Ethnological section was attached to the establishment of the Chief Magistrate . . . with a view of instituting research into the history, ethnology and present day conditions of the tribes . . . On the one hand it is intended to build up a body of detailed and accurate information which will be of use to the administration and to science, and on the other to investigate specific problems for the Department.[53]

In the commissioner's report lay the most salient features of state formation in the twentieth century. An important challenge of government increasingly centered on the issue of economic management and colonial rule, the precise relationship between economic policy and "ethnological matters."[54] The state's tribalism, culminating in apartheid, became a central feature of its social engineering – indeed, the political hinge upon which swung the doors of labor control and the rehabilitation of the reserves. Retribalization began in the 1920s, especially with the 1927 Native Administration Act. That Act not only marked a decisive shift towards segregation on Lugardist principles of indirect rule but, importantly, was also explicitly authoritarian. Section 5 of the Act, for example, allowed authorities to remove from the district Africans whom they decided had become "recalcitrant"[55] so as to preserve "good order."[56]

The shift towards tribalism was especially pronounced in the Ciskei, where Africans were now ruled by decree by the Native Affairs Department and not by parliament. Rule in the Ciskei was thus brought into line with native policy in the Transkei. As one official stated to a meeting of Africans in 1933, in which he attempted to explain the benefits of segregation: "If I were a Native I would rid myself of European bodies, and look to Native bodies." Perhaps, he continued, some may "have objected to law by proclamation." But "they will appreciate this when the local council has been introduced . . . Matters of a trivial nature like land regulations in the Ciskei could not always be referred to Parliament – this would take years to rectify such matters." It was, he argued in a language of means and ends, simply "impossible to wait for parliament in other administrative matters. Law by proclamation is absolutely necessary."[57]

Armed with rule by administrative decree, the state returned in the 1930s to the issue of the council system first envisioned in legislation such as the Glen Grey Act. The direction of the state was now to reverse the earlier "policy of emasculating the power of Native Chiefs" and "the weakening of Native custom restraints."[58] Legislation such as the 1927 Native Administration Act permitted the NAD to create tribes where they had not existed. Through retribalization, with headmen and, increasingly, chiefs at the local apex of the system of rule, the state sought enhanced administrative efficiency.[59] Custom thus not only became a mode of colonial control, but was also central to the expansion of bureaucratic power and the state's grand fantasies. Weakened by policies pursued by the state in the years of conquest, chiefs found it difficult not to hitch their futures to the authoritarian state in which, ultimately, they remained powerless before the NAD. Since their income under the new legislation derived largely by the number of taxpayers in their district, chiefs tended to support the very policies that brought such ill-health to the people they ostensibly ruled. At the same time they became inextricably tied up with the migrant-labor system, a development that had begun earlier in the century. Where once chiefs had "been against their followers leaving their locations," the migrant-labor system increasingly came "to work through the chiefs."[60]

Chiefs occupied a central role in the formation and composition of district councils. Moreover, bureaucrats planned on using the council system, the new structure of local government, to introduce betterment and other development programs. Both the council system and the new economic policies entailed the creation of a substantial bureaucracy. For example, a host of new positions emerged with the formation of the agricultural development branch that trained Africans as "agricultural demonstrators."[61]

As in the past, officials ideally sought the endorsement of the people living under their rule when appointing chiefs and headmen. They might, for instance, solicit nominations for successors and then take a vote of the location inhabitants. This attempt at generating consent and muting conflict became increasingly difficult as officials introduced policies concerning rehabilitation and retribalization. Rule, in short, became increasingly despotic. In the 1920s particularly, meetings between NAD officials and location inhabitants became tense and, at times, uproarious. In 1926, for example, the magistrate at Sterkspruit held a meeting that began by pointing out the role of headmen in implementing the state's policies of controlling "noxious weeds." The meeting quickly moved on to complaints by people about the Native Bills being introduced in parliament and their implication for access to land. Shouts and tumult ensued. The magistrate revealed his hand, in a tone that well represents the slide towards authoritarianism. "If such disorder ever again occurs at my meetings," he declared with a mix of frustration and intolerance, "I shall close the meeting and never call another." "I do not need the meetings," he continued. "I can rule

[the] district without consulting the people and will do so if they show so little respect."[62]

The Great Depression and the Second World War delayed the introduction or muted the effectiveness of the state's new policies of segregation and retribalization. In some areas officials put the council system to a vote to gauge popular sentiment. In 1933, an official presented the following question: "Are you in favor of replacing the constitution given you by Queen Victoria by the council now offered?" He was less than happy with the response. "At the present moment," he wrote, "the advantage lies with the people" whose leaders saw the council system as destroying any vestige of the rule of law. But on the "very clear" question of "whether the district is to be ruled by the people or by the State through its Administration," the official knew where he stood. He suggested removing those who were "a danger to the Administration."[63]

Through the 1940s the councils that had been installed remained for the most part relatively weak. The state's betterment polices typically met with something less than uneven success. What was clear, however, was that the state sought, if it was unable to secure, "absolute control" or, more euphemistically, "securing the efficiency of [the] system."[64] This situation of state weakness, ongoing administrative indecision, and lack of clarity as to just how far officials should govern according to rule by decree changed dramatically in the 1950s with the beginning of apartheid. If "segregation was a response to vastly changed social conditions in the first two decades of this century," Dubow has written, "so apartheid emerged out of the massive social, economic and political dislocation of the 1940s and 1950s," particularly "industrial expansion . . . a profound resurgence in African political resistance" and the continuing economic collapse of the native reserve economies.[65]

What is especially striking about the latter period is the certainty with which officials devised and prosecuted native policy, and their willingness to use force if necessary. In 1951 the National Party government passed the Bantu Authorities Act; the Bantu Laws Amendment Act entered the law books the following year. Along with other legislation these laws continued the decentralization of power to local (tribal) authorities that had begun earlier with the 1920 Native Affairs Act and the 1927 Native Administration Act. With this legislation the era of apartheid had begun. Under the Bantu Authorities Act the state created "Tribal Authorities" designed in accordance with "Native law and custom"[66] and headed by chiefs. The new system of tribal authorities superseded the system of councils. Tribal authorities, introduced in most of the Transkei by 1957, took over the unenviable responsibility for implementing rehabilitation; implementation very often required considerable coercion.

The Bantu Authorities Act represented the zenith of colonial social engineering, at the center of which was African culture itself, or more precisely the minute spatialization of culture. "The aim and object of Bantu Authorities is, therefore, to foster the development of your own culture," one official lectured in the early 1960s, "your own language, your customs, laws and administration." *"Remember,"* he continued, that a *"Nation without its culture is a nation without its soul. A nation who does not develop its culture will deteriorate and eventually die."* For

> Chieftainship is a very valuable asset because it binds the people and, therefore, the tribe together. Each community must have an able leader and the Chief or Headman must ensure that through his deeds, actions and behaviour, he is regarded by his people as their natural leader . . . The Chief of a tribe and, as such, the head of a tribal authority, is the political, administrative, executive and priestly head of the tribe.[67]

"You have by now all heard," the official began to conclude, "of the huge five-year plan through which the Bantu homelands will be further developed in order to increase the carrying capacity and productivity of the soil and to improve the economic position of your people."[68] Tribalism, in short, had become the servant of development, ethnicity a scientific truth.

It is striking how in apartheid the science of culture – anthropology – was so powerfully joined to the state's concern with health and agriculture. At the five-day 1952 native chiefs' education conference, for example, chiefs viewed an ethnographic film on the Chagga of Tanganyika that was intended to demonstrate "how the influence of wise chiefs helps bring prosperity to the people." The conference then proceeded to the subjects of education and disease. Three of the five days were devoted to rehabilitation.[69]

By this time the NAD had published numerous ethnologies and anthropologists had become enmeshed in the apartheid state's tribalism. Certainly, describing tribes, defining tribal territories, creating chiefs, and creating apartheid rule had become intertwined. To apartheid's architects the creation of a paramount chiefship among the Bhele, as happened in 1959, must have seemed a happy day. For "today," the chief Bantu affairs commissioner for the Ciskei declared, "you are given not only a head of the Tyumie Tribal Authority but at the same time a Chief of the amaBhele Tribe and, as such, Head of the Dikeni Regional Authority."[70] Even apartheid became an excuse for a party.

Ends, beginnings

We will explore the triumph of authoritarianism in greater detail in later chapters. Here I return to the issue of rationality and rule. In the broad period from conquest to apartheid two political developments stand out. The first is the increasing frequency in the encounters people had with the colonial government. Many of these encounters could be quite commonplace – for example, paying a tax. Others – for example, forced removal – were very often devastating. Avoiding the demands of the state represents an engagement with it. Even feigned consent is still consent. The colonized, in short, increasingly came to "live in the shadow of the state."[71]

Second, colonial rule became far more bureaucratized. Power came to be "hidden in [the] institutions"[72] of a bureaucratic state in which administrative functionaries implemented state policies that reached into new and increasingly more intimate areas of social life. Beginning in the 1920s with rule by decree, and especially in the 1950s with the rise of apartheid, state rationality became increasingly instrumental. That is, the logic of administrative practice became untethered from ethical consideration, so that, for example, issues that came before the state became technical challenges. The very language of apartheid – "redundant people," "endorsed out," "temporary sojourners," "influx control" – points to this development and to the triumph of an authoritarian social engineering in South Africa.

We are accustomed to seeing bureaucracy as part and parcel of the rise of reason, the victory of the empirical, and the decline of mysticism and charismatic forms of domination. Bureaucracy marked the triumph of reason against the forces of irrationality manifested in, for example, witchcraft. Weber, for example, contrasted bureaucracy with charisma and with patriarchal and other forms of domination where "norms derive from tradition: the belief in the inviolability of that which has existed from time out of mind."[73] In liberal democracies, bureaucracy has been seen as central to the organization of a "neutral" state, a form of power that was somehow less arbitrary than the systems of rule that had preceded it. But in much of the world, where people have remained subjects and not citizens, the opposite has been the case. Authoritarianism has triumphed and bureaucrats have imposed their visions on prostrate (and typically poor) populations.[74] Apartheid shared with other authoritarian regimes in the twentieth century a commitment to "five-year plans."

The people's increasing encounters with the state and the changes in bureaucratic practice had important implications for their experience of colonial rule. Prosaically, the modality of rule became far more textual – receipts for various taxes, censuses of people and stock, registration of land, memoranda, telegrams, transcribed testimonies, and, of course, the pass book. Increasingly, this material was produced mechanically using typewriters and telegraphs: the reduction of knowledge to mechanically reproduced typescript. Rule, in turn, became more remote as the "bureaucratization of administration . . . diminished the emphasis" that had been "placed on the 'personal touch'."[75]

As we have seen, nineteenth-century encounters with the state were of a more personal nature, a colonial world less of paper than of face-to-face relationships where the character of colonizer and colonized powerfully shaped the emerging local colonial order. In 1889 Stanford had lamented that "the most successful Magistrates are those who act illegally. They seize stock summarily at the Kraals and hold it as security until the amount due is paid."[76] Stanford's observation speaks to the limits of colonial power in the nineteenth century, and its replication of ostensibly premodern forms of rule. Stanford was in effect accusing his colleagues of acting like African despots.

At times in that earlier period, white magistrates wore the political mask of the people they were conquering. In the case of Hamilton Hope and others, at least some Africans believed that Europeans had access to and control over magic. Here a different logic of power came into play, a logic in which Africans brought Europe into their own, longer conversation about the world around them.[77] But what of the future? How might the colonized have folded the authoritarian state into their own, changing, political discourses, elaborating a politics of evil in the face of outrage? How might they have enchanted the authoritarian order, adorned its prison house of rationality with a culture of their own making, creating a space within which to critique the state as illegitimate and evil?

Part 2

States of emergency

4 Prophecies of nation

The tradition of the oppressed teaches us that the "state of emergency" in which we live is not the exception but the rule. We must attain to a conception of history that is in keeping with this insight.

Walter Benjamin, *Illuminations*, 257[1]

Informers, we will kill you. Hayi! Hayi!
Witches, we will burn you. Hayi! Hayi!

Liberation Song, 1980s[2]

Queenstown is located in an impoverished Eastern Cape farming area that few South Africans, let alone foreign visitors, today frequent. The main highway passes through it, bringing people and possessions north to Burgersdorp and into the flat lands of the Free State, or south to the Indian Ocean and the port city of East London. Founded in the early days of colonial expansion, the town still bears the marks of the Victorian age of British conquest. Many years ago the region boasted some of the wealthiest wool farmers in South Africa, who pastured on conquered lands large flocks of merino sheep and shipped wool to the industrial centers of England. That prosperity, now seen in the remaining nineteenth-century buildings and a few old farmhouses, has long since gone. Poverty is now what makes Queenstown famous, though visitors to the area might not know it. Instead, Queenstown is a convenient resting spot for travelers, a place to stretch one's legs, grab a snack, and fill the car with petrol before going someplace else.

In the days of apartheid the town sat at the northern tip of the "white corridor," an area of colonial settlement sandwiched between the Ciskei and Transkei bantustans. From time to time, the town has awoken from its apparent sleepiness and entered the national and international glare of reporting on violence and politics in the country. In the final convulsive days of apartheid the Azanian People's Liberation Army (APLA), the armed wing of the Pan-Africanist Congress (PAC), detonated a bomb in the local Spur, a greasy fast-food steakhouse frequented by whites who ate their meat and drank their beer and mostly complained about the Africans who seemed to be taking over the country. The blast reverberated across the country, creating among some whites

115

a fear that their way of life was collapsing and, worse still, raising the specter of race war in the "new South Africa."

During the 1980s many died at the hands of the security forces in Queenstown and across the Eastern Cape, from the smallest towns and villages to the big cities of Port Elizabeth and East London. In seemingly quaint Aliwal North, not too far from Queenstown, approximately twenty-four people died in one massacre. One paroxysm of violence in Queenstown itself, in which at least eleven people died, ended with bodies "stacked upon each other" and "blood running from under the [mortuary] door."[3]

During the 1980s and early 1990s at least twenty thousand people died nationwide as a result of political conflict. Some of the worst bloodshed took place in the Eastern Cape. During this convulsive period Queenstown became known as the "Necklace Capital of the World." In the space of just four years, at least thirty-nine people had been beaten, bound, and burned to death with old tires and gasoline rags and to chants of revolution by young and murderous ANC supporters.[4] Some died because the comrades, South Africa's "young lions," had suspected them of being police spies. Others perished because they had become the targets of one of humankind's more powerful emotions – jealousy.[5]

Death by fire very often involved accusations of witchcraft, in the Eastern Cape and elsewhere in the country.[6] According to one journalist, "these youths" who destroyed people accused of being witches or wizards were, and still are, seen by others in the community as "selfless heroes committed to 'freeing' people from 'supernatural evils'."[7] In one amnesty application before the Truth and Reconciliation Commission, concerning the deaths of twenty-six people in Venda, ANC supporters "claimed that they perceived the victims as persons who were practising witchcraft in their area and in doing so, working hand in hand with politicians of the Venda government to strengthen them and keep them in power."[8]

Tragedy and violence run deep in Queenstown, as if bloody pasts lay buried in shallow graves easily disturbed by the living. Not far away are Sada and Ilinge, the notorious "transit" or "resettlement sites" created by the apartheid government to house those who had been dispossessed or otherwise "endorsed out" of white South Africa. Between 1960 and 1983, the state forcibly "resettled" over 3.5 million people to such places of death.[9] These were the rural dumping grounds for apartheid's unwanted and dispossessed, people who in the state's eyes represented so many technical problems that could be solved through the appropriate policies. By the early 1980s some 40,000 people lived in Sada alone, a vast grid of boxes in a desolate area. The great majority of Sada's inhabitants were, and are, unemployed, and virtually everyone lives there in the loneliness of dire poverty.[10]

In 1962, a famous battle had taken place at the Queenstown railroad station between the police and members of Poqo, then the armed wing of the PAC.

Poqo fighters had infiltrated the nearby forests as well. Their ritually scarified bodies (see chapter 8 below) and pronouncements of war struck fear in the minds of both the African collaborators they targeted and whites with their racist visions of African savages running amok. This was not first time that whites had spoken of African madness or, sadly, that terrible violence had flowed across the area. Some four decades earlier, police and army troops had opened fire on the religious community of the Israelites at the Ntabelanga location about twenty miles from Queenstown. One hundred and sixty-three died and ninety-two were wounded. The slaughter of the Israelites, which came to be known as the Bulhoek massacre, was South Africa's first modern political massacre.

Today all that remains is a monument and the memory of the massacre in the minds of the people. It is difficult to reconstruct the history of that period or, given its economic backwardness today, to imagine that in the early part of the twentieth century Queenstown had bustled with activity. The arrival of trains on the iron tracks of modernity had transformed a town serving local farmers into an important way station in a rapidly industrializing South Africa. Men first began laying down rail in the 1860s. In the 1870s and 1880s the pace of railroad construction quickened considerably. Railroads ultimately destroyed the livelihoods of the African transport riders who plied the roads of the region, but they also created jobs for many people who struggled to feed themselves and their families. In 1882 at least a thousand people from the Middledrift area alone worked on railroad construction; without their wages they would "not have managed to eke out an existence."[11] Seven years earlier there was "no difficulty... in procuring a sufficient supply" of labor for the rail line connecting the port of East London to Queenstown.[12] Chiefs and headmen assisted the state in helping to secure a steady supply of labor, but most men went to work of their own accord, and sought labor "on their own terms."[13] Few worked for an entire year; many would quit their jobs and return home when they were needed to turn the earth to plant maize. While building the railroad tracks they kept track of time by observing the moon and by marking each day of labor with a small notch on a stick.[14]

By the 1890s a thin scar of land cut by steel and stitched by wood ran through Queenstown on its trip northwards from Port Elizabeth to Kimberley and the Rand, to the industrial centers of South Africa. There the trains deposited workers who burrowed deep into the earth searching for diamonds and gold. In the early decades of the twentieth century trains running east and west connected Umtata to the main trunk lines so that virtually all of the Eastern Cape had access to these wondrous bellowing machines of steel, steam, and smoke. Men who had once built the railroads now traveled on them – to the diamond mines of Kimberley, to the gold mines of the Rand, to the bustling port of Cape Town.

In this torrent of economic change, in what was one of the world's most rapid industrial revolutions, Queenstown formed a kind of eddy, where people from all over the region gathered together before voyaging to more distant places. People who once had lived in relatively isolated communities now found themselves meeting others with whom they shared similar experiences: the difficulties of getting the land to produce its bounty, familial misfortunes, the travails of securing passes, the persecutions of the colonial state, the anxieties of leaving kith and kin. By the beginning of the twentieth century more than a thousand migrants took the trains each month; certainly some came from places like the neighboring Glen Grey district, which had been the object of such state attention. In subsequent years that number increased dramatically: one thousand had grown tenfold.[15] Many migrants camped near the train station. Others established their own locations, such as the Basotho migrants who walked down from their highland homes, settled temporarily in Queenstown, and awaited the trains that brought them north into the interior. Still others attempted to settle in locations or sought comfort and a temporary abode in crowded places like Bulhoek.[16]

Still others came to Queenstown to participate in the culture and sensibilities of the African Christian elite. In the Eastern Cape, Queenstown was second only to the Kingwilliamstown–Fort Hare corridor in terms of the density of European mission stations. Religious change seemed to follow the railroad tracks of capitalist development. Queenstown became the local terminus of people and of ideas. (It also had two mental asylums, a remarkable fact given its size.) For example, the African-American Church of God and Saints of Christ, of which the Israelite prophet Enoch Mgijima had been a member and eventually a leader, based itself in Queenstown early in the second decade of the twentieth century. Near the town lay an important training institute for African clergy. Awash in Christianity and the religious discussions and disputes of the time, Queenstown not surprisingly became an important locus of subaltern religious visions and of elite politics. It was an obvious choice for the ninth annual congress, held in 1920, of the South African Native National Congress (SANNC), which soon became the ANC, now the party of government in South Africa. The organization both critiqued and made claims on the state by deploying the rights-based universalist language of official nationalism. At the congress the elite discussed such weighty matters as the segregationist state's land and labor laws, increasing labor militancy, the pass system and the color bar, the high cost of living, barriers to decent education, and heard a report on the organization's memorial to the British king.[17]

Quite literally down the road, the Israelites spoke of how the land had died and engaged in rituals that seemed utterly foreign to the Christian elite and to colonial officials. While SANNC leaders discoursed on rights and laws, on the individual and the invidiousness of segregation and a racial oppression that located them as so many members of tribes, the Israelites' subaltern speech addressed the problems of evil and good, sorrow and hope. We can imagine what some of their questions might have been like. Why was a world ruled by God and protected by the ancestors filled with so much anguish and cruelty and death? Why did so many children perish so young? What was this disease that in 1918 had struck down so many so quickly, even the strong? Why was there so much sickness among people and the animals they depended on? Where lay the evil that seemed to reign so triumphant over the land? And what of these prophecies of a nation that would vanquish evil and usher in a just world?

One did not need to go far to discover ample evidence of death, misfortune, and discord. Poverty had taken over many areas of the Eastern Cape. The 1918 influenza pandemic had struck down more than a quarter of a million people in South Africa alone. In some areas of the Eastern Cape the dead would be "lying in the same hut as the living, who are, themselves too weak and too indifferent with pain, to try and move them . . . hundreds [were] dying from sheer hunger and exhaustion."[18] A severe drought and an unusually cold winter had struck the region. The Israelites knew of, and sympathized with, the labor disputes that had erupted across the country, led by railway workers, miners, sugar plantation workers, and dock workers.[19]

By 1921 the Israelites had built three hundred homes where, just three years earlier, only twenty-six huts had dotted the commonage. Now between seven hundred and fifty and a thousand people lived there. Some brought their stock, ploughed the commonage, and struggled to raise a crop from an unforgiving land. Most of those who "squatted" on the commonage were desperately poor; the Israelites comprised a community of South Africa's impoverished and destitute. The commonage offered little material respite. In 1921 disease insinuated itself into the community; many succumbed to typhus. Beneath the commonage in the cemetery the Israelites had created lay the bodies of some 170 people. And yet despite the hardships of daily life and the omnipresence of death, despite being "packed like sardines"[20] like other neighboring communities, their numbers increased "daily."[21]

On this scrap of common land – on "God's ground not the Government's"– the Israelites created a community that sought the restoration of social health to a world that had gone terribly awry, a world that was in very basic ways profoundly evil.[22] The community of the faithful centered on the Tabernacle, at first simply a "bush enclosure"[23] that housed their Ark of the Covenant. The Israelites marked off their community; only those who had "permission from Jehovah . . . might enter the village."[24] The prophet called the believers to prayer. In April people "from all parts" of the region came to a six-week celebration of Passover, the coming of resurrection of the Lord Jesus Christ who had been persecuted by the Romans.[25] Tents and bush served as homes for the faithful.

During midnight water baptisms, adherents entered a community whose members' faith promised a better world. There, in the night, they shared a "kiss of peace." The Israelites knew that "black people . . . were God's chosen."[26]

Their faith, their membership in a "Black Nation," would redeem them from a world of poverty and racial oppression and bring order to a world of wickedness and chaos.

The colonial state thought differently. Officials had become irritated by the Israelites' refusal to submit to the state's will to know, to have their people counted. Local white farmers alleged thefts of stock and grain as the Israelite community's numbers swelled.[27] As early as 1919 local colonial officials surveilled the community. The Israelites were "squatters," and the state declared their settlement on the commonage illegal. There was official concern with the possible spread of disease among so many poor so crowded together, particularly in the aftermath of the influenza pandemic.

Visions of prophets and talk of a black nation were perhaps even more alarming than the alleged pilfering of stock. The Israelites proclaimed that "the punishment of Jehovah would soon fall on unbelievers, and the end of the world was near, and so they had gathered at this place of God's choosing to prepare for this day."[28] To colonial officials, indeed to many of the African elite as well, the ideological work of the Israelites seems as incomprehensible as the communities they had created. Ntabelanga seemed like a chaotic mess of a community, and a disease-ridden one at that. The visions and pronouncements of the Israelites were those of mad, detribalized people – people who had lost their mooring.

One Israelite lived in Glen Grey to the east, in the district that had been so important to the state's new policies of segregation and economic intervention, where people had seen boundary marks sunk into the earth and people dispossessed of their land. Converts from Ntabelanga had arrived in Glen Grey and had "introduced a new religion," a religion solely "directed to the black man." "Many of our people were converted to the new religion," the man later testified. "We were told that all of God's children were to be in one place." He heard of the prophecies of "a bloody war beteen [*sic*] whites and blacks." At Ntabelanga the man was baptized. He also prepared for the coming war. With others he manufactured swords and spears that would defeat the white man's "bullets that would be turned into water." Men engaged in "drilling exercises" directed by the *mpati mkulu*, the "Commander-in-Chief." The Israelite army, dressed in their religious uniforms, was divided into five divisions led by officers, the organization of these religious forces reproducing the military organization of the colonial army; and, like that army, the call of the bugle awakened the Israelites to battle.[29]

"I am a messenger before the blood," the prophet Mgijima declared. "The whole world is going to sink in the blood."[30] And it did. On 24 May 1921, Israelites went into the nearby mountains where they made fires that served as a signal that "the land was dead," that the war against the whites "had been declared."[31] Armed with rifles and a maxim gun, colonial troops and the South African police opened fire on the attacking Israelites who had, quite literally, hammered swords from the springs of carts. In a "very deadly fire ... the charging Israelites dropped in large numbers." And yet, as one policeman later reported, the "charge was not stopped and those who could keep on their legs, amongst them being some badly wounded men, persisted in attempting to reach our lines. It was not until the foremost Israelites were within about 20/25 yards of my troops that they were shot down. I shot two with my revolver at close quarters."[32]

Less than a week after the massacre, troops had demolished 213 "unauthorised dwellings" in an action nearly identical to the forced removals of the apartheid era. "By the time the demolition operations were completed" the village seemed to have "undergone a severe bombardment." The "unauthorised residents of Ntabellanga village had left, with the exception of a few who were too ill to be moved, and whose houses were, in the meantime, spared destruction."[33]

The other conversion

The Israelites elaborated a vision of a black nation as they critiqued a colonial order that sowed evil and misfortune. Theirs was not the only one. Later in the decade, for example, the illiterate prophetess Nonthetha ("the one who speaks") expounded on a world gone awry, but also spoke of the dawn of a new world centered on social health and the black nation. "A nation ... is coming," she prophesied in the area near Kingwilliamstown:

Pray that it should find you with God already, if that nation will find you without God, you will experience too much hardship. You will be bound. Even the church will bind you. You will even feel that it was better before the church came than before the church era. The nation that is coming to you knows hardship and bondage – for that is where it started.[34]

What do we make of these visions of evil and misfortune and, especially, this talk of a black nation? The Israelites and the adherents of the prophetess Nonthetha spoke of God and of the black nation. Both would bring succor, as Weber wrote, to the "sufferings of the present."[35] The black nation as transcendent subject offered a new, alternative source of social health, at the same time as it connected people's present to a mytho-historical past. People envisioned themselves as members of a community both local and national that suffered the indignities of an oppressive political order. This represented a radically new shift in rural political culture, reflecting not simply a growing macrocosm but also, and importantly, "a crisis of identity."[36] There was, as Greenfeld has argued in a much different context, an increasingly "fundamental inconsistency between the definition of social order it [traditional identity] expressed" and people's everyday "experiences."[37]

Subaltern politics, I argue here – and speculatively – unfolded as a form of conversion. Its discourse was theodic in that it was centrally concerned with the problem of evil, much as revolutionaries in the 1980s fighting for the liberation of their nation sometimes perceived their enemies as witches who perpetrated evil in their work for the state. It is precisely subaltern nationalism's theodic nature that helps explain its engagement with social health, with evil, and, as we shall see, ultimately with the intricacies of modern state formation. This fusing of theodicy and modernity produced diverse and hybrid political visions and social movements. It allowed for the emergence of a subaltern politics centered on the creation of a just world, the return of *ubuntu*. But it also gave rise to a kind of fundamentalism that demands unwavering obedience, sees violence as not only necessary but central to political society, and sustains acts of horror such as necklacing.

A crucial issue is in the relationship of mimicry, appropriation, and other forms of engagement with state formation to the creation and expression of new definitions of self and community.[38] Mimesis and the idea a black nation both comprise important facets of the colonized's autoethnography, ways of seeing and representing self and other that "*engage with* the colonizer's own terms."[39] The stories of the Israelites and Nonthetha and their prophecies of nation in a world of evil speak to resistance and, especially, to the culture of subaltern agency in the twentieth century. In others words, what is the relationship between colonialism and African ideas about evil and politics? What do we make of this new black nation that offered the promise of social health in a world of evil, and of the many social movements that exploded in the Eastern Cape from the late nineteenth century? What is the relationship between subaltern culture and consciousness and colonial state formation? Why would movements such as the Israelites appropriate facets of a state that oppressed and, ultimately, killed them in a brief moment of terrible violence? To begin answering these questions is to write a "political history from below."[40]

Nationalism is a notoriously vexing subject; the study of subaltern nationalism is particularly so. The very triumph of a particular and bourgeois nationalism in the world makes it hard to conceive of alternative inventions of nationalist consciousness, especially so when that consciousness does not have as its central aim control of the state.[41] We are accustomed to seeing nationalism as a quintessentially secular phenomenon, in the colonial world a discourse derivative of the secular rationality of the West. The very idea of a peasant nationalism appears "oxymoronic."[42] Nationalism as religious experience seems to stretch credulity to the breaking point. The powerfully theodic quality of subaltern nationalist consciousness – the issue of the nation as confronting the problem of evil and offering the promise of social health – distinguishes it from the seemingly more secular nationalist vision of the African elite that sought access to the authoritarian state, if only to democratize it.

It is to that latter nationalism that scholars have devoted most of their energies. Historians of Africa and elsewhere in the colonial world have tended to conceive of nationalism as having percolated down from the middle classes to the popular masses, and not as a series of nationalist imaginings in which previous institutions, interactions, and conceptions shaped new ideological constructions of community and polity. Thus, as Hobsbawm has argued more generally, "whatever the nature of the social groups first captured by 'national consciousness', the popular masses – workers, servants, peasants – are the last to be affected by it."[43] For Anderson, in his influential *Imagined Communities*, nationalism is a political ideology of the literate, in the colonial world the armies of clerks and the word-conscious elite. Print capitalism, and the institutions associated with it, allowed for the emergence of the homogenesis time necessary for the development of nationalist identity.

Research undertaken by Africanists almost always has focused on the rise of the middle class and their role in the formation of political movements. In South Africa, scholars have written of the Christian mission station as the cradle of the modern African middle class. On the mission stations Africans gained literacy, participated in the creation and spread of a culture of "print capitalism," and imbibed in the nationalism of Europe. The narrative moves from religious experience to secular politics, where in the latter the state becomes the *telos* of national imagining. Thus the mission stations' more articulate and more fortunate progeny often took up posts within the colonial state and, like Sol Plaatje, became the founders of the first black political organizations.[44] This narrative of the nation essentially parallels arguments set out in Anderson's *Imagined Communities*, where the "armies of clerks" – bilingual, educated, and responsible for the day-to-day functioning of empire – were central to the invention of colonial nationalism because it was through their "bureaucratic pilgrimages" within the colony that the nation came to be imagined.[45] The masses were on the receiving end of these ideological developments, caught, as it were, in the "stupefied bondage" of the old order.[46] Borrowing the work of George Rudé and continuing in the footsteps of Eric Wolf's *Peasant Wars of the Twentieth Century*,[47] Marks, for example, argued that

for smouldering peasant discontent to flame into revolt, if not revolution, it is necessary in general for popular protest to fuse in some way with a more systematic, "derived" set of structured beliefs, beliefs that could transcend the parochialism and fragmentation inherent in peasant life . . . "derived" [ideas were] usually brought in by the literate bourgeoisie or petty bourgeoisie.[48]

This approach offers little possibility for alternative visions and inventions of nation, and it assumes what is parochial and what is national. But if subaltern nationalism was not simply derivative, how precisely did it come about? What is clear in the work of Anderson and others is the centrality of the modern state to the formation of nationalist consciousness. In an important sense in much of the colonial world the modern state came before the modern nation. Certainly it is a truism that modern nationalist movements in virtually all of sub-Saharan Africa unfolded within territories established by the colonial state. Certainly also the "bureaucratic pilgrimages" of the elite were important to the invention of nationalism and to the creation of the first modern political organizations that espoused a politics that both contested the state and sought access to it.

The state was also deeply sedimented in the lives of the subaltern, even if they flouted its laws and delayed the implementation of key policies, and politicians stumbled and fought among themselves on the perpetual subject of native policy. The elementary forms of state formation – land beacons, telegraphs, censuses, trials, taxes, and the plethora of paper produced by an expansive authoritarian state – comprised one part of a wider political geography wherein the state has shaped in microscopic ways the constitution and experience of its subjects. The magistrate's office, the police station, the telegraph, the postal service, and the railroad constituted the subject and disseminated the power of the state. Each comprised a node within a complex political geography organized around stable, impermeable boundaries. Going to the magistrate's office for a pass, being arrested by the police, having a letter written or a telegraph sent to kith and kin, or taking a train that operated on the basis of "clock and calendar"[49] – all of this created a new subject and crucially shaped the ways in which people came to narrate their experiences, both individually and collectively.

The state helped create and shape the local and supralocal geographies within which the subaltern moved. The modern colonial state powerfully shaped the experiences of its subjects, braiding its presence with the ways people have evidenced their experiences.[50] The pilgrimages of the poor were walks and train journeys to and from work, in the early decades of this century usually but certainly not always males. The political geography of the state mediated these journeys. Its bureaucracy powerfully shaped and very often violently interrupted them. In the twentieth century the political geography of the state has been entwined with the development of industrial capitalism. The state was the great disseminator, and enforcer, of homogeneous time. This can be seen most obviously in the pass system, train schedules, due dates for taxes, and, ultimately, in the labor bureaux system in which the state controlled the movement of labor into and out of an economy based on modern industrial conceptions of time.[51]

Capitalist development in South Africa resulted in a radical dispersal and circulation of people, especially men, who moved within a space emphatically circumscribed by the colonial state and increasingly according to new conceptions of space and time. The worlds of the poor were greatly enlarged, but enlarged in very specific ways. This growth in scale in social interaction opened the possibility for people to begin perceiving that they were members, even if anonymously so, of a wider community that shared a common identity. To take one early, phantasmic example, in the early years of the twentieth century, people throughout the Eastern Cape spoke of a winged animal, usually a pig, that would fly through the region from its origin somewhere in Zululand. One official wrote that a headman had "heard from a Tembu who is on a visit from Tembuland, that a witchdoctor living at the Kraal of the Paramount Chief of Zululand, has sent word throughout the Colony to destroy all pigs and fowls." The animal would "fly over the country and where ever a pig or fowl answers to their call all the people living at that Kraal will die . . . most of the natives residing in the Transkei were doing away with their pigs and fowls."[52] Those who participated in this ritual slaughter thus became members of a privileged and clearly supralocal community. People could imagine others whom they did not know killing their swine and chickens, and entering a sacral community. In the 1920s there was again talk of a winged pig and of ritual slaughter. By this time the community of the faithful proclaimed themselves members of a "black nation." Their registering in a populist discourse of "this black nation of ours" made new forms of community real: and new forms of collective action possible.[53]

Like the Christian God, the nation has, as Herzfeld argues, a "transcendent status."[54] Yet where the first is intrinsically unbounded the nation emerged in a close relationship to colonial state formation, in the complex workings of the institutions of rule. The state did precede the nation, both in its elite and subaltern inventions. At the same time, however, subaltern nationalism, specifically its therapeutic and prophetic qualities, continued in a radically different key an ancient pattern of thought and discourse that linked power and authority to fertility and social health. Ultimately, subaltern nationalism confronted a state of evil, engaged with modernity, and continued older yet ongoing conversations about power and the political world, about hope and despair, about why the clouds did or did not surrender their tender rains to the earth.

Entering an "extensive moral wilderness,"[55] missionaries had communicated a conception of evil that stressed humankind's inherent sinfulness. In this Christian world, we are all already touched by evil. Stained by original sin but cleansed by baptism and guided by church leaders and sacred teachings, good Christians take control of their spiritual life. Others, however, succumb to Satan and become evil by committing sinful acts. This way of conceiving of good and bad permitted, among other things, the emergence of the secular and the sacred, the world of Caesar and the world of God. It also stressed the omnipresence of evil, which must be fought constantly and vigilantly. Missionaries, for example, preached "that sin was the greatest sorcery, having bewitched all mankind, and would destroy all who continued under its dominion."[56]

Not surprisingly, witchcraft became the site of conflict between missionaries and the people they sought to convert. According to one missionary, "we had

8 The devil (photo by author; original located in household of Mhlaba, Fort Beaufort)

come into their land with a Word that was opposed to every sinful custom and practice." But one man said "they did not know God," while another "appeared to be confused, but pointed out the woman as having murdered his brother by witchcraft and said he thought they had a right to punish her accordingly. Thus the contention between us lasted for more than two hours."[57] Sometimes this conflict seemed to center around procedure. For example, missionaries decried the torture and murder of witches because, among other things, it did not entail a "law proceeding" as in other cases of dispute.[58] It thus "perverted judgment, and . . . God would requite their unrighteous proceeding."[59]

At other times the clash of Africans and missionaries exposed important conceptions of the world. In one case, a "prophetess" had foretold that a witch "had taken the ground upon which he had made water and the blood of his brother and that these two being thus mixed and hid were the cause of his sickness." The healer found the bewitching substance. The missionary, however, proclaimed that "all the poison is not yet found but the great prophet Christ is on his way to find it and woe that man who has it hid when he cometh." The missionary then interrogated the healer. He was especially interested in how she could identify the source of the witchcraft.

"How do you know that?" he asked in the good spirit of Western empiricist logic.

"I was told so in my sleep," the healer responded matter-of-factly.
"What told you so?"
"A Lion," the healer replied.

To the missionary, of course, this was pure poppycock. Everyone knows that lions have neither the capacity to think nor to speak. Incredulous, the missionary continued:

"What[,] can a Lion talk?"
"Yes[,]" she said.
"Does a Lion know better than you[?]" he persisted.
"Yes."
"How is it that the Lion never converses with other people besides you?"
"I know not," said the healer.
"How does the Lion know these things?"
"I know not," she continued, "but perhaps he has fellowship with God and and he had thought proper to make known these things to us by a Lion."

The missionary ended the conversation by asking "her to confess that she was a deceiver before all the Caffres and to seek forgiveness of sin and friendship of the great prophet Christ before he came to chastise her for her falshood [*sic*]." The healer, however, wanted to know "where Christ was."[60]

Christ was not the only person to elicit quizzical ripostes. Sin and the devil frequently emerged in the early relationships between Africans and British evangelists. In a conversation between a missionary and Chief Ngqika during a long drought, for example, the chief asked "how those who first existed were made and what were their names." Ngqika then inquired as to "how came it to pass for so many nations to exist." The missionary began his answer by invoking original sin, humankind's "natural dislike to God." The chief "then asked who the devil was? I answered he was one of Gods [*sic*] chief servants [since] they have no word for angel." But, Ngqika queried, if the devil was God's servant, why "was he cast into hell?"[61] To the chief the missionary's concept of good and bad simply made little logical sense.

Missionaries attempted to impart a conception of the world separated into the sacred and profane, joined only by religious faith that awakened God's presence, and the devil who weighed on the souls of the righteous. Heaven and hell existed, but they did not exist here, in the sensible world. Lions were certainly God's creation, but just as certainly they had no powers of prophecy. One of the most powerful ideas missionaries conveyed to prospective converts centered on a paradox, a paradox Ngqika seems to have been aware of. God might be omnipotent, and his presence is everywhere, yet sin and evil nonetheless remained pervasive: the devil continued his work, more or less successfully. The very fact of original sin, and the omnipresent temptation to turn away from God, augured the grim prospect of evil's triumph.[62]

Traditional conceptions of evil stressed the use of forces to defeat those that bring life and peace and thus, in their victory, to sow misfortune and suffering among the innocent. Witches were "bad persons who enter league with wolves, jackals, baboons and some imaginary beings and can from them get what will enable them to injure their fellow men."[63] Here there was no original sin, no devil, no all-powerful and all-knowing God. At the same time people could act most devilishly and malefically, for example by communing with animals, stealing the hair or blood of their victims, or by placing inside a person a terrible animal that could cause death. Moreover, "people made no distinction between natural and supernatural. All was pervaded by divinity," that is, by spiritual forces.[64] Lions could speak to people in their dreams – and dreams were real.

These ideas did not mean, for instance, that all illness resulted from malevolent magic. Africans made empirical judgments, but these were according to their own rational ordering of reality. In 1827, for example, a healer conceded that "witches [had] laid their bewitching matter to destroy Soko and old Tzatzoe." But "the chief cause of" Tzatzoe's "illness was a blow that had been given him when hunting about Twenty Years ago." Soko's case was different. He "was very much against their making any further search for bewitching matter." Soko "said the persons who had been endeavoring to murder him by such means would, by the discovery of their plans, be more enraged and would certainly destroy him."

Nonetheless, the search for the witch proceeded. The "substance of" the witch-finder's "speech produced a great discussion and a division in the Judgement of the Counsellors," so that the final identification and punishment of the witch or witches remained unresolved. But not for long. Soko's illness progressed. Four people were accused of witchcraft. One man who had been caring for Soko was tortured and put to death. His wife "produced all the bewitching matter that was required of the Caffer Doctor." "The poor woman, however, could not produce the Head and part of the back bone of a Man, which the Doctor stated he had in his possession, as also some of the flesh of the woman that had been put to death" earlier.[65]

Both productive and destructive forces pervaded the world, and at times became intertwined. This meant that the issue of evil went beyond that of simply the malevolent actions of the individual, or of neat divisions separating secular from sacred. The problem of evil was an ancient one for people living in a region prone to drought, temperamental rains, and the random, destructive violence of lightning. There was a tendency in this envisioning of the world to emphasize ways of identifying and defeating forces that destroy and of securing those that brought about health and harmony. People enlisted ritual specialists to reorder symbolic space and thus restore health, order, and tranquillity. A man whose cattle were dying, for example, might ask that his kraal be doctored to send the owls back "to the bush"[66] and away from the domestic space of the household. Ritual specialists would require sacrifices to ancestors, who helped ensure the safety and productiveness of the household. Prophecies frequently created "considerable excitement." They also could attract substantial followings to those who "firmly believe" that the healer was "gifted."[67]

Witchcraft was the idiom for explaining misfortune: suspicious deaths, crop failure, the death of cattle, devastating rains and lightning. In such cases witchcraft unfolded in the domestic domain, in the suspicions and jealousies of kin roused by tragedy. "I wish to make a statement regarding what I have done," said one man in the early 1950s. He had taken his "sick child to a witch doctor." According to the man's testimony, it was "the senior wife of my brother in the right hand house who was causing the illness of the child." He "asked the woman whether she would be able to restore the health of the child she was killing and she said she did not know and that it would depend on her 'lightning bird' (*impundulu*)." The man "caught her, took off her doek, put her on the ground and tied the doek round her throat and throttled her with that. When I considered her to be dead I tied the doek in a knot at the back of her neck so that she could not recover."[68]

Witchcraft became a constant, indeed an indissoluble, feature of social life in the twentieth century. While the data are admittedly scarce, it would seem that Christian ideas of good and evil helped create more starkly rendered beliefs about witchcraft, nourishing and sustaining a bleak perception of a world overrun by a darkness that could be combated only by exceptional faith and extraordinary action. In short, there arose a subaltern Manichaeanism, a social reality of terror and prophecy, perdition and delivery, the abyss that is the present and the possibilities of salvation somewhere in the future.

Certainly not everyone believed equally in the pervasiveness of witchcraft. Some, indeed, rejected it. Committed members of established churches, typically members of the African elite, looked to Christian teachings of the devil, humankind's exile from the Garden of Eden, Jesus Christ, and the promise of deliverance. Witchcraft signified for them a barbarous past they had transcended. The vast majority, however, remained steadfast in their belief in magic and witches. In 1922, for example, a magistrate wrote that people "appear to be practising or taking part in witchcraft on a large[r] scale than they have done in years past."[69] As witchcraft insinuated itself ever more deeply into people's lives, as evil became ever more common and more palpably felt in their misfortunes, the eradication of witches became more violent. Ethnographic material from the precolonial period, for example, suggests that the persecution of witches rarely entailed murder. People typically simply burned witches out of the community. Torture (to elicit confessions and to purge the evil) and murder usually took place in instances of witchcraft accusations relating to drought, chiefship, or unusual crises. In such cases the victim might be "stretched on the ground" and tortured by stinging ants and hot stones.[70]

In the twentieth century, people accused of witchcraft have met with deaths that are as elaborate as they are violent. One method of murder, for example, is to ram a long stick or metal rod up the anus, viewed as a location of evil, of the accused female witch with such destructive fury that the weapon perforates the intestines and punctures various organs in the stomach cavity. In excruciating agony the victim bleeds to death.[71]

Fire, however, has continued to be a basic way of dealing with witchcraft, a strategy of doing away with evil, ultimately also a temporal marker separating past and present. But whereas fire had earlier been used to cleanse the locale of witchcraft, the body itself has increasingly come to be seen as a central locus of evil. Importantly, to destroy the body by fire was also to destroy the soul and thus prevent to it from returning to haunt the living.[72] Here, for example, is a description of 1986 triple murder in East London, in which a woman and her daughter "were accused of having bewitched their son and brother" who were involved in the United Democratic Front. "The two Dikana women and a third woman were abducted by a crowd and taken into a house while a fire was built in the road nearby." According to an eyewitness,

[A man] was placing iron rods approximately one metre long into the fire. He seemed to be handling two or three of these rods. When these rods were red hot they were taken and handed over to [another man]. All the time I could hear screaming and pleading for help coming from inside the house. These rods were passed in and out for a period of about one hour. Throughout this hour the screaming and shouting for forgiveness never stopped . . . The following morning when I arrived I saw a large crowd of people gathered there. In the road I saw the same three females I had seen the previous evening lying in the roadway [Three men] were standing next to the bodies and were placing tyres on top of the bodies.[73]

The problem of evil and its eradication often unfolded within the domestic sphere, but it also often involved the intricate and competitive politics of power and authority. This has been the case in the present, in the violence of comrades fighting the apartheid state and its black cronies, and in the past with respect to agricultural fertility and, more generally, social health. Chiefship, we recall, was intimately bound up with rain and agriculture. Chiefs, masters of magic, were the "sons of heroes"[74] who defeated leopards and, in making peace with the First People, brought rain and fertility to the land. These mythic connections were unstable. Chiefs renewed their relationships to autochones, and chiefs and their subjects came together at crucial ritualized moments to ensure rains and bountiful harvests. But in their avariciousness they were also capable of great malevolence that would bring social conflict and drought to the land. One's ancestors were relatively powerless in the face of such evil; people sought ritual specialists, the supreme being who, as it were, lurked "in the wings,"[75] and, especially, autochones who lived in the hills whence the rain came.

Colonialism profoundly and in many cases irrevocably ruptured the connection between chiefs and the First People. It also largely destroyed those ritualized relationships, so important to the constitution and reconstitution of political society, between chiefs and commoners that helped ensure agricultural fertility. The capacity of people to ensure plentiful rains declined precipitously. Magistrates of course made no attempt to establish relationships with the First People and did not create or knowingly participate in (and indeed struggled to ban) rituals that brought rain and fertility. They possessed the land but they were not its "owners," the "sons of heroes."[76] The retribalization that began in the twentieth century, the return to political prominence of colonial chiefs, the rise of "decentralized despotism," did nothing to restore the relationship between chiefship and social health: quite the opposite. Chiefs, headmen, and others became crucial to the state's vast program of social engineering; they were employees of an authoritarian state responsible for instituting policies ranging from villagization and stock culling to the control of migrant labor. They were, in a very real sense, the local embodiment of authoritarianism.

Colonial policies such as villagization had deep and enduring implications for agricultural fertility and, more generally, for social health. Particularly in the twentieth century the region saw an extraordinary explosion of poverty and rising destitution and the terrible "violence of everyday life" that accompanies it. Where poverty had once been cyclical it now became a permanent feature of people's lives. Not surprisingly, people believed that evil reigned triumphant. The explanation of why this was so constituted a central feature of the ideological work of the subaltern, the ways in which the poor spoke about power and misfortune in their lives.

This search for an explanation for evil and its banality occurred during a time in which the scale of social interaction had enlarged massively. The precolonial world was largely a localized one; for most people the district typically represented the most distant yet still important boundaries. Microcosmic boundaries were strong and macrocosmic ones weak.[77] In the space of a very short period of time this changed. Colonial rule and the emergence of a state expanded the macrocosm considerably. Labor migration to places as far afield as Johannesburg, Cape Town, and even German South West Africa obviously did so as well.

The issue facing the colonized – and here, again, I do not include the Westernized elite – centered on how to explain evil in the context of such massive social change and, simultaneously, how to seek new sources of social health. For Weber the problem of theodicy emerged out of the paradox that "the more the [religious] development tends toward the conception of a transcendental unitary god who is universal, the more there arises the problem of how the extraordinary power of such a god may be reconciled with the imperfections of the world that he has created and rules over."[78] In short, the problem of theodicy lay in explaining the presence, and at times the seeming triumph, of evil in a world ruled by an omniscient God. Weber outlined a number of possible solutions, one involving "messianic eschatologies" that promised "a political and social transformation of this world."[79]

The adoption of the Christian God, a ubiquitous feature of the historical landscape of the late nineteenth and early twentieth centuries, represented a central innovation in the quest to explain evil and secure social health. As Horton argued many years ago, conversion to Christianity usually followed "a marked weakening of microcosmic boundaries."[80] In the Ciskei, for example, widespread conversion to Christianity occurred only after the 1856–7 Cattle Killing – that is, immediately after the extension of colonial rule and a very considerable weakening, if not in many areas an actual collapse, of local society. Suddenly Christianity was "in great demand."[81] In the late 1860s, in the years surrounding the Taylor Revival, there were "sudden," large, and "unprecedented ... conversions"[82] "characterized by a highly emotional, ecstatic conversion experience."[83] In the 1890s, an African evangelist, who would soon break with his European-dominated church, wrote of the "signs of awakening among the people" in the area around Alice, particularly among women.[84]

Especially from the 1880s converts seceded from the established and increasingly segregationist European-controlled churches. One of the most important churches, the Ethiopian church, had as one of its founding members a man who hailed from Queenstown.[85] In 1897 another separatist leader, James Dwane, who subsequently founded the Order of Ethiopia, convened a conference of Ethiopian ministers in Lesseytown, a few miles from Queenstown. By the early years of the twentieth century thousands of Africans had joined separatist churches that, increasingly, critiqued the state's racially oppressive laws. The Ethiopian church, for example, "signalized themselves by their bitter expressions against the White people for legislating in connection with the Plague on racial lines." Members, moreover, enunciated "the opinion that the Native races were the original owners of the soil and would one day free themselves from [the] European tyrant and establish a Government for their own on the land unlawfully taken from them."[86] In the area around Victoria East, the center of separatist Christianity in the Eastern Cape, by the early 1900s perhaps as many as sixteen thousand had joined separatist churches, especially Mzimba's African Presbyterian church.[87] Elsewhere, for example in Herschel and throughout the Ciskei, membership in these churches skyrocketed. In Albany "the Order of Ethiopia has spread through this district and has a large number of followers."[88] In Port Elizabeth there was a church by the name of "Native Independent Persuasion." In Pondoland there was also significant appropriation of Christianity.[89] In neighboring Qumbu, some 280 people had joined separatist churches by 1902; there were at least 2,188 – and almost certainly more – converts in the Transkei by this time.[90]

Localized identities have become tied up with the very historical forces that would appear to destroy them, such as migrant labor. At the same time, supra-local identities – of nation, of a shared sense of oppression, of a common person, of a "black people" – have been elaborated locally and often in the most intimate of places. Churches comprised a privileged space within which the colonized imagined itself, narrated its experiences, assembled supra-local identities, and thus brought new subjectivities into being. This was certainly the case for the Christian elite and for other converts who, especially from the end of the nineteenth century, formed their own separatist churches, as well as for the churches such as that of Nonthetha.

This second wave of religious change was less separatist than syncretic, what has been glossed in the scholarly records as the rise of millenarian Zionist churches. As in the case of the Israelites or the prophetess Nonthetha, these churches emphasized prophetic visions and the healing of a world gone terribly wrong. Theodicy lay at the ideological epicenter of these religious movements. For the Israelites, for example, the "land was dead"; it had been overcome by evil. For Nonthetha God "had been watching all the evil that you have done . . . He decided to destroy you so that he could create anew."[91]

Whereas generally speaking the elite remained faithful to the established mission-based churches and those neither terribly poor nor particularly privileged joined separatist churches, the very poor overwhelmingly comprised the ranks of Zionist faiths. Beyond seamlessly incorporating Christianity with older forms of belief and practice, including witchcraft, Zionist churches created a rich iconography of space that placed exceptional importance on water baptism. Water was perhaps the most elemental connection to the past; indeed, to the very beginnings of the world. Humanity emerged out of Hlanga, described as a marshy area near the banks of a river. Water also was a central component of the process by which people became healers.[92] The element had been important to the religious visions of the middle of the nineteenth century; now, in the twentieth century, water became the quintessential element that created and welcomed the person into a community of the faithful that was ineluctably connected to, and sustained by, the past. For the Israelites, the use and control of water, an ancient symbol associated with political power, signified their autonomy and sovereignty.[93] Water, which symbolically restored social health, made that which was barren fertile again, also created a new political subject, a member of a black and oppressed nation. Water transformed person, reawakened "the mysterious sense of human connection between things,"[94] relocated the faithful within a fabric of history ultimately rooted in the very birth of humanity – a time, we should note, that people associated with proper morality.

Baptism created a new subject. And words had the capacity to "bring into being the events or states they stand for."[95]

Baptism by immersion in water represented a creation of community that stood in opposition to the more established churches. In 1925, for example, Walter Rubusana reported how a number of people belonging to a Zionist order gathered in front of a minister's house and only 30 yards from Rubusana's church. They belonged to an order called "Christ's Church," headed by one Mpini who had served time on Robben Island. Many of his followers were alleged to have been "the remnant of Mqidima's sect. of the Bullhoek affair." According to Rubusana, one man said to the gathered crowd:

You say there are ministers, I say there are no ministers either white or black. They are a lot of robbers, liars and scroundrels who have big bellies from the wages they robbed from the hard earnings of widows. They distort the Scriptures, and are teaching you lies. They have instituted marriage although Adam and Eve were never married, just to get money from you. Today we have come to teach you the truth as they have been teaching you lies all along. They sprinkle you with water. That is not baptism, which is taking you to the river and immersing you.[96]

In the trial that followed one of the accused refused to be sworn but assured the court he was speaking the truth: "I preach the word of God as written in the Bible. My teaching is the [sic] people should be baptized by immersion and invite people to come to God without funds. My teaching is everybody should work hard for his living and that the preachers should not make their livelihood from the earnings of other people. That's all I wish to say."[97]

Religious innovation went one step further than water baptisms. Securing agricultural fertility, for example, generally drifted away from chiefs and towards the Zionist churches. The Christian God, after all, gave "you the rains from heaven and fruitful seasons . . . filling you with food and your hearts with joy."[98] And the "river of the water of life, bright as crystal, flowing from the throne of God," nourished the world, brought forth fruit and crops "and the leaves of the tree [that] are for the healing of nations."[99] In some cases, the annual first-fruits ceremony shifted to the church and the minister, who blessed the crops. "In this way" the congregants "thank the ancestral spirits for the grain. We take our custom a little from them but especially from the Cain and Abel story in which the fruits were brought from God."[100] The Holy Spirit appeared in dreams to offer advice on the medicines to be used to heal people who had been bewitched or whose ancestors had abandoned them. A special emetic or laxative might then be administered to purge the body of the illness and evil.[101]

With the syncretic churches Christianity seems to have contributed not to the creation of a world separated into the sacred and the secular so much as to a conviction of the banality of evil, a diabolization of the everyday that emerged as a result of the combining of "indigenous and Christian concepts of evil."[102] Certainly the problem of evil and the centrality of social health to the Israelites' and Nonthetha's vision is unmistakable. They believed the world to be awash in evil and depravity. It was, in a way, socially dead. Their community of the faithful stood in critique of a world over which they struggled to gain control. In the settlement at Ntabelanga, for example, Africans reasserted control over space and time. Comaroff has written that the "primary mnemonic" of Zionist churches such as the Israelites, the ways in which they understood and invested the world, is located in the "physical body and its immediate spatiotemporal location,"[103] in the case of the Israelites the commonage, their distinctive uniforms, and their water baptisms. On the commonage, on God's holy ground, the faithful awakened memory, produced history, and elaborated a vision of the world and a black nation.

This complex ideological work involved appropriation and mimesis, a way to "get hold of something by means of its likeness."[104] Mimesis represented a central feature of many of the social movements sustained by a conception of a black nation. Importantly, it engaged with the colonial state. For example, the Israelite "army" mimicked the colonial one. The Israelites believed that God, not the state, had conducted a census. In short, their ideological work unfolded at the very epicenter of the state's attempt to make its subjects visible and knowable, using rational, indeed scientific, modes of surveillance, to lock them in modernity's "iron cage." The Israelites, however, did not simply reject the colonial state's will to know, to render the colonized legible to its instrumental power. Rather, they reproduced the issue of legibility as counter-hegemonic discourse by shifting it from an evil state to a just God.

We remember how, in the early 1880s in the context of colonial conquest, rebels took control of magisterial buildings, confiscated and adorned themselves with the clothes of their European rulers, and staged mock colonial trials. The death of Hamilton Hope was also the appropriation of his body and the institutions he represented. Mimesis was a double, and doubled, portraiture. In incorporating the state – its artifacts and its procedures, even the bodies of bureaucrats – the subaltern represented both itself and, simultaneously, the political world of the colonizer. Mimicry represented one way by which Africans attempted to comprehend, and to gain mastery over, the world of the Europeans they encountered. Mimicry wove together state formation, indeed modernity itself, and subaltern culture and consciousness. This process entailed identification and distinction, the translation of the modern state into indigenous political vocabularies and distinguishing the state as "other" and evil. The modern state thus became both similar to and different from earlier forms of power and authority.

Joseph and Nugent, writing on Latin America, have pointed out that the "state, especially the capitalist state, has been of signal importance in providing some of the idioms in terms of which subordinated groups have initiated their struggles for emancipation."[105] These idioms are clearly located in the political visions of the Israelites, as they are in other social movements in twentieth-century South Africa. Mimetic representation engaged with, and critiqued, the colonial state's quest for information and simplification. As we have seen, from the end of the nineteenth century Africans and the rural landscape they inhabited were subjected to a colonial social engineering that required a growing bureaucracy in the form of the NAD and other administrative agencies. Rule in this period became increasingly textual. Receipts for various taxes, censuses of people and stock, registration of land, memoranda, telegrams, transcribed testimonies, and the pass book all involved paper and print and mechanically reproduced knowledge. The region was quite simply papered over by the state's bureaucracy. This paper was an ineluctable part of the state's will to know, and to control in ever more detailed ways, the subjects of its rule.

A striking facet of Israelite ideology concerned the central features of bureau-cratic rule: writing, census, space. The Israelite community stood in opposition to the state's surveillance, categorization and accumulation of information – its will to know. They believed that the state's will to know was intimately related to the presence of evil and misfortune. The idea of a commonage, the Israelites' "holy ground," repudiated the state's interest in the ever more precise mapping of space. Their land, the land of a "black nation," had in an important sense been mapped by God. The Israelites also adamantly refused the state's attempt to conduct a census. For a census already had been conducted, a subject created, a knowledge produced. The Israelites' "names were written in God's book."[106]

Both the Israelites and Nonthetha and her adherents sought out and created a space that was sacred in part precisely because it was free from the state's field of vision. That field of vision, we remember, sought to make representations lived realities, to colonize consciousness. From the end of the nineteenth century space became increasingly racialized and, in the native reserves, organized on the basis of the state's fantasy of discrete tribes occupying equally discrete spaces. The shift towards indirect rule and, in the 1950s the beginnings of apartheid, made the colonial organization of space an essential feature of state formation and policy. The state's expanding regulation of labor made control of space an absolute necessity. Commonages, however, were relatively free from the more detailed mapping of the state. As early as the late 1890s, in the context both of new state intervention and spiraling poverty and landlessness, they had become sites of a new politics and religious sensibility. To the state squatting was of course a metonym for illegibility. But for those who lived on them commonages offered the possibility of addressing a world that had gone astray.

Subaltern movements refused to submit to the state's will to know. They also elaborated a counter-hegemonic discourse that deployed key idioms, images, and procedures of the state they contested. In the Griqua Le Fleur movement of the late 1920s, concerned with the restoration of land expropriated by the state, adherents were to obtain "passes"; passes were the epitome of colonial rule, the document required of all African men and perhaps the single most hated document of the colonial and apartheid eras. But here they were endowed with magical properties that could overturn the colonial order. Possession of these documents that mimicked those of the state ensured that people would magically obtain land to plough. While those without passes would, with whites, "either be burned or driven out of the land," people with them constituted an imagined community held together by paper and the word.[107] Adherents were also to destroy "all their pigs"; the presence of swine would "prevent the working of such [magical] mixture" that would "drive all the Europeans away from Umzimkulu."[108]

In the 1920s, then, social movements appropriated facets of the state they contested. This process, this grasping the state "by means of its likeness,"[109] began in the years of colonial conquest and continues today. In the 1950s subaltern movements appropriated and reproduced the institutional language and procedures of the state they resisted. They had their own committees, judges, secretaries, treasurers, police, and courts – even their own system of taxation. Mimicry ultimately deauthorized the state and, by the late 1950s, catapulted much of the rural Eastern Cape into open rebellion.

Social movements evinced a distinctive political hybridity. The "power of the mimetic faculty"[110] formed part of the attempt by the colonized to penetrate the hidden abode of colonial power and to create a space within which to critique the authoritarian colonial state. Africans saw the bureaucratic state as a ritual order operating on the basis of magic; indeed, very often on the basis of witchcraft, just as they had seen chiefs deploying magic in the intensely competitive politics that allowed for the massing of nourishing symbolic power but also for the misfortune competition so often brought. Witchcraft constituted African representations of otherness, a simulacrum of evil. It was also a profoundly political discourse that often, though not always inevitably, conjoined questions of power and social health.

We have speculated that at least some Africans believed that early magistrates had access to magic. The colonized had made these associations in ways in which, initially at least, the ambiguous relationship between power, authority, and magic was maintained. Particularly from the 1920s, the decade that ushered in a new era of tribalism centering on chiefs and rule by decree, Africans began associating the colonial state with witchcraft.[111] The state, for example, operated on the basis of "crafty measures."[112] People referred to the poll tax, introduced in 1925, as the *impundulu*, the lighting bird and the quintessential exemplar of witchcraft.[113] Rumors of anti-colonial uprisings invariably included reference to the use of fire to destroy the houses of Europeans and, often, railways and telegraphs as well. When Africans "were going to make an attempt to get rid of

white people . . . houses were to be burnt and the children killed."[114] Africans
began using ritual specialists in legal cases heard before the white ruler. These
"witchdoctors," ritual specialists who identified and neutralized bad magic,
were always "about the village when cases are being heard." When possible
they doctored the courthouse bench with "herb water" to protect people from
the colonial state's powerful magic.[115] Independent Industrial and Commercial
Workers' Union (ICU) adherents invariably sought possession of membership
papers which they believed empowered them in their struggles against the colonial order.[116] At meetings of the Independent ICU (IICU) speakers described the
state as "satan." They also referred to the state as a "bloodsucker," using a word
that was common in anti-capitalist movements elsewhere in the world. Luise
White has suggested that "vampire beliefs emerged out of witch beliefs."[117]
Certainly to refer to the state as the devil is to view it as evil. But did the subaltern also see the state as a kind of vampire, a parasite that fed on the flesh
of the living, that took without returning and left its victims weakened and
hollowed?

The incorporation of the European's world in the colonized's rituals of social
healing has been a common feature of the colonial world, from Cuna healing
figures in the Americas to the Hauka of West Africa.[118] Mimicry became a
way of penetrating the power of the modern state, mimesis a central feature not
simply of resistance but also of a social healing in a world of human misery.
The state came to be seen as a source of evil, its employees purveyors of magic.

The promise of a new nation

One of the most important movements to emerge in this period was that of
Wellington Buthelezi and his Africanized Garveyism. Born in Natal, and briefly
educated in Lovedale, Buthelezi spent much of the 1920s traversing the greater
Eastern Cape region. He learned of Garveyism in eastern Lesotho from a West
Indian who had established "a branch of the Universal Negro Improvement
Association."[119] It was also in Lesotho that Buthelezi became a healer.

By the early 1920s "Americanism" and the Garveyite prophecy of the return
to Africa of all those who had been lost to it had become an important theme for
many in the Eastern Cape. "Americanism" had surfaced in the Le Fleur movement, as well as among the Israelites and in Nonthetha's church. Buthelezi in fact
visited Nonthetha during her incarceration in Pretoria. According to a 1922 issue
of *Abantu Batho*, "the Negroes are making preparations for returning to the land
of their ancestors – Africa . . . These men (Negroes) desire to regain Africa."[120]
"Redemption is coming," speakers would say in the Transkei in the 1920s.[121]
"Something is coming. All the eyes will see it."[122] "Go in front of God," a minister instructed one meeting, "cry to God as a nation as Africans."[123] "Today,"

one Pondoland man said in 1927, "the word America (iMelika) is a household word symbolic of nothing else but Bantu National freedom and liberty."[124]

Buthelezi's "movement spread at an extraordinary rate" throughout the Transkei.[125] "A large proportion of the Natives believe that American Negroes are coming in Aeroplanes to assist them to drive the whites into the seas."[126] He became involved in local struggles in the Mount Fletcher district and in Herschel. In 1927 the state deported him from the Transkei; thereupon he begins to disappear from the archival record,[127] although Garveyism continued to be an important source of resistance in the region.

In Buthelezi's movement can be found the themes of mimicry and magic, the problem of evil, and the creation of new political subjectivities centering on an illusive black nation. He enjoined his followers to create a new social order free from colonial rule. His social order in many respects mimicked and symbolically inverted the colonial order. Members were to establish their own churches, solemnize their own marriages, and establish their own schools, in short to create an alter-society separate from that controlled by the state, a society that would "be released from the Government."[128] They were not to pay the poll tax, and instead were to pay 2s 6d to join the movement. In return they would receive badges or buttons that would signify their membership in the new movement, protect them from evil, and ensure their salvation.[129]

A striking feature of Buthelezi's movement was its appropriation of the artifacts of modernity, especially those relating to endlessly reproducibly quality of modern representation, in the vision of a new world. He was as much a "modernized herbalist"[130] as a herbalist of modernity, a master of magic posing as a "doctor of medicine." At one meeting he "sent for his handbag . . . to tell the meeting the secrets."[131] He used a battery to heal people with electric shocks. Photographs, the printed word, and other adornments attained a magical aura. Buttons and badges were "supposed to be worn to save themselves from being slaughtered when the Americans come."[132]

What is important here is the place of magic in the critique of colonialism and in the creation of new identities. As a kind of counter-appropriation of modernity, magic became an instrument to probe modern power, to understand the evil of whites who were seen as the "descendants of Cain, accursed by God."[133] In addition to his battery, Wellington Buthelezi had "what must have been a type of camera obscura." He instructed people "to gaze into the glass." There they saw "numbers of aeroplanes and motor cars filled with negro troops sailing in the sky, awaiting the call to land to he and his hearers assistance. A native assured me that he did as he was told and saw machines loaded with troops."[134]

Glass and reflective surfaces had long held the fascination of the colonized. Mirrors, for example, have been important to witchcraft-eradication movements. "Divination by looking glass," the Comaroffs have argued *pace* Audrey

Richards, "seems to have been especially appropriate for identifying and capturing a hidden malevolent" using a "quite explicit deployment of European tools and techniques." More generally they have argued for the importance of the mirror to the constitution of the divided self. "The image of the mirror blocked out the encompassing world, turning the self back on itself, dissociating the ego from its context, and fragmenting a formerly continuous perceptual universe."[135]

In the West until the end of the nineteenth century and the crisis of modernism, the camera obscura remained perhaps the quintessential instrument of objective representation, the very epitome of empiricism, rationality, and modernity. None other than René Descartes used a "camera obscura to reproduce the observed world."[136] The camera obscura's projections were as timeless as they were incorporeal, their objectivity guaranteed by their impersonal production, the science of optics producing a transcendent truth. The formulation of the rules of perspectivism that the camera obscura made possible, moreover, may ultimately have shaped the "rationalizing practices emerging in commerce, banking, book-keeping, trade, and agricultural production under centralized land management."[137] The camera obscura thus returns us to such mundane activities as surveying and other measurements that we have seen were so central to colonial state formation.[138]

With Wellington Buthelezi's camera obscura, however, we have not simply the issue of reflection and individuation, the creation of the alienated bourgeois self, the splitting of mind and body, the ocular triumph (quite literally) of Enlightenment – at least not quite. Perhaps the projected image Buthelezi's followers saw was a doubled image capable of endless duplication and, importantly, association. Perhaps it less alienated and individuated than associated and conjoined peoples and places. Perhaps gazing at the image people could imagine their place in it, could have an ineffable feeling of comity and communion, could believe that black troops were "sailing in the sky" to liberate them from their oppression. If so, then here was a transcendence radically different than the promise of science and Western rationality, yet using one of its most classic exemplars.

The Wellington Movement, as it was called, was but one of a series of movements in the 1920s that appropriated and mimicked the state, science, and modernity and sought social health in magic that would contest the power of whites and bring into being a black nation. People who participated in "Americanism" typically also participated in other social movements, particularly the Ethiopian and Zionist churches that blossomed in this period. The movement in fact appropriated some of the symbols of the Ethiopian churches,[139] and many of its supporters in places such as Herschel participated in separatist Christianity and in localized movements that contested the colonial state's authoritarian high modernism.

Briefly, in the 1920s and early 1930s, and as we shall see in later chapters again in the 1950s and early 1960s, prophetic nationalism intersected with, and at moments substantially radicalized, more conventional elite-based movements such as the African National Congress and the Industrial and Commercial Workers' Union. Of particular concern to both movements was the new regime of taxation that began in 1925 and the torrent of segregationist legislation that flowed from the state. Formed in Cape Town shortly after the end of the First World War, the ICU became South Africa's first mass-based social movement with a membership of close to 150,000 by the end of the 1920s. The union, and its independent branches, were especially active in Port Elizabeth and in East London where it led important struggles against low wages and racial oppression.[140]

As the ICU's following expanded, its ideological content changed. Local ICU leaders fought for higher wages, but they did so increasingly in the prophetic language of the subaltern. Lambasting whites and the state as the purveyors of evil, the union offered salvation and social health and assistance in bringing together the "black men of South Africa" as "one big nation."[141] One speaker "advised his hearers not to go the Mines or to allows their relatives to do so, not to listen to their Magistrate who was nothing but a snake, to cease paying taxes and [to] join the ICU ... In the very near future he would compel the Magistrate to leave the District, force the Veterinary Department to cancel all restrictions on the removal of stock and to abolish the dipping regulations."[142]

The early history and politics of the ANC and its predecessor in the Cape are well known.[143] Early on the SANNC largely concerned itself with issues of land tenure, the native vote, ensuring "our political rights by electing Members of Parliament," and with the "Progress of Civilization."[144] Land issues became more acute with the 1903–6 Native Affairs Commission. From Glen Grey, for example, the recently reconstructed SANNC telegramed the prime minister to express their "disfavour" with the "method whereby irresponsible native witnesses are summoned by govt to give evidence on matters of general importance affecting the native people," particularly with regard to the all-important Glen Grey Act.[145] This concern arose again in the 1906 the SANNC meeting in Queenstown's Native Baptist hall.

The 1913 Land Act and Hertzog's Native Bills awoke the SANNC from the slumber of liberal politics. With the 1920 annual conference in Queenstown it began engaging directly the state's policies of segregation. In his presidential address Safaka Mapogo Makgatho described the government as "despotic" and spoke of the Native Affairs Department as the "Native Persecution Department."[146] This meeting was especially concerned with wages and the racialization of subject and space. Where "older members of the organization" did "not mind the presence of Europeans at their meetings," some of the newer ones were "of a totally different type."[147] One speaker invoked the idea that "the land originally belonged to the natives" and "that all the wealth which is being obtained from the land at the present time is taken and controlled by other nations."[148]

By this time ANC meetings included the subaltern, and, importantly, some local leaders were able to bridge the gap separating elite politicians and the colonized poor. At the local level the two nationalisms – one oriented around access to the state, the other centered on magic and social health – blurred. It is at this point that ANC leaders began speaking of the organization as embodying the "black nation." In 1923, for example, at a meeting in East London James Ngcuka said of the congress: "We are the principals of the black nation in South Africa."[149]

Later in the decade, in the relatively few areas where the ANC remained active, the movement found itself entangled in the state's land policies, the new regime of native taxation, and, especially, the introduction of the council system and the reworking "traditional" rule as envisioned in legislation such as the 1927 Native Administration Act. In Herschel, for example, there was considerable resistance to the introduction of the council system and, particularly, taxes and land registration. In 1926, recently dismissed headman Makobeni Mehlomakhulu, who claimed the local Hlubi chiefship, led a deputation to the magistrate protesting at the state's segregationist policies. Mehlomakhulu and the others believed "that in their experience [land] registration, Bunga and survey were usually associated one with the other, and it was their fear that registration would bring survey and also the council."[150] The headman also objected to the manner by which land "was being allotted by the Magistrate without reference to the Headman and was being granted only to people who were willing to register" their lands.[151]

In part Mehlomakhulu was reacting to, or more accurately attempting to appropriate, subaltern resistance against the state's new policies. Initially he and other ANC members were successful. In 1928 close to a thousand people attended ANC meetings in Herschel; one meeting the following year counted close to five times that number.[152] The ANC had become the effective center of political struggle in the area, fusing elite and subaltern politics and, in doing so, becoming embroiled in the politics of local office. Showing their ANC tickets subalterns dictated their complaints to the organization's chief clerk;[153] they believed the ANC had the power to confront the state successfully.

Mehlomakhulu and others argued for what was in effect a modernization of headmanship in ways that were not dissimilar to the direction of state policy. Headmanship, they argued, "should not be for an indefinite period, but for a stipulated term so that the people might have an opportunity of asserting their preference when a Headman lost his popularity owing to bias and neglect of the location interests."[154] At the same time they argued against the council system, the new regime of taxation established by the Native Taxation Act, and the other policies prosecuted by that most "dangerous department in the Union," the Native Affairs Department.[155]

But this melding of elite and subaltern politics proved ephemeral. The ANC sought access to state power, not its repudiation; as James Thaele put it, "we want our rights which we are entitled to."[156] So also did individuals such as Mehlomakhulu whose challenge lay in accessing the power of the authoritarian state and, locally, with developing a basis of legitimacy. It proved a largely impossible challenge. Many ANC leaders owed their careers to the state: some were headmen, while others were dipping foremen,[157] clerks, or policemen. In 1925 the magistrate at Herschel had written that it was "only natural that the more enlightened and progressive section of the natives in this District should desire the establishment of a Council."[158] This overstated the case and simplified the situation. The segregationist state's policies, especially those entailing retribalization, its decentralized despotism, held their own attractions. Thaele, the Garveyite-inspired Cape ANC leader, saw Hertzog as "the man of the hour." He lauded Hertzog's industrial policies and, especially, the possibility that under segregation "natives could buy land . . . and become territorially independent as never before."[159]

The radicalization of the ANC in the Eastern Cape continued into the 1930s, though it was unable to sustain its connections to the African poor. In 1930, in the context of increasing harassment by the state, J. T. Gumede deployed South African Communist Party (SACP) rhetoric and the importance of class struggle.[160] But to little avail: this radical language failed, among other things, to address the problem of evil and fertility. The ANC lapsed into near irrelevancy, caught as it was between the Scylla of demanding rights in a state that sowed evil and the Charybdis of seeking legitimacy at the local level. ANC leaders invoked the heroic struggles against colonial conquest, but this was, as it were, in a "borrowed" and hollow "language."[161]

The dreams of the elite, as Fanon noted long ago, were derived, very often enviously so, from the colonizer's world. From its earliest days the ANC had committed itself to the civilizing mission first enunciated in the nineteenth century, a liberal politics in which the law applied to all equally (at least theoretically) and Africans held inalienable rights and responsibilities as individuals. This "register of *radical individualism*" was not the only meter of modernity; apartheid and its crucial emphasis on tribe and custom was in the most fundamental ways also quintessentially modern.[162] Liberal modernist sensibilities remained exceptionally important in shaping the political imagination of the African elite. Throughout much of its history the ANC remained an elite – and very often an elitist – organization. As is well known, its critique of the state was less radical than reformist, that all individuals should have access to the state irrespective of race. The ANC did not see the modern state as intrinsically wrong: quite the opposite. Segregation, from the 1920s, and apartheid, from in the 1950s, was wrong because they denied Africans rights within, and democratic access to, the modern state. This was a classically liberal, indeed Lockean, politics that ultimately justified violence – revolution even – in the name of bourgeois modernist rights. The ANC finally turned to violence in the early 1960s in the face of tyranny and the denial of representation in a unitary and neutral state.[163] Bloody revolution was not the intent of this violence. Rather, ANC leaders hoped to wake the authorities from their authoritarian slumber so as to initiate dialogue and political reform, and so to use reason to end the nightmare of racial oppression.

Subaltern nationalism had little to do with the bourgeois rights of the individual or with a conception of the state as neutral arbiter and protector. At the same time the African elite did not see the state as practicing witchcraft; in fact, ANC leaders disdained and dismissed such sentiments. Nor did it believe that the state's policies were responsible for drought. To have envisioned the state as the subaltern did would have required the elite to turn its back on the secular vision of state and nation, indeed a conception of social reality, that it had borrowed from the West. Not surprisingly, subaltern nationalism perplexed and troubled African political elites who saw the movements they had helped create being transformed by a vision of the world they scarcely understood.[164] For in the 1920s and early 1930s, and as we shall see in later chapters again in the 1950s and early 1960s, prophetic nationalism intersected with, and substantially radicalized, more conventional elite-based movements such as the ANC and the ICU. This intersection allowed for the emergence of the ANC and ICU as mass-based, though inherently unstable, social movements.[165]

Elite and subaltern conceptions of the political were thus not entirely incommensurate. Elite nationalism's origins lay in the bourgeois political history of the West. The roots of subaltern nationalism, however, resided in indigenous African conceptions of power and authority and the belief that supernatural forces pervaded the world. These conceptions, though of extraordinary power, were not unchanging. Christianity, seen especially in the Zionist churches, fused with earlier conceptions to create a terrifying vision of a world awash in an evil and inequity that could be cleansed only by unwavering commitment to God, the ancestors, the "black nation" . . . and to the eradication of witches.

There are other comparisons. Both the ANC and ICU engaged with many of the same state policies, though the subaltern believed these policies were responsible for the presence and, it seemed increasingly, the triumph of evil in their lives. Both the discourse of an African nation and of a workers' republic entailed the creation of a transcendent subject as well as an engagement with the state's racialization of domination. Secular politics was never particularly so; both nationalist and socialist politics entailed belief in, and the bringing into being of, a transcendent subject that would end oppression and begin the world anew.

5   Government acts

Authoritarianism triumphed with the introduction of apartheid in the 1950s. The first half of the decade saw a dizzying cyclone of legislation from the National Party government that came to power in 1948 and which solidified its control in its electoral victory of 1953. The Population Registration Act and the Group Areas Act, both passed in 1950, classified people by race and forced people outside the reserves to live in racially demarcated areas. Various pieces of security legislation, such as the 1954 Riotous Assemblies Act, heralded the creation of a police state; importantly, this law represented not an authoritarian patina but a central component of the state's massive social engineering. By the end of the 1940s police already "seemed to delight in persecuting and arresting people."[1] In the early 1950s the government passed the Bantu Authorities Act and the Native Laws Amendment Act; both, as we shall see, became intricately interconnected to rule and to controlling labor in the reserves. The Native Laws Amendment Act greatly increased the state's control over African labor and would become a "principal pillar" of what came to be known, in the quintessentially technical language of grand state planning, as "influx control."[2] The legislation, as Posel has pointed out, gave the state "an unprecedented degree of control over the distribution of African labour."[3] The Bantu Authorities Act, introduced in the Transkei in 1956, marked a crucial moment in a more general process of retribalizing the reserves. This process culminated in the grand apartheid policies of separate development that saw, for example, the extension of a sham "self-government" to the reserves beginning, in 1959, with the Promotion of Bantu Self-Government Act.

It was a time of enormous political change, of which the Native Laws Amendment Act and the Bantu Authorities Act formed only a small part, however important. In the context of exploding poverty and prolonged drought in the reserves, the state prosecuted a battery of betterment and other policies aimed at "stabilizing" and "rehabilitating" the rural economy: new settlement patterns; new agricultural schemes; anti-soil-erosion works; stock culling, and so on. From as early as the late 1940s, the state began forcibly relocating large numbers of people within the reserves in an attempt to rid "white" South Africa of its undesirable and unwanted black population. These efforts became maniacal in the 1960s and 1970s as the state poured ever greater resources into influx control and created various resettlement camps across the country to house the dispossessed.[4]

Authoritarianism and the social engineering that so often accompanies it had its most immediate roots in the 1920s, in legislation such as the 1927 Native Administration Act. The 1950s, however, saw not simply the application of policies formulated earlier but also, and most importantly, the "bureaucratic reinvention of Native administration, a process distinguished by concerted attempts to convert the DNA (Department of Native Affairs) into a 'state within a state'."[5] Officials were "now handed" an "aggressively interventionist brief"[6] with which to prosecute with near impunity a social engineering the scale of which was (and remains) unparalleled on the African continent. The department amassed vast new powers symbolized, in 1958, with its renaming as the Ministry of Bantu Administration and Development.

All of these developments had deep historical roots, some going back to the early years of colonial conquest and the first era of colonial state formation when the state began organizing administrative space on the basis of its vision of "tribal society." The late 1920s had seen the beginnings of rule by decree and the decisive shift towards remodeling domination on the basis of Lugardist principles of indirect rule. The 1927 Native Administration Act marked this turn to retribalization, segregation, and authoritarianism. This period also saw the rise of betterment and other policies aimed at reconstructing the rural economy, for example the 1936 South African Native Trust Act, which greatly increased the state's control over and management of African land, and the 1939 Betterment Act.

The dream of most bureaucrats is a pure concordance of policy and practice, but in reality there is always a space between them, keeping the designs of administrators and policies separate from what actually unfolds "on the ground." The authoritarian state insists on making the dream a reality, and in so doing creates a nightmare for all those subjected to its rule. The Great Depression and the Second World War frustrated and, in many areas, delayed the state's implementation of the legislation it had so energetically passed in the 1920s and 1930s. After the war, however, South Africa emerged with a far more powerful and advanced economy. The state had within its grasp a greatly enlarged coercive capacity. It was now capable of intervening far more powerfully in the lives of its subjects. But the era beginning in 1950s represented more than just a continuation of developments rooted most immediately in the period of segregation. The very scale of social engineering, perhaps most visibly seen in the creation of resettlement camps, sets it apart from the earlier period. In the 1920s and early 1930s retribalization and rural development ran more or less parallel to each other. In the 1950s they converged in a tornado of political and economic change. A second distinguishing feature of the period was, of course, the rise of Afrikaner nationalism, spearheaded by the National Party. Ultimately, authoritarian rule in the reserves and the racist nationalism of the National Party, so liberally imbibed by the great majority of white South Africans, became inseparable. In the name of racial exclusivity and ethnic purity the South African state pursued one of the twentieth century's greatest and most tragic experiments.

Apartheid involved both an attempt at reconstructing the rural economy and the radical reworking of the structures and daily practices of rule. Locally, apartheid introduced a new and at times seemingly frenzied era of political competition and conflict, particularly in the Transkei, the cornerstone of the regime's policy of separate development. Many, though certainly not all, chiefs and headmen and those who aspired to such positions sought access to the state. Other people created new social bases from which to launch social movements. This was an era of "many meetings" and much discussion as people jockeyed for power, attempted to mark out domains of authority, made "claims for chieftainship,"[7] or organized resistance. More generally this period saw an extraordinary rise in resistance and violence, much of it quite protracted, from seemingly local disputes over property to the outbreak, in 1960, of the Pondoland Revolt, to the beginning of the armed struggled waged by the militant wings of the ANC and the PAC.

The 1950s thus represented a crucial moment of state formation in South Africa – both a culmination of processes that had been unfolding in the region since the mid-nineteenth century and a decisive turning point in its political history.[8] Indeed, the decade bears an odd resemblance to the earlier era that had seen the first extension of colonial rule. At the center of both periods lay the most basic issues of rule, from the organization of political space and the definition of political subjects to the allocation of scarce resources such as land. Both periods entailed a radical reworking of political society. In a sense apartheid represented a grand reconquest of the region that entailed, among other things, a return to the expansive politics of paramount chiefs now supported by the most powerful state on the continent. The technologies of colonial rule – particularly map, census, and the production of ethnographic information – were central features of both periods. The nineteenth century also became tangled up in the 1950s in obvious ways. For the introduction of apartheid awakened historical memory and discussion of the years of colonial conquest. Thus, as we shall see, in the region around Tsolo and Qumbu, the nineteenth-century story of Mhlontlo and the plight of the Mpondomise reemerged and shaped people's understanding of the beginning of apartheid in South Africa.

Many rural people in the Eastern Cape grappled with more than the new policies and institutions introduced by officials of the apartheid state. Not only were they living in a world of police, agricultural officials, passes, labor bureaux, relocation, and the courts, but the great majority were stuck in lives of dire poverty, hardship and outright misery, the indignities of landlessness, economic insecurity, malnutrition, premature death. Roughly "half the children born in most Reserves were dying before the age of five," noted a 1966 government report that described life in the Bantustans "as one of abject poverty."[9] To make things worse, the region entered an especially dry period. The years of the British conquest in the Transkei had corresponded with a global period of poor rains and pathetic harvests. Such was the case in the 1940s and 1950s also. A severe drought hit the Eastern Cape in 1945, just three years before the National Party victory. For the rest of the decade and into the 1950s drought struck much of the region, in some places creating considerable famine. The drought of 1955–6 was especially punishing, "the greatest within the memory of the present generation."[10] At the very same time the state began introducing its apartheid policies, at this crucial moment of state formation, the rains failed.

People grappled with all of this and much, much more. There were familial tensions, jealousies, hatreds. There was the malevolence of witches who secreted evil among the innocent, sowed misfortune, employed zombies, sent animals into the bodies of victims, flew with the *impundulu*. "Why do we suffer so?" "What is the source of our daily afflictions?" Both the historical record and contemporary evidence point to witchcraft as a central feature of social life, an intractable problem even, for many people in the Eastern Cape and, indeed, elsewhere in South Africa. Missionary evidence from before the period of colonial rule – that is, before the state outlawed, and drove underground, witchcraft and other customs its officials deemed "barbarous" – points to what most Westerners might view as a world filled with supernatural forces and mysterious beings. These conceptions continued into the colonial period, as people sought ways of combating evil and securing social health. In the Zionist churches especially they fused with Christian ideas of sinfulness and of a Manichaean world of good and bad and helped refine a conception of the world as profoundly evil, perhaps even socially dead.[11]

In the previous chapter I argued for the centrality of the theodicy problem within subaltern thought. This problem centered on explaining the persistence of evil, whereby the intentional deployment of occult power brought harm, disorder, and destruction to both individuals and communities, and of developing ways of overcoming it. I argued, partly by inference, at times by speculation, that the theodicy problem became bound up with two interrelated developments. First, the problem of evil shaped the invention and elaboration of new identities, for example that the subaltern were members of an oppressed "black nation" in a world gone wrong. Second, subaltern conceptions of evil and the supernatural shaped perceptions of the colonial state and its formation.

We now begin turning to the question of resistance in the era of apartheid. We have suggested that each pivotal moment in state formation led to new forms of resistance and cultural invention among the colonized. Colonial conquest and the era of segregation marked two such pivotal moments. Apartheid represented a third. The more recent past is a fourth. An important feature of cultural invention centered on belief in a world filled with occult powers, witches, and magical beings. These beliefs, we have argued, had their own history and at times shaped people's actions. The resistance of the 1950s and 1960s, it is suggested here, continued historical patterns of subaltern representation and agency that were centrally concerned with the problem of evil and its relationship to modern state formation. The very hybridity of African resistance speaks to people's ongoing engagement not simply with protesting against discrete policies but also with probing and exposing to critique the nature of state power and state formation, and with grappling with the evil that dominated their lives.

The politics of retribalization and development

In 1955 the Transkeian Territories General Council (Bunga), first envisioned under the Glen Grey Act, accepted the Bantu Authorities Act passed by the South African government four years earlier; the state began introducing the new system the following year. The secretary for native affairs believed that "we must go ahead now and get Bantu Authorities going while the iron is hot."[12] Throughout this period the Transkei represented the prototype of the state's new policies, and so the state expended considerable energies and monies (including a great deal of propaganda and the deployment of information officers "to convert the Bantu people") to ensure its success.[13] The Bantu Authorities system which the legislation introduced represented "the first legislative crystallization of ethnos theory in Native administration,"[14] the idea that people were members of distinct and fixed cultural groups who should live in "live in contiguous areas."[15] In the earliest years of conquest magistrates had attempted to create ethnically pure areas even as they were determined to destroy chiefship as an institution. Officials in the 1920s, as part of the turn to segregation and the rebuilding of chiefship, had likewise pursued the dream of a concordance of tribe and space. But in both cases the state simply did not have the capacity to enforce its policies consistently.

This situation changed after 1948. By the end of the 1950s the vision of making space and ethnic identity identical had evolved into the grand apartheid policy of separate development. Under legislation such as the 1959 Bantu Self-Government Act, the reserves were to become self-governing nation-states. In one sense the plan entailed marrying the modern state with the putatively ancient "form of Bantu Government and Tribal administration" which was, as Bantu Affairs commissioners were instructed to deliver at meetings throughout the region, "nothing new."[16] These changes culminated in 1963, when the Transkei received its first parliament, though the South African government provided virtually all of its financial support and tightly controlled the political and institutional structures of its puppet state.[17] The Ciskei received its sham independence in 1976. Ominously, during the events celebrating Ciskeian independence the flagpole on which the new flag was hoisted promptly fell over.

The Bantustan policies of separate development rested on the 1951 Bantu Authorities Act. This legislation reworked the system of government in the reserves by introducing a pyramidical and overlapping structure of local and territorial "authorities." At its apex stood the Territorial Authority, headed by a paramount chief. An African – indeed, a traditional leader – would thus take over the position that had been occupied by the chief magistrate of the Transkei. Below the Territorial Authority stood a series of ethnically defined regional and district councils followed, finally, by local tribal authorities. Organized around discrete "tribes" comprising a number of locations controlled by headmen, tribal authorities replaced the districts first created by the colonial state in the immediate context of conquest. They constituted "the basic units of administration and allegedly reverted to the boundaries of chiefdoms that had formerly constituted the different 'tribal units'."[18]

Headmen were, according to one official document, "the tribal authorities best friends and collaborators."[19] As with chiefs, the Bantu Authorities system offered headmen considerable powers. Importantly, the process of selecting those who would serve in the tribal authorities unfolded "without the tribesmen's consent."[20] Headmen remained important to the allocation of land, though now their chief political linkage lay with the traditional authority, the chiefs, and not the resident magistrate. After 1956 headmen were prohibited from allotting new residential sites unless the tribal authority had agreed to "planning under the Department's stabilisation policy."[21] This immediately placed them on the front line of the state's new policies. They were instructed, for example, "that under no account should *widows* be allowed to call themselves heirs." Crucially, headmen were instructed that lands for which people did not hold proper certificates could be transferred by the tribal authority. Location sites that had not been used for two or more years were to be converted to commonage and "can under no circumstances be allotted unless the location is stabilised."[22] Headmen were thus invested with not inconsiderable powers to reallocate land in the context of extraordinary poverty and landlessness. Given this broader context, they had considerable room for corruption, for example by turning their backs on land consolidations or by accepting bribes for land.

Precolonial boundaries differed radically from the fixed borders established by Europeans in the nineteenth century or, for that matter, created under the Bantu Authorities system. (Indeed, officials were well aware of the artificiality of their ethnic engineering.) The porous, shifting, and overlapping boundaries of the precolonial period were incompatible with the formation, not to mention the existence, of a modern state. The reversion to putatively preconquest boundaries utterly contradicted, though it certainly did not erase, precolonial theory and practice. Apartheid was thus very much a political fantasy that imagined fusing a modern industrialized state to an African political world that either no longer existed or had become utterly perverted. That said, apartheid returned to some of the most basic issues of political space – the establishment of domains of rule. These issues had been very important in the early years of conquest when Europeans mapped chiefdoms and created the first magisterial districts. In the 1950s they again returned to the forefront of local politics.

Headmen, chiefs, and paramount chiefs were at the very center of this re-organization of political space, this tribalization of the colonial state, especially since a major feature of apartheid was to get members of discrete, seemingly immutable, tribal groups to live in a single area.[23] Chiefs appointed location headmen and headed the various tribal authorities. They also largely constituted the regional authorities. Because members of the various regional authorities comprised the Territorial Authority, under the Bantu Authorities system chiefs and other "traditional" leaders in theory had control over all levels of govern-ment: "In theory" because the South African state retained command of key features of the Authorities system, continued to control the means of coer-cion, and were more than willing to install cooperative chiefs whose claims to authority were dubious.

The destruction of chiefship had been a major feature of nineteenth-century colonial rule, even as officials invested considerable energy in creating ethni-cally pure administrative areas. In general chiefs had been demoted and con-verted into location headmen. The twentieth century saw the resurrection of chiefship, though it was only in the 1940s and especially in the 1950s that this process gathered steam. The Hlubi chief Charles Ludidi, for example, had once been a headman, but with Bantu Authorities he now had the power to ap-point them. Doing so, however, led to conflict, particularly as he had proceeded "without consulting the people of the locality concerned."[24]

The elevation of chiefs to the center of rule completed a process of retrib-alization that had been initiated in the 1920s. In other respects, particularly regarding the council system, the Authorities system had historical roots in leg-islation such as the 1894 Glen Grey Act. The 1927 Native Administration Act and other legislation passed in the 1920s and early 1930s marked a decisive shift towards strengthening chiefship, expanding the council system and, together, creating a system of "decentralized despotism."[25] While the Transkeian Terri-tories General Council had originally had a mostly advisory function, it became an increasingly powerful (and conservative) institution composed of "the over-lapping categories of bureaucrat-headmen, chiefs and richer peasants."[26] This shift also marked the emergence of a more clearly patrimonial system in the reserves. Patrimonialism was impossible without the existence of a state. What began unfolding in the twentieth century was the process by which authority

that previously "had appeared as a pre-eminent group right" increasingly became a "personal right" which chiefs and others assumed "in the same way
he would any ordinary object of possession."[27] Indirect rule, most classically
in the northern Nigerian emirates and Rwanda, was preeminently a patrimonial system because it combined "traditional" authority based on a codified
body of custom with a clearly delineated state that regularly intervened in the
economy.[28]

The Bantu Authorities system thus represented both an extension of earlier policies and a crucial turning point in the creation of a patrimonial system.
It greatly increased the powers of chiefs, and especially of paramounts.
"Chieftainship," proclaimed a document entitled "Bantu Authorities: Their Aim
and Object and the Place of the Chief or Headman in these Authorities," which
was read out to chiefs and headmen, "binds the people and, therefore, the tribe
together." Chiefs would "be guided by the laws and traditions of his people."[29]
Chiefs were, in effect, patrimonial authorities and the people they ruled their
subjects. As set out in Proclamation 180 of 1956, succession to chiefship automatically meant also succession to the head of a tribal authority.[30] The great
deal of "communal integration" that had once characterized political society,
and, importantly, the capacity of commoners to "vote with their feet," all but
disappeared with the rise of patrimonialism. Moreover, under the earlier Bunga
system many councillors had been elected and thus had attempted to secure
some popularity. This electoral aspect largely faded in the new system of Bantu
Authorities. It was, according to one NAD official, "contrary to the Government's policy to have . . . 'elections'."[31] At the same time, the practice of using
chiefs in native courts, begun under the 1927 Native Administration Act, was
greatly expanded. Chiefs, for example, could now retain a portion of the fines
they levied; and, crucially, they were central to the implementation of a new
battery of betterment legislation. Finally, there were various other state incentives for chiefs to accept the new system, including the offer of extra arable
land.[32]

Apartheid, therefore, was retribalization on a grand scale, in which chiefs
were central to the new system of government. Bantu affairs commissioners
created the "pedestal" upon which chiefs and paramounts sat.[33] The ethnological section of the NAD expended great energy collecting ethnographic information, assembling chiefly genealogies, and demarcating "tribal" boundaries.
When "questions of hereditary succession arose" the NAD's "ethnology section
devoted itself to investigations of royal pedigree."[34] In some areas it became necessary to "to create a chieftainship."[35] At the same time the state was more than
willing to overlook its own research for reasons of political expediency. This
became very obvious in the protracted conflict between the Thembu paramount
Sabata Dalindyebo and Chief Kaiser Matanzima. Sabata enjoyed considerable
popular support and, while he rejected the state's new policies, nonetheless

remained interested in expanding his power. Much more willing to throw in his lot with apartheid, Matanzima used the considerable resources of the state and its new policies to his advantage. Ultimately officials pursued expediency. In order to implement Bantu Authorities, it became imperative to have the "Paramount Chief's influence . . . removed."[36]

Patrimonialism is uniquely suited to corruption and tyranny because the decline of "communal integration" takes place at the same time patrimons have greater control over the distribution of state largesse and power. What was striking about the 1950s was not only the scale of retribalization and the extraordinary resources the state contributed to its new policies, but, crucially, that retribalization became an absolutely central feature of authoritarianism. The entire edifice of state rule and regulation rested on "traditional authorities." Rule by "decree" had begun with the 1927 Native Administration Act, legislation that had also empowered officials to invent tribes. In the 1950s, however, the state began embarking on a level of intervention never before experienced. Chiefs and headmen became the central agents for implementing and enforcing state policies that ranged from land and stock management to the introduction of Bantu Authorities. As one subaltern text put it, clearly establishing both the absence of any communal integration and the fact that Africans had been transformed as subjects of supposed traditional rule, "You gave us Kaizer so that he must kill us."[37]

Chiefs did not automatically agree or comply with the state's new policies. In Lusikisiki the headman and the secretary of the tribal authority participated in the 1960 Pondoland Revolt;[38] and in 1961 at a meeting with the paramount some 1,000 Thembu chiefs criticized the state's rehabilitation policies. But most of those recognized chiefs found themselves caught between two perils: not cooperating with the state – with the inevitable result of the loss of office and income – and collaboration, which brought substantial material rewards but also the prospect of popular resentment. Most chose the latter. In the context of extraordinary poverty the material temptations the state proffered were hard to turn down, and access to the quite considerable power of the state was seductive.

There was thus a concerted effort on the part of officials, on one hand, to recreate an African tribalism and, on the other hand, of some Africans to amass power and participate in the authoritarian state. In 1958, for example, the chief native commissioner for the Transkei wrote that in Pondoland his "main pre-occupation . . . has been to restore and rejuvenate the prestige of Paramount Chief Botha Sigcau and the allegiance of the loosely-knit clans to him."[39] This was especially difficult since many believed that the "rightful" paramount was Nelson, not Botha.[40] The official, Ramsay, had earlier headed the first Central Labour Bureau, created in 1953 with the "task of rationalizing and centralizing information" on the state's African subjects.[41] An accomplished and dedicated social engineer, Ramsay nonetheless appreciated some of the complexities of

African society and was well aware of the artificiality of the state's retribalization. "Most of these clans," he wrote, "were not originally Pondos but 'brought
themselves in' during the upheavals in Natal during the last century . . . These
imported clans came in under their own chiefs, who until now have not been
recognised and were merely headmen of their locations."[42]

Ramsay faced a twofold challenge in somehow engineering a system in which
ethnicity conformed with administrative space. On one hand he hoped to make
these "imported clans" more "Pondo," in an important sense to erase difference.
On the other hand he sought to create a system of centralized rule, centered on
paramount chiefs, that simply had not previously existed. The official knew that
the "Paramount Chief was a distant, never-felt entity." Indeed, most chiefs "did
not admit any right on his part to interfere with their local affairs."[43] Yet this
was precisely what the Bantu Authorities system was introducing, a system of
rule in which paramount chiefs had greatly enhanced powers.

Local architects of apartheid such as Ramsay ultimately reawakened a classic
issue in the political history of the region, albeit in a radically new way. A feature
of precolonial politics had been the attempts by chiefs to expand their power and
of paramounts to extend their control over outlying chiefdoms. Those attempts,
as we saw in the first chapter, typically failed. Neither the Transkei nor the
Ciskei saw the emergence of a centralized state in the precolonial period. The
district remained the largest enduring political unit. Apartheid in a quite basic
way returned to this classic pattern but now, of course, in the context of a
centralized modern industrial state. With Bantu Authorities paramounts began
attempting to amass and extend power by controlling appointments to the new
state structures, by receiving and redistributing monies from the state, and by
collecting fines. The state drew up plans for enlarging the "grazing area for
royal herds" as "an extension of royal power."[44] Judicial appeals were now to
be heard at the Great Places of the various paramount chiefs. More generally
the judicial system became more centralized; for example, the introduction of
Bantu Authorities entailed the abolition of the small, local headmen's courts.
This meant, among other things, that litigants had to travel much further to
attend cases.[45]

People often concluded that under the Bantu Authorities system individual
locations lost their political voice and, ultimately, control over their communities. Certainly, corruption increased dramatically. The collection of court fees
and other fines by paramounts quickly led "to abuse."[46] Chiefs were "open
to bribery," extortion, and other malfeasance.[47] There was, quite simply, an
explosion of "corruption" that was "deeply resented by the tribesmen."[48]

One important official responsible for introducing apartheid wrote that chiefs
had once simply "paid" the paramount "lip service." With the "essential incur-
sion of" Bantu Authorities, however, "matters became different."[49] Sigcau, for
example, had at his disposal the power to help reorganize much of Pondoland

into the various tribal authorities as provided under the Bantu Authorities Act. According to the official the paramount "recommended Head (of tribal authorities) and appointed members without in any way consulting the people concerned." He split up clans and, at least in one case, "recommended a commoner as head of a tribal authority where there was a chief."[50] Not surprisingly, the situation very quickly became volatile. In the case of one tribal authority the official intervened, but the situation remained extremely tense and helped lead, in 1960, to the outbreak of the Pondoland Revolt.

The situation was especially acute in places like Lambasi, an area comprising some 32,000 morgen with "approximately 185 kraals." Crucially, the "residents were there" on the sufferance of the paramount chief and did not have "the right of tenure of the residents of an ordinary location in the Transkei. Many of them were stock thieves, many of them Zulus, some Basutos, Bacas and Hlubes [sic]." Moreover, "many had obtained rights of residence illegally during Sigwebo's headmanship."[51] In other words, Lambasi had continued the historic pattern of being both a frontier area and central to royal power. Under Bantu Authorities, the paramount attempted to extend his power, especially in Lambasi, in part by claiming large amounts of land for grazing his "royal herds." To do so, however, was to "expect resistance."[52] In fact, by 1957, just after the introduction of Bantu Authorities, people began making public declarations of resistance. Throughout these years many "felt that Chief Botha was selling our country, so that it no longer belonged to us, and you are going to be paid for the sale."[53] When, for example, the chief tried to persuade people to accept rehabilitation in 1958, he "had to run away as there was violence."[54]

In Pondoland, and indeed elsewhere in the Eastern Cape, the state was well aware of the fictitiousness of its new ethnic policies. In Bizana district, for example, there were "tribesmen of non-Pondo origin" who had "occupied a homogeneous area and had preserved its identity intact." "Some of them have in the past not given complete loyalty to the Paramount Chief of Eastern Pondoland who, in common with his predecessors, rarely visited their areas." The result was simply that "they look upon him as someone nebulous."[55] Bantu Authorities changed all of this because it involved the growth and extension of chiefly power, especially that of paramount chiefs. In Bizana district alone the state created no less than eight different tribal authorities. "In an endeavor to link the people ... more closely with the Paramount Chief" the state appointed seven sub-chiefs to head them. These were all "installed by the Paramount Chief."[56]

As the official put it, "When tribal authorities were being established ... the clannishness referred to showed strongly ... in almost every case each clan wanted its own tribal authority."[57] The situation in Bizana, and indeed elsewhere in the Eastern Cape, was not so much that of parochialism, but rather arose out of concern with the growth of paramounts' power and the increasingly competitive politics that Bantu Authorities ushered in. For members from these seemingly clannish communities were in fact holding mountain meetings to organize large-scale resistance against Bantu Authorities. They were identifying those supporters of tribal authorities who were to be burned out, and they were collecting money for the employment of attorneys.

We will begin exploring resistance to Bantu Authorities shortly. Suffice it to state here that the local tribal authorities represented the linchpin of the entire Bantu Authorities system, the central point at which rule was being transformed and, importantly, the crucial intersection of retribalization and development. As the chief official in the Transkei put it in mid-1960, "we have reached the stage where we have satisfied the Chiefs and their satellites that these authorities will work. As paid administrators of their people they have everything to gain and little to lose." But "we have not always satisfied the commoner that the authorities are for his benefit as well. It is difficult for him to see that there are mutual benefits available for the Chief" and commoner alike. "He feels, very often, that the Chiefs and Councillors are paid Government servants, while he, the taxpayer, is receiving little or no benefit from the 'New Order'."[58] Perhaps the "greatest objection" to Bantu Authorities centered on the "granting of jurisdiction and considerable authority to the Chiefs," particularly in the tribal authority courts.[59]

Indeed. Despite knowing its unpopularity, officials remained steadfast in their determination to introduce the "new order." In many areas of the Eastern Cape people correctly associated Bantu Authorities with the advent of authoritarian rule. Even in areas that accepted Bantu Authorities, a significant portion of the local population was typically "not prepared to commit themselves."[60] The new government, put simply, was one that did "not believe in consultation."[61] Bantu Authorities had been "thrown into their midst."[62] With Bantu Authorities "too much authority has been vested in those in power . . . The Pondos . . . had not appointed the Paramount Chief – he was appointed by the Government."[63] Chiefs "seem to associate very much more with police men than they ever did before."[64] This was an astute observation. In the late 1950s, and especially with the 1960 Pondoland Revolt, chiefs supporting apartheid not only asked the state for guns but requested that the "licenses of all persons who possess firearms . . . should be cancelled."[65] They also wanted "the powers that the Police possess" and assistance from the Special Branch of the South African Police. In short, chiefs should, as Matanzima argued, "be permitted to suppress any rising and thereby nip any trouble in the bud."[66]

Or as one person put it in 1960, neatly summarizing the rise of patrimonialism:

Paramount Chief Botha Sigcau is very loyal to the Government, but he has lost contact with the tribe. The motor car has spoilt him. He used to come to the village years ago with approximately 400 tribesmen. That does not happen now. If he installed a Headman, he would spend the night there. Now he arrives in his car for the installation, takes the meat given to him, and leaves.[67]

Spoilt indeed. Never before did so few have access to so much. With Bantu Authorities the entire edifice of rule was reworked and tribalism, in effect, became ever more bureaucratized. The "new order" represented a fundamental reorganization of political society and the creation of an authoritarian tribal order. Bantu Authorities, however, constituted only one, admittedly crucial, part of a broader set of political and institutional changes that ushered in the authoritarianism that was apartheid.

A striking feature of the Bantu Authorities Act and the Bantu Laws Amendment Act was the extraordinarily wide range of issues they addressed, from authorizing chiefs to levy taxes to prohibiting African worship in European churches. Equally striking was the centrality of economic intervention and management. Both laws created three-tiered pyramidical structures, the first to reorganize the system of rule, the Bantu Laws Amendment Act to control African labor. The latter act created a "system of 'local', 'district', and regional labour bureaux" that entailed a reworking of the pass system and the rise on the part of the state of a far more disciplined system of influx control.[68] "All work-seekers were required," according to Posel, "to register, so that the local labour bureaux would have the information and control necessary to ensure that migrant workers were not taken on until local labour had been used up."[69] The Central Reference Bureau was, as Ramsay noted, "virtually the Bureau of Census and Statistics for Natives."[70] These changes occurred alongside others relating to labor, for example the 1952 Native (Abolition of Passes and Co-ordination of Documents) Act which greatly increased the state's control over the black working class.

The rivers of retribalization and economic control and labor regulation thus began coursing together in the 1950s. The decade, however, saw not only increasingly control of and surveillance over migrant labor but also the introduction of vast new schemes aimed at shoring up the collapsing reserve economies. In a now classic article Wolpe argued that a defining feature of apartheid centered on the attempt to reconstruct the reserves to maintain their functional relationship to the major industrial centers of the country.[71] While the argument suffers from excessive reductionism, many of its major points remain true. Just before the introduction of the Bantu Authorities Act the South African government issued the Tomlinson Commission report. The report's charge was to investigate the reserve economies and to recommend to government policies that would reverse spiraling poverty and economic involution. The report represented part of a genealogy of government interest and intervention in the reserve economies going back, for example, to the 1930 Native Economic Commission that had influenced legislation such as the 1939 Betterment Act. The report recommended a vast program of social engineering in the reserves bankrolled by some £104.5 million in government funding. It outlined policies to increase employment within the reserves, attract white investment, promote the formation and growth of an African bourgeoisie, and create an industrial base in these impoverished rural areas. At the same time the report set out "a comprehensive revitalization programme . . . involving the revision of communal land and the introduction of freehold title in order to promote a class of capitalistically oriented peasants," while "non-farmers" would be "transferred to urban settlements where they would be employed by the expansion of industry."[72]

The idea of industrializing the reserves represented a radical departure in government policy. Much of the commission's report, however, continued policies elaborated in the 1920s, 1930s, and 1940s, as officials became increasingly alarmed with the scale of African poverty and ecological degradation. The 1943 Social and Economic Planning Council report, for example, had raised these issues, as had other government studies. What was new in the 1950s was the very scale of the proposals, their fusing of tribalization and economic management, and the capacity of the state to make them a reality, even in the face of protracted African resistance. As it turned out, the National Party government rejected a number of the Tomlinson Commission report's proposals, and severely modified others. The state backpedaled on initiatives to attract white capital and pursued the industrialization of the reserves at best fitfully. It also rejected the commission's funding estimates, paring down the figure of £104.5 million by two-thirds.

The National Party thus for the most part rejected any progressive recommendations contained in the Tomlinson Commission report, opting instead for what the party considered to be the minimal requirements for maintaining control over the reserves and continuing the economic exploitation of the people living in them. At the same time, in legislation such as the 1958 Taxation and Development Act, the state shifted the burden of funding its plans for economically reconstructing the reserves to the African population; indeed, in 1959 there was a big push to collect taxes which included collection "tours" throughout the reserves.[73] By this time, with Verwoerd at the head of government, the state had committed itself to reworking the political economy of the reserves within the narrow parameters it had set. "Rehabilitation" of the homelands, wrote the chief magistrate of the Transkei in 1960, was "priority No. 1."[74]

That population, as we know, could scarcely bankroll the apartheid state's grand plans; indeed, the population had few resources to provide for the most basic of needs. The Eastern Cape had one of the densest rural populations in Africa. Poverty was widespread. Population densities far exceeded those of Kenya or even Lesotho. One report described the Transkei as "an urban country."[75] In 1948 a state research officer wrote that the "land is restricted, population is far more dense [than white areas], every ploughable piece of ground is turned over for human food production; the veld is stocked to its maximum, and the soils are hopelessly unstable."[76] In the area around Queenstown the situation remained "very bad." So dense was the population and so desperate their economic misfortune that people were "ploughing over all the flats and up the steep slopes into the mountains."[77]

Such was the scene across much of the Eastern Cape. Virtually every part of the region depended heavily on migrant-labor remittances; indeed, in many places this had been the pattern since the early part of the century. Population growth and agricultural production were moving "in opposite directions." The "food supply position of the people" had "markedly deteriorated." "Most cows give no milk for human consumption," so that even households who maintained "fairly large herds of cattle ... nevertheless have no milk for domestic usage." In the Transkei, in excess of "40% of all native families own no cattle." Livestock mortality was unusually high, with many animals perishing from "thirst and starvation." The distribution of livestock ownership was highly skewed. In one area, for example, 0.3% of stock owners possessed 70% of the sheep and half of the cattle. Upwards of 60% of households owned no stock whatsoever. So dire was the situation for the great majority of people that much of the population was "malnourished," and, in the months just before harvest, "many people ... especially children" were "starving."[78]

Landlessness, of course, had long been a problem. In the 1950s it reached a level never before experienced. With the rise of urban influx control and relocation a sizable class of people who were either landless, or virtually so, came to distinguish communities throughout the Eastern Cape. Many grown men essentially lived at their father's homes when they were not working on the mines or in other forms of urban employment. At the same time, older men struggled, and it seems increasingly failed, to maintain access to the bulk of wages earned by their sons. By the 1940s, in some areas perhaps even before, earlier practices aimed at socializing the youth about sexuality, while still prohibiting and preventing vaginal intercourse, began to collapse. Illegitimacy skyrocketed. Men and women simply bypassed customary initiation ceremonies, eloped without paying bride-wealth, and struggled to establish households independent of the control of their families.[79]

After the Second World War the state had begun a five-pronged assault on the reserves aimed at preventing further soil erosion and improving agriculture, and reducing the numbers and improving the quality of livestock. The state began, as it always had, with map and census, the first two prongs of the assault. In the 1950s agricultural demonstrators began erecting land beacons prior to introducing betterment measures such as contour farming that, in many areas, reworked the allocation of land. Land registers had existed before, "but registrations had not been effected for many years."[80] The new policies introduced in the 1950s attempted to reverse this administrative "drift."[81] The state increased its surveillance of land allocation and of livestock numbers. At the same time it submitted the rural population to a battery of censuses. The state's effort to count people accelerated in the decade and received a final push in 1960;[82]

censuses were widely resisted and became an important part of the grievances behind the Pondoland Revolt.[83]

As the state began collecting and codifying this information it pursued three additional areas of intervention. First, in the name of stabilization it began moving people and relocating them on so-called Trust lands that had been established in the 1930s with the 1936 Native Trust and Land Act. Second, the state tightened up considerably its control over the movement of livestock in the hope of preventing overgrazing. Finally, it set out to reduce the numbers of livestock through culling. All of this – maps, censuses, and a plethora of measures to improve agriculture and livestock – cost a great detail and required considerable labor. To meet these needs the state increased taxation and began commandeering labor to build fences, dams, and the material edifice of betterment.

"Kill us once more"

In the past, officials noted, Africans often did not observe colonial "land regulations" and headmen "allotted arable land and kraalsites to people regardless of the regulations . . . there has been general laxity in all administration."[84] This "laxity" had allowed, for example, considerable settlement on lands deemed by the state as commonage. For years people had expanded agriculture by having "little lands" "tucked away in the hills."[85] In the 1920s the state began attempting to reduce these "little lands" and adding them to commonages.[86] These efforts often ended in frustration. In the context of exploding poverty Africans continued settling on commonages, and, whenever possible, sought additional arable lands.

After the end of the Second World War, however, and particularly in the 1950s, the state exerted renewed effort to close these possibilities and to more systematically implement its development plans for the reserves. In August 1945, to take just one example, it began a concerted action against residents in one location who were refusing to be relocated from Mount Currie district to farms owned by the South African Native Trust in neighboring Matatiele. At their new location, however, they found their stock being impounded and, in addition, "they did not like the way in which they were being instructed to plough their lands by the Agricultural Officer."[87] The rules and regulations were "unbearable."[88] "We do not want Trust property and their regulations."

If a man dies the wife and family are told to leave and their land and kraal site are confiscated. The family of a dead husband and wife are told to go where they like. That is after the death of both parents. If this heir is a single man he is told to leave. He is considered a child if he is not married. This has happened at Makoba's [new] location . . . These children of these families live anywhere all over. Their kraalsites and lands have been reallocated.

Their lands in the new location were much smaller. Moreover, their new arable lands, located some distance from their kraals, were fenced; so also were their grazing areas.[89]

> The difference in living at New Makoba's Location to that in Old Makoba's Location is that the allotment of lands and kraal sites is now in the hands of the Agricultural Officers[;] the Headman has no power whatsoever. We also object to being told to plough our lands in certain ways and to graze our stock at different places ... That is why we feel there has been no exchange of ground, because we are not living under the same conditions.[90]

Some refused to move to the new location and, in October 1945, "as an act of defiance" people began ploughing.[91] Others soon returned to "rebuild" the old location. It was, they said, "their ground and they were willing to die" to defend it. The state did not relent. In 1946 the men ended up in court where they faced prosecution under the Native Administration Act of 1927. The struggle did not end there, however. Later in the year the conflict collapsed in bloodshed between the state and location residents who were rebuilding their homes. "I spoke to these natives," stated a member of the South African Police, and told them "that they were trespassing on property that was [now] Trust property." He then "informed them that I was arresting them for trespassing." The men became angry and "armed themselves ... Some of them pointed at their foreheads saying that they can shoot them there today." At this point the police retreated and subsequently phoned the district commandant for further instruction. The commandant instructed the police to arrest the men "at any cost." That cost, in violence that erupted later the same day, was four lives.[92]

The struggle did not stop in a brief moment of gunshot. The movement's leader and head of what came to be known as the Makoba Council, Alois Mate, wrote to the minister of justice in May 1946 of their intention in October to "erect our kraals in the old Makoba Location." "On that date," he said, "you may again send your constables and kill us once more."[93] The government stood its ground. "Is our blood of no spiritual feeling to the Government," wrote Mate in 1950, "or there is no government for the orphans and poor, because he shuts his ear not to hear, his eyes to see, his mouth not so speak to our complaints and requests."[94] In 1951 the state attempted to take a census of livestock in the location. The Makoba Council, however, had instructed residents not to allow stock to be counted. It "had issued instructions that nobody was to take stock to the count, and to ensure that these instructions were carried out they had posted their men along the roads to the dipping tanks with orders to kill anyone ... who was taking stock for counting." "As we passed along the road," wrote the official, "we observed several of these guards, armed with shields and sticks, and some of them also carried assegais."[95] At one stock-dipping tank,

I estimate the men at about 75 and the women at about 50. They hurled insults at me and my officers and swore at the officials. The women were dancing and singing a song about not bringing cattle for counting, while one man was conducting for the other men to sing a song they have compiled about returning to the old location. There was no stock there when we arrived . . . Members of "The Council" have informed the Agricultural Foreman that the stock will never go out of the gate; the officials may round it up but they will be killed before they drive it through the gates.[96]

Across the entire expanse of the Eastern Cape officials encountered similar examples of protracted, often violent, resistance against the state's betterment policies. Near Alice, for example, in 1950 location residents threatened Trust officials sent to repair and build dams. (The location had been declared a Trust area in 1948; a new wave of resistance began almost immediately.) In another incident, residents impolitely informed Trust officials that "if you put that Tractor to work here you will not see the day out we will kill you . . . Take your machines and fuck off."[97]

Resistance in this area continued for a number of years. It is clear from judicial and other records that from the beginning residents had complained about "the Trust," going back to 1939.[98] But in the 1950s the state remained utterly committed to implementing its policies. In 1952, an incident arose involving the erection of a fence, a common point of conflict elsewhere in the Eastern Cape.[99] A number of men (including his son) forced the headman, Alexander Ngwabeni, to confront the Europeans who, with a number of African workers, "were putting up the fence and to ask them why they were working there." The headman's son said, "We have brought our father to ask you on what authority you are working here." But when the headman clearly expressed his tepid lack of support, two of the resisters, one of whom was his son, struck him and knocked him unconscious.[100] The men also assaulted an African worker; at one point there was gunfire. The court records reveal not simply resistance against the state but also the local struggles over headmanship which pitted father against son. The headman later testified that "my son and I have been enemies since I returned from Umtata where I was a Policeman" and took over the headmanship from his son.[101]

Incidents similar to these occurred all over the Eastern Cape, particularly as the politics of retribalization joined those of development. This inevitably meant that headmen and chiefs became more and more central to implementing state policy. Cash incentives might be a helpful political lubricant, but accepting state monies for enforcing rehabilitation typically brought on the ire and rebuke of others living in the location.[102] There was considerable unrest, for example, in Tsomo in 1956 and 1957. In one incident a people attacked a police patrol. When the magistrate introduced the chief magistrate of the Transkei, who had arrived to discuss "stabilisation," he was "continually interrupted" by "jeers and boos." "Go away," people yelled. "We did not ask for you to come here. We do not want the Government on our locations. Later they yelled, "Let him go. We'll govern ourselves." They also "howled down" Chief Nkwenkwezi: "Who are you? We don't want any chiefs. You're just a Government Tool."[103]

When people condemned the Bantu Authorities system they at once condemned taxes, the passes, and the state's new betterment and rehabilitation policies. Taxes, increased twice in the 1950s, had "gone beyond" most people's "means."[104] Bantu Authorities

brought about the purchase of arable allotments, forest produce, thatch grass and kraal sites. It has encouraged free movement of women without the consent of their husbands, and the absconding of our sons. It has resulted in long delays in the hearing of our cases . . . rehabilitation . . . has caused many deaths. The land has always been stable by the act of God – there is no other God – that is going to create the land afresh.[105]

By middle of the 1950s many areas of the Transkei and Ciskei teetered on the edge of rebellion. At the top of the list of grievances was tribal authorities, followed by the stock rate, general levy, general tax, the installation of chiefs, allocation of land, court cases, territorial authority, agricultural shows, reference books, rehabilitation, and influx control – in other words the entire edifice of separate development. People accused tribal collaborators like Sigcau of "selling our country."[106] At this point people in various areas of the region "decided that all who are doing Govt. work should be attacked . . . if we want to fight the Bantu Authorities, we should kill the appointed members."[107] This is precisely what began to happen. From the middle of the decade headmen and others became the targets of assassination. In Willowvale in late 1958, for example, an attempt on the headman's life ended in the death of his brother. A group earlier had emerged to resist the state's rehabilitation schemes. There was much "propoganda [sic] . . . spread in secret amongst the residents"; on a number of occasions people had cut the location's boundary fence. The situation escalated in 1957 with the beginning of contour ploughing, a central feature of the state's plan to reconstruct the reserves economically. Fencing, however, remained the greatest complaint. Soon the faction that had been" "agitating against the erection of fences" had gathered "quite a following." There were meetings at night and a collection for money in case they needed to employ an attorney. As the situation deteriorated the men decided to hire a "tsotsi from East London to murder the headman and the subheadman" so that fencing would come to a stop.

The state began introducing its grand plans for retribalization and economic reform during an exceptional drought. In 1955–6, drought resulted in the "failure of at least 80% of the mealie crop. Unprecedented numbers of Bantu were compelled to leave" in search of incomes to support their families.[108] Incidents of disease, malnutrition, and infant mortality spiraled upward. People's control over their world seemed in inverse relationship to the government's acts to control ever more precisely where they lived, what they farmed, how they worked, where they moved. Collecting information had become an obsession of officials – white employees of the NAD as well as chiefs, headmen, and other collaborators – who submitted the colonized and their landscape to a new barrage of censuses, surveys, and other instruments of definition, surveillance, and control.

In very real ways, therefore, the introduction of apartheid represented a veritable reconquest of the region, reproducing in a new key many of the basic features of conquest that had unfolded in the nineteenth century. In that earlier period what in fact constituted the state was unclear, in part because Africans translated colonial political institutions and practices into indigenous grammars of power and authority. Even at its most despotic, the colonial state remained "blurry" precisely because it so depended on ostensibly traditional political models. This very blurring, however, meant that African resistance inevitably extended well beyond contesting discrete policies. Resistance was shaped by, and sustained, the historic conversation people had over the nature of power and the relationship between politics, fertility, and social health. People reasonably concluded that something was terribly wrong, that evil and mendacity had managed to triumph and, in so doing, had wrought misfortune and drought. To combat evil, to restore social health, to bring the rains entailed far more than simply protesting against the state's policies. It involved ridding the world of wickedness.

6   Conflict in Qumbu

The 1950s thus witnessed rising violence in both rural and urban areas of the country. Serious violence, for example, broke out East London during the 1952 Defiance Campaign, in which young men murdered and set on fire a white nun. Elsewhere in the country the second half of the decade saw bus boycotts, demonstrations, police arrests, and, at least in the Eastern Cape, an increasing number of African assaults on whites. The rolling tide of conflict breached both urban and rural areas. The region around the towns of Tsolo and Qumbu saw some of the most protracted and striking violence in this period, as various social tensions ranging from jealousy to landlessness became tied up with state formation and the rise of apartheid.

We have discussed this area in some detail in the first chapter, in the story of the death of Hamilton Hope at the hands of the Mpondomise chief Mhlontlo and the widespread African resistance to colonial conquest at the beginning of the 1880s. Even seventy years later people still felt that "the Government still holds Hope against us."[1] Certainly the Mpondomise paid dearly for the killing of a colonial official and a white man. Mhlontlo survived the conflict, but died a pauper in a community of paupers. Following the conflict, in which colonial troops killed a not inconsiderable number of people, destroyed crops, and confiscated cattle, the colonial state deposed chiefs, doubled the hut tax, disarmed men, and confiscated and redistributed land to loyal "Mfengu." In the early decades of the twentieth century there was violence that has been managed in the colonial archive as "tribal" conflict, mainly between those Bhele and Hlubi (typically referred to as "Mfengu") who did well out of colonial annexation and the Mpondomise, who suffered as a result of Hope's murder.[2]

While relatively far from the centers of organized political activity, the area has never been politically quiescent. Independent churches have been very active in the area around Qumbu village and in Sulenkama, the traditional seat of the Mpondomise paramount chief and the location of intense political discussions for over a century.[3] In the 1920s, Garveyite discourses powerfully shaped political conflict. During this time the ICU was active in the area. In the early 1950s the ANC held occasional meetings in Qumbu. More generally, throughout the twentieth century there has been near-constant conflict over a variety of rural "betterment" policies aimed at controlling livestock, allocating land and reorganizing rural space, and preventing soil erosion, and state policies aimed at reconstruction chiefly rule.[4]

These struggles have become inextricably tied up with the wider political economy of South Africa, and especially the poverty that characterizes so many rural areas in the country. Most importantly there has been the issue of land and the ability, or the inability, of households to produce sufficient food. The era following colonial annexation saw enormous differentiation and increasing landlessness. There have been fundamental shifts in the organization of land and in the settlement patterns of rural people. Disputes around land invariably became struggles over and commentaries on the organization of households, custom, the role of headmen, and, ultimately, the relationship between local political office and the colonial state.

Access to land declined precipitously in the twentieth century. The region has long been "very thickly populated"[5] and awash with complaints of landlessness and the specter of economic collapse.[6] By the 1920s people in Tsolo and Qumbu had long been relying on migrant labor to support their households. Younger males typically first migrated to the sugar plantations of Natal, then in subsequent years north to the diamond mines of Kimberley and to the Rand gold mines.[7] This participation in a wider economy had four major impacts on communities. First, and most obviously, was the increasing dependence of rural households on wages earned in faraway places. Not only did men migrate north in very substantial numbers, over the course of the twentieth century they remained away for longer and longer periods of time.[8]

Second, migrant labor increasingly became tied up with, and in turn reshaped, the dense web of ongoing disputes over land and authority. These disputes took place not only within locations but also between them, especially in the context of population pressure and closer patterns of settlement. Third, stock, and especially cattle, became more valued. Migrants typically converted a substantial percentage of their wages into cattle, a preserve of men. Storing wages in cattle allowed men to maintain, however insecurely, patriarchal control of the homestead even if they were only there for a few weeks each year.[9]

Last, there were important changes in how individuals and households managed, or failed to manage, participation in the wider economy. In addition to disputes over land, the twentieth century saw rising conflict between and among neighboring households, between husbands and wives, and between fathers and sons and youths and their elders.

These issues of landlessness and poverty, patriarchy and power, fortune and misfortune, very often inflamed feelings of envy. Why did one's child die when another's thrived? Why did some remain healthy while others fell to sickness, especially to the coughing and hacking that comes with tuberculosis and pneumonia? Why did some possess more property than others? How was it that the crops of one person withered on the stalk while another's stood green and strong in the African sun? Why did some men return home from the Rand with money in their pockets and commitment to their families, while others came back ruffians who had squandered their wages on booze, women, and cheap clothes?[10]

Envy and hatred could be expressed in many ways, including witchcraft accusations.[11] In Qumbu, "Witch 'Doctors'," wrote one official, "still carry on their nefarious practices and all classes of Natives believe in witchcraft." In nearby Bizana "witchcraft continues and is very difficult to deal with as the law Officers fail time and again to get evidence against those practicing it. The natives now take to burning out the accused persons instead of killing,"[12] which brought in the police and invited very stiff penalties for those convicted. While fire continued to be central to the struggle against witches, murder did not disappear. People might be killed for a range of reasons. In 1961, a man believed to be a witch had his homestead burned down. Then, on his way to church, a number of men stopped and killed him. One of the accused "hated the deceased." Indeed, "the deceased was so disliked in the locality." Another of the accused said that "now I have got the man I have been looking for who was killing my children."[13]

These patterns of stratification and conflict became ever more acute in the 1950s with the combination of spiraling poverty and landlessness, the economic recession (and drought) that began in 1956, and the state's influx-control measures which sent increasing numbers of Africans, especially men, back into the reserves. One of the results of these changes was an extraordinary rise in stock theft. For centuries pilfering stock has been a common feature of masculine identity and male politics throughout the Transkei, indeed, throughout much of Southern Africa. The deft seizure of beasts demonstrated one's prowess within the community. What happened in the 1950s, however, was altogether a different matter. By 1956, thieves were stealing hundreds of head of stock each month.[14] This epidemic of stock theft was no ordinary case of upstart young men demonstrating their masculinity within the community, an innocent raid on the unsuspecting. Stealing was one thing, robbery quite another. What was especially evident in the 1950s was that thieving had, in fact, become a way of life, occasionally even an occupation passed from father to son.[15] As members of Makhulu Span wrote to the resident magistrate of Qumbu, three years after the formation of the organization in late 1956,

In Qumbu . . . stock theft started in 1952 and by 1956 & 1957 . . . it had reached outrageous proportions. A large number of stock (both large and small stock) was removed every week from many locations. It became clear that thieves *not* [only] *stole in the old sense but robbed*, coming as they did by night, eight to ten armed men, awakening the kraalhead and telling him they had come to remove his stock and that he should defend it if he could. The frightened kraalhead would only be too pleased that his life had been spared.

Thieves were committed for trial but were acquitted through lawyers. In desperation, the people decided to punish them by burning their kraals. This move did not end stock theft but lessened its intensity considerably.[16]

Sometimes the thieves might leave a "letter at your door" telling the person that "he must not attempt to look for his stock because it has been taken by" the thieves. Those looking for their stock risked being murdered. Thieves bragged about their exploits and extorted money from people who wanted to avoid having their stock stolen. They also burned down kraals and huts, especially of those whom they thought might speak to the police.[17]

By 1956 stock theft had become "unprecedented." A number of thieves were among the most wealthy people in the region. The Tsolo School of Agriculture "lost about £2000 worth of stock in the last two years." In most cases "thieves either cannot be detected or escape conviction when prosecuted. The Qumbu criminal roll is so heavy that cases often are not concluded until months have elapsed from the first arraignment. The accused must be allowed on bail, and by the time the trial takes place witnesses have disappeared and good evidence has deteriorated."[18] The nocturnal and notorious outlaws of Tsolo and Qumbu reigned victorious. So confident were they that the robbers "constituted themselves into a sort of aristocracy which did not mix with lesser folk and at beer drinks would sit apart. They blatantly called themselves stock thieves."[19] According to the chief colonial official in the Transkei,

The cult of the rural "Tsotsi" [thugs, gangs, derived from zoot suit] has become so acute that many *parents and other adults* are now afraid of them. *It is an unheard of occurrence for boys to attack men.* Many influential Natives . . . tell me that *many boys evade or postpone circumcision which will convert them into men and so preclude their associating with the gangs.*[20]

"These young men have no respect now," testified one man. "We are today being ruled by this element."[21]

Thieves usually referred to themselves as the "Nephews" (*abatshana*; also *abafana bomoya*: "young men of the wind").[22] So also did those who persecuted them. This deployment of kinship terminology points to the importance of masculinity, generational tensions, and kin disputes in struggles over stock and theft. The Mpondomise and most other patrilineal peoples in Southern Africa have privileged a male's relationship to his uncle's family on his mother's side. On the one hand, this relationship comprised an important and distinct domain within which male youths tested and learned about the boundaries of civil conduct and respect in a way that extended beyond the orthodox and more obviously charged patrilineal politics and sanctions of the homestead. On the other, a nephew's connections with his mother's brothers were far less formalized than agnatic relations. These relations allowed for a far wider range of behavior than would be acceptable to a male's father and his family. Nephews could be disobedient, for example by being impudent or by making selfish demands on the resources of the uncle's household. As one man told me, a nephew "could get anything" he "demanded or asked for."[23]

In the 1950s many people believed that young men willfully and permanently transgressed the boundaries of community. They were, in effect, out of control, a society of impudent, lawless nephews. The thieves of Tsolo and Qumbu in effect engaged in the invention of new kinds of community that were for many others in direct conflict with conventional society. Thieves were "known by their balaclava caps and great-coats."[24] They deployed commodities and symbols associated with urban *tsotsi* and migrant-worker culture. The Nephews bear close relation to rural *indlavini* male gangs in Pondoland and in the area around Mount Frere. Both groups adapted and modified older forms of social organization in ways that allowed them to flout the authority of senior men in the community, in many cases even their own fathers. In the past males had participated in groups that provided ways of learning about, and controlling, sexuality. *Indlavini* groups, on the other hand, engaged in acts of sexual bravado and predation that left "respectable" people aghast. In many areas migrants participated in complex rituals that reaffirmed their responsibility to the household and to the ancestors. The Nephews, composed largely of people deeply entwined in South Africa's migrant labor system, effectively ruptured the social organization of migrancy that had become central to the economic life of the household.[25]

Oral evidence makes it clear that migrant labor and urban living were important parts of the thieves' world. The movement of pilfered stock out of the area followed precisely the same paths that migrant laborers took to the mines. Yet instead of using incomes generated by migrant labor to acquire land and establish rural households, the Nephews stopped migrating and instead came to depend largely on theft of stock. The thieves, these "urban boys," "didn't plough."[26] Instead, they used the money generated by theft to hold huge parties called *tshawe* or *spolo*, which one man defined as "to be free" or "to connect themselves freely." Both married and unmarried men and women, "loose and free" people, attended *spolo*. One informant described the females who attended these parties as "girls" and women who had "deserted from their kraal," by which he meant unmarried females and women who had left their husbands. In addition to drinking, eating, conversation, and love-making, competition was at the center of *spolo*. On the one hand, success was measured by *ifashion* – that is, by wearing the most popular township clothes. On the other hand, masculinity and gift-giving became inextricably linked. It was important to be decked out in the latest fashions and to lavish gifts on the women one desired; men would "steal rather than appear poor in the eyes of their girlfriends."[27]

What had thus emerged by the middle of the 1950s was a kind of aristocracy of thugs whose predations, flouting of authority, lasciviousness, and lavish consumption of food and drink in an area of deep poverty sowed conflict and exacerbated an already volatile situation. They seemed, moreover, somehow immune from prosecution, above the law. Indeed, while we know virtually

nothing about how thieves viewed the magical world of their nocturnal exploits, we do know that they had their own ritual specialists who "doctored"
them so that they would succeed in their pilfering and would be untouched
by the legal system of the whites. Given the widespread belief in magic it is
reasonable to conjecture that many people would have perceived thieves as
having access to and use of malevolent magic. In addition to secreting paper
into the domestic space of the household, thieves typically attacked homesteads
in the dark of night. This was especially outrageous because people were supposed to be indoors safely, enjoying the comforts of their abode. The night
was the time when witches did their evil work, when cold zombies walked the
land. People sought the safety of their homes precisely to protect themselves
from malefic beings. To attack at night, to sow evil and conflict under cover of
darkness, was at best commune to with witches and, at worst, actually to be a
witch.[28]

Makhulu Span officially emerged in the closing days of 1956.[29] Initially
residents living in a number of neighboring locations formed "committees"
representing the *ibandla*. People had often used the term to describe those who
acknowledged the authority of a chief. This changed in the twentieth century,
however, as chiefs increasingly became functionaries of the state and people
looked for new ways to ensure social health in the context of rising poverty. Now
ibandla applied to the religious congregation of Zionist churches, a community
of the faithful who very often saw themselves as members of a black nation. In
the case of Makhulu Span, however, it took on yet another meaning, representing
the moral community of a number of contiguous locations.

The first Makhulu Span attacks on the Nephews may have taken place in the
light of day, though these may have been largely spontaneous revolts against
thieves. A hundred people or more might descend on the homesteads of robbers.
Their stock and property would be confiscated, the people driven from their
homes, and their kraals and huts set on fire. Typically stock was redistributed
among the locations, then slaughtered and eaten. Once dispossessed, thieves
fled the area and, in many cases, attempted to seek safety within the locations
of other comrades in crime. Nephews thus deployed a complex web of social
relations and corporate networks that grew out of migrant labor and older forms
of male association, but which now were sustained by robbery and affirmed in
ritual and social practice.[30]

The leaders of Makhulu Span were "honest people of good record" who
wanted to put a stop to stock theft.[31] Residents of a particular location elected a
committee member, a fully constituted committee representing seven or more
locations. Each committee was organized around the judge, secretaries, and
treasurers who took note of proceedings and collected dues that could be used in
hiring lawyers. Most committees later appointed their own constable, detective,

prosecutor, attorney, in addition to the "Judge of [the] people." Committees kept very precise written information that recorded not only the amount to be paid by those convicted before the courts of Makhulu Span, but also the names and amount of those who subscribed to the organization.[32]

The blowing of a whistle or the ringing of a bell indicated that the "Court of the 'mbandla' [*ibandla*]" was about to meet. Trials typically took place on hilltops from seven to eleven in the evening. Committee members seated themselves in a semi-circle. The spatial organization of the committee quite closely mimicked the meetings of headmen and chiefs. Most committee members, who were always male and like their enemies had participated in migrant labor to the mines, were in their thirties, with ages ranging from twenty-five to sixty. By the time the accused, who had been summoned to appear before the court, had made his appearance one hundred or more people might have gathered to hear the proceedings. The presence of so many people provided Makhulu Span with an air of popular legitimacy. With the accused standing before Makhulu Span, a member of the committee announced the charges. The accused was then asked to respond to them. He was then beaten and forced to provide stock and/or cash equivalent to the property he was alleged to have stolen. The accused also paid money for court fees and money and stock to "cleanse" his name of the evil he had perpetrated. The burning of huts followed the trial and conviction of thieves; the group also began murdering suspected robbers.[33]

Sitata Nontso, a secretary of one of the Makhulu Span committees, described the institutional architecture of the organization. Note the discipline and organization of Makhulu Span, its emphasis on writing and on purification, and the importance of appearing as a legitimate authority in the community.

I was once instructed to carry my books to the meeting . . . *In these books I was required to make entries of* [the] *subscription fees paid by various persons . . . I also kept a record of payments made by the stock thieves for the cleansing of their names* . . . These bigger amounts had been paid by stock thieves for the *purpose of cleansing their names*. A total amount of £78–15/- was collected at the various meetings . . . It had been decided by the committee that a fund should be available in the event of any member of the committee becoming involved in any prosecution . . . *The committee gave the appearance of being a lawful authority* . . . The original meeting referred to by me was called with a view to putting an end to the stock thieving that was prevalent. At this meeting the stock thieves undertook to restore possession to the rightful owners of the animals . . . I am unable to say whether the committee members would be assaulted and fined by *the community if they failed to carry out their mandate from the people*. The subscriptions in the sum of 2/6d. were given voluntarily by the persons concerned.[34]

These were deeply gendercd and violent spectacles of men trying men before the community. Mile Sejossing, a member of the audience, recounted the case of Sibute Tamako, who "was alleged to be a thief" and who was tried before the committee on the same day when Natives Duma and Dasi paid their fines in the sum of £10-each. He was alleged to have stolen sheep . . . He denied having stolen these animals. He was then assaulted. He was beaten with a stick across his buttocks . . . After he had been beaten several time[s] he stood up pleading for mercy. He still denied any knowledge of the animals in question. He was ordered to lie on the ground and was again assaulted. He continued to deny any knowledge of the sheep and lamb. On a whistle being blown by a member of the committee, all members at the meeting would be required to stand up and await further instructions from the committee. The committee instructed that on the whistle being blown the 4th. time, all persons present should strike Sibute Tamako. When the whistle had been blown the 2nd, time, a certain Native . . . stood up and requested to be allowed to speak to Sibute. He was allowed to do so . . . The latter [Tamako] then admitted the theft of the sheep and lamb. He offered to pay a sum of £12-as compensation for the theft of the 5 sheep and the lamb. He also offered to produce a beast for the purpose of cleansing his name.

What is striking about Sejossing's statement is that, having been in the audience during the court's proceedings, he was subsequently tried and convicted by Makhulu Span. Like Tamako, Sejossing denied having stolen stock. He was forced to remove his trousers and was assaulted by the committee. He "then admitted the theft of the animals . . . for the sole reason that I was being assaulted."[35]

It is difficult to discern whether those who denied having stolen stock were, in fact, innocent. In some instances it is clear that such denials were disingenuous. It seems clear, however, that Makhulu Span did not only punish people whose guilt was unequivocal.[36] Certainly Sejossing's statement raises a number of important issues. First, participants in Makhulu Span trials also became its victims. There is the possibility that stock thieves were not only brought before the courts but were close observers of its proceedings, if not simply because not attending the meetings was seen by others as evidence that they were one of the Nephews. The very people who brazenly attacked homesteads and pilfered stock also may have watched, and indeed participated in, the proceedings of Makhulu Span.

Second, some of the people who burned down homesteads did so out of fear. Lagamfula Gwazilitye, a victim of the burnings who had, in fact, been charged with stock theft in the magistrate's court, described how "a great friend of mine" informed him that his homestead was to be destroyed. Some two hundred people participated in this incident of incendiarism, including his "great friend." Following the burnings Gwazilitye and his companion remained "on friendly terms in spite of the fact that he burnt me out. He told me he was compelled to do so."[37]

People participated in the trials and the burnings either because of direct threats or because they believed that by not doing so they would themselves fall victim to Makhulu Span. Each man of the location "was supposed to be a member" of the organization. If not, he was "threatened"; Makhulu Span "would come back to them."[38] Wilson Sitemela described how he had been "called upon" to pay his "contribution" which he also described as a "protection fee." By becoming a member of the "committee" Sitemela meant that his due allowed him to participate in the proceedings as an observer, not as a member of the court. He then witnessed the trial, conviction, and beating of two of his paternal uncles, one of whom he described as a stock thief and the other as a suspected thief.

Sitemela added that "any person defaulting on his contribution was warned or threatened with assault."[39] Failing to pay one's contribution meant that the person "would no longer be recognised as a member of the Ibandla,"[40] that he stood outside and in opposition to the community. In fact, people who failed to pay their contributions to the committee, neglected to carry their spears, or failed to attend meetings of Makhulu Span were subsequently brought before the court. They received much the same treatment as stock thieves.[41]

Even those members of the committee who failed to whip victims with suffi-cient severity were themselves beaten. Indeed, the court sessions became mass trials, wherein all sorts of people – from stock thieves to people who for one reason of another did not want to participate in the trials; from those involved in land disputes to committee members themselves – appeared before Makhulu Span.[42] From the beginning the courts developed a number of authoritarian proclivities that had little direct bearing on larceny.

By March 1957, just a few months after its formation, Makhulu Span had burned down as many as four hundred huts in Qumbu and one hundred huts in Tsolo. The Nephews did not take lightly to the actions of Makhulu Span. Their nocturnal predations and arson continued. The entire area was described as being literally on fire. There is a sense in the records, and in oral testimony, of a fabulous, almost surreal war of the night, much of it organized around writing and the circulation of written texts, a storm of violence that engulfed the region in robbery and retribution, fire and magic.[43] Both the court proceedings and the incendiarism that illuminated the night skies of Tsolo and Qumbu were elaborate theaters, perhaps more accurately newly invented rituals, that concerned authority and community, purity and pollution, cattle sacrifice and morality, mendacity and masculinity, the night battles of men and their magic.

The evidence relating to Makhulu Span and witchcraft is tantalizing if in-complete. We know that witchcraft had been a constant issue, an indissoluble feature of social life for the great majority of people living in the region. We know also that poverty and misfortune on the one hand, and accumulation on the other, often inflamed jealousy and hatred and could lead to accusations of the evil use of magic. Witchcraft might afflict the individual but it destroys the community. It is also clear that the Makhulu Span movement did not primarily focus on the issue of the violation of individual rights. Rather, it concentrated on healing the open wounds of the community. It did so by chasing deviants away as well as reincorporating those who had violated the norms and expectations of the *ibandla*, a moral community that, ultimately, had its ancient origins in the beginnings of chiefship.

Finally, the issue of fire is unmistakable. Fire, of course, is a practical way to destroy something or someone. However, given the large numbers of people involved there were other ways to destroy huts swiftly and effectively. The question of practicality, moreover, cannot be easily separated from the symbolic import of people's actions, as if rational choice remained immune from concept and culture. Makhulu Span remained thoroughly committed to the use of fire, even when it was raining. We know that many people considered fire to be an important part of the arsenal combating witchcraft. It seems reasonable to conclude that many who participated in the activities of Makhulu Span may have perceived their struggle against thieves as similar to, or at least closely paralleling, ongoing community attempts to control and eradicate people who used magic to do harm.

In the spectacle of Makhulu Span we are reminded, moreover, of the subversive possibilities of mimicry and of the carnivalesque as quotidian.[44] The organization of Makhulu Span mirrored, and even mimicked, that of their enemies the Nephews and other forms of male organization in rural areas throughout the Eastern Cape. Nor was this all. Makhulu Span deployed discourses and practices associated with the chief's and headman's court; and, importantly, it appropriated categories and much of the institutional language and practice of the state. The trials became a kind of improvisational theater and ritual. They also became dramas which mocked collaborationist chiefs and headmen, and exposed the false legitimacy of the apartheid state by borrowing its emblems of law and order.

Makhulu Span and the apartheid state

Ultimately the violence of the 1950s resurrected events of almost a century earlier: the 1880 murder of Hope and the Mpondomise rebellion. The assassination had taken place at Sulenkama, the location of the Mpondomise paramountcy of Mhlontlo. Hope was killed at the hands of Mhlontlo and Mditshwa, the Mpondomise leader of Tsolo.[45] Colonial retribution had involved not only the confiscation of substantial lands and the introduction of a range of policies and practices such as tax collection that insinuated the state into the most intimate domains of the household, but also the destruction of Mpondomise chiefship. As elsewhere in the Eastern Cape, state-appointed headmen became the most important holders of political office.

Beginning in the 1930s, however, the state began to reconstitute the Mpondomise "traditional" order. In 1935 it recognized Chief Lutshoto as head of Tsolo district. Earlier, the state had accepted Isaac Matiwane as acting paramount. He sought to "wipe away" the blood of Hope. Certainly Matiwane cooperated with the introduction of betterment policies. His son, Sigidi, was less sympathetic to the authorities. In the early 1950s, for example, he criticized the implementation of betterment policies. In 1954, in a context of near rebellion, the government dismissed him. The pliant Isaac Matiwane returned as paramount according to the recently introduced Bantu Authorities Act. There were, however, constant "rumblings of discontent," especially at Sulenkama, "due to the dissatisfaction of the people with their being under the rule of descendents [*sic*] not of the direct Royal Line."[46]

Those who joined Makhulu Span associated the Nephews and their anti-social behavior with a political order that lacked popular legitimacy. Makhulu Span directed considerable energy to attacking chiefs, headmen, and others viewed as collaborating with the state. For example, headman Mpiyonke Quvile, of Tsolo, was "said to be one of the ring leaders of the stock thieves," but his powerful magic meant that "nothing can be proved against him." He was considered to be the "King of Thieves." But in 1958 this headman of roughly sixty years old feared for his life. Makhulu Span was out to get him. Quvile hired a bodyguard. The European magistrate suggested, and the headman agreed, that he leave the location for six months; in other words, the state unwittingly became an accomplice in theft.[47]

In another example, people accused Hlubi headman Velelo Mgobozi of siding with thieves. "There are many people attacked by night," they complained, but "the headman have [*sic*] never taken steps." Mgobozi's accusers lodged two other complaints in addition to the issue of stock theft. First, they argued that his authority was illegitimate "because according to our grandfather's custom of the Hlubi's one cannot be appointed to rule people whom they do not like." Mgobozi's authority was considered particularly illegitimate because he replaced the sub-headmen with people "who are thieves."

Second, the headman appointed his son as a ranger and as the registrar of births and deaths. Not only was his authority at best questionable, not only did he surround himself with thieves, but his son also worked for the apartheid state. He denied that he was "sympathetic towards" the Nephews, though he did "not permit" Makhulu Span "to burn out the suspected stock thieves." He knew that his legitimacy was questionable because his he acted "without consulting [the] men of the location." He also knew that Makhulu Span "threatened to kill me as well as my son."

Certainly Mgobozi's accusers linked his son the ranger with the loss of stock. Nor was this case unique. In Balasi location, for example, a ranger's huts "were completely destroyed." The incendiarism had a powerful impact on the ranger who received a cash wage from the state, collected written statistical data on livestock holding, and enforced betterment. The ranger developed a "guilty concience [*sic*]. I was a ranger before and have arrested many people. I thought the people might want to get their own back."[48]

These examples point to the ways in which Makhulu Span became involved in disputes around authority and political office. These disputes became ever more volatile in the closing years of the 1950s and, especially, during the early 1960s. In 1957–8 the state arrested and convicted in very well-attended trials scores of Makhulu Span members on charges ranging from murder to arson and public violence. Makhulu Span subsequently attacked people perceived as police informers. It continued assailing headmen defined as collaborators or seen for one reason or another as lacking popular legitimacy. The movement rained much venom upon chiefs Matiwane and Majeke, whose rule was seen by many as based on subterfuge and wickedness. Both were threatened with violent death.

Throughout the early 1960s Makhulu Span remained active. Fire consumed the nights as the organization burned out suspected thieves, collaborators, informers, and others. Makhulu Span continued its attacks on thieves and considerably expanded its critique of collaborators, the introduction of the Bantu Authorities Act, indeed the entire apartheid state. Chiefs Majeke and Matiwane constantly received death threats. There were other developments. In Qumbu, Makhulu Span began organizing workers on the South African Native Trust Etwa Plantation. Workers were told "to demand payment for days they were required to sleep on the plantation premises but for which they received no pay – failing payment they were advised to go on strike." A two-day strike ensued.[49]

The chief Bantu commissioner for the Transkei wrote to his superiors in Pretoria that, in Tsolo, "Makhulu Span is rapidly gaining control of this District." In one wave of arson the organization destroyed some 194 huts in just four locations.[50] By this time Makhulu Span had appropriated the nationalist language of formal African political organizations. Chief Mditshwa, Tsolo's equivalent of Isaac Matiwane, wrote that if the members of Makhulu Span did

> not like a certain person in the district he is accused of stock theft, even if he has never been convicted . . . Large sums of money [are] demanded from him and should he not pay his kraal is burned down . . . [Makhulu Span] are also against the implementation of bantu authorities or any of the Government Scheme[s] for the betterment of the Bantu in the Tsolo district. There [sic] object is that I be put in a bad light with the Government Officials so that they might think that I am incapable of ruling my people . . . I have today gathered information to the effect that these three men [alleged leaders of Makhulu Span] have told the Pondomisis [sic] that all the bantu people, instead of having all these different Chiefs, should strive to be under one chief and that chief must be ALBERT LUTILI [sic] [then president of the ANC] . . . No european should rule them. Taxes are not to be paid to the europeans but to chief LUTILE, the bantu man, who should rule the whole of South Africa.[51]

By 1962 Makhulu Span had expanded to nearby Engcobo district, where a number of brutal murders by the organization raised considerable panic in the community.[52] Wherever it operated the organization quickly divided people into supporters and collaborators. The latter faced murder, the destruction of their homesteads, and the confiscation of their property, even if they had nothing to do with stock thieving. In Tsolo, in a 1961 letter to the district commandant a number of people wondered, "Why does the Government set chiefs and heads of tribal authorities on us Bantu?" Clearly they did not support the introduction of apartheid into rural South Africa. But they were not supporters of Makhulu Span either, for they asked the official, "Will you please investigate this extortious action or else we will be forced to defend ourselves against this barbarous rape of our scant pennies . . . the so called secretary is the headman of Jenca location the headquarters of Makhulu span. He has already made a fat profit of over £1000 as fines."[53]

Makhulu Span disappeared after 1962, in large part because of the arrest and conviction of many of its members and the government's declaration of a state of emergency in the Transkei following the 1960 Pondoland Revolt. In a document relating to that revolt an official observed that "agitators are now collaborating with Makuluspan to murder" Chief Majeke.[54] By this time much of the Transkei was, in effect, in a state of open rebellion, with headmen "afraid to walk . . . for fear of being assaulted or killed."[55] This situation would continue into the early years of the 1960s. And the hatreds borne of jealousy and tragedy, the malevolence of witches, and the persecutions of the apartheid state would continue their rule in this impoverished land.

It is, however, to the great revolt in Pondoland that we now turn.

7   The men of the mountain

Elliot Lumbe get away from among the Tshezi people if you wish to live long. We must not hear again that you are a secretary of your Tribal Authority. We have travelled round the country to put things in order. You are busy giving away the country to the Europeans . . . On the 8th July, we will visit you from Lusikisiki. We want to put an end of your [Bantu] Authority . . . In one night we shall murder three of the Headmen. We come from Congo . . . We take no notice of a white man . . . We want our country back from the white people, we being Africans.[1]

1960. "Here are the people – they have come. You are going to die."[2] A crowd of more than two hundred angry people stood near the doorway of the house of Chief Vukwayibambe Sigcau, brother of Paramount Chief Botha Sigcau and head of the Ntlenzi tribal authority in Flagstaff district, Pondoland, created under the Bantu Authorities Act. It was a Sunday night, the evening of the Lord's day. Beams of light from flashlights illuminated the rain and mist and flitted nervously across the land.

Mlahlwa closed the door, turned on his heels and ran to the back of the house. "Wake up," he shouted to Vukwayibambe. "The people have come . . . Take the gun and shoot." Someone shattered one of the windows. A shot rang out in the house. But the chief could not find his weapon. He had been deceived – a "young man has taken it away."

Panicking, concerned with saving his own life as much as the chief's, Mlahlwa hid underneath the bed. The house, however, was on fire. Reaching the thatch from inside the broken window, someone had set fire to the roof. Composed enough to put on his overcoat and shoes, Vukwayibambe stepped through the entrance of his house to face his accusers.

"I am asking for forgiveness from you chiefs," he pleaded to the crowd, affecting deference to the mob, "don't kill me."

Mkatazo, who stood just outside the door, screamed to the men: "Here is Vukwayibambe." A man of some forty-four years, Mkatazo gripped in his hand an axe or a knife used by workers to slice the tough cane on the sugar plantations of Natal. He struck Vukwayibambe as he stood outside his house. The weapon shattered the back of his skull, cutting a deep, mortal wound to the chief's brain.

Then Mkatazo, or someone else, took the chief's right hand and severed each of his fingers where they joined the palm; the rebels also cut off his left ear.

Vukwayibambe's body lay crumpled in the mud. Blood gushed from his broken skull and the deep trauma to the brain, mixing with the rain and the soil. Mkatazo stood over the dying chief. "You have shitted now."[3] "You are the man who" called "the Police vans on us."

A moment of consideration interrupted this blaze of violence in the dark. "Look, men, see that the children are not burnt in the hut," someone said. Mlahlwa, who had moved from under the bed and now hid behind a wardrobe, told the children inside, "Go, go out."

Mkatazo yelled to the boys to "Come out of the hut."

The children ran out. The men stopped one of them. "No, this is a man, this is a man." "No," someone else said, "this is a child." Released, in terror the children ran until they reached the main road, then sat down, exhausted, and watched the kraal go up in flames. Mlahlwa also had escaped, barely, and fled in the direction of his home.

"We are finished the work here."[4]

The fire destroyed the house. Vukwayibambe either fell or was dragged close to the house, so that the fire consumed his face and most of the right side of his body. Two of the chief's bodyguards lay dead and burnt as well. Some time elapsed before what remained of the chief's mutilated body was retrieved. Animals had eaten away at the burnt flesh . . .

The day before a large crowd of people had met on Ngqindilili hill. Dodd Mzozoyana, a retired school teacher, attended the meeting. He had heard about the meeting from Wilson, when they "had gone to attend a church service." "It was said that everybody was required to attend the meeting, and if a person did not attend, there was a threat." A person might be killed and his kraal burnt down by the "men of the mountain," the Congo. At the meeting Mkatazo, Vukwayibambe's murderer, proclaimed that "we have decided that an informer should have his throat cut and thrown over a cliff" as chiefs had done to witches and enemies before the white man had arrived in their land.

Mzozoyana arrived late. The meeting had begun. He paid his 2/6 to one of the leaders of the Congo, his sub-headman Julius Vaku. Then "we heard the warcry from the women, so it was said that everybody should sit down and remain and see why the women were raising this warcry." Mzozoyana "waited and five Police vans arrived. They stopped just across the stream, then they started coming to us again. We remained sitting down. When the Police vans arrived, something which had a smoke was thrown to the crowd."

The teargas created a lot of commotion; people fled in every direction. At this point the police opened fire. Chief Vukwayibambe had accompanied the police. He too fired on the crowd. In a brief moment a number of people lay injured; at least one died of his wounds.

The following day Mzozoyana attended another meeting at Ngqindilili hill. People agreed that they should get together again on Sunday – and they should bring their guns. They would "find out where the Chief was, the man who shot at the people," Vukwayibambe. On Sunday night, riding his horse, Mzozoyana joined the group of men "moving towards the Chief's place." Mzozoyana had his gun. It made him feel, he later testified, "like a man." The men converged on a dipping tank near the chief's kraal. Mzozoyana and "another religious minister" said a prayer.

"After that, somebody said we have been waiting" at the tank "a long time. They said other men should go forward, leaving four men at the spot to wait for the people who were expected to come from Bizana district."

When the crowd – a few on horseback, most walking – reached Chief Vukwayibambe's "Great Place ... it was said [that] some people should remain near the stock kraal and keep a watch-out for persons coming out ... and some other people should go to the huts" to kill the man who "fires on his people."

"Here are the people – they have come. You are going to die."[5]

The origins of the Congo and the spread of resistance

Twelve years earlier, in 1948, the year of the National Party victory, the agricultural officer for Mount Ayliff, J. Brinkles, had penned a rather anxious letter to his superior. Brinkles was in charge of implementing "betterment" policies ostensibly aimed at preventing the continued involution of the rural economy. These policies, as we have seen in previous chapters, became part of a brazen attempt on the part of the state to restructure the "reserves" in the name of continued economic exploitation and intensifying racial oppression. Brinkles was but a minor official in a rapidly expanding bureaucratic machine, but men like him were the ones responsible for the rise of an authoritarian order that had so much contempt for the people whose lives it frequently ruined.

Stock culling increasingly formed an important component of the state's interventions in the Eastern Cape. It was to economic management what the 1951 Bantu Authorities Act was to political engineering, an attempt to reorder the African world on the basis of rational – indeed scientific – principles, to create a lived world that corresponded with the state's detailed fantasies of the way things should be. Very few Africans supported stock culling or, for that matter, any of the other policies the state pursued in the 1940s and 1950s. Brinkles wrote that the "Kongo movement made it known that any person found driving stock to the sales yards would be attacked." The movement's power had been "sufficient to dampen" the "enthusiasm" of people willing to part with their animals. Presciently, Brinkles argued in his letter that the government "greatly underestimated" the "influence of this small but armed group in local affairs." Indeed, he wrote, "until" the government "successfully dealt with" the Congo, "thousands of potential supporters of progress will continue to exhibit an apathetic attitude for fear of reprisals."[6]

The Congo had been operating in the Mount Ayliff area since at least 1947, and almost certainly well before then. Its beginnings, like the beginnings of many other groups organized around labor migration, masculinity, and the rural homestead, lay most immediately in the 1920s when migration to the Rand became a more constant fixture of the lives of Transkeian men. At work in the city, migrants typically invested considerable energy in maintaining connections to their rural homes. These new social groups – whether the Congo, *indlavini*, *izitshozi*, or the infamous Nephews of Tsolo and Qumbu – had still older roots in institutions organized around gender and generation. The *intlombe* of circumcised young men, for example, had their own "laws" and became important sites within which people assembled, discussed, and imparted from one generation to the next knowledge on and about the world: authority, community, economy, responsibility, sexuality, and, increasingly, the ways one negotiated a racially oppressive world.

They were also important sites around which male aggression was organized. These "schools" were a place where young men "learn many things,"[7] including how to fight. "The young people," Mayer has written, "speak of the 'laws' of *intlombe* or *mtshotsho* with much the same kind of respect one expresses from the 'laws' of one's community in the wider sense. And the adults, who have been through it all themselves, fully approve of this."[8]

The *intlombe* is called a training school (*Isikolo soqeqesho*) of the Red people. All the life of our people is led by order of the law. There is not a single organisation that has not a pattern of law designed for it. If you go to a beerdrink the people will talk about the law. At the *inkundla* people talk about the law. We *abafana* talk about the law ... The *intlombe* teaches the members to respect the law of the people which is there for everyone's welfare and good. It teaches us to respect anyone who is chosen or appointed to any position of authority.[9]

Groups such as the *intlombe*, composed of males from their teens to their thirties, very frequently had senior men who served as "special advisers whom the senior youngmen can consult about *intlombe* 'law' when necessary."[10]

In the Transkei, labor migration had become an important part of the ritual of manhood probably early on in the twentieth century. Certainly migration became an important moment in the graduation to *intlombe* groups. Following circumcision, for instance, a young man might migrate "to town for a few months to earn money and buy himself new adult-style clothes (*ukutshintsha*, 'to change' clothes). He starts attending *intlombe* as soon as he is home again."[11]

Congo groups represented one among a number of similar and frequently overlapping associations that emerged in this period, typically formed by male migrants from local areas who would "migrate together and seek employment in the same institutions."[12] In the Transkei east of Umtata, most of these groups emerged in the 1920s or 1930s, at a time of extraordinary hardship, skyrocketing poverty, increasing reliance on migration to the Rand, and profound political and ideological change.[13] It is quite clear that *indlavini* members had spent considerable time working on the mines or in cities, and frequently found themselves in prison. Sometimes they referred to themselves as *amakhasmen*, "Case men," referring to the "many cases they commit."[14]

It is difficult to distinguish these groups as either "red" or "school," as much of the anthropological literature, and indeed the state as well, has attempted to do. McAllister, for example, argues that Congo groups were "exclusively for 'reds'," whereas "non-traditionalists belong to the *indlavini* group."[15] The evidence does not bear out this assertion. What is perhaps most distinctive about the Congo and other groups is precisely their cultural hybridity, and particularly the ways in which they appropriated and mimicked aspects of the world that oppressed them. We have encountered this hybridity before and its centrality to the ways people envisioned and refashioned their world; indeed, it has been a feature of the cultural history of the region since the years of colonial conquest and control, for example in the murder of Hamilton Hope and the rebellions of 1880–1. Hybridity comprised a central feature of ideological innovation in the 1920s and 1930s, particularly in the invention of new identities that were both supra-local and, simultaneously, spoke to issues of social health and local authority. It was also a feature of Makhulu Span and the world of their enemies, the Nephews. Likewise, *indlavini* "elected" their own "magistrate" or "president," and had their own policemen, sergeants, even their own courts.[16]

This anthropological material sheds some light on Brinkles' anxious letter. In the 1940s Congo groups, which had their origin in quite localized male associations, rural impoverization, and the rise of a migrant working class, had become a powerful force in local political society. They began organizing resistance to the implementation of state economic policies, especially stock culling and changes in the distribution and tenure of land, and they participated in struggles over the legitimacy of local political leaders. In their secluded hilltop meetings the Congo became an alternative site of political imagining. Indeed, it began to elaborate a structure of authority – polity even – that stood in opposition to the chief and, ultimately, to the apartheid state itself.

Serious resistance broke out in the Mount Ayliff area in 1947. The previous year the state had declared the district a betterment area. In early February 1947, with the area already seething with discontent, the state recommenced culling stock. Violence broke out almost immediately. A raucous meeting at one location ended when a number of Africans "adopted a truculent attitude and broke up the meeting by refusing to listen to any explanations and by shouting down the Interpreter and finally standing up and marching away."[17]

Congo members threatened police and government officials, and injured a few native police constables. When officials summoned the "offenders" to court they failed to appear; a police patrol sent out to get them was stoned. By this time there was serious commotion in the entire district. Finally the leader of the resistance, Ntlabati Kwalukwalu, who had been at the meeting, turned himself in with twenty-one others. All but one were tried and convicted that same day.

Ntlabati was the "son and heir of the late Kwalukwalu who was a son of the late Mfundisi, the eldest son of the first wife married by the late Chief Jojo." In 1925 the state had appointed him headman of Dundee location, though he also had control over two neighboring locations. Location residents considered his position as "of considerable importance," wrote the native commissioner for Mount Ayliff. Ntlabati was, in effect, considered "chief" of the three locations. Four years later, however, the state convicted him of stock theft and duly stripped him of his position as headman. Ntlabati hoped for reinstatement and, especially after the death of Chief Mbizweni in the late 1930s, became more involved in the always complex politics of ethnicity and hereditary rule. His efforts, however, came to naught.

In the 1940s, with the implementation of stock culling and other policies of rural "rehabilitation," Ntlabati returned to "prominence." By the end of the decade, and probably much earlier, Ntlabati had become a leading member of the Congo. Angry at the chief, people turned to "the second kraal of the late Chief Jojo." This was Ntlabati's chance to recoup his losses and to amass power in the area. Many people certainly saw him as the leader, as chief, and Ntlabati in fact worked with the magistrate to help calm the increasingly tense situation. In return he received the name "Valigazi," the "preventer of bloodshed."[18] Certainly, despite being stripped of his official position, Ntlabati "in any case exercises and will continue to exercise" the position of headman as long as "he resides at the second kraal of the late chief Jojo."[19]

With the Second World War ended, government officials renewed their attention to the reserves, hoping to continue implementing policies going back to the 1927 Native Administration Act and the 1939 Betterment Act. After the earlier disturbances in 1947, in early July Ntlabati, with seven other leading men accompanied by between eight hundred and a thousand people, converged on the magistrate's office. All of these men were Congo members. They lodged a series of complaints before the magistrate. Monqoba said that an additional "thing which disappoints us is that we find our district being surveyed without our knowledge . . . We are altogether against the rehabilitation scheme. We will fight wars for our cattle."

Another recounted the recent political history of the area. He pointed out that many had fought alongside the government in the war with the Griqua. The man also asserted that Ntlabati was the rightful "head of the Xesibe's." Others pointed out how Chief Gaulibazo failed in "consulting the people." Mgalela declared that "we ... know [that] he [Ntlabati] is head of the Xesibes. If he was not the head of the Xesibes he would have died ... The cause of the trouble is the Bunga."

At this juncture Ntlabati spoke:

We were selected as committee members of the rehabilitations scheme by the Chief. We were told we would be taught in the office. Before we were taught about the culling we were called to the great place. We were told all small stock – sheep and goats – should be done away with. The Xesibes were against it because this was not made clear to them. I say the rehabilitation scheme has not been made clear to the people. Some of the Xesibes say the chief is the cause of the friction ... The Chief also assaults people.

The magistrate asked if people were sure they really understood the rehabilitation policies. At this point Mpongo Jonas, chairman of Congo in Dundee, yelled out that "we do not want any explanations of the scheme. We say this – bring your rifles and shoot us and then you can rehabilitate the locations over our dead bodies." The magistrate replied that he would inform the chief of their feelings and that "perhaps the Chief would like to say something."

The Crowd: The meeting was called for us. We do not want to hear what he has to say. He had nothing to say here.
The Crowd then separated leaving the chief with about 150 followers and in view of the attitude taken up it was decided to conclude the whole meeting.[20]

By the middle of the month the Congo had made plans to burn the kraal and to kill Chief Kaiser Jojo, though the plans were never put into effect.[21] Ntlabati left the area to work in Witbank.

In early 1949, roughly eighteen months after the affrays in Mount Ayliff, Congo meetings were still taking place in Dundee location. At one meeting of at least 241 men held at Ntlabati's kraal, one member "said that the members of the 'Kongo' were tired of having their meeting in the mountains and that they have now come to ask Headman Nqubela if they could have the meetings in his location." Then Elias Mabodla stood up and declared that "we have come to appoint a Chief here today." Some commotion followed, in large part it seems because of disagreements over whether they should speak to the chief and magistrate. Another man shouted that "we will appoint our Chief on that day even if they refuse to let us hold our meeting here."[22] The Congo subsequently approached Ntlabati and "asked him whether he would be prepared to accept the Chieftainship ... he ... agreed if he was elected."[23]

The Congo, and especially Ntlabati, continued to control the political situation in Mount Ayliff into the early 1950s, especially with regard to issues around access to grazing and impounding of stock found "illegally" grazing on the village commonage; in one 1951 incident, for example, Congo members "rescued" impounded stock.[24] By this time the Congo had a well-developed organization, with a secretary and a treasurer who collected money to employ an attorney "to fight their case to have Ntlabati elected as their chief." At one May 1950 meeting, while the "money was still being paid, Ntlabati arrived escorted by a number of men. On his arrival the whole meeting stood up and raised their hats and arms and shouted 'bayete' and remained standing until he took his place alongside that of Elias Mabodla."

Much of the meeting centered on three points:

(1) What is to be done to the chief Jojo and the headmen who failed to attend the meeting when called upon to do so by the tribe;
(2) What to be do about the magistrate who is separating the chief and headmen from the people and remarking that the present chief and headmen are more concerned by becoming the magistrates' policemen than they are concerned over their people;
(3) Suggestions were made that a certain day to be appointed when all present should escort Ntlabati to Mount Ayliff and there to declare him as their chief in the presence of the magistrate.

That the chief and headmen had not attended the "orderly and open" meeting especially incensed the men.[25]

In February and April 1951 the group played a central role in two large meetings of the magistrate, Chief Jojo, and Ntlabati. The people who attended the February meeting, in all roughly a hundred or so people, were "all well know[n] 'Kongo-ites' and it was clear that they were antagonistic." People expressed particular concern with the way the Native Commissioner handled grazing and boundary disputes. For Wilberforce Jojo, headman of Bethswana location, these issues should be "discussed in the presence of the Chief." The official disagreed. "This is not a tribal matter," he argued. Another resident of the location then protested, saying that "we cannot understand why we are called here. The meeting should have been held at the Great Place. We want the Chief to be present." Beginning to lose his cool, the native commissioner closed the meeting, saying that "I am in charge of this district and [am] the only bull in the kraal. I am not prepared to take instructions from you."[26]

Ntlabati, as putative chief and as leader of the Congo, subsequently interceded on the residents' behalf, though to little effect.[27] By the second meeting the situation had become far more charged. The struggles for political office came to a head, even if they remained unresolved. Chief Kaiser Jojo chaired the meeting, attended by the native commissioner, Ntlabati, and between five and six hundred others. Jojo hoped that his political supremacy would be affirmed; that, in effect, Ntlabati would publicly renounce his claims to the chieftaincy. But the situation was more complex than that. For Ntlabati argued that "the Chieftainship of the Ntlavini belongs to me."[28] "Ntlavini" is remarkably similar to *indlavini*, the male migrant association that was very active in the area, though one document defines the word, again with wonderful ambiguity, as the "second kraal of the late chief Jojo."[29] Was Ntlabati referring to *indlavini*, and was he suggesting that he/*indlavini*/Congo, or some combination thereof, was the legitimate successor to Jojo, or at least a central node of political authority? In this context of fluid contestation, what might be meant by someone claiming to be a chief of the *indlavini*?

Ntlabati continued. "I have brought the 'Kongo' here because it is said that I have taken them away from the Great Place . . . I am disappointed when the Chief tells me that I am his younger brother. I am his eldest brother. Mfanombana is his younger brother. The family history is not correctly described. I have brought the Chiefs [*sic*] people. I now claim from him the stock which belonged to the estates of the late Mfundisi [his grandfather's family] and the late Makweni. I want to settle this amicable [*sic*] so as to prevent a case."

Jojo was, understandably, livid. His authority had been flouted, the very basis of his political position subverted. Moreover, Nltabati had "told me that he [Ntlabati] desired to break all his connections with the 'kongo'. He also told the magistrate that he wished to break with the 'Kngo' . . . The matter Ntlabati has mentioned is not a thing he called us for today. I declare the meeting closed."

The native commissioner interceded. He did not want the meeting to end without Ntlabati renouncing his membership of the Congo. Turning to Ntlabati, the official asked, "Does he not intend to make the declarations?" Ntlabati: "I thought I made it clear that I will have nothing to do with the 'kongo' in the future. I also do not claim the chieftainship. I only claim the estate stock of the late Mfundisi and the late Makaweni . . . before the magistrate goes I intend to leave the meeting. I am leaving the people who came with me here," in other words his Congo followers. "I am going home myself."

But others would have none of this. They had appointed Ntlabati as chief. "We advised the magistrate by letter that we appointed Ntlabati. We cannot be thrown into the air. If Ntlabati leaves we go with him to his kraal. (Roars of assent from the crowd.)"[30]

Struggles such as these continued through the 1950s and into the 1960s. Most directly they emerged as a result of the frenzied political competition and conflict unleashed by the state's new political policies. Invariably, however, resistance also involved issues ranging from surveying to stock culling. In 1952, for example, the Congo threatened workers fencing the Mount Ayliff commonage with death and the destruction of their homes. Some of these "threats were made in a rather peculiar fashion. A strange native would wait along the hill and way lay me . . . and as I stop to find out what he had to say he would say 'Do not continue with this work [or] you will be killed.'" The Congo also confronted the work gang. The laborers were "scared stiff."[31] In 1961, resistance in the area resulted in incineration of the magistrate's office, two schools, and a church in one Mount Ayliff location.[32] Throughout this most tumultuous time the Congo continued to play a central role in the politics of the region. Indeed, in many respects it was the central political player in Mount

Ayliff, having elaborated a vision of polity that stood in opposition to the chief and to the state itself. Not surprisingly, during the Pondoland Revolt the "men from the hill" usurped the state's authority and took control of the distribution of land.[33]

The Mount Ayliff "disturbances" were not simply localized "peasant" movements. For the Dundee Congo linked up with other groups in the Transkei. Joseph Mangqoba, for example, moved to Mount Ayliff district after the First World War. In early 1947 he began attending meetings of the Congo in Dundee location. At his first meeting Mangqoba was elected secretary. Like *indlavini* groups the Congo met regularly on Saturdays, collected dues, and met at the same spot. Mangqoba recounted that there was some discussion of resisting the implementation of rehabilitation schemes, but it was decided instead to collect money with the idea of employing a lawyer. In addition, they sent out a delegation.

Our instructions were to meet a similar delegation from the Qumbu organization, which has similar objects. Thereafter the delegation from here and the delegates from the Qumbu organisation were to proceed together to Cape Town . . . On arrival at Qumbu it was decided that Mgqaqama [a member of the Mount Ayliff Congo] should return to Mount Ayliff as certain forms (Petition forms containing the names of persons who had signed them) were lost with the haversack when I lost my £12. Mgqaqama was to again get a petitioned signed . . . [Two weeks later] when [he] returned [there was] a meeting of the Qumbu Natives at Shawbury. Ntlabati was present at this meeting. He did not speak. It was a meeting similar to those we of the "Kongo" organisation hold in Mount Ayliff District . . . The instructions we got from our organisation was to ask the Attorneys to fight the following things:- (1) Culling of stock (2) Fencing of Locations (3) Removal of Kraal sites and (4) the appointment of Ntlabati as Chief instead of Gawulbaso. The object of the Qumbu organization was chiefly the fighting of the rehabilitation scheme in general.

The structure of the Congo in Dundee subsequently became more elaborate. By the middle of 1948 the group had amassed a sum of £100–200, and had hired lawyers to represent their interests to the magistrate. Some portion of this princely sum appears to have been collected on the mines by Ntlabati. Mangqoba made four other pertinent points. First, "some men had arranged to kill" Chief Gawulbaso, who was seen as a collaborator. Second, one of the Congo's rules was "that no stock will be taken to the periodical sales organised by the Government." Third, Mangqoba observed that "the membership of the Kongo is increasing. I estimate the present membership at 500." Finally, he noted that at one meeting of the Congo, a committee member had passed around a copy of *Torch*, the magazine of the All-African Convention (AAC) published in Cape Town, where it had widespread interest among the black population.[34]

Under the leadership of Isaac Tabata, who hailed from Queenstown, the AAC espoused a Marxism that looked for "the main social forces for revolution . . . in the countryside." In the 1940s and 1950s the AAC was busy "promoting the cause of peasant resistance to state land rehabilitation schemes."[35] According to Bundy, in the 1940s "there was considerable competition between the African National Congress (ANC) and the All-African Convention (AAC) in reaching and directing rurally based movements in the Transkei." Certainly the AAC "identified the African reserves as areas of potential revolutionary activity."[36] It was more an "umbrella" organization than the ANC. Organizations such as the Cape African Teachers' Association (CATA) were affiliated to the AAC and, in Pondoland, the Congo aligned itself to the organization.

There is no indication, however, that either the ANC or the AAC had any direct role in forming groups such as the Congo, though ANC members such as Govan Mbeki worked hard to involve the organization in the Pondoland Revolt after it had broken out.[37] Rather, just as subaltern social movements were appropriating the state, so also were they acutely aware of elite nationalist politics in the country. The Defiance Campaign had been especially powerful in the Eastern Cape cities of Port Elizabeth and East London; serious violence had broken out in East London. Certainly people who joined the Congo knew about, and in a number of cases participated in, the Defiance Campaign and were well aware of nationalist politics both in South Africa and elsewhere in Africa.[38] Just prior to the outbreak of the Pondoland Revolt resistance and violence had engulfed Cato Manor, Durban, and areas in Harding district in Natal. CATA had affiliated to the AAC in 1948 and was active in parts of the Transkei, spearheading resistance to Bantu education as well as the introduction of rehabilitation.[39] One "very active member of the Congo" was alleged to be in close contact with N. Honono, an important leader of CATA in the Transkei and, indeed, was distributing CATA pamphlets in his location in Lusikisiki.[40]

By the late 1950s resistance and violence had washed over much of the Eastern Cape. Groups similar to the Congo had emerged across the region. As we have seen, by early 1957 anti-stock-theft crusades had spread from Tsolo and Qumbu to East Griqualand. Like Tsolo and Qumbu, the East Griqualand movement was preceded by a wave of stocktheft, what a member of the security branch described as "intense activity on the part of Stock Thieves." In a fifteen-month period ending in March 1957, "175 cases of Stock Theft was [sic] reported to the Police" in Mount Fletcher district. Once the crusade began, cases reported to the state declined by 80 percent. By the end of July 1957, ninety-five kraals of "know[n] and reputed" thieves had been burned to the ground. Eighteen suspects had been murdered. In neighboring Matatiele, seventeen kraals were destroyed by fire and five reputed thieves killed.[41]

The police officer observed further that people were forming "groups and organising them on the pattern of the Vigilance Associations, who act along the lines set at Qumbu." "Although the drastic and barbaric methods employed by the anti-stock thieving faction cannot be condoned," he argued, it must be pointed out that for a long time now the honest and hardworking peasants have been the victims of unscrupulous Stock Thieves whose activities have deprived them of their savings in Stock. Many of these Thieves are known to the victims, but because of the lack of evidence against them, they have succeeded in evading being brought to account and have continued their Stock Thieving activities. Others who have been arrested, have been acquitted on technicalities that the unitiated natives do not understand.[42]

Similar developments characterized Kentani, Willowvale, Tsomo, and Pondoland. There was considerable violence in Tsomo in 1956, when people attacked a police patrol, and again in late 1957. Here the Tsomo Vigilance Assocation led the movement against the introduction of apartheid. In July 1957, the association declared "that they opposed categorically and unreservedly the implementation of the Bantu Authirties [*sic*] Act in this district, which they expressed in shouts and yells, etc., and which they were not allowed by the Native Commissioner to express by voting against it."[43] In October, a meeting of 1,000 people with the magistrate – ten times the usual number of people for a quarterly meeting – became "very unruly." "At the mention of the word 'stabilisation' there were jeers and boos." At times "shouts from the rear ranks . . . caused" the magistrate "to keep silent for a long as ten minutes." "We'll govern ourselves," people yelled out. Much of the resistance seemed to be led by young men; generational tensions certainly were evident. Tsomo "had many young men . . . employed at Port Elizabeth and on their return are flooding the district with African National Congress propaganda . . . sometimes schoolboys along the roads will shout the ANC slogan 'Mayebuye Africa' to passing European cars."[44]

Like Tsomo, areas such as Willowvale had strong and enduring connections with East London and Port Elizabeth, crucial sites for the rise of worker unionization and, most centrally, the meteoric rise of the ANC in the wake of the 1952 Defiance Campaign. In Cafutweni location, resistance to betterment and the reorganization of residential sites was informed by both the AAC and (especially) the ANC, though again there is little evidence of any explicit connection between local resistance and nationalist movements. The three suspected of destroying a fence worked in "great secret" and were not, as far as one local teacher knew, members of either the AAC or ANC, though he suspected that they might be getting "advice from some educated politician and I know that they associate with the attorney CANCA at Willowvale who is their attorney."[45] The men "had quite a following."[46] There was a botched attempt on the life of the headman – his brother ended up dead – and there appear to have been plans to employ a thug from East London to assassinate him.[47] As elsewhere stock theft played a central role in the sensibilities of people and in the organization of violence. In this case, however, people seen as collaborators had their stock stolen as "fines" for their participation in apartheid.[48]

By the late 1950s the level of violence had thus reached quite exceptional levels throughout large areas of the Eastern Cape. Chiefs, headmen, low-level functionaries, police, and even white officials had become targets of groups resisting retribalization and the economic restructuring of the reserves. Stock thieves, many of whom people considered to have links to the state, also became the targets of violence, including murder. Fire, as we have seen and will see again shortly, had become a common feature of violence throughout the Eastern Cape. Writing had become an important feature of the culture of resistance. Groups often sent "anonymous letters to intended victims." Most of these letters went to reputed thieves and to people seen as collaborating with the apartheid state. The "anonymous letters" created great "fear" in the minds of those who received them.[49]

The people of Tsomo had silenced their magistrate with the shout we shall "govern ourselves." But what had they really meant? And what was the imagined community or communities they and other groups claimed to represent? Were the rural struggles in Tsomo and elsewhere so many "backward-looking" peasant revolts mired in "traditionalist phraseology"?[50] The very complexity of these social movements suggests a different interpretation. One striking feature centers on both the seizure of the "traditional" institutions of chiefship and the duplication of the institutional forms of the colonial state such movements critiqued as unjust and illegitimate. These were both outward- and inward-looking movements. At the center of the Congo's subaltern political philosophy lay an appropriation of dominant institutions and political symbols, whether the colonial state, formal African political organizations like the ANC, or even of occupations like lawyers – or, even more amorphously, though no less powerfully, the appropriation of past and present.

Especially important in this respect were political developments both inside and outside the country. People involved in rural movements such as the Congo either had heard of, observed, or even participated in movements such as the 1952 Defiance Campaign that had been so very powerful in places like Port Elizabeth and East London. Thus a treasurer of the Congo in Bizana had participated in the ANC struggles in East London; "he was used to such gatherings at East London where he was a Member of Congress."[51] The 1959 Cato Manor riots reverberated throughout the eastern half of the Transkei, whose inhabitants worked in Natal, either in the sugar fields or in cities like Durban. Indeed, quite a few of the people who participated in the Pondoland uprisings lived in Cato Manor.[52] (Some of the rebels' weapons may have come from the Durban area.[53]) Then, of course, there was the political resistance lead by the PAC in the Vereeniging area, and in Langa and Nyanga in the Cape, which culminated respectively, in the Sharpeville massacre and a massive demonstration in Cape Town.[54] In each case, rural people knew of these developments and talked about them; in doing so they made them part of their world.

Externally, the late 1950s witnessed the cascade of independence throughout much of Africa. Ghana had received its independence in 1957. By 1960 it had become the center of African nationalism on the continent. Closer by, the Belgian Congo was on the cusp of independence – and a crisis that would involve intervention by the United Nations. Here, for example, is the testimony of Albert Somadlangati, a Lusikisiki resident, a teacher and a member of the 1,500-strong Congo group that burned down the kraal of headman Gladwin Sigcau, cousin of the paramount and head of the Mtshayelo tribal authority. (Somadlangati, who "caused great trouble," would be "convicted of imputing witchcraft."[55])

You will agree with me that it is the wish of the United Nations that the smaller nations should be given freedom these days. You will have noticed that the big powers like England and France have granted independence to their former colleagues. Ghana, on the same continent as Africa – last December there was a big conference at Accra – many South Africans were present. Among the resolutions taken at that Congress was that colonisation should be wiped out in Africa . . . The whole Africa is moving. In other countries the black people are getting independence – Natives are being appointed Postmasters in Ghana – lots of people want to go to Ghana to work. I wish to refer to the Conference in Addis Abada [sic]. It was decided that the African states should be united like the United States of America . . . In 1958, Dr. Nkrumah spent Christmas in India – when strikes take place, the Indians and the Bantu work together . . . Russia is also sympathetic with Dr. Nkrumah.[56]

This cultural and political innovation included religion. The Eastern Cape had experienced profound religious innovation, especially with the rise of Zionist churches over the course of the twentieth century. Evangelists took part in the Pondoland Revolt. Certainly many Congo members also participated in one of the many Zionist churches in the region. These churches, we argued earlier, centered on the belief that the world had fallen to a tyranny of evil, a tyranny that, ultimately, would be overturned with the triumph of the "black nation." This concern with the problem of evil had other important political implications. Where the chiefs had once played a central role in ensuring nourishing rains, for example, increasingly people turned to God in their attempt to secure agricultural fertility. Religious leaders now became important interlocutors, blessing the harvests of their following (ibandla) and working to bring the sweet rains that succored the soil.

The Congo and other groups throughout the Eastern Cape were thus imagining their world by "looking over the shoulders" of the dominant forces in their lives, appropriating in often enigmatic ways symbols and social processes that cohered in new, enduring, and, as we shall see, potentially revolutionary forms. These political languages were neither peasant discourses centered around the restoration of lost worlds nor derivative of the formal nationalist struggles of the AAC, ANC, or, for that matter, any other formal political organizations

9 Men praying, during the Pondoland Revolt (reproduced with permission from the Mayibuye Centre, University of the Western Cape)

in South Africa.[57] Their creativity, their cultural sycretism, emerged in large part precisely because of their relative autonomy from the forces that otherwise dominated their lives, and their origin in practices aimed at social definition and incorporation. This very autonomy offered the possibility for the rise of new, largely autonomous sites of political imagining where people surveilled the wider political world, gave voice to the dominant broad social, economic, and political forces, and elaborated a structure of authority – of polity even – that stood in opposition to chiefly rule and, ultimately, to the apartheid state.

In the meetings of the Congo and other groups people elaborated a critique of the state and its local collaborators. And they gave voice to a politics at the center of which lay the ancient and enduring problem of authority and social health. These sensibilities had been embedded in the idea of a black nation, a political identity both parochial and global, that confronted evil and brought health to the world. Here, then, was a subaltern politics that sought less the capture of the state than its rehabilitation, less the destruction of chiefship than its moral reconstruction, less the seizure of power than the ecstacy of healing and catharsis. The Congo especially emerged as a kind of polymorphous polity that had attained a popular legitimacy. Summoning chiefs, headmen, and colonial officials to its meetings, and ultimately in violence itself, the Congo struggled to refashion a world that had gone terrible awry.

"But his soul was mad"

Authoritarianism and rebellion

By the end of the 1950s much of the Eastern Cape teetered on the edge of rebellion. Areas such as Qumbu and Tsolo already were quite literally ablaze in protracted conflict. Across the Transkei people "felt that Chief Botha was selling our country, so that it no longer belonged to us, and you are going to be paid for the sale."[58] With the state's new economic policies the "land would gradually be taken away from them."[59] The apartheid state pursued its policies of retribalization and economic transformation relentlessly, despite the fact that legislation such as the Bantu Authorities Act greatly increased political tensions and competition. Whatever room for maneuvering and compromise may have existed at the local level disappeared as local officials, backed by a vastly more coercive and more centralized state, attempted to make their political fantasies the maniacal reality of apartheid.[60]

By 1957, in Pondoland the Congo already had become not only a powerful center of political critique but, ultimately, also a new and competing node of political authority in the region. Indicative of their confidence and stature the Congo *summoned* chiefs, headmen, and magistrates to their meetings.[61] In April 1960, the Congo in Bizana decided that "we should not start burning immediately but that we should first go to the chiefs, headmen and Tribal Authority Councillors and invite them to the mountain. We should do this at least twice and if they refuse then we should start burning their kraals." Messages went out of the meeting at Ndlovu (the elephant) hill, what would become the epicenter of revolt. Over a thousand people were present. The chiefs, headmen, and councillors, however, refused to attend. The most important to have refused were two heads of tribal authorities, one of them Makasonke Sigcau, the head of the AmaDegane tribal authority and the paramount's half-brother.[62]

Two days later another meeting took up the issues of taxes and Bantu Authorities. One of the leaders "told them to talk to their Headmen and sub headmen and ask them to come to the mountain and if they refused then we would know what to do with them." Speakers assured people that they would be able to employ top attorneys, Canca "and others from Durban and Johannesburg." They collected money from various areas. Lastly, "it would be arranged with the Magistrate to attend the following meeting."[63] That meeting took place the following month, May. The leaders of the Congo "told the Magistrate they were against Tribal Authorities, increased taxes, increased stock levies etc."

The Magistrate tried to explain and he mentioned rehabilitation and then the crowd stood up and became annoyed and said that they did not want to hear anything about that and if he wanted to talk about that he must not come to our meeting and he would not again be invited. The Magistrate then left.

Only after summoning chiefs, headmen, and councillors, and then meeting with the magistrate – in other words those responsible for introducing Bantu Authorities – did the men reach their fateful decision to begin burning kraals.[64] Soon people "decided that all who are doing Govt. work should be attacked . . . if we want to fight the Bantu Authorities, we should kill the appointed members."[65]

The revolt began in earnest in early March, 1960, in the Isikelo tribal authority, Bizana district, on the very day the tribal authority was to begin functioning there. The Isikelo location, one of six comprising the authority of the same name but by far its most populous, had some of the least support for Bantu Authorities in the entire district; according to one official document a mere 1.9 percent of the population favored Bantu Authorities.[66] A particularly tense issue concerned "amalgamation," the forced inclusion of outlying locations into the tribal authority, "in spite of total opposition on the part of the location residents" who were, quite simply, faced with a "*fait accompli* . . . something that has been forced on them by the Paramount Chief."[67]

In some respects the situation in Isikelo differed from other locations across the Transkei where chiefs and headmen often hitched themselves to the Bantu Authorities system. In Isikelo the recently appointed, and young, chief Mhlabuvelile did not support the new system and had canvassed the area for a very large meeting "called for the purpose of finally abolishing the Tribal Authority."[68] Mhlabuvelile had become chief following the dismissal, and then, and importantly, the mysterious illness and unexpected death of Tandabantu, whose father had quarreled with the paramountcy.[69] Tandabantu had gone to Qaukeni "to be made chief. Shortly after that," however, "he took sick and died."[70]

The sickness and deaths of chiefs historically have been moments of flux, competition, and potential conflict. These were times of great suspicion and sustained rumor, as people spoke of witchcraft and the machinations of the powerful, and worried over the redrawing of political boundaries and the relationship between authority and social health. Would the political world be dominated by evil men, purveyors of witchcraft who would consign the land

and its people to hardship and drought? Or would legitimate leaders emerge and the rains appear? We can speculate that at least some people may have suspected the paramount of causing Tandabantu's death. What is certainly clear is that Tandabantu's death, and Mhlabuvelile's appointment by the state, had come at the very moment the state was introducing the Bantu Authorities system – and the paramountcy was busily attempting to mass power while drought punished the land. Mhlabuvelile appears to have bristled at the attempt by the paramount to extend his authority over Isikelo through the appointment of councillors. As one man put it, people became councillors "by playing about," by successfully manipulating the increasingly competitive political arena created by the Bantu Authorities system.[71]

The situation reached a crisis in March, at a meeting convened by Chief Mhlabuvelile. At the meeting the chief told the assembled company that Bantu Authorities "had been forced upon him." He then said "Here are the members – ask them."[72] At this meeting the Congo "arraigned" three Bantu Authorities councillors. The Congo charged the men with "selling the country." "They were sentenced to death and brutally assaulted by those present."[73] Following additional mountain meetings, attacks on other councillors and "traitors" ensued. According to the Bantu affairs commissioner of Bizana, one of the major "reasons for the disturbance" was that

the Paramount Chief appointed the Councillors as members of the Isikelo Tribal Authority without the knowledge or consent of either the Chief [Mhlabuvelile] or of the residents of Isikelo Location. It appears that a public meeting was not held and the residents of Isikelo Location did not agree to their appointment. It follows from this that the Councillors did not enjoy either the support or the confidence of the Chief or the people. They feel that the Councillors have been thrust upon them to run the affairs of the Tribe without their consent. It is rumoured that these persons were appointed as Councillors purely on the recommendation of Saul Mabude.[74]

Mabude was, according to one official, "intensely disliked and hated by the Eastern Pondos. He is not a Pondo."[75] "The people say that Mabude would never have come back as a councillor if the people had been consulted."[76]

According to one official report, "'cells' sprang up in each location and a determined effort was made by the rebels to subvert the whole district." Meetings of the Congo continued to be held on the tops of hills, money for "the defense fund" was collected, and traitors punished and rehabilitated. "Prominent people who had assisted the Government in any way in the past were fined £5. If they refused to pay they were told that their kraals would be burned." Those who did not participate in the incendiarism of the Congo were deemed traitors, and their kraals destroyed. The Congo "had its own 'People's Court,' its own leader, who was both Prosecutor and Judge, and its own Treasurer." Rebels from all over the district, indeed it seems from all over Pondoland, and perhaps from other places in the Transkei, attended meetings at Ndlovu hill, the "National Headquarters of the Rebel movement," their "Holy Court."[77]

Rebels produced and distributed to each cell "a list of grievances" that included virtually the entire edifice of separate development, from taxes to the legal system, from Bantu Authorities to influx control.[78] The "Reference Book was like a spring which holds a man down in his locality," one man later testified. "Now the Government officials come along and use the order of the gun and they kill us."[79]

Throughout March and April rebels destroyed the kraals of chiefs and headmen they believed supported Bantu Authorities. Chiefs and headmen seen as enthusiastic supporters of Bantu Authorities, or who were perceived as corrupt, were singled out. By this time the Congo had supplanted chiefship as the locus of political authority. Some chiefs, for example, accepted its authority. In the Isikelo area, Chief Singwata's kraal had been destroyed by the rebels. In March, and again in September, the chief asked the Congo "for forgiveness" and asked to rebuild his kraal.[80] The Congo, the chief stated, "had greater powers than Government."[81]

Into late April and early May, the magistrate for Bizana, Eric Michael Warren, managed to meet with the rebels. By May, the South African Police had moved into the district in some force. Warren's meeting with the rebels ended when he refused to have the police vans removed from the district. By this time much of Pondoland had erupted into open rebellion. In addition to destroying the kraals of traitors, and occasionally killing them as well, rebels erected road blocks and dug trenches to entrap SAP vehicles, destroyed telephone poles, and cut telephone wires. They shot at police vehicles and burnt one magistrate's office to the ground. The South African government responded by declaring a state of emergency.

One of the most brutal murders occurred in Imizi location. Rebels, "between 1000 and 3000 strong, streamed toward his kraal and put" Stanford Nomagqwatekana and three other men "to death."[82] Nomagqwatekana died from a massive blow to the brain that quite literally crushed his skull; another victim had an axe lodged in his head. Nomagqwatekana had only just succeeded his father, who had died in March 1960 as the revolt was beginning. His father had only just been elevated from headman to chief and head of the Amazizi tribal authority. Stanford "was not well-liked by the majority of the Mzizi tribe,"[83] though the tribal authority council appointed him chief as his father's health deteriorated. A number of people, including some who would later be accused of his murder, preferred another son. Indeed the father may have "expressed the wish that the youngest son . . . should be his successor."[84] So disliked was Stanford that following his accession as chief "a large number of tribesmen . . . walked away showing their disrespect even before this word of greeting had been decided upon."[85]

Death had thus enlivened disputes over political succession. For reasons that are not clear Stanford seems to have curtailed the mourning period from one year to three months. His decision, however, "was not recognised by some members of the tribe."[86] Instructions came down from the mountain, from the Congo, to continue mourning. These were met with counter-instructions from Stanford.

The period immediately following a chief's death was always fraught with the possibilities of conflict. This was a time when the broader political landscape could be substantially reworked and people might fret about the relationship between power and production, agnatic conflict and agriculture. People buried their chiefs in forests. Memory has it "because it was ordered by the first doctors because of their medicines."[87] Chiefly graves received especially vigilant protection. Among other things people wanted to prevent witches from acquiring their bones and turning the dead chief into a zombie and the witches' slave.[88] While the data are admittedly limited, we may presume that Stanford Nomagqwatekana's behavior created anxiety among many people and raised serious questions not only about his conduct but, ultimately, about the very nature of the chiefship.

Certainly he had become "haughty." Among other things he snubbed "the advice of the elders of the tribe." He "claimed to be the embodiment of tribal law," though the new chief "failed to preserve order at tribal meetings and allowed members of his family to insult tribesmen."[89] He "told the elders that he was now the law, and what he said was going to be done and not what the Counsellors advised him."[90] Clearly he ascended to power at a most tumultuous time. Clearly also many people already disliked him. At a meeting with the magistrate in August a man had stood up and declared that "Chiefs and Headmen have been chased out of locations in other parts of the district – we have not chased out our Headmen but you need'nt [sic] think that that is going to continue. It will not take much and we will chase out our Headmen too."[91]

Nomagqwatekana also associated with men widely believed to be stock thieves, brigands who, like the Nephews of Qumbu, succeeded in escaping arrest and conviction. As elsewhere in the Eastern Cape, stock thieving had been increasing throughout the 1950s. Despite protests from location elders, however, the chief continued associating with men most people reviled.[92] One of them had a long record of violence and theft.[93] At beer drinks people discussed Stanford, his association with criminals, and the imminent arrival of Bantu Authorities. People also began holding mountain meetings. There, on the mountain, "insults ... were hurled at him."[94] He attended at least one of these meetings; there is evidence he was summoned to appear before the Congo. He, however, would have none of this. At meetings at the Great Place, the chief "denounced" the leaders of the movement against him; he also had people's kraals raided, including those it seems of the rebel leaders, appropriating stock, "chasing people away," and refusing permission for people to live in the district.[95] At one meeting Stanford allegedly said that he planned to eject "foreigners" from the location, "that he was going to get assistance from some locations in Natal to drive . . . people out."[96] Indeed, he so terrorized people, mostly in night raids, that "they were sleeping in the veld."[97] Around this time his bodyguards had armed themselves; people saw this not simply as yet more evidence of his arrogance, but also as illustrative of his political illegitimacy.

On 25 November, the chief magistrate of the Transkei and the native commissioner and magistrate of Bizana addressed a meeting at the Great Place. There Stanford shook hands with the white officials, symbolizing to many his acceptance of Bantu Authorities. He told the officials and the assembled crowd of some 600 people "that he was dismayed at the death of Chief Vukayimbambe," in Flagstaff district, and lauded the government's efforts to squelch the resistance.[98] Eight days later the chief lay dead.[99]

One of the men who would be sentenced to death for Stanford's murder was a forty-six-year-old evangelist. Born a few years before the great influenza pandemic that swept away so many so quickly, Barnabas Maqawana came of age in the period when Pondoland began collapsing into poverty and increasing numbers of men relied on migrant labor to make ends meet. Interested in tribal authority matters,[100] Maqawana led the rebels to Stanford's kraal. Wearing the white collar of a minister, Maqawana administered medicine along the way to "strengthen us to be brave and our knees not to weaken."[101] Once they arrived at the chief's kraal they set fire to the huts. As people crawled out of the burning and collapsing buildings and attempted to escape they were caught and killed. Stanford appeared with his gun. The crowd retreated, then he ran for the darkness. The crowd followed. "We have finished the job," one man recalled someone saying, "God has worked."[102]

By the time of Stanford's death the revolt spread through much of the rest of Eastern Pondoland. The rebellion was especially pronounced in Lusikisiki district, location of the Great Place for Eastern Pondoland at Qaukeni. Qaukeni was the location of the paramount of Eastern Pondoland and the historic center of the Pondo polity, the nineteenth-century Great Place of none other than Faku.[103] In Lusikisiki there was an illustrative combination of events and personalities, the madness of apartheid and the ferocious tensions it unleashed. The magistrate, J. Fenwick, behaved in an especially "autocratic manner."[104] He had become utterly "obsessed by the [Bantu Authorities] System" that was crumbling before him. Convinced "of his own infallibility," Fenwick believed that "only he can do this job of forcing natives to accept Bantu Authorities and rehabilitation." He "caused unnecessary trouble," for example, by having "people picked up for things which have nothing to do with him." The magistrate instructed the chiefs to "impose heavy fines in their courts, in order to build up their treasury." The frequent delay in cases, so "Witch-doctors say," became a way that chiefs could extract more money.[105]

Fenwick descended into paranoia, obsession, and delusions of bureaucratic perfection, the insanity of social engineering run amok – a crazy avatar of authoritarianism, a twentieth-century Hamilton Hope. "His soul was mad," but Fenwick "intended to accomplish great things."[106] The more obsessed with control the more uncontrollable he became. His increasingly thuggish behavior not surprisingly caused widespread consternation. He drank "very heavily" and, "in fact," was "seldom sober."[107] Soon he had "lost touch with the everyday niceties of life" as he ranged about the area persecuting people, trying to make apartheid a reality. But to no avail. In May 1960, he received a letter "threatening" him with "assassination."[108] By this time he had collapsed into "a maniacal frame of mind."[109]

In the 1950s, Lusikisiki had seen a "bitter and acrimonious dispute" over the paramountcy There were two rival claimants – Botha and Nelson Sigcau – and their claims ended up before the Supreme Court in Cape Town. The court ruled in favor of Botha, who subsequently became paramount. Many in Pondoland, however, clearly believed that "despite our protests" the "Government forced" Botha "upon the people and appointed him at the point of the rifle."[110] Tensions had increased throughout the 1950s, as in much of rural South Africa at the time, and the situation was especially volatile with regard to the position of chiefs and headmen. Much of this tension centered around headman Segwebo Mhlanga, member of the royal family, whose father had been regent in the early part of the century and who "claimed chieftainship and the right to place his sons [as head] in a number of locations."[111] There were, however, conflicting claims and intentions that continued from the 1910s and which were made even more Byzantine by the colonial state.

Mhlanga became headman of Lambasi "which fell under the Qaukeni Regional Authority" established by Bantu Authorities.[112] Lambasi was of great historical importance. Located in the coastal plain, it had since the 1830s been the customary winter grazing area for the paramount's herds. According to Beinart, this "pattern of distribution was not determined by ecological considerations alone ... It was essential for them [chiefs] to distribute cattle to the homesteads if they were to maintain their followings and secure access to services" such as wives and male and female labor.[113] Lambasi historically had been a frontier zone and yet central to the dynamics of the Pondo polity. In the 1950s Lambasi was composed of some 32,000 morgen with "approximately 185 kraals." "The residents were there in the gift of the Paramount Chief and had not the right of tenure of the residents of an ordinary location in the Transkei. Many of them were stock thieves, many of them Zulus, some Basutos, Bacas and Hlubes [sic]." Moreover, "many had obtained rights of residence illegally during Sigwebo's [sic] headmanship."[114] In other words, Lambasi had continued the historic pattern of being both a frontier area and central to royal power. To the state, however, Lambasi represented another case of African illegibility

10 March on Bizana during the Pondoland Revolt (reproduced with permission from the Mayibuye Centre, University of the Western Cape)

and flew in the face of the apartheid fantasies of creating ethnically pure tribal areas.

Under Bantu Authorities, the paramount attempted to extend his power in Lambasi. The idea was to "plan the location in order to put it to the use for which it was intended," as a grazing area for royal herds. When this was told to the people, Fenwick was "informed" that he and others "could expect resistance."[115] In fact, by 1957 – that is, just after the introduction of Bantu Authorities – people began making public declarations of resistance and expressing their hatred for Paramount Chief Botha Sigcau who was "carrying out orders like a soldier."[116]

In the late 1950s Segwebo Mhlanga had returned to Vlei location, located near Mhlanga location – where his father had lived – and at the northern edge of Lambasi. At Vlei he took control of the location following the murder of his half-brother, a murder in which Gladwin Sigcau was implicated.[117] Mhlanga was appointed acting headman in 1958, having virtually seized the position. He then claimed head of the Mtshayelo tribal authority, now held by Gladwin Sigcau, and insisted that "all the locations which had originally fallen under Mhlanga to be constituted into a Tribal Authority under the Vlei, [sic] location."[118] By the outbreak of violence in 1960, Mhlanga stood in clear opposition to Gladwin and the paramount, both intensely disliked.

People detested Bantu Authorities. Many believed that "since Bantu Authorities...too much authority has been vested in those in power...The Pondos...had not appointed the Paramount Chief – he was appointed by the Government."[119] They added a volley of other complaints. Taxes, for example, had "gone beyond our means." Bantu Authorities "brought about the purchase of arable allotments, forest produce, thatch grass and kraal sites...It has resulted in long delays in the hearing of our cases...rehabilitation...has caused many deaths." "The land," they continued, "has always been stable by the act of God – there is no other God that is going to create the land afresh."[120]

Many of the local leaders of the Congo had been sub-headmen. The "people of the location have confidence in the sub Headmen."[121] At the same time, under the Bantu Authorities system sub-headmen were being increasingly marginalized and the powers of headmen and chiefs increased. "What would happen is this," one defense attorney testified, "the representative would call the men of the location together, that is including all the sub-headmen of the various localities, and then they would be able to appoint leaders from amongst their group and invariably a sub-headmen...would be appointed as a leader...and the sub-headmen of the various localities would also in some cases have the responsibility of collecting the funds."[122]

The people of Vlei location had formed "a committee which controls its own affairs, and...a Select Committee which deals with special matters."[123] According to one resident, Albert Somadlangati, a teacher who described himself as an "educated man," Mhlanga headed the resistance. Somadlangati, we recall, had discoursed on the United Nations, Nkrumah, Russia, India, and African nationalism and decolonization. (There was in fact a formal appeal made to the United Nations.) He also believed in witchcraft and played an active part in the rebellion.[124] Two men went to Bizana "to study the movement," and a "sub Headman was sent to Lambasi in order to start a second movement, which is working there." At a "very big meeting" at the end of May, 1960,

Chief Sigwebo [*sic*] stood up and made a report, bringing in the two men who had gone to Bizana. He told what they had learnt in Bizana. They explained the constitution which controls this movement. Each members of this movement, who is not a member of the Bantu Authorities should contribute 1/-, and one who is has been a member . . . should pay £5.1.0 – the £5 is to cover himself and his kraal so that he should not be burnt out . . . A man who is regarded as a traitor . . . is fined £14 when he is discovered. This money is collected, and the fund for the impi is built up.[125]

According to Somadlangati, the people of Lambasi "were in full agreement with us. . . . we could safely go to Qaukeni and burn the Paramount Chief."[126]

During the revolt 1,500 people, many "walking four deep," others on horseback, marched to Gladwin's kraal and burnt it to the ground.[127] "The procession was about 1 $^1/_2$ miles long." Again the Zionist churches played their part. The men had been "doctored" by a herbalist. Evangelists "also prayed for blessing." Once they had said " 'Amen' the men must jump up and take their arms."[128] Men carried guns, sticks, knob-kerries, and bush knives. Women patrolled the area and were instructed to "send word across to warn us that the [police] vans were coming." A man with binoculars also monitored the situation. The men burnt four of Gladwin's five huts, saving one that kept grain for the children. "We were not fighting against the children," a man later testified. "The Chief," he continued, "who is a Chief under the Bantu Authorities, cannot pay money to save his life – the constitution [of Congo] says that. His throat should be cut."[129]

As "the flames were leaping sky high" a helicopter appeared; so also did a number of police vans. A serious clash ensued, with the police and military using teargas and arresting a number of men involved in the destruction of Gladwin's huts. Much of the resistance was organized from Nqusa hill, near Vlei location. Here there would be a serious clash between the Congo and the police using teargas and helicopter, which included Congo members from Bizana and Flagstaff.[130]

Gladwin survived the attack. Many others were burned out, however, and a number of people were murdered by the Congo. "All the Chiefs who were appointed under the Bantu Authorities with their followers and the members of the Tribal Authorities, were to be burnt out – right up to the Paramount Chief – [and] also all who co-operate with the Government officials."[131] There was even talk of an attack on Qaukeni.[132]

By October 1960, throughout the Transkei there was "tremendous general agitation against many of the Chiefs, Headmen and the Tribal Authorities." Pondoland was in a state of open revolt. In the Gcaleka regional authority "signs of active opposition are appearing." Other areas were "also likely trouble spots."[133] In Thembuland people held mountain meetings where they organized resistance against Bantu Authorities; "any one who refused to join them or who refused to contribute to their fund will be shot and his kraal burned." Each location "was to elect its own committee." They were to assassinate police informants, "kill Government servants and burn their kraals," and "fight against Bantu Authorities."[134] At the beginning of 1961 "a group of men" "brutally murdered" the chairman of the local district authority at Bashee location, headman Spalding Matyile.[135]

One official neatly summarized the developing resistance. Beginning with "general agitation" against Bantu Authorities, threats and the actual use of violence against people participating in Bantu Authorities followed. "At the same time pressure is brought to bear on the Europeans in the district by means of boycott and threats of boycott." "After success has been achieved," he continued, "the people form their own courts and resist all attempt on law and order. They refuse to pay taxes or comply with any of the requisites of Government-controlled administration."[136] They had, in short, delegitimized the state. But the official was only half right. Resistance typically began at the very point where the state was attempting to render African space and African subjects more legible and thus more compliant to its instrumental rule. Thus fencing, surveys, and censuses were among the first things people resisted. The sensibilities that created this resistance flowed directly into the formation and structure of the Congo.[137]

Delegitimization took a number of forms and very often entailed considerable violence. According to one lengthy analysis of the revolt in Bizana, "the National Headquarters of the Rebel movement was at Ndlovu Hill in Entsinbini Location. All Rebels from all over the district were expected to attend the meetings at Ndlovu Hill. From those meetings each 'cell' returned to its own location to carry out the decisions made at the National Headquarters."[138] Beginning with its own body of laws[139] the Congo, as we have seen, developed what was in effect a system of governance that stood in opposition to Bantu Authorities. It had its own system of taxation and a court system, a "People's Court," that had assumed the right to take life. The Congo also, importantly, began distributing land.[140] The fifth law of the Congo, for example, dictated that the group should be responsible for allocating land for agriculture and for erecting homes.

Rebel "cells" based primarily in individual locations met on the tops of hills, first during the day and increasingly at night. People who refused to attend meetings found themselves threatened and very often burned out of the location.

The Congo, as we have noted, collected money for "the defense fund." This money was also collected, so one man later testified, "for the Nation to guard whatever can happen to the Nation."[141] Again, refusal to pay met with serious threats.[142] People identified by the Congo as collaborating with the apartheid state were fined £5; refusal to pay led to their kraals being burned. In addition to these fines, however, the Congo required alleged collaborators to attend meetings to "prove [their] loyalty." The Congo also required them to burn "the kraals of Government supporters" when instructed to do so.[143] The mountain was the source of the law, as one man put it "here is Law coming out of Ngquza Hill."[144] The "chiefs are no more ruling," another testified, "complaints should be brought to them at the hill."[145] "Everything," one man testified, "is decided on the hill-tops."[146]

By the end of 1960 rebels held meetings virtually every day. In Bizana the Congo held court on Mondays. "They tell the people that they are the Mountain Court and that there are no Chiefs."[147] "The Mountain Court has usurped my powers and functions," one chief complained. "They intimidate the people so that the latter do not attend my Court but they hold their own Court."[148] At other meetings the Congo planned attacks on people supporting Bantu Authorities or who were suspected of being traitors. As with Makhulu Span, the Congo turned on people who were not employees of the state but who also became the targets of violence. People who refused to participate in the Congo found themselves the targets of violence, including murder. There appear to have been considerable threats to force people to participate in violence. "People who did not attend Congo meetings would be cut up," one man stated; they would be killed.[149] And they were.[150] Failure to pay money to the Congo also met with violence; as one man put it, the Congo was "extorting money from the people."[151]

Incendiarism represented a central feature of the Congo movement. Warren wrote that "every single person who had joined the rebel movement was required to become a member of the burning party";[152] failure to participate in the violence held dire consequences. The Congo attacked collaborators with the apartheid state, people they considered to be enemies, and, in addition, witches. This incendiarism very often involved many people, at times upwards of seven hundred. Interestingly, sometimes the firings took place on a Sunday, as if the Lord's day of purification was also the ideal moment to cleanse the community of evil.[153] A typical act of incendiarism was the attack on one sub-chief. People began assembling at dusk. Once they got close to the kraal, the leader "said that all those who had firearms had to stand of the side as they (numbering some seventeen people) had to approach the kraal ahead of the others." "When we got to the cattle kraal" one rebel "fired and we all fired thereafter. We did not see any persons at the kraal and we shouted to the others to come. We turned all the cattle out of the kraal. When the crowd got to the kraal they set the huts alight. The whole kraal was destroyed."[154]

It would be easy to explain the use of fire as simply an effective way of dealing with one's enemies. However, it is important to note that hut burnings invariably followed, instead of preceding, murders. Killing a person was not enough. Rebels went to rather elaborate lengths to ensure fire destroyed homesteads. Even when rains had soaked the thatch, making it difficult to ignite the material, the commitment to fire was unwavering. Rebels dismembered their victims' bodies or dragged the warm corpses into burning huts to destroy their souls. Combatants forced one man to drink buckets of water until he began vomiting. Like fire, purgatives have long been important in the struggle against witchcraft. In this case the man ended up being stabbed in the chest, limbs cut from his body, and his corpse placed in a hut that was then set on fire.[155]

This evidence and other data, such as the ritual administration of medicines to strengthen rebels, suggest that magic and witchcraft formed an important feature of the revolt, if not for everyone then probably for most. Certainly throughout the region people spoke of magic. Politicking across eastern and western Pondoland, Segwebo Mhlanga had amassed power and directly competed with Gladwin. He enlisted a ritual specialist to "strengthen him," to good effect. For after one meeting Gladwin "became speechless and collapsed . . . This was hailed as another victory for Sigwebo [*sic*] whose witch doctor, so all the Bantu people believed, had overcome Gladwin." Then the secretary of the Mtshayelo authority also fell ill "and fearing that he was also bewitched, handed in his records and ceased to function."[156] A meeting called for by the magistrate in early March 1960 was canceled because Fenwick's condition had become so severe.

For those who believed in magic, neither Gladwin's sudden muteness and fainting nor Fenwick's disorders were simply the results of mere physical or mental ailments. These were rather the consequences of powerful magic confronting evil. It is likely that such people perceived chiefs and others working for or cooperating with the introduction of Bantu Authorities, perhaps including magistrates, as using witchcraft. In Amandengane location Congo members murdered a sub-headman whom they described as a thief, as someone who "worries us about the allocation of lands," and who was married to a witch who caused the death of a child.[157] At the same time Congo members employed ritual specialists to protect them in their coming battles. An important Congo leader at Ndlovu hill, for example, had "a big reputation" as a "well-known witchdoctor." "All of the people of Amadiba Location," one man stated, "are afraid . . . because he is a powerful witch-doctor and they are afraid that he will send their lightning."[158]

The revolt, it seems, was as much about getting rid of the Bantu Authorities system as it was ridding the world of the evil that had so overcome it. Occasionally officials noted the "religious slant" of the movement, though the archival record carries scant data on the crucial issues of magic and evil. A number of

important Congo leaders were also native evangelists, people who believed in
the existence of a black nation that confronted evil and which promised rain and
social health. At times people referred to the court at "their National Headquarters at Ndlovu Hill as a 'Holy Court'."[159] Meetings were begun with prayers in
which rebels "prostrate themselves on the ground with their foreheads touching
the ground." Rebels "found a list under a stone containing the names of the
Tribal Authority Councillors and this list was placed there by the Deity."[160] "It
would almost seem," one official wrote but could not quite understand, "as if
the Rebels are under the impression that they are conducting a Holy war and
that what they are doing has the approval of the Deity."[161]

Aftermath

In November 1960 the apartheid government declared a state of emergency,
which remained in effect until the end of apartheid itself some three decades
later. Soon after the declaration a "large body of Police" were "concentrated
in the troubled areas."[162] The police action involved mass arrests, the use of
teargas, and the use of planes and a helicopter. According to one man police
assaulted "women and children" and confiscated property.[163] Some of the most
violent police action was at Nqusa hill, where a number of people were shot.
"The Government officials come along and they use the order of the gun and they
kill us," one man testified. "How can we go to them now with our grievances,
because it is the Government who causes our death."[164]

The authorities largely succeeded in breaking up the meetings of the Congo
and other groups. The police conducted "continuous raids . . . to ensure that law
and order be observed and that taxes, etc. are paid." The permit system, an
important component of the authoritarian state's attempt to control people in
the reserves, was enforced with far greater force. Chiefs received "increased
power" and protection. And the state began generating "lists of persons deemed
undesirable . . . in order that these persons can be suitably dealt with."[165] Despite
the widespread support for the revolt, headmen and chiefs singled out people
for expulsion from their locations.[166]

By January 1961 the army and police had quashed resistance in Pondoland,
though the "law and order" that had "been restored . . . may be superficial."
In Lusikisiki the situation remained very unstable, and in Mount Ayliff the
Congo had yet to "be dealt with." But over 3,500 people had been detained
in Pondoland alone; they were either released or charged. Approximately 281
people had died in the conflict.[167] Some 160 "listed persons" were also arrested,
though "there are still many who have so far escaped arrest."[168] Following the
police crackdown, for example, Segwebo Mhlanga had fled to Durban.[169] In
Bizana the state had prosecuted over 2,200 people on charges ranging from
murder to failing to produce their passbooks. Sixty-five people were arrested

on charges of murder or culpable homicide. The vast majority, however, were arrested for offenses related to taxes.[170] People who had accepted lands from the "Men from the hill" were also being dealt with.[171] The taxes in many areas of Pondoland were being "well paid and large sums are being collected."[172] But beneath this veil of compliance, however, there was still "a tremendous effort" at resisting Bantu Authorities and reclamation.[173]

Officials evinced surprise at the extent of African resistance and the depth of anger at the Bantu Authorities system. "I have never known of another instance in the Transkei," wrote the chairman of the commission of inquiry, "where various clans or districts simultaneously come up with the identical grievances."[174] Many officials suspected the ANC of being responsible for fomenting rebellion.[175] There is precious little data to support such ideas of conspiracy. Even the chairman of the commission of inquiry admitted that it was "difficult to determine" whether the revolt "has been inspired by some communistic organisation or the ANC."[176] By May 1961, however, the ANC leaders were attempting to appropriate rural resistance in Pondoland. The obstacles were enormous. The ANC, and indeed the other major political organizations in the country, had been banned. Congress leaders faced the fateful decision of forming Umkhonto we Sizwe, its armed wing, the Spear of the Nation. The South African Communist Party already had committed itself to an armed guerrilla struggle. Such a struggle would require a rural base; the Transkei, already seething in discontent, could be central to a violent struggle to overthrow apartheid.[177]

Early in May, Govan Mbeki arrived at Quagga's Nek via Lesotho. At a meeting with three others Mbeki "told us that he had been instructed by the Head Office of the National Action Council . . . that a Sub-Office under the Port Elizabeth Branch . . . should be established." Mbeki instructed the men that the region would be divided into four zones and that their purpose would be to organize resistance against Bantu Authorities and Bantu education.[178] Mbeki was not the only ANC official to visit the region. A Lusikisiki man recalled that an ANC member arrived in his area from Lesotho. "He mentioned some names of the leaders, but . . . the only name I can remember . . . is that of Mandela. He explained to us," continued the man, "that our Congo Movement during the Unrest was similar to their 'Congress' movement. He further said that we should get all the people in our district to join his 'Congress' movement."[179]

A commission of inquiry was held at the Bizana aerodrome where people were invited by the state to "air their grievances and submit any complaints."[180] Five thousand people came. As before, people recited the usual litany of grievances: rising taxes, new and often more costly controls on labor, especially the pass system which often forced a "holder of a reference book . . . to borrow money to proceed to the labour centres,"[181] changes in the legal system, and, again, that Bantu Authorities had been foisted on them. With Bantu

Authorities, "Chiefs were appointed and also Councillors without consultation with the people."[182] The committee "found that some of these complaints were quite justified."[183] But nothing came of their grievances.

By January 1961 Pondoland was, in effect, under military rule. The army was busily arresting people for failure to pay taxes. A "steady stream" of laborers began heading off to the mines. Others tried to plant crops. In one area in Flagstaff the SAP reported men dressed "in female attire" trying to hoe their lands.[184] Violence continued in Pondoland well into 1962. In September rebels opened fire on the police who had come to arrest a suspect in Bizana.[185] Congo meetings may have continued into 1963. In Bizana district one man "said [that] anybody who did not attend Congo meetings must be killed." He also prophesied that "a pig will come from the sea with firearms."[186] Others said that "the Russians were going to give us freedom ... we were going to be given firearms."[187]

The state condemned some twenty rebels to death by hanging. A few had their sentences commuted; in one case the accused was acquitted on appeal and released from jail. Many more had risked their lives fighting the apartheid state, only to find themselves languishing in prisons whose infamy would become legendary. According to the Truth and Reconciliation Commission "torture was a key part" of the mass detentions in the wake of the revolt.[188] At the time a number of accused rebels testified they had been tortured. To try to elicit confessions officials had administered electric shocks to their bodies. This was the first use of torture by the authoritarian state.[189] The men's screams would in later years be joined by many others.

8   Flights of the lightning bird

I am here to warn you, whilst at the same time I am advising you that the
road you are taking being that of the so-called "Bantu Authority", to retard
the progress of the Blackman, is a dangerous one. The oppressors are bravely
shouting that this country of ours does not belong to the Blackman. So, as the
indigenous person of this country, what is your opinion, or are you one? Not in a
distant time, the Blackman is going to be a master in his own country . . . Chief,
I still put it to you that after this time, only chiefs like Hintsa, Dingaan, Moshesh
and Cetywayo will survive and enjoy the fruits of freedom.[1]

The meetings, beginning in 1961, took place late at night, after men laboring
hard in the factories and manufacturing businesses of the Western Cape had
returned to their bachelor compounds and hostels in Langa and Nyanga, the
sprawling black townships just outside Cape Town. A number of men, "strange
men," one later stated,[2] would enter a room wearing balaclava masks, demanding to see the influx-control permits and passes of the residents. Then the men
announced their purpose, to gather recruits for a new organization that would
fight with arms to "conquer the Europeans and take our country back from
us as they had stolen the country from us."[3] The new organization, Poqo, the
military wing of the Pan Africanist Congress (PAC), means to be "pure" or to
stand or be "alone." Along with other political organizations and trade unions,
the PAC had been banned by the apartheid government in 1960 in the context
of the Sharpeville massacre, the Pondoland Revolt, and the wave of African
resistance that coursed over much of the country. In the official mind Poqo
was a terrorist organization that, moreover, confirmed the African's essential
madness and irrationality.

Over a number of months nightly meetings took place across the Western
Cape townships; the extensive recruitment succeeded. Men joined the new
organization, discussed the coming armed struggle, began preparing for battle.
A number of the members had recently lived in Mbekweni, the township outside
the agricultural town of Paarl, where many worked in places such as the local jam
factory or in small businesses, such as Tractors Spares. Between 1959 and 1962
Mbekweni had become the site of a paroxysm of resistance and repression.[4]
Others had witnessed or had participated in the great march to parliament in

Cape Town to protest against the pass laws in early 1960. A "large number of" the marchers were "peasant-type demonstrators," a Liberal Party member wrote, migrant workers who were "the section of Africans hardest hit by the pass laws."[5]

One of the most urgent topics of conversation among the workers concerned developments in the Transkei hundreds of miles to the east: the introduction of the Bantu Authorities system; the labour bureaux system; influx control and the state's increasing control over labor; and the rise of Chief Kaiser Matanzima, recently appointed by the apartheid state paramount chief and head of the Thembu tribal authority, and soon to be head of the Transkei National Independence Party and authoritarian ruler of the Transkei homeland. The new Poqo members explicitly connected Matanzima to the prosecution of influx control in the Western Cape as well as rehabilitation and resettlement in the Transkei.[6] By early February 1962, the decision had been reached to "send Poqo armies . . . to kill all the Europeans, Coloured, Indians and people not of our race . . . All the chiefs particularly Chief Matanzima," as well as headmen and the magistrate at Cofimvaba, "had to be killed."[7]

In early December 1962, some thirty-odd men bought train tickets headed east for Queenstown. They brought with them an assortment of weapons which they hid in the train's ventilation shaft: a few pistols, knives, machetes, and homemade weapons such as a hoop iron sharpened at both ends. They had also received ritual protection. Small incisions near the scalp, into which some substance, probably gunpowder, was placed, would project them from the lightning bird and the white man's bullets. In the following days others boarded trains for the Transkei. By the time the first group arrived Poqo was already active in Thembuland and in other parts of the Transkei and Ciskei. The "advance army" left the Cape on Sunday evening and arrived in Queenstown the following Tuesday morning.[8] There they boarded a bus that snaked its way first up to Lady Frere and then towards Qamata, stopping along the way to disgorge travelers and especially migrant workers who labored in the Cape or on the Rand. Late in the afternoon the men got out at a bus stop five or ten miles outside of Qamata, near the Indwe River and the base of a series of mountains rising to an elevation of over 4,500 feet. The men climbed up into the mountains, received additional ritual protection, and slept the night in one of the many caves in the area. Many years before Thwa hunter-gatherers also had used these caves, often embellishing them with paintings of eland, trance dances, and, occasionally, pictorial stories of the colonial conquest that led to their extermination.

Once they had made camp the leader sent some of the men to return to the Queenstown railroad station "to meet reinforcements from Cape Town" and to nearby locations where Poqo was active.[9] The following morning the men awoke to overcast skies and approaching rains; by late afternoon soft and nourishing rains had turned heavy so that a thick mist enveloped the mountains.

The men moved into the forests where some fashioned weapons from "plain sticks."[10] The plan was to wait for reinforcements before the Poqo army attacked Matanzima's village. The police, however, had caught wind of the intended attack. Soon some sixty "uniformed men [were] coming up the mountain."[11] There ensued, in the words of the divisional commissioner of police, a "most vicious deliberate attack ... I have never seen anything like it before."[12] The Poqo men rushed the police with their ragtag weapons "screaming and shouting war cries."[13] One of the men stabbed a white warrant officer with a home-made sword; in total the Poqo fighters injured three men, one seriously. The police killed six Poqo fighters. The other men, many of them bleeding from gunshot wounds, fled back into the forest. Over the following days they moved from mountain to mountain and then attempted to blend back into their rural communities.[14]

As the advance army combed the forest a fierce battle between Poqo fighters and the police had erupted at the Queenstown railway station. The police had stopped, as they disembarked from the Cape Town train, a number of men who, unlike most migrant laborers, had not brought with them their trunks and blankets. The police led the men "in dribs and drabs in a bunch" through the general exit.[15] As the police were trying to get the men to form a line against the outside railway building wall shots rang out. Four people died, including one white policeman who "was hacked to death with pangas near the entrance to the station as he tried to escape from the mob."[16] Four other whites and ten Africans lay wounded in the hospital; the police had shot dead three of the Poqo fighters. The rest fled into the town and, over the next few days, tried to elude capture and struggled to return to their rural homes. The police commissioner sent out armored cars to patrol the streets of Queenstown and began an air and land search for the fleeing Poqo fighters.

These were not the only Poqo attacks in the Eastern Cape. Although Poqo was especially active in Thembuland the secret militant organization oper-ated throughout much of the region. Poqo was implicated in the murders of at least two headmen. In the districts of Uitenhage and in Lady Frere and in Kingwilliamstown, Poqo planned to kill whites, cut telegraph wires, and destroy police stations and Bantu Administration offices; there was even a Poqo group in the small town of Graaff-Reinet. In Mqanduli, Poqo leaders spoke of decolonization and freedom, and ended the meetings of some thirty to forty people "with the words 'our country' while the participants raised their hands."[17]

In early February 1963, Poqo struck at whites who were camping in caravans along the banks of the Bashee River. After throwing petrol bombs at the caravans the Poqo fighters attacked the inhabitants, hacking five people to death.[18] The state's response to these attacks, particularly the Bashee River murders, was swift. By June 1963 over a hundred people had been convicted of murder;

another seventy-seven were still awaiting trial. Over a hundred Africans had been charged with attempted murder; fifty-three people had been detained with regard to the Bashee River murders alone. In total the state had arrested more than three thousand suspected Poqo members.[19] The 1962 Sabotage Act came in especially handy: by June 1963 over a hundred people had been convicted under the new legislation; over five hundred awaited trial.[20]

Poqo was not the only organization to engage in violence. In 1961 the African National Congress formed Umkhonto we Sizwe, the Spear of the Nation. A number of its important leaders, including Nelson Mandela, left South Africa and received military training abroad. In the middle of December 1961, Umkhonto bombs exploded in Johannesburg, Durban, and Port Elizabeth. Over a period of some eighteen months Umkhonto launched some two hundred attacks, virtually all of them in urban centers. Most of these attacks involved small bombs and incendiary devices aimed at police stations, magistrate's offices, and other public buildings, or the destruction of telephone wires and railway signals. While the Umkhonto leadership intended to avoid bloodshed, indiscipline at the lower ranks resulted in attacks on policemen and suspected informers.[21] The vast majority of Umkhonto attacks took place in large cities, especially in Durban and in Port Elizabeth, where the ANC had substantial followings. Port Elizabeth saw the greatest concentration of attacks (fifty-eight). Here Umkhonto set fire to the police station, severed telephone wires, and tampered with the railway line.[22]

In the context of the Pondoland Revolt and ongoing rural resistance, the ANC continued its attempts, begun especially in the 1950s, to extend its control beyond its historic urban base of support and into the countryside. Other nationalist organizations also stepped up their interest in rural areas, especially the All-African Convention (AAC). Particularly in the 1950s the AAC successfully linked up with local organizations such as vigilance associations and, especially, the Cape African Teachers' Association (CATA), which helped spearhead resistance to the introduction of the Bantu Authorities system.[23] The AAC helped shape resistance to Bantu Authorities, rehabilitation, and Bantu education. Only from the late 1950s, however, did the ANC begin to emphasize rural areas. In 1955, the national executive committee resolved that "the question of organising the peasants must be tackled."[24] In a secret 1958 letter, the police expressed concern that Africans entering the Transkei "were organising members of the African National Congress and that they were distributing subversive African National Congress Pamphlets at night."[25]

In 1960 the ANC had expressed its support for the revolt and had called "upon all the people of the Transkeian territories to pledge their solidarity with the people of Pondoland by immediately launching in their respective areas the resistance campaign against Bantu Authorities."[26] By this time, and in the context of rising radicalization and persecution, the organization well recognized the importance of rural protest. The magistrate at Tsolo received a letter from Langa, Cape Town, ostensibly written "under the instructions of the African National Congress" protesting against the Trust, accusing the police of corruption, and demanding an end to the scourge of stock theft in the area.[27] The ANC, however, was for the most part unable to harness the anger and ongoing rural struggles unfolding across much of the Eastern Cape, from the Congo meetings that continued into 1963 to the ubiquitous struggles against rehabilitation, registration, and the Bantu Authorities system.[28] Indeed, even as it reluctantly embraced violence as a political instrument, the ANC remained committed to a bourgeois politics that, ultimately, had roots in the political culture of conquest during the nineteenth century. That political culture, or at least one part of it, had been universalist in orientation. One facet of conquest, that concerned with the civilizing mission of the British, had scripted the African as a bourgeois individual with inalienable rights in a political world in which the state was conceived of as neutral arbiter and protector. Even in violence the ANC remained committed to this essentially liberal-democratic vision of nation and state.

The PAC was much different. By the early 1960s the organization had adopted a Maoist ideology that embraced violence and spontaneous insurrection. It saw the world in apocalyptic terms, a Manichaean struggle against the forces of evil. The oppressor was not simply to be defeated, but was rather to be obliterated. Only by eliminating the oppressor could the dream of a new, liberated, and just order be realized. Violence thus had a fundamentally purifying role, ridding the world of evil at the same time as it recreated the colonized as a new, whole, person. This recreation, this reconstruction of humanity, entailed not only the death of the white oppressor, but also the renunciation of their culture which had destroyed the soul of the colonized. South Africa was a colonial society. Freedom would come only by purging the country of every trace of colonialism. Committed to an apocalyptic violence, the PAC's ideology underscored the importance of the everyday miseries the colonized lived and their unrealized revolutionary capacities. Through both organized resistance and spontaneous violence, the colonized could overturn oppression and bring a "return of power to the indigenous 'sons of the soil.'"[29]

These issues resonated with the men who joined Poqo, as they did for many other people in the Eastern Cape for whom the problem of evil occupied an important part of their moral and political imagination. Poqo attacks had little to do with the bourgeois rights of the individual or the reformation of the state, but rather with the return of a world destroyed or suppressed by colonialism and its tyranny of racial ideology. It was in part precisely the otherness of Poqo – its seeming barbarousness and madness, its epitomizing the essential irrationality of the native – that so troubled the authorities: not to mention many nationalist elites. Poqo thus formed part of a longer history of the critique of power not simply circumscribed by colonial conquest and rule. In this sense the movement both engaged colonial domination and transcended it; the consciousness of Poqo members cannot be reduced to a mere effect of colonial power; rather, it formed part of the Africans' historic conversation about power and authority.

We have discussed this historic or ancestral conversation many times. We located its beginnings in the migration of Bantu-speaking agriculturists into the region, their complex mythic and historic relationships with the First People, and especially in the hero-founders who slew lions and leopards and reconciled their presence with the First People, and who helped ensure rains and bountiful crops. Polity and production were thus inextricably intertwined, a fragile double helix held together by history and ritual and the human imagination but susceptible to being torn apart by avarice and the chaos sowed by those who wield destructive magic. The cupidity of man brought instability to the world even as it created a world of possibility. People grappled with the problem of evil that lurked, always, in the shadows of their lives, in the world just beyond the homestead.

The problem of evil, and the rich discourse it produced, was a historic one and, as we have seen, continued into the colonial period. It became a way by which the colonized scrutinized colonial power and, in so doing, translated the colonial state into indigenous concepts and practices. Those concepts and practices had their own history. The horrors of colonialism joined the promises of Christian redemption to reshape people's everyday beliefs and their engagement in the world, offering at once a vision of a better future even in the face of a profoundly evil, perhaps even socially dead, present. And now the rhetoric of violent revolution nourished this fertile imagination and the hopes, anxieties, and sorrows it sustained.

For Poqo the issue was not just that apartheid was wrong, that it denied Africans their natural rights within the modern state. Or that it confiscated property arbitrarily. Or that passes and the labour bureaux system had produced a draconian control over people's movements. Or that the Bantu Authorities system created a new wave of insecurity over people's access to land. Or that the same system reduced their ability to seek legal redress. Or that it led to rising corruption among chiefs and other apartheid collaborators. Or that Bantu education was an education of servility, a pedagogy of submission. Or that apartheid created such terrible pain and hardship in the daily lives of its subjects. All of this is true . . . but there is more.

In the imagination of Poqo insurgents it was not simply that apartheid was wrong, a violation of their rights, a regime of prejudice. Apartheid was *evil*, profoundly so, which could only be addressed by a purifying violence. It is this issue of evil that ties the history of Poqo, the eastwards journeys of men from the townships of the Western Cape, and the battle in the forest and at the

Queenstown station to PAC ideology as well as to the historic conversation of Africans concerning the nature and location of wickedness in the world – and how best to battle it. For Poqo elaborated a vision of violence as a purifying force, a kind of fundamentalism that fused evil with modern nationalism. Many of the participants in the Pondoland Revolt ultimately had turned to violence reluctantly, and only after near-constant pleas to state officials. Poqo, however, relished the prospect of a bloodshed that would somehow set right historic wrongs. Their actions form part of a tradition of violence that connects, for example, Poqo to the necklacings of the 1980s and 1990s.

A ubiquitous feature of Poqo were the rituals fighters participated in, both in the Cape and in the Transkei. These rituals usually entailed small incisions on the head and upper back, and were intended to protect them from the white man's bullets and also from the *impundulu* bird, the magical animal invariably associated with witchcraft and the work of evil. Such incisions were not unusual; what was new was their inclusion in a violent social movement. They typically were made "because you have some ailment or other and the mpundulu bird worries you."[30] People suffered from aches and pains when the lightning bird "troubled me," one Poqo member testified.[31] Other Poqo members, all of them migrant workers, spoke of being troubled by the *impundulu* bird while in the Cape and away from their rural homes. "When I got to Capetown," one man testified, "the Mpundulu started, I think the power of the incisions was failing."[32] The return to the Transkei and the attack on collaborators such as Matanzima was one way of getting rid of "this sickness."[33] Another testified that "whenever I leave home I get incisions, when i [sic] leave my place of employment going home I get incisions in order to drive away evil spirits."[34]

These practices, then, were an important part of the culture of labor migration. Now they became a central feature in the men's struggle against apartheid. Matanzima not only "has sold our land"[35] but, it seems, was seen as one source of the "evil spirits" that troubled the souls of migrant laborers in the Cape. That he was viewed as manipulating occult power is not surprising. The accretion of political power was often seen as accompanied by the use (and abuse) of magic. And, as we have seen, the subaltern had endowed the modern state with magical powers – the modern state as witch and Matanzima as a witch chief. Matanzima escaped murder because he had been successfully "doctored."[36] Collaborators used evil magic. One was accused of being a vampire who drank "the last drop of their blood."[37]

To confront magic requires magic. In the secret Poqo meetings in the Cape the fighters were bathed and incisions made on their bodies, into which were rubbed medicine to strengthen them and protect them from the *impundulu* bird. In the forest the men were again "treated," their bodies "washed with doctored water,"[38] and a black powder pressed into the incision. "We were told we were going to be treated so that the bullets do not hit us," a Poqo fighter testified.[39]

The incisions were "to make me strong and kill the chief and everybody who wants to fight us including the Europeans."[40]

Beginnings, endings

Kaiser Matanzima's rise to power had begun in the 1940s, and had accelerated in the 1950s with the introduction of the Bantu Authorities system and the triumph of authoritarianism in South Africa. The chief magistrate of the Transkei officially installed him as chief of the Hala clan of the Thembu in 1940. This was, in Matanzima's words, "the first time in the history of the Emigrant Tembus to have a chief in line of succession installed under the Native Administration Act of 1927."[41] That Act, as we have seen, represented a crucial moment in the invention of tribalism and the rise of a patrimonial authoritarianism in the reserves. At this juncture Matanzima acknowledged that he was subordinate to Paramount Chief Dalindyebo Sabata (whose nephew is Nelson Mandela), though during the 1940s he had lobbied the Native Affairs Department to be recognized as senior chief over Thembu in Emigrant Thembuland. This the state did by 1952. As Matanzima put it, this was a "time when I was marshalling and consolidating my administrative and judicial duties as set out in the 1927 act."[42]

Officials, however, well knew that Matanzima's authority scarcely extended beyond his district and that "conferment of additional authority . . . would no doubt make him more loyal to the Government" but would likely create "dissatisfaction" among various groups.[43] They looked to anthropological wisdom to uphold their position, specifically the ethnological publications produced by the state ethnologist J. Van Warmelo. Yet despite these and other misgivings – officials knew exactly the artificiality of their various tribal creations – this is precisely the road the state traveled. Of course Matanzima encouraged precisely this course of action. He wrote, in 1953, that he "was under the positive impression that the Government would shoulder me with more administrative and judicial duties so as [to] test the efficiency of the African Chiefs in running their affairs in according with the Government's policy of Apartheid. I built the tribal offices with that object in view."[44]

Certainly by 1954 Matanzima was using "his powers of ruling" to extend his control over people who did not recognize his legitimacy.[45] As we have seen, Bantu Authorities unleashed a wave of contestation over the structure and character of so-called traditional authority, not simply chiefs but especially paramount chiefs who ostensibly headed the various tribal authorities. The situation further deteriorated from late 1955. At a meeting in December attended by Sabata and Matanzima, in which the paramount was to appoint a chief in the district, Sabata in frustration said to Matanzima: "My younger brother, despite the announcement I made in the meeting, you want more. Is it so brother? What more do you want?"[46] Kaiser wanted more, much more. The minutes of subsequent meetings illustrate clearly Matanzima's jockeying for power, in large part by raising the specter of the growth of Paramount Chief Sabata's power. "The property of one house cannot be appropriated by another," one man declared. "The cattle belonging to one house cannot go to another. Matanzima has his rights here [in Cofimvaba]."[47]

Sabata was interested in expanding the power of the paramountcy. He was, however, caught between the perils of collaboration – and inevitable delegitimization – and the expansive politics of a traditional political institution whose viability increasingly rested on cooperation with the state. He equivocated, in part because he sought out reasonable positions.[48] But he also failed. Authoritarianism and principle seldom are on speaking terms. By the mid-1950s "modernizing" chiefship inevitably involved complicity with the apartheid state, including its considerable coercive apparatus. Matanzima suffered from no such doubts; such are the prerogatives of upstarts and wannabes. In 1956 there had been "a violent quarrel between Paramount Chief Dalindyebo Sabata and Chief Kayser Matanzima...regarding areas of jurisdiction and allegiance."[49] In a November 1956 meeting of the two chiefs Matanzima had affronted Sabata by having his praise singer compete "against his own."[50] This situation continued to deteriorate, in terms of Matanzima's relationships with Sabata and with Chief Victor Poto, paramount chief of western Pondoland. By the end of the decade Matanzima had thrown in his lot with the apartheid state. Indeed the "pedestal he sits on was created by the influence of the Bantu Affairs Commissioner."[51]

Clearly the state was intimately involved in the rise of Matanzima. It was also intimately involved in his disputes with Sabata, Poto, and others. The state's agricultural policies – especially stabilization – became points of conflict around the extent of Matanzima's power and his embattled relationship with Sabata. In 1962, to take but one example, once Sabata heard of the plans for stabilization "contemplated in this District he sent messengers to stir up trouble...and before long the residents started agitating against stabilisation and a crisis was only averted through prompt action taken by the Bantu Affairs commissioner and Chief K. D. Mantanzima."[52] As elsewhere the strongest support typically came from people who found themselves "obliged," the state euphemism for forced, "to move their residential allotments in conformity with approved planning."[53] In this case the state managed to have Sabata's influence "removed." According to the Bantu Affairs commissioner "the result is that the Bantu have all now accepted not only reclamation but rehabilitation and they are whole-heartedly co-operating in carrying out the planning of the District."[54]

State support was thus "the crucial factor in securing" Matanzima's "political base."[55] This became ever more crucial in the years leading up to the 1963 elections and, following the elections, Matanzima's formation of the Transkei National Independence Party (TNIP), which furthered his aim at attaining control of the Bantustan state. Matanzima, Southall has remarked, "was reputed to be ruthless, brutal and authoritarian." The chief "campaigned in favour of separate development."[56] His major opponent, Chief Victor Poto, sympathized with the ANC and, not surprisingly, "strongly repudiated separate development, apartheid and all the racial divisive politics of the Republic."[57] A full discussion of this election is beyond the scope of this book.[58] Three points are apposite. First, Matanzima quickly abandoned any hope of gaining popular support and, instead, managed to secure the allegiance of chiefs who, as we have seen, increasingly had cast their lot with the apartheid state. This allowed Matanzima to procure sufficient support within the assembly to emerge as chief minister (and later prime minister and then state president) and, more ominously, to begin his patrimonial consolidation of the authoritarian Bantustan state.

Second, the election formed an integral part of the process of state formation. At its most basic level it required the registration of voters, in short a new wave by which the state attempted to render its subject ever more legible. The push to register voters in the early years of the 1960s thus should be seen as an intrinsic part of state formation in this period, part of a broader set of developments that included land registration, the labour bureaux system, and various rehabilitation policies. NAD officials assiduously pursued voter registration. "The Registration of Voters," one official wrote, "has not been proceeding at all well. Elements in the locations have bee totally opposed to registration of voters." However, a push by the NAD officials, the commissioner general, and Matanzima "have gone a long way to dispel their suspicions."[59] Officials, for example, handed out pamphlets about voter registration, often at the same time as they distributed anti-Poqo literature; people often displayed a "greater interest" in the latter.[60]

The third point concerns the emergence of political parties, a process that was also unfolding in the other Bantustans. Following the 1963 election, and the formation by Poto of the Democratic Party, Matanzima formed the TNIP. Although this party never had any popular support it was unofficially, and substantially, bankrolled by the South African government.[61] Nevertheless it "became unchallengeably dominant" – and corrupt and authoritarian. The party, importantly, did not stand outside the authoritarian state. Rather, it was an intrinsic feature of its formation. The TNIP, moreover, was important to the continued creation of a weakened civil society unable to confront authoritarian rule, a society already weakened by the rising coercive powers of chiefs and headmen. Under the election laws, to take but one example, Africans who did not write were required to state their voting preference before the polling officer and witnesses. The scope for abuse was very wide indeed. And, since "people fear the chiefs because of certain threats, namely that they will be deprived of their rights as well as of their arable allotments . . . they are not prepared to go to the polling station."[62]

It was in this context of the massive social engineering of apartheid and the rise of Matanzima that the Poqo men began meeting in the Cape and planned their journey east. Matanzima became synonymous with apartheid: the new tribalization of the reserves that forced people from their homes; the increasing powers of so-called traditional leaders who now had the full backing of a powerful modern state; the massive stabilization schemes that, among other things, vastly increased the state's surveillance and control of people and property; and the labor-bureaux system that greatly expanded state control over labor and mobility. Matanzima was the quintessence of instrumentality, an avaricious person capable of sowing misfortune among people laboring far away in the Cape.

By 1963 the state had smashed Poqo, as it had virtually all the other political movements in the country. It mounted a vigorous propaganda campaign to combat Poqo. This campaign became an opportunity to have the "power and prestige of the Tribal Authorities and the Chiefs and Headmen . . . maintained and increased." Where "needed," officials were encouraged to mount police raids; after all, "nearly every Kraal has a crime hidden away, whether it is a tax offence or having illegal weapons etc." Controls over Africans working in the Cape were increased. Propaganda warned that Poqo would bring destruction, crop failure, violence, starvation. According to one directive, "Full use should be made of Bantu superstition. The disaster of Nongqawuse (1857) and the horrible results that followed should be made to realistically indicate what will happen to the Bantu who follow methods such as this [Poqo]."[63] The state also distributed some 250,000 pamphlets that connected Poqo to death.[64] These pamphlets, ostensibly invoking the irrationality of the traditional, were distributed "in connection with the registration of voters."[65] Never had the state acted so efficiently, if also so ironically.

In less that three years the apartheid state had arrested over 10,000 people in the rural areas of the Ciskei and Transkei. It had charged thousands of people with crimes ranging from murder and sabotage to failure to pay taxes. In the privacy of the jails police shocked men into submission, the wails of humiliated victims trapped by cemented walls. The state of emergency became the rule of everyday life.

Conclusion

We place our vision of a new constitutional order for South Africa on the table not as conquerors, prescribing to the conquered. We speak as fellow citizens to heal the wounds of the past with the intent of constructing a new order based on justice for all.

Nelson Mandela, Inaugural Address, 9 May 1994[1]

Before the Law stands a doorkeeper. To this doorkeeper there comes a man from the country and prays admittance to the Law. But the doorkeeper says that he cannot grant admittance at the moment. The man thinks it over and then asks if he will be allowed in later. "It is possible," says the doorkeeper, "but not at the moment."

Franz Kafka, "Before the Law," *The Penguin Complete Short Stories of Franz Kafka*, ed. N. N. Glatzer (New York, 1983), 3

Democracy has arrived in South Africa. But drought has returned to the Eastern Cape. Between the country's first elections in 1994 and the end of the millennium, drought struck the region not once but twice. By December 1999 close to 60,000 cattle had died of various diseases related to the drought. Cattle perished from lack of water, some after they had become stuck in the mud of depleted stock dams. Sheep abandoned young they were unable to feed. Some areas had received less than half the average rainfall. Farmers compared the drought to 1933, for them the worst drought in living memory. According to one agricultural official, 1999 had the "second-lowest rainy season since 1955,"[2] just before the introduction of Bantu Authorities in the Transkei and the beginning of widespread resistance to the authoritarian state. Nature in the Eastern Cape, it seems, rarely cooperates with modern state formation.

Neither the Transkei nor the Ciskei Bantustans exist as political territories; they now form part of the Eastern Cape Province, one of the new political divisions in the new South Africa. The reincorporation has not been smooth. In many areas the civil services – hospitals, police services – have all but collapsed. Taps serving clinics have dried up, laundry remains unclean. Scarce funds have mysteriously disappeared; political corruption and patrimonialism continue. Stock theft is rife throughout the region; people have taken the law into their own hands. In discussing the current wave of theft, violence, and lawlessness, older men and women in Qumbu and Tsolo recall an earlier era of theft and retribution, the Makhulu Span of the 1950s. Invariably also they return to a still more distant past, the 1880 death of Hamilton Hope – whose monument remains surprisingly well kept, surrounded by tall trees protecting it from the African sun.

People just trying to live a decent life have been swept up in violence. In June 1993, on my way to conduct research on Makhulu Span, I gave a ride to a man whom I shall call "J. M." A very personable individual, J. M. told me how he had worked in the big city of Durban for a few years, then as a truck driver plying the roads of South Africa, and was now the owner of a small shop in Idutywa, one of Transkei's dusty towns. In a desperately poor area like the Transkei, J. M. is a successful, self-made man who is trying to make the best of the cards life has dealt him. He is married and has two daughters. He spoke of his hopes that they would go to college, that their futures might be bright.

When I told him that I was heading to Qumbu he seemed surprised, perhaps even a bit perplexed. He was born in Qumbu and still held a plot of land there on which he kept some stock. I told him that I was conducting research on Makhulu Span. He knew of Makhulu Span, but our conversation quickly turned to stock theft in the 1990s. I asked him if he had lost stock. Yes, he nodded. He then told me that recently a wave of stock theft had swept across the area of Tsolo and Qumbu, just as had happened some four decades earlier. J. M. described the thieves as well-organized young men armed with AK-47s. He alleged that they were aligned with the militant Pan-Africanist Congress. He then explained the purpose of his trip to Umtata. The apprehensiveness I had sensed when we began discussing Makhulu Span became clear. He was to appear in court. Two months earlier, following a rash of larceny, he and seventeen others had captured and, with exceptional ferocity, murdered two men suspected of stock theft.

There is great sickness and tragedy in places such as Qumbu, where since the death of Hamilton Hope so much sadness has reigned. Machine-gun fire and masculine anger possess the land. There is torture, murder, robbery, rape, a universe of shadows cast by the fires of hatred and jealousy and retribution and a grinding poverty to which there seems no end. There has been so much violent death in Qumbu area that the government has created a special court just to deal with the murders. Witchcraft has a ubiquitous presence. There are rumors of the beginning of a new era of frontier wars, a refighting of epic conflicts that took place over a century ago. There are apocalyptic and genocidal visions that demand the obliteration of the evil that is this world before the rebirth of worlds denied and suppressed and yet oddly proximate, as if goodness and health lies just over the next hill, just over the horizon of one's vision. In South Africa, perhaps in most political conflicts where there is also terrible poverty, violence has both ruptured temporality and produced too much history, too much memory, too much anger – perhaps also too much hope.

In the face of today's terrible horrors it is worthwhile pausing and reflecting on the violence modern states are capable of generating as well as the hatred and violence that can be unleashed from among the colonized. Here again South African history provides an exemplary example. Apartheid was evil written in the ink of bureaucratic memoranda, laws, and procedures of a governmental state that stripped the humanity from people officials considered represented so many technical problems. Apartheid, however, was not so much a perversion as one possible consequence of modernity, an endpoint in rationality untethered from morality, a bureaucracy of perfectionism gone perfectly mad. In this sense apartheid was a politics of evil.

At the same time, however, there emerged from within the colonized a complex imagining of the problem of evil. The subaltern politics of evil critiqued the state and summoned a vision of a socially just world, the return of an Africa where the rains fell and in the bounteousness of the earth people could lead a life they deemed worthwhile. But it could produce just the opposite. The fusing of theodicy to politics, of evil and what to do about it, can be productive of justice and injustice, of the reaffirmation of one's humanity as well as a crude legitimization of terror and inhumanity. The politics of evil sustained the peaceful visions of the prophetess Nonthetha. She believed evil had overrun the world and had caused terrible suffering and misfortune. But Nonthetha had another vision, a vision of a new age of peace and equality and harmony.

The subaltern politics of evil, however, also sowed passions of hatred, suspicion, and jealousy. It has nurtured the horrible violence of men who celebrate brutal murder and the burning of flesh. Necklacing is precisely the politics of evil played upon the bodies of its victims by people whose intolerance is directly related to a Manichaean vision of a world of evil and good. In this respect perhaps fundamentalism today is precisely a politics of evil waged in the broken rubble of world history.

The sham boundaries of the sham nation-states of the Transkei, Ciskei, and the other homelands no longer appear on political maps. But of course history is not so easily erased. Signs have been removed, but the earth – that great palimpsest – speaks still. The magisterial boundaries first created in the nineteenth century, and then reworked in the twentieth century's nightmare of segregation and apartheid – the fantasies of tribalism and authoritarianism – in fact remain intact, powerfully so. So also do the various "traditional authorities" that comprised South Africa's "decentralized despotism."[3] Indeed, paramount chiefs continue to head the regional authority courts, convicting people still defined as "Transkei citizens." None other than Chief Kaiser Matanzima heads one such court in western Thembuland.[4]

What to do with the political structures of the former homelands – structures that I have argued are now over a century old – is a subject of considerable discussion and debate in the country, especially given the brute facts of horrible poverty and institutional collapse. As early as 1994 the ANC recognized the importance of transforming local government, both to addressing social and economic challenges and, importantly, to establishing regime legitimacy. "Perhaps the most crucial [challenge] is the establishment of credible and effective Local Government . . . Without this, implementation of development programmes will be seriously hindered."[5] Yet in neither the former Ciskei nor Transkei is local government credible or effective: quite the opposite. Moreover, the political compromise of 1994 led to the ANC taking a distinctly conservative route with regard to political structures in the former homelands where "customary power" remains fundamentally "unreformed."[6] The state may have been deracialized. It has yet to be democratized.[7]

The constitution of South Africa, which took effect in February 1997, enshrined the compromise reached three years earlier. The section on traditional leaders is as unclear and tentative as it is breathtakingly short. The role of such leaders was entirely couched in the conditional voice, including the possible creation of national and provincial "house[s] of traditional leaders."[8] These in fact were created in 1998. It soon became clear, however, that the national house "wants to become a full-time body and to play a more significant role in policy formulation and the finalisation of legislation," and that the provincial houses "have made it clear that they want to play a more substantial role."[9]

The government has now begun to address more substantially the issue of "traditional leadership." In April 2000 it issued "A Draft Discussion Document towards a White Paper on Traditional Leadership and Institutions."[10] The document represents less a departure from current practice than an attempt to legitimize the *status quo ante*. It is in many respects a peculiar text. It fantasizes precolonial polities as "absolute monarchies," a position shared by traditional leaders looking for greater powers in post-apartheid South Africa to secure access to state largesse and the monies flowing from various international development agencies. The document invokes a cultural relativism entombed in various international agreements going as far back as the 1948 Universal Declaration of Human Rights and its enunciation that all people have "the right to participate freely in the cultural life of the community." The text deploys a language of modernization while affirming, effectively in the same breath, the resilience and continuing importance and relevance of customary rule.

The problems of traditional rulers and local government have come together in the attempt by the state to redraw local political boundaries ahead of the 2000 elections. Legislation passed in 1998 and 1999 led to the creation and refinement of local demarcation boards. The process of reworking political space has been highly controversial, especially in former homelands of Ciskei and Transkei. Traditional leaders – who, we should remember, have for close to a century been joined at the hip with the state – threatened to boycott the elections. They claimed that they had not been fully consulted on many basic issues of the demarcation process and, importantly, expressed alarm and frustration with the fact that the process has proceeded slowly and haphazardly. Some traditional leaders "complained that the tribal boundaries have been tampered with and their land demarcated into wards."[11] Others, for example some chiefs in Tsolo, backed the process – or at least how it was described by the local ANC member of parliament: "This process has not come to rob chiefs and other traditional leaders … of their dignity and status, but to enhance them to the level in which they were during the pre-colonial era … The delimitation process aims to address the imbalances of the past by speeding up delivery to improve living standards"[12] Indeed, in early September 2000 the Eastern Cape House of Traditional Leaders endorsed the new system because, according to one reporter, "the new municipal system would broaden the influence and role of traditional leaders."[13]

It is too early to determine where these discussions and changes will in the end lead. Certainly custom and culture will continue to be at the center of the government's attempt to reorganize political space locally.[14] Currently there is precious little evidence that suggests that the government intends on embarking on reforms that would democratize local political structures in the former native reserves. Instead, the government appears simply to want to reconfigure the relationship between the local and central state in such a way as to produce the political consent to ensure that its policies and programs will not be "seriously hindered." The government has, for example, failed to support elected officials in the former homelands of Ciskei and Transkei: many traditional rulers have seen democracy as challenging their power; they protested and lobbied; the government has acquiesced. Crucial issues such as land reform, land allocation, and the resolution of minor disputes remain largely in the hands of traditional rulers. A commitment to social and political democracy seems to be fading into the hills, promises qualified or forgotten, as so many rural people continue to live in squalor and die in the wretchedness of their poverty.

The state of emergency in fact continues. Tuberculosis remains hyper-endemic. Babies perish at alarming rates. Today there is a largely silent history, itself part of a wider moral imagining, that is born and sustained in pain and in whispers and lamentations by women who know that their loss is part of a deeper history of infant death. The violence of desperation, of relentless poverty, ruptures the relations among people: domestic violence, rape; violence against the young and the elderly; the ubiquitous murders and petty larcenies; the gasoline flames of hatred and brutality. Most have witnessed at close quarters extreme forms of violence. Many have participated in it. Violence and misfortune are deeply sedimented here, much of it born out of the collapse of institutions but especially because of a poverty whose hunger seems without end. And now AIDS tyrannizes the land.

These are moments in the state of emergency that is the quotidian. There are others. People waiting for a bus to go to Umtata are gunned down by machine-gun fire, children perish, a minibus overturns, at night in a hidden place men torture witches. The lightning bird flies again. Wretched poverty, the death of infants, the fury and the Furies that consume the living and the dying, all of this is entwined with a violence and a state of emergency that, until recently, was promulgated by decree and orchestrated in daily actions of the state. The arbitrariness of corrupt officials. The arrests for petty offenses. The destruction of communities. The mass detentions for political crimes. The thick acrid smoke of teargas wafting through townships. Men and women and children chased through the street and beaten with *sjamboks*, then rubber bullets, shotgun blasts, and high-powered rifle fire. Massacres. The military occupation of entire communities. And there is the state violence that until recently unfolded in a world of whispers and screams. Wet burlap bags placed over the heads of enemies of the state. Electric shocks. The mutilation of bodies. Assassinations. Disappearances. Only time will tell if these horrors have been consigned to the past.

The *ancien régime* of colonialism and apartheid persists in other less obvious but in no less enduring ways, shaping the struggles people have over access to scarce resources such as land and water, sculpting the landscapes that pass before people as they set out in search of work, fashioning memories of the past that so powerfully inform their hopes for the future. Memory is preserved, awakened, and opened to conversation often in seemingly enigmatic ways, but in ways that have been subtly shaped by the modern state. Cooking, drinking beer, the unveiling of a shoebox of artifacts long forgotten, walking to work, riding in the bus, funerals: these become sites of historical production that, at crucial junctures, gain wider political salience. The past is also etched into the land. All along the main road in the Transkei, for example, are the faint outlines of abandoned kraals and plots. They are like so many scratches in the land, some quite distinct, others almost invisible as the sun, wind, and rain bleach them into the earth. To the historian they speak of the fantasies and designs of the state and its failed policies of betterment, and of economic involution and dependence on the famished roads that lead to distant places: Cape Town, Natal, the diamond mines of Kimberley and the gold of the Rand. These faint lines in the dirt reawaken for some, at times intentionally, at other times unexpectedly and seemingly unconsciously, memories on and about the past – production, migrant labor, family, policies, officials, political struggle – and, in so doing, unveil the lively and enduring functioning of historical sensibility in a distant corner of the impoverished Other world.[15]

Certainly in South Africa there is no escaping politics or history; both are ever-present. The political past remains indissolubly linked to the social and the cultural, indeed, to the very ways people define themselves and others. At a time when the academic practice of history has all but collapsed in South Africa, the people's history has assumed an extraordinary public purpose, both nationally, as in the case of the Truth and Reconciliation Commission hearings, and locally.[16] In January 1999, for example, Chief Jongibandla Mditshwa of the Mpondomise, of the area near the town of Tsolo, died. The grave site subsequently became a center for "traditional religion and worship."[17] His death occurred in the context of extraordinary violence and at the beginning of a new period of ethnic politics unleashed by the collapse of apartheid, the ANC's electoral triumph, and the state's attempts to reorder rural political space. Two months earlier Mpondomise leaders had called for the "restoration of its lost kingdom,"[18] in effect a return to imagined precolonial borders and a heroic history. Increasingly people spoke publicly of a Mpondomise past, of valorous chiefs, and, especially, of the loss of land at the hands of British conquerors. They invoked sacred symbols and awakened a vision of politics that connected historical and political legitimacy to the land and the rains that originated high in the hills and mountains of Lesotho, a politics not of evil but of fertility and social health. Miraculously, five mole snakes "made a mysterious appearance at the laying of a tombstone of Mditshwa's grandfather." The serpents' appearance was a harbinger of "peace . . . and an occasion for joy." In welcoming the snakes "prayers for rain were also offered. Before the end of the day, it was raining cats and dogs."[19]

In the face of so much hardship there is a quiet hope – a conviction, even – that the voices of the poor will be heard, their eloquence acknowledged by the giants that have for so long towered over them, that their dreams will be realized, that the world will be set aright. Since the middle of the nineteenth century, visions of the imminent arrival of worlds less lost than unrealized have been a constant presence within the imagination of the poor. The ubiquitous political chant *Mayibuye iAfrika, iAfrika Mayibuye*, "Come back Africa, Africa come back," registers both the pain of loss and the declaration that one day a legitimate community will be born.

Such a day is unlikely to come soon. It is to be hoped that South Africa, a country in which most people lack the means to secure housing, jobs, and food, will not become a country of monuments and memorials to serve the ends of politicians. Perhaps it is now the case that "just when they seem engaged in revolutionizing themselves and things," as Marx so presciently wrote, "in creating something that has never yet existed," politicians "conjure up the spirits of the past to their service and borrow from them names, battle cries and costumes in order to present the new scene of world history in this time-honoured disguise and this borrowed language." How will South Africa "let the dead bury their dead?"[20] The ANC had hoped that the Truth and Reconciliation Commission would become a memorial to its struggle. When the commission began exposing the movement's own gross violations of human rights, however, the ANC promptly filed suit and attempted to delay the commission's report. Mandela himself only reluctantly accepted the report from the Archbishop Desmond Tutu.[21]

Politicians rename streets and dream of monuments, manipulate the past to serve their pursuit of power. Certainly much in South Africa has changed. But much remains the same. In the Eastern Cape, the Bantu Authorities system, that colossus of social engineering and tribalism, remains firmly in place.[22] Tribalism itself is resurgent. Few seem willing to discuss the ANC's tribal politics. But the government's refusal to support elected rural officials adequately, and its concessions to and increasing cooperation with traditional rulers, suggests the willingness of the ANC to play the tribal "card" even at the expense of its commitment to democracy. Thus, while beginning a new era of state formation in the country, the ANC government is, in a quite fundamental sense, renewing a tradition of rule begun in conquest and continuing in the twentieth century with segregation and apartheid.

Contemporary South Africa is faced not simply with the wreckage apartheid created but also with colonial political boundaries, structures, and processes over a century old. An enduring feature of the Eastern Cape, especially the former Transkei, is that it was conquered by a fully modern state, indeed by a bureaucratic agency. Few of these boundaries, structures, and processes created by colonialism's civil servants were utterly new, formed *de novo* by the white bearers of modernity. They were instead powerfully shaped by an ancient political history of some one thousand years old, a history that continues to this day.

Even at its most violent, even when the differential in coercive power was most marked, the political order colonialism entailed much more than foreign imposition. Conquest, I have argued throughout, is best analyzed as a cross-cultural encounter involving complex acts of translation, appropriation, and misunderstanding. Viewing conquest in this way raises difficult theoretical and historical questions about what the state really "is." Until recently the answers to such questions seemed patently obvious. "State" had a solidity that other words in the sociological lexicon, such as "nation," seemed to lack. Ernest Renan's famous question, "what is the nation?" identified precisely the ambiguity and murkiness of the concept; its solidity required, in Renan's ironic formulation, a great deal of forgetting.[23] Scholars have had far fewer problems with the state, its analysis requiring neither irony nor, for that matter, any other literary device. Debates over its definition – and there have been many – have centered on its function, the state's role in economy and society, not its materiality. In contrast to the nation one could, as it were, point to the state as a thing, as a set of interlocking institutions that had "a legitimate monopoly on the use of force," or which acted in the interests of a particular class, or which mediated the contradictions produced by capitalist development.[24] Scholars, in short, "have come to take the state for granted as an object of political practice and political analysis."[25] States are strong or weak, a thing citizens in democratic societies should respect, subjects in authoritarian orders should detest, and revolutionaries everywhere should smash – if only later to reform in their own image.

On the edge of empire, however, what the state "was" actually was seldom clear. The very contingencies and messiness of history – including the fact that Africans were busily translating and appropriating into indigenous concepts and practices the Europeans coming among them – created for rulers acute problems as they struggled to render Africa legible to modern power and, in so doing, create the subjects of their rule. Here the problem of knowledge and rationality become central. There is of course a quite considerable theoretical literature on both. What is much less understood is how the will to knowledge and the forms of rationality unfolded "on the ground," as it were, and how various historical actors understood them. Yet this is central to understanding political history in South Africa and, I suspect, elsewhere in the modern world.

A recent astute observer of African politics has argued that apartheid was the logical culmination of the "decentralized despotism" first begun with the rise of indirect rule in the early decades of the twentieth century.[26] Once we shift attention away from charting the genealogies of policies, however, the roots of apartheid go still deeper into the past. They are located not in the twentieth century but in the nineteenth century, when Europeans first extended control over the region. The road from the bureaucratic rationality of the nineteenth century to the instrumental rationality of the twentieth century was paved by the violence of conquest, European fantasies of control, and an intolerance for people who imagined the world differently. Hamilton Hope was both an avatar of modernity and of authoritarianism, of the terrible beauty and violence of Western civilization and its many discontents. It is important to remember that Hope both sought knowledge and was more than willing to beat his subjects unmercifully; indeed, he was willing to use violence in pursuit of knowledge and the illusion of mastery he thought it conferred. Fenwick, the mad master of apartheid, was Hope's successor. Like Hope, Fenwick became obsessed with making real a set of political fantasies, of making the model the reality.

That apartheid was evil is a trite banality conveniently invoked by those who sit in padded seats still warmed by the former rulers who so recently occupied them. Seeing apartheid as a consequence, and not simply a deviation or perversion, of modernity raises troubling issues. Certainly in the South African case "Enlightenment rationality" was "a logic of domination and oppression,"[27] though post-modern pessimists too often push the point too far. The challenge politicians now face is how to reimagine politics progressively and in ways that acknowledge the long and continuing conversations people have had about power and legitimacy, about the location of good and evil in their lives. A durable democracy will in part rest not simply on the success of policies but also on the ability of leaders to understand how citizens conceive of their world. Indeed, this empathetic imagination, this ability to experience difference, may well be necessary to the formulation of policies ranging from land tenure to health care.

Political history too often has restricted itself to the study of policy formulation and a kind of "biography" of the state.[28] It has typically not been interested in examining state formation as a cultural process, full of the ironies and surprises that so often reside at the center of cross-cultural encounters. Social history, or history from below, has been preoccupied with analyzing how the colonized reacted to foreign domination, how the thrust of the colonial state was met with the riposte of the oppressed. It is surprising just how often political history in effect reproduces the state. And it is surprising how irrelevant, in the current political moment, social history has become – and how sad. By focusing on rule and on the intertwined histories of state formation and popular culture, I hope in this work to have begun to chart an approach that outlines a new political history that brings together, and simultaneously attempts to complicate and reinvigorate, older ways of "doing" history from "above" and "below."[29]

At the center of the kind of political history undertaken here is the attempt to understand both the broader process of state formation and the conversations people have had, and continue to have, about the world they inhabit. At the center of the ancient conversations people have had, and the popular culture it shaped, were the historical problems of power, of good and evil, and their relationship to the political world. What is power and how have people acquired it? What is the relationship between power and people's ability to create and to destroy? Where does ultimate power lie? How have conceptions of good and evil changed over time, and what impact might they have had on people's understanding of, and participation in, the world of power and politics? If there is a God, and if the ancestors are to protect us in our daily lives, why is there so much cruelty and sadness and evil in the world?

These questions and the political imagination they nourished, it is important to recall, spoke of the land and the rains and of people's relationship to the earth. Farmers considered the hunter-gatherers of the hills to be of the land. The rest of us are but visitors. Humankind's very transience compelled respect for the elements that could ensure sustenance or, in but a furious moment, bring destruction. The land in the Eastern Cape has all but died. As elsewhere in the world authoritarianism has augured ecological collapse. But democracy has arrived. Will the rains return?

Historians generally are averse to writing about good and evil, topics they believe are best left to "Continental" philosophers and theologians, less scientific thinkers. Instead, they typically deal with good and evil metonymically, the heroic struggles for social justice by individuals and movements representing one side, the oppression and exploitation of the powerless denoting the other. But this is not enough, not now, not in the world in which we live, a world of such horror and bloodshed. Today the problem of evil directly shapes the actions of people who see the world in Manichaean terms, a politics of evil unfolding on the stage of world history and invoked in messianic declarations and horrific terroristic violence, or in the smug pronouncements of politicians who speak of an "axis of evil."[30]

A new political history will have to address more directly good and evil as historical problems in their own right, problems that have their own histories. It will have to explore the conversations people have had about their environment and the powers that so often lorded over them. It will have to explore the historical location of joy and sorrow and of hatred and the many terrors hatred unleashes. It will have to analyze the presence and shape of wickedness, past and present, the politics of evil locally and globally. At the center of a new political history will be an exploration of the relationship between politics and suffering, about social health and a political world of many centers, a history of people's seemingly infinite capacity for hatred as well as their hope that the future will be different, that their lives and their histories somehow will have mattered.

Notes

INTRODUCTION

1. Quoted in Allister Sparks, *Tomorrow is a Different Country* (Chicago, 1995), 227, 229. Unless otherwise noted, all archival sources are located in the Cape Archives (CA), Cape Town.
2. For overviews of the transition see Sparks, *Tomorrow*; Anthony W. Marx, *Lessons of Struggle: South African Internal Opposition, 1960–1990* (New York, 1992); Martin Murray, *The Revolution Deferred: The Painful Birth of Post-Apartheid South Africa* (London, 1994). For statistical material on arrests and deaths see *Race Relations Survey* (Johannesburg, 1984–94.)
3. Francis Wilson and Mamphela Ramphele, *Uprooting Poverty* (New York, 1989), 16–18.
4. See Wilson and Ramphele, *Uprooting Poverty*; J. May, *Poverty and Inequality in South Africa: Summary Report prepared for the Office of the Executive Deputy President and the Inter-Ministerial Committee for Poverty and Inequality* (Pretoria, 1998). In this work I will be using Eastern Cape and Eastern Cape Province synonymously.
5. *Daily Dispatch*, 29 June 2000, 25 May 1999.
6. The above information is based on interview with J. M., 21 June 1993, and conversations with Jeremy Pickering.
7. Adam Ashforth, *Madumo: A Man Bewitched* (Chicago, 2000), 16. For a much earlier period see J. B. Peires, *The Dead Will Arise: Nongqawuse and the Great Cattle-Killing Movement of 1856–7* (Johannesburg, 1989), esp. 2, 196–8.
8. Isak Niehaus, "Witchcraft, Whites, and the 1994 South African Elections," unpub. seminar paper, Institute for Advanced Social Research, University of the Witwatersrand, 1995.
9. Peter Geschiere, *Modernity of Witchcraft: Politics and the Occult in Postcolonial Africa* (Charlottesville, 1997), 7. See also John and Jean Comaroff, eds., *Modernity and its Malcontents: Ritual and Power in Postcolonial Africa* (Chicago, 1993); Luise White, *Speaking with Vampires: Rumor and History in Colonial Africa* (Berkeley and Los Angeles, 2000).
10. See Laurine Platzky and Cherryl Walker, *The Surplus People: Forced Removals in South Africa* (Johannesburg, 1985); Wilson and Ramphele, *Uprooting Poverty*; Cosmos Desmond, *The Discarded People: An Account of African Resettlement in South Africa* (Harmondsworth, 1971).
11. Desmond, *The Discarded People*, 3.
12. Quoted in *Truth and Reconciliation Commission of South Africa Report*, 5 vols. (London, 1999), I, 95.

13. See below, pp. 121–32, and Birgit Meyer, *Translating the Devil: Religion and Modernity among the Ewe in Ghana* (Trenton, 1999); Geschiere, *Modernity of Witchcraft*.
14. The distinction between good and evil, so powerfully drawn in Western culture, is less clear in the African context. See chapter 1; Geschiere, *Modernity of Witchcraft*.
15. ACC 793, letter book of Major Gawler, letters of 29 and 31 October 1856. See also Ashforth, *Madumo*. Ashforth speculates whether Madumo's travails as an accused witch may be related to his association with the author and his not inconsiderable resources.
16. Andrew Silk, *A Shanty Town in South Africa: The Story of Modderdam* (Johannesburg, 1981), 12.
17. Sean Redding, "Government Witchcraft: Taxation, the Supernatural, and the Mpondo Revolt in the Transkei, South Africa, 1955–63," *African Affairs*, 95 (1996): 555–79; Govan Mbeki, *South Africa: The Peasants' Revolt* (Baltimore, 1964), 108.
18. Monica Hunter, *Reaction to Conquest: Effects of Contact with Europeans on the Pondo of South Africa* (London, 1961), 489.
19. Geschiere, *Modernity of Witchcraft*, 7–8. See also Niehaus, "Witchcraft"; Tim Lane, "'Jele Tšhelete': Witchcraft, Chiefs, and the State in the Northern Transvaal, 1900–1930," in Clifton Crais, ed., *The Culture of Power in Southern Africa: Essays on State Formation and the Political Imagination* (Portsmouth, 2002). Hunter wrote that "there are individuals who do not believe in witchcraft or supernatural magic, but they are rare": *Reaction to Conquest*, 488.
20. Ashforth, *Madumo*, 16.
21. See also White, *Speaking with Vampires*.
22. Tzvetan Todorov, *The Conquest of America*, trans. Richard Howard (New York, 1982), 249.
23. I take "contact zone" from Mary Louise Pratt, *Imperial Eyes: Travel Writing and Transculturation* (London and New York, 1992).
24. Here I paraphrase Robert Borofsky, "Cook, Lono, Obeyesekere, and Sahlins," in Robert Borofsky, ed., *Remembrance of Pacific Pasts: An Invitation to Remake History* (Honolulu, 2000), 420–42, 440.
25. Jean and John Comaroff, *Of Revelation and Revolution, vol. I: Christianity, Colonialism, and Consciousness in South Africa* (Chicago, 1991), 29. On experience see Joan Scott, "The Evidence of Experience," *Critical Inquiry*, 17 (Summer 1991): 773–97. For a useful essay on culture see William Sewell, "The Concept(s) of Culture," in Victoria E. Bonnell and Lynn Hunt, eds., *Beyond the Cultural Turn: New Directions in the Study of Society and Culture* (Berkeley and Los Angeles, 1999).
26. See, for example, the debate between Gananath Obeyesekere, *The Apotheosis of Captain Cook: European Mythmaking in the Pacific* (Princeton, 1997), and Marshal Sahlins, *How "Natives" Think, about Captain Cook, For Example* (Chicago, 1995). See also Edward LiPuma, *Encompassing Others: The Magic of Modernity in Melanesia* (Ann Arbor, 2000).
27. See Carlo Ginzburg, *History, Rhetoric, and Proof* (Hanover and London, 1999), who argues for the utility of rhetoric to historical understanding.
28. Ann Laura Stoler, "Rethinking Colonial Categories: European Communities and the Boundaries of Rule," in Nicholas B. Dirks, ed., *Colonialism and Culture* (Ann Arbor, 1992), 321.

29. See, for example, Comaroff and Comaroff, *Of Revelation and Revolution* (1991, 1997); Paul Landau, *The Realm of the Word: Language, Gender, and Christianity in a Southern African Kingdom* (Portsmouth, 1995). One critique can be found in Terence Ranger, "Africa in the Age of Extremes: The Irrelevance of African History," in Simon McGrath, Charles Jedrej, Kenneth King, and Jack Thompson, eds., *Rethinking African History* (Edinburgh, 1997). For recent works on the political history of South Africa see, for example, Adam Ashforth, *The Politics of Official Discourse in Twentieth Century South Africa* (Oxford, 1992); Belinda Bozzoli, *The Political Nature of a Ruling Class: Capital and Ideology in South Africa, 1890–1933* (London, 1981); Saul Dubow, *Racial Segregation and the Origins of Apartheid in South Africa, 1919–1936* (Oxford, 1989); Deborah Posel, *The Making of Apartheid* (Oxford, 1991). For an attempt at a reworking of both political and social history see Allen Wells and Gilbert Joseph, *Summer of Discontent, Seasons of Upheaval: Elite Politics and Rural Insurgency in Yucatan, 1876–1915* (Stanford, 1996). Recent work on cross-cultural encounters has emphasized the importance of missionaries to the "colonization of consciousness": Comaroff and Comaroff, *Of Revelation and Revolution*. As we shall see, however, missionaries played a somewhat less important role than many have assumed, and the consciousness of the colonized remained unfettered by the intrusion of European modernities.

30. Philip Abrams, "Some Notes on the Difficulty of Studying the State," *Journal of Historical Sociology*, 1, 1 (March 1988): 58–89. See also George Joseph and Daniel Nugent, "Popular Culture and State Formation," in George Joseph and Daniel Nugent, eds., *Everyday Forms of State Formation* (Durham, N.C., 1994).

31. Philip Corrigan and Derek Sayer, *The Great Arch: English State Formation as Cultural Revolution*, foreword G. E. Aylmer (Oxford, 1985), 2.

32. Corrigan and Sayer, *The Great Arch*, 3.

33. Kenneth Minogue, "State," in J. Kuper, ed., *Political Science and Political Theory* (London, 1987), 239–40. See also John L. Comaroff, "Reflections on the Colonial State, in South Africa and Elsewhere: Factions, Fragments, Facts and Fictions," *Social Identities*, 4, 3 (October 1998): 321–62, and, esp., Philip Corrigan, "State Formation," in Joseph and Nugent, eds., *Everyday Forms of State Formation*, xvii–xix. See also Michael Taussig, *The Magic of the State* (New York, 1997).

34. Todorov, *The Conquest of America*, 250.

35. Alice Truax, "When Cultures Collide: Winning and Losing in Nineteenth-Century Borneo," *New Yorker*, 14 Sept. 1998, 9. Dirks has written that "colonial knowledge both enabled colonial conquest and was produced by it": *Colonialism and Culture*, 3. See also LiPuma, *Encompassing Others*, esp. 153–85.

36. See also Mahmood Mamdani, *Citizen and Subject: Contemporary Africa and the Legacy of Late Colonialism* (Princeton, 1996).

37. James Scott, *Seeing Like a State: How Certain Schemes to Improve the Human Condition have Failed* (New Haven, 1998), 2, 5. For a useful critique of Scott see Fernando Coronil, "Smelling Like a State," *American Historical Review*, 106, 1 (February 2001): 119–29. See also Michel-Rolph Trouillot, "The Anthropology of the State in the Age of Globalization: Close Encounters of the Deceptive Kind," *Current Anthropology*, 42, 1 (February 2001): 125–35. In 1929 Smuts had argued that policies that sought to "de-Africanize the African" were misplaced and insisted

on a "new policy" based on "specifically African foundations": quoted in Mamdani, *Citizen and Subject*, 5.

38. Dirks, ed., *Colonialism and Culture*, 7.
39. See Scott, *Seeing Like a State*, 4, 88–9.
40. Scholars typically have stressed the second half of the eighteenth century and the nineteenth century as crucial historical moments in its creation and ascendency. For a useful introduction see David Harvey, *The Condition of Postmodernity* (Oxford, 1990).
41. Foucault, Michel, "Governmentality," in Graham Burchell, Colin Gordon and Peter Miller, eds., *The Foucault Effect: Studies in Governmentality* (Chicago, 1991), 104.
42. For a discussion of Weber as well as more recent sociological writing see Richard Bernstein, ed., *Habermas and Modernity* (Oxford, 1985); Theodor Adorno and Max Horkheimer, *Dialectic of Enlightenment*, trans. John Cumming (New York, 1979). See also Harvey, *The Condition of Postmodernity*. On the Holocaust see Hannah Arendt, *Eichmann in Jerusalem: A Report on the Banality of Evil* (Gloucester, Mass., 1964).
43. Michel Foucault, *History of Sexuality: An Introduction* (New York, 1990), 142–3.
44. Foucault, *History of Sexuality*, 140–3. See also Burchell et al., eds., *The Foucault Effect* .
45. Ann Laura Stoler, *Race and the Education of Desire: Foucault's History of Sexuality and the Colonial Order of Things* (Durham, N.C., 1997), 207. Mitchell, for example, has demonstrated the place of panopticism in European colonialism in Egypt. See Timothy Mitchell, *Colonising Egypt* (Berkeley and Los Angeles, 1991). A striking feature of culture in the colonial context was its reducibility to space and to numbers. As Said argued with regard to Orientalism, it "is absolutely anatomical and enumerate; to use its vocabulary is to engage in the particularizing and dividing of things Oriental into manageable parts": Edward Said, *Orientalism* (New York, 1979), 72. See also Frederick Cooper and Ann Stoler, eds., *Tensions of Empire: Colonial Cultures in a Bourgeois World* (Berkeley and Los Angeles, 1997).
46. Mamdani, *Citizen and Subject*, 61.
47. Ivan Evans, *Bureaucracy and Race: Native Administration in South Africa* (Berkeley and Los Angeles, 1997), 298.
48. Roughly the same as the official urban African population in 1962: Posel, *The Making of Apartheid*, 120. By this time prison labor had become an important part of the white farming economy. See Evans, *Bureaucracy and Race*, 112.
49. Comaroff and Comaroff, *of Revelation and Revolution*; Stoler, "Rethinking Colonial Categories." See also Albert Memmi, *The Colonizer and the Colonized* (New York, 1965).
50. Ranger, "Africa in the Age of Extremes."
51. Corrigan, "State Formation," xvii.
52. Mahmood Mamdani, *Politics and Class Formation in Uganda* (London, 1976), 142. See also his *Citizen and Subject*.
53. Both subjects have produced important works. See, for example, Tom Lodge, *Black Politics in South Africa since 1945* (London, 1983); William Beinart and Colin Bundy, *Hidden Struggles in Rural South Africa: Politics and Popular Movements in the Transkei and Eastern Cape, 1890–1930* (Berkeley and Los Angeles, 1987).

54. Ranajit Guha, "On Some Aspects of the Historiography of Colonial India," in Ranajit Guha, ed., *Subaltern Studies I: Writings on South Asian History and Society* (Delhi, 1982), 4.

55. Michael Herzfeld, *The Social Production of Indifference: Exploring the Symbolic Roots of Western Bureaucracy* (New York, 1992), 37.

56. The suggestion here is to move beyond the current fascination with missionaries and the Christian god that has fascinated some scholars but has done surprisingly little to reinvigorate Southern African studies. See, for example, Comaroff and Comaroff, *Of Revelation and Revolution*; Landau, *The Realm of the Word*.

57. Redding, "Government Witchcraft." On mimesis see Michael Taussig, *Mimesis and Alterity: A Particular History of the Senses* (New York, 1993), 21, paraphrasing Benjamin: "Every day the urge grows stronger to get hold of an object at very close range by way of its likeness, its reproduction." See also Achille Mbembe, "The Banality of Power and the Aesthetics of Vulgarity in the Postcolony," *Public Culture*, 4, 2 (Spring 1992): 1–30; Jean-Francois Bayart, *The State in Africa: The Politics of the Belly* (London, 1993).

58. See Ashforth, *Madumo*; Niehaus, "Witchcraft."

59. Herzfeld, *The Social Production of Indifference*, 62. Ashforth, *Madumo*, 132, quotes a healer who says, "People, they know that there *is* witchcraft. So if the government says 'There is no witch,' this means that they are protecting this witchcraft so that it must grow, grow, grow." For a parallel see chapter 6 on suspicions that the state was protecting thieves who used magic.

60. Ginzburg, *History, Rhetoric, and Proof*.

61. This is a very long period; Europeans conquered most of Africa in just a few decades. For background see John Galbraith, *Reluctant Empire: British Policy on the South African Frontier, 1834–54* (Berkeley and Los Angeles, 1963); Jeffrey Peires, *The House of Phalo: A History of the Xhosa People in the Days of their Independence* (Berkeley and Los Angeles, 1981); Clifton Crais, *White Supremacy and Black Resistance: The Making of the Colonial Order in the Eastern Cape, 1770–1865* (Cambridge, 1992); Beinart and Bundy, *Hidden Struggles*; Timothy Stapleton, *Maqoma: Xhosa Resistance to Colonial Advance* (Johannesburg, 1994).

62. Daniel R. Headrick, *The Tools of Empire: Technology and European Imperialism in the Nineteenth Century* (New York, 1981), 100.

63. See Gordon Pirie, "Railways and Labour Migration to the Rand Mines: Constraints and Significance," *JSAS*, 19, 4 (Dec. 1993): 713–30.

64. NA 158, Shaw, report, 31 Dec. 1877. On shipping and telegraphy see Daniel R. Headrick, *The Tentacles of Progress: Technology Transfer in the Age of Imperialism, 1850–1940* (New York, 1988), 18–48, 97–144.

65. See David Landes, *The Wealth and Poverty of Nations: Why Some are so Rich and Some so Poor* (New York, 1998), esp. 168–291.

66. For an overview see Howard Rogers, *Native Administration in the Union of South Africa* (Johannesburg, 1933).

67. For a general, if flawed and uninspired, overview see Leonard Thompson, *A History of South Africa*, rev. ed. (New Haven, 1995), esp. 70–153.

68. E. H. Brookes, *A History of Native Policy in South Africa from 1830 to the Present Day* (Cape Town, 1924), 98.

69. Brookes, *A History of Native Policy*, 118.

70. Quoted in Brookes, *A History of Native Policy*, 92.
71. The large-scale migration of people into what became Fingoland and Emigrant Thembuland created significant instability and drew the state ever more deeply into African political processes. From the 1850s, and especially in the following decade, at least 30, 000 Mfengu migrated from the west and some 20,000 Thembu moved in from the southeast, with Xhosa under paramount Sarhili increasingly confined to the area around Willowvale and Kentani. These migrations took place in the context of colonial expansion. Together they led to the outbreak in 1877 of the so-called Ninth Frontier War.
72. 1/COF 9/1/44, extracts from the report of the Government Commission on Native Laws and Customs, Jan. 1883.
73. CO 4521, Elliot to under secretary for native affairs (NA), 4 Apr. 1881.
74. (UCT) BC 293, D 10, MS of Rev. E. J. Warner containing the history of his father, Rev. Joseph Cox Warner, n.d., t.s.
75. CO 4521, copy, office of resident magistrate (RM) with Gangelizwe, 28 Oct. 1875.
76. Evidence of Robert W. Stanford, G. 4-'83, *Report and Proceedings of the Government Commission on Native Laws and Customs*, 1883. The commission took place in 1881, in the immediate aftermath of the rebellion throughout much of the Transkei.
77. G. 4-'83, 22.
78. CO 4521, Graham, Unannexed Tembuland, n.d. [1881–2]. The Cape Colony annexed Thembuland in 1885.
79. Sir Walter Stanford, *The Reminiscences of Sir Walter Stanford*, ed. J. W. Mac Quarrie (Cape Town, 1958), I: *1850–1885*, 18.
80. 1/IDW ADD 1/1/1, Colley to chief commissioner (CC), 4 Dec. 1858.
81. The state deposed and attempted to arrest the Thembu paramount in 1876 and reinstalled him all within the space of a few months. See (UCT) BC 293, A 70, Stanford to Judge, 11 Sept. 1876. See also Stanford to Wright, 26 Aug. 1877. There was considerable variability in colonial rule, even in such basic issues as the appointment of headmen.
82. Testimony of Dick, special magistrate, Tamacha, G. 4-'83.
83. See, for example, (UCT) BC 293, A 70, Stanford to Brownlee, 3 May 1877.
84. CMT 1/147, Rules and Regulations.
85. See Beinart and Bundy, *Hidden Struggles*, 139.
86. Ibid.
87. See material on the Glen Grey Act located in NA 225. See also Rogers, *Native Administration*; Evans, *Bureaucracy and Race*, 184.
88. Barrington Moore, Jr., *The Social Origins of Dictatorship and Democracy: Landlord and Peasant in the Making of the Modern World* (Boston, 1967), 435.
89. Evans, *Bureaucracy and Race*, 108.
90. Evans, *Bureaucracy and Race*, 88.
91. See Clifton Crais, *A Century of Sadness: Poverty and Power in Rural South Africa* (Portsmouth, forthcoming).
92. See Sara Berry, *No Condition is Permanent: The Social Dynamics of Agrarian Change in Sub-Saharan Africa* (Madison, 1993).
93. See GH 8/34, Maclean to secretary to High Commission, 18 Jan. 1858; BK 72, Brownlee to Maclean, 4 Aug. 1860; BK 73, Brownlee to Brownlow, 17 May 1865.

94. See, for example, GH 8/36, Miller to Maclean, 1 Nov. 1858; BK 86, Miller to Maclean, 2 Dec. 1858; BK 87, Miller to Maclean, 3 Aug. 1859.

95. NA 195, Dick to acting CC, 15 Jan. 1883.

96. (UMT) CMT 164, Nqwili and others to RM, Qumbu, 7 Dec. 1924.

97. (UMT) CMT 164, RM to [?], 23 May 1923. See also 1/QBU 7/1/8–9, Maraule to RM, Qumbu, 18 Jan. 1938.

98. See BK 28, Wild to Brownlow, 7 Nov. 1862; GH 8/34, Census of the Crown Reserve, 1 Jan. 1858; GH 8/27, Maclean to Southey, 27 Aug. 1855; GH 8/36, Brownlee to Maclean, 12 Dec. 1858.

99. (UMT) CMT 164, Meeting held at Qumbu, 15 May 1924 re: complaints against headman.

100. (UMT) CMT 164, Nqwili to RM, Nov. 1924.

101. (UMT) CMT 164, statement of Maxalanga, 27 Apr. 1925.

102. NA 658, Preston to Secretary of Labour, 19 Oct. 1904. See also Partha Dasgupta, *An Inquiry in Well-Being and Destitution* (Oxford, 1993), esp. 290–4 on the "tragedy of the commons"; Beinart and Bundy, *Hidden Struggles*; Jack Lewis, "An Economic History of the Ciskei, 1848–1900" (Ph.D. thesis, University of Cape Town, 1984), esp. 422–512; Jack Lewis, "Rural Contradictions and Class Consciousness: Migrant Labour in Historical Perspective," paper presented to Centre for African Studies, University of Cape Town, 27 Feb. 1985.

103. 1/IDW ADD 1/1/2, journal book, Warner, special magistrate, 4 Nov. 1864.

104. Quoted in Thomas J. Winslow, "Paying the Price: Women and Domestic Conflict in Late 19th Century Thembuland," unpub. paper presented to the History Department, University of Cape Town, n.d. [1989], 18; CCK 25, Apthorp to secretary for NA, 12 Mar. 1932. Winslow discusses a case where, in 1899, a Thembuland woman killed herself after every one of her four children died in infancy.

105. (CL) Ayliff, Report of the Heald Town Circuit for 1859.

106. CMT 1/143, minutes of meeting, 10 Mar. 1885.

107. See William Beinart, *The Political Economy of Pondoland, 1860–1930* (Cambridge, 1982); Elizabeth Elredge, *A South African Kingdom: The Pursuit of Security in Nineteenth-Century Lesotho* (Cambridge, 1993). For many who have owned stock, from the 1850s to the present, the issue has been not whether their cattle would succumb to sickness and die, but simply when. Other diseases, such as red water fever, s were also serious. Sickly and scrawny, cows often stopped producing milk. On economics and the domestic politics of cattle see James Ferguson, *The Anti-Politics Machine: "Development," Depoliticization, and Bureaucratic Power in Lesotho* (Cambridge, 1990), esp. 135–66.

108. (WITS) AD 843, Dr. E. Jokl, *A Labour and Manpower Survey of the Transkeian Territories* (SAIRR, 1943), 6.

109. NA 464, Jenner to under secretary of NA, 26 Sept. 1885.

110. NA 464, RM, Butterworth to chief magistrate (CM), Transkei, 11 March 1885.

111. NA 464, RM, Willowvale to CM, Transkei, 11 Sept. 1885.

112. NA 196, Nightingale to under secretary of NA, 6 Feb. 1883; NA 541, Bowker to chief inspector of native locations, 24 Feb. 1902.

113. (CL) MS/PR 8496, Mzimba to Ross, 1 Sept. 1880; NA 195, Dick to acting civil commissioner, Kingwilliamstown, 15 Jan. 1883.

114. See also F. William Fox and Douglas Back, "A Preliminary Survey of the Agricultural and Nutritional Problems of the Ciskei and Transkeian Territories with Special Reference to their Bearing on the Recruiting of Labourers for the Gold Mining Industry," unpublished MS, 1943, 183, 190.
115. Jokl, *Labour and Manpower Survey*, 8–9.
116. NA 229, Sweeney to ?, n.d. [1895].
117. NA 225, Musgrave to CC, Glen Grey, 20 Nov. 1895.
118. NA 225, Kelly to RM, Glen Grey, 7 July 1897.
119. NA 734, Vershuur to Secretary of NA, 30 Jan. 1907; NA 734 Whitfield to Secretary of NA, 7 Sept. 1908.
120. NA 657, Ellis to RM, East London, 9 July 1906.
121. NA 708, petition of residents to prime minister, n.d. [1908].
122. CMT 3/679, typewritten bits, 1910–11.; NA 708, petition to the prime minister, n.d. [1908].
123. NA 555, Blakewood to secretary for NA, 15 Feb. 1906. See also CMT 3/679, typewritten bits and pieces, n.d. [1910–11].
124. NA 725, Ulana to "My Dear Brother," 9 Sept. 1907; NA 725, Cross, short statement made by natives working at the Cambrian Coal Mine, n.d.; NA 724, payment of compensation, n.d. [1908].
125. 1/ALC 5/1/1/2, comparative statement, 1909 and 1910; NA 723, "Labourers employed on Mines and Works and Other Employ . . . 1903–09." See also Beinart and Bundy, *Hidden Struggles.*
126. NA 687, complaint of ill-treatment . . . from "Cata Location" of Kingwilliamstown, March 1906.
127. NA 555, Roberts to secretary of NA, 17 Dec. 1904. See also NA 554, RM, Dordrecht to secretary for NA, 18 Sept. 1902, (BR) 455, Bradford to secretary, Rand Mines, 5 Mar. 1907; NA 556, Erskine to Secretary of NA, 28 Dec. 1904; (BR) 455, Davies to Steil, 4 Nov. 1908.
128. See, for example, (BR) 455, Martienssen to secretary of central administration, 6 July 1908.
129. NA 531, Elliot to secretary for NA, 26 Sept. 1900.
130. CMT 3/679, typewritten, n.d. [1910–11].
131. 1/NKE 7/1/60, report, 28 Sept. 1926.
132. CCK 120, report on conditions, 18 Oct. 1932.
133. CCK 105, Collett to Native Commissioner (NC) (Herschel), 4 Mar. 1934.
134. CCK 105, NC (Herschel) to A. L. Barrett, 1 Feb. 1934.
135. (CL) Uncat. material from magistrate's office, Keiskammahoek, rural research report ending for year 21 Dec. 1948.
136. CCK 26, Hartley, report on the district of Keiskammahoek, 23 Dec. 1932.
137. See Saul Dubow, "The Elaboration of Segregationist Ideology," in Saul Dubow and William Beinart, eds., *Segregation and Apartheid in Twentieth-Century South Africa* (London and New York, 1995), 147–8.
138. Evans, *Bureaucracy and Race*, 2.
139. 1/ELN 67, Bayky and Norton to minister of NA, 3 July 1914.
140. Rogers, *Native Administration*, 46.
141. NA 658, Martley to Preston, 1 Nov. 1904.
142. Mamdani, *Citizen and Subject*, 191.

143. Mamdani, *Citizen and Subject*, 17, *passim*.
144. For background see Beinart and Bundy, *Hidden Struggles*; F. Hendricks, *The Pillars of Apartheid: Land Tenure, Rural Planning and the Chieftaincy* (Uppsala, 1990) Evans, *Bureaucracy and Race*.
145. Evans, *Bureaucracy and Race*, 284.
146. Evans, *Bureaucracy and Race*, 169.
147. Mamdani, *Citizen and Subject*, 71.
148. Quoted in ibid.
149. See Scott, *Seeing Like a State*.
150. Scott, *Seeing Like a State*, 11.
151. Comaroff and Comaroff, *Of Revelation and Revolution*.
152. Benedict Anderson, *Imagined Communities: Reflections on the Origin and Spread of Nationalism* (London, 1983, 1991). See also Mitchell, *Colonising Egypt*.
153. Antonio Gramsci, *Selections from the Prison Notebooks of Antonio Gramsci*, ed. Q Hoare and G. N. Smith (New York, 1971), 110; also used in Sparks, *Tomorrow*.
154. Evans, *Bureaucracy and Race*, 305.
155. For example, hospitals have struggled to provide food, clean linen, and access to basic medicines. In a recent example a Lusikisiki hospital, whose electrical bills were outstanding, had its power cut off without warning. A number of premature babies "became hypothermic": *Daily Dispatch*, 1 Aug. 2000.
156. Department of Provincial and Local Government, "A Draft Discussion Document towards a White Paper on Traditional Leadership and Institutions," 11 April 2000. See also Mamdani, *Citizen and Subject*.
157. Mamdani, *Citizen and Subject*, 61.
158. Thus while both the Ciskei and Transkei have been incorporated into Eastern Cape Province, the local boundaries largely remain in place.

1 THE DEATH OF HOPE

1. Quoted in Harold Scheub, *The Tongue is Fire: South African Storytellers and Apartheid* (Madison, 1996), 223.
2. CMK 1/152, Hope to CM, Kokstad, 14 Oct. 1880. See also CMK 1/152, Hope to CM, Kokstad, 19 Oct. 1880; RM Maclear to CM, Kokstad, 22 Oct. 1880.
3. Hope to Davis, 19 Oct. 1880, in "Historical Record of the Murder of Hamilton Hope," typescript originally compiled by W. C. Henman.
4. NA 20, Davis to secretary of NA, 29 Oct. 1880.
5. See Michael W. Doyle, *Empires* (Ithaca, 1986), 142, for statistical material on British imperial expansion.
6. CMK 1/152, Hope to CM, Kokstad, 22 Oct. 1880; W. T. Brownlee, *Reminiscences of a Transkeian* (Pietermaritzburg, 1975), 82.
7. NA 20, Davis to secretary of NA, 29 Oct. 1880; Brownlee, *Reminiscences*, 82.
8. NA 20, Davis to secretary of NA, 29 Oct. 1880.
9. Brownlee, *Reminiscences*, 83; *Fort Beaufort Advocate*, 5 Nov. 1880, in "Historical Record."
10. Brownlee, *Reminiscences*, 83.
11. Emphasis mine. NA 20, Davis to secretary for NA, 29 Oct. 1880.
12. Brownlee, *Reminiscences*, 84.

13. Brownlee, *Reminiscences*, 84; NA 20, Davis to secretary for NA, 29 Oct. 1880.
14. NA 20, Davis to secretary for NA, 29 Oct. 1880; (UCT) BC 293, Stanford to?, 23 Nov. 1880.
15. *The Eastern Star*, 23 Nov. 1880, in "Historical Record."
16. Ibid. "The fowls of the air (aasvogels) should eat them, or the witch doctor's medicine would not act": *The Port Elizabeth Telegraph and Eastern Province Standard*, 26 Nov. 1880, in "Historical Record."
17. Brownlee, *Reminiscences*, 88.
18. Stanford, *Reminiscences*, I, 131. See also 1/ECO 4/1/1, statement of Mangele, 8 Mar. 1881.
19. Quoted in Scheub, *The Tongue is Fire*, 265. See also NA 20, Davis to secretary of NA, 29 Oct. 1880.
20. Brownlee, *Reminiscences*, 92.
21. "Historical Record."
22. Quoted in W. D. Hammond-Tooke, *Bhaca Society: A People of the Transkeian Uplands, South Africa* (Cape Town, 1962), 47.
23. Sahlins, *How "Natives" Think*, 188.
24. A. C. Jordan, *The Wrath of the Ancestors (a Novel)*, trans. Priscilla P. Jordan (Lovedale, 1980), 108.
25. Greg Dening, *Islands and Beaches* (Honolulu, 1980), 20.
26. See below for further discussion. In addition, there is no data today that suggests any relationship between Hope and magic.
27. Dening, *Islands and Beaches*, 6, 43.
28. Comaroff and Comaroff, eds., *Modernity and its Malcontents*, xvi. For a critical overview of the concept see Talal Asad, *Genealogies of Religion: Discipline and Reasons of Power in Christianity and Islam* (Baltimore, 1993), 55–82. On boundaries see Dening, *Islands and Beaches*. I am using boundaries somewhat differently than does Dening.
29. Here we should remember as well more prosaic but no less important boundaries. A central feature of colonial conquest and the sovereignty of empire was the creation of permanent unmoving borders in a world of once-fluid boundaries. See below, pp. 68–87, and also Anthony Giddens, *The Consequences of Modernity* (Stanford, 1990), esp. 73.
30. Missionaries were not the only people to charm the minds of the colonized. Recent writing has forgotten this. See, for example, Comaroff and Comaroff, *Of Revelation and Revolution*, Landau, *The Realm of the Word*. On cross-cultural encounters see Sahlins, *How "Natives" Think*; Obeyesekere, *The Apotheosis of Captain Cook*; Todorov, *The Conquest of America*; Borofsky, *Remembrance of Pacific Pasts*.
31. See Christopher Ehret, *An African Classical Age: Eastern and Southern Africa in World History, 1000 BC to AD 400* (Charlottesville, 1998), esp. 209–43; Christopher Ehret and Merrick Posnansky, eds. *The Archaeological and Linguistic Reconstruction of African History* (Berkeley and Los Angeles, 1982); T. S. Robey, "The Ecology of the Iron Age in the Transkei," report on archeological research in the Mbashe River catchment, University of Cape Town, February 1985.
32. See, for example, Jan Vansina, *Paths in the Rainforest: Toward a History of Political Tradition in Equatorial Africa* (Madison, 1990).
33. Sahlins, *How "Natives" Think*, 73.

34. Brownlee, *Reminiscences*, 88.
35. See also, for example, Vansina, *Paths in the Rainforest*; David Lan, *Guns and Rain: Guerrillas and Spirit Mediums in Zimbabwe* (Berkeley and Los Angeles, 1985).
36. The locations of chiefs very often differed little from those of commoners. They tended to be somewhat larger, and the pace of activity was greater. What was clear is that chiefs' residences were distinguished by the presence of the tails of lions and leopards, ancient symbols of political authority. See H. Lichtenstein, *Travels in Southern Africa*, trans. A. Plumptre, 2 vols. (Cape Town, 1928–30), I, 354: "The habitation of the king is not otherwise distinguished than by the tail of a lion or a panther [leopard] hanging from the top of the roof." See also (SAM) Smith 3: "Thus the cattle kraal is often ornamented with the tail or ear of an elephant, which, when the animal is killed, is always carried to the king, they have also sometimes the tail of a tiger drawn on a stick and placed by the door or in the thatch of their hut."
37. *Transactions of the London Missionary Society. Volume 1, From its Institution in the Year 1795, to the End of the Year 1802. The Second Edition. Published for the Benefit of the Society* (London, 1804) Van der Kemp, "Second Attempt to Enter Caffraria," 394. Van der Kemp also noted that Ngqika "had in his hand an iron kiri," another historic symbol of political authority.
38. John Ayliff, *The Journal of John Ayliff*, ed. Peter Hinchliff (Grahamstown, 1971), 64.
39. James MacDonald, "Manners, Customs, and Superstitions, and Religions of South African Tribes," *Journal of the Anthropological Institute*, 19 (1889), 282.
40. Ludwig Alberti, *Alberti's Account of the Xhosa in 1807*, trans. W. Fehr (Cape Town, 1968), 77.
41. See also Vansina, *Paths in the Rainforest*, 71–128.
42. The common stem (Guthrie's C. S. 1101–1102) is *-koci*, "chief," "lion". The Mbeti (spoken in north-western Central Africa) word for lion is *nkosi*. The Luba (spoken in the south-central Central Africa) word for chief is *makofi*. According to Guthrie, "the fact that the source-item of C.S. 1102 has the same shape might seem to suggest a common origin with a mutation of meaning due either to the honorific use of the term for 'lion' to refer to 'chief' or to the pseudonymic use of the term for 'chief' to refer to 'lion', but as the two area of distribution are in different parts of the field this seems unlikely": Malcolm Guthrie, *Comparative Bantu*, 4 vols. (Amersham, 1970), III, 289. The contemporary word for lion is *ingonyama*.
43. The source for "leopard" is C.S. 866. See Guthrie, *Comparative Bantu*, III, 229, 221. See also Vansina, *Paths in the Rainforest*, 277: "Proto-Bantu. The leopard is thoroughly identified with political leadership." The words for celebration and to celebrate are linguistically closely related to the word for leopard. The contemporary word for leopard is *ingwe*, and to celebrate is *ukuguya*. Again, it is unlikely Xhosa speakers today, and indeed probably in the past as well, would be aware of the linguistic connection between "leopard" and "celebration".
44. Highly visible images and practices associated with cattle braided around these ancient and elusive symbols of political authority; together they created a tradition shared by peoples throughout the Eastern Cape. People spoke of the powerful as bulls. Those who could used cattle in the creation of alliances, among chiefs and between chiefs and their subjects. Political rituals invariably involved cattle sacrifices. Cattle were, and in many areas remain, vitally important to the creation and

maintenance of social ties, the "glue" through which social relations and society is made and remade. Marriage, for example, required cattle in the form of bride-wealth. Bovines bounded past to present; men propitiated male ancestors through cattle sacrifices. In their representations of African society European observers stressed the centrality of cattle. In the early nineteenth century Alberti, for example, defined the Xhosa as a people who "live[d] principally by cattle-breeding." A man's "cattle is the foremost and practically the only subject of his care and occupation, in the possession of which he finds complete happiness" (*Alberti's Account*, 54). Modern scholars continued this tradition of seeing cattle as "the lynch-pin of . . . social structure," extending an emphasis on cattle into their reconstructions of political society (Peires, *The House of Phalo*, 4). At the same time they have drawn a wall separating cattle as the preserve of men from agriculture as the world of women, in short a strict sexual division of labor. Yet both the "bovine mystique" and the sexual division of labor, as supposedly timeless features of African society, emerged at a particular moment in the colonial encounter, and in the European construction of African anthropology and history. See Ferguson, *The Anti-Politics Machine*. This was especially so in the late nineteenth and early twentieth centuries, with the rise of migrant labor and the revalorization of cattle, by African men, in the context of colonial conquest and an explosion of rural poverty. Migrant labor seemed to reiterate a sexual division of labor and the centrality of cattle as quintessential features of African society. Since agriculture related to women and used "less valued labor," and politics concerned men, scholars focused more on cattle linkages than on agricultural fertility and its relationship to political society. See Comaroff and Comaroff, *Of Revelation and Revolution*, I, 135.

45. I am indebted to Professor Benjamin Schumacher for providing astronomical data.
46. MacDonald, "Manners, Customs, and Superstitions," 283.
47. Transactions, "An Account of the Religion, Customs, Population, Government, Language, History, and Natural Productions of Caffraria, by Dr. Vanderkemp," 433.
48. Igor Kopytoff, ed., *The African Frontier: The Reproduction of Traditional African Societies* (Bloomington, 1987), 53.
49. Quoted in Jeff Opland, *Xhosa Oral Poetry: Aspects of a Black South African Tradition* (Cambridge, 1983), 187; (SAM) Smith, 3, 4.
50. (SOAS) MMS 309 (9), Shaw, miscellaneous papers, 1854–7.
51. Vansina, *Paths in the Rainforest*, 56–7. See also Randall Packard, *Chiefship and Cosmology: An Historical Study of Political Competition* (Bloomington, 1981); Kopytoff, *The African Frontier*.
52. Vansina, *Paths in the Rainforest*, 56.
53. (SOAS) MMS 309 (9), Shaw, miscellaneous papers, 1854–7.
54. And of course in many other areas of Africa. See, for example, Packard, *Chiefship and Cosmology*; Linda Heywood, "Towards an Understanding of Modern Political Ideology in Africa: The Case of the Ovimbundu of Angola," *Journal of Modern African Studies*, 36 (1998): 139–67.
55. I borrow exalted status from David W. Cohen, *Womunafu's Bunafu: A Study of Authority in a Nineteenth-century African Community* (Princeton, 1977), 163–5.
56. (SAM) Smith 3, 4.
57. Peires, *The House of Phalo*, 33.

58. Andrew Steedman, *Wanderings and Adventures in the Interior of Southern Africa*, 2 vols. (London, 1835), I, 42. See also William Shaw, *Journal of William Shaw*, ed. W. D. Hammond-Tooke (Cape Town, 1972), 181.

59. Hunter, *Reaction to Conquest*, 79.

60. Hammond-Tooke, *Bhaca Society*, 177.

61. Quoted in ibid.

62. 1/MFE 8/1, RM to CM, Umtata, 25 Mar. 1913.

63. CMT 1/27, Cumming to acting CM, 13 Feb. 1878.

64. Scheub, *The Tongue is Fire*, 235 and *passim*; Frank Brownlee, *The Transkeian Native Territories: Historical Records. Compiled by Frank Brownlee, Resident Magistrate, Mount Agliff* (Lovedale, 1923; repr. Westport, Conn., 1970), 123.

65. Steedman, *Wanderings*, I, 261. See also MMS 309 (9), Shaw, miscellaneous papers, 1854–7.

66. (SAM) Smith, 4. See also Anon., "Kafir Belief in the Existence of a Deity," *Cape Monthly Magazine*, 3 (Oct. 1880), 253.

67. See also Comaroff and Comaroff, *Of Revelation and Revolution*, I, 159.

68. See below on the Mpondomise and Hammond-Tooke, *Bhaca Society*, esp. 173–97.

69. Max Gluckman, *Rituals of Rebellion in South-East Africa* (Manchester, 1952). On the Bhaca, see Hammond-Tooke, *Bhaca Society*, esp. 173–97. See also T. O. Beidelman, *Colonial Evangelism: A Socio-historical Study of an East African Mission at the Grassroots* (Bloomington, 1982); Packard, *Chiefship and Cosmology*.

70. Surprisingly little has been written about magic and political process and structure in Southern Africa; it will be a recurring theme in this book. Until recently, literature on the occult has tended to focus on misfortune and social inferiors, especially women. See, for example, Leroy Vail and Landeg White, *Power and the Praise Poem: Southern African Voices in History* (Charlottesville, 1991). Discussions of magic and polity are mostly absent in, for example, Beinart, *The Political Economy of Pondoland*; Beinart, *Hidden Struggles*; and virtually so in Peires, *The House of Phalo*.

71. See below and Peires, *The House of Phalo*, 46–7; Stapleton, *Maqoma*; Hunter, *Reaction to Conquest*; Scheub, *The Tongue is Fire*. Elsewhere see Vansina, *Paths in the Rainforest*; Packard, *Chiefship and Cosmology*; Robert Harms, *River of Wealth, River of Sorrow: The Central Zaire Basin in the Era of the Slave and Ivory Trade, 1500–1891* (New Haven, 1981); Lan, *Guns and Rain*.

72. Peires, *The House of Phalo*, 46–7; Crais, *White Supremacy and Black Resistance*, 27–8; Stapleton, *Maqoma*, 214–15. The chief's mother "has become a rain maker": (SOAS) LMS 21 (3) B, Kayser to Tidman, 7 Oct. 1845. See also (SAM) Smith 4: "There are some families in each tribe who lay claim to the power of making rain and they maintain that the father has the power of transferring the secret to his son. This power or believed power of making rain gives the possessor of it a high rank and influence amongst the people."

73. Quoted in Scheub, *The Tongue is Fire*, 230.

74. 1/MFE 8/1, RM to CM, Umtata, 25 Mar. 1913; Hammond-Tooke, *Bhaca Society*; Ashforth, *Madumo*, 167. See also (SOAS) LMS 13 (3) C, Kayser to directors of London Missionary Society, 12 July 1833. For a recent case see *Daily Dispatch*, 16 June 2000.

75. *Transactions* "Transactions, of Dr. Vanderkemp, in the Year 1800," 418, 423, 426–7; also Steedman, *Wanderings and Adventures*, I, 41–5. See also (SOAS) LMS 13 (3)

C, Kayser to directors of the London Missionary Society, 12 July 1833. And, later, see (SOAS) LMS 18 (2) D, Kayser to Tidman, 24 Dec. 1841: "the young King has made a body of his people together to ask for rain from *their* rainmaker."

76. See also Kopytoff, ed., *The African Frontier*; Packard, *Chiefship and Cosmology*; Meredith McKittrick, "To Dwell Secure: Gender, Generation and Christianity in Northern Namibia," unpub. MS. McKittrick notes that good rulers "often are remembered as rain-makers who brought fertility and prosperity to the land, while bad kings reigned alongside famine or made unreasonable demands" (fol. 40). On magic and agriculture in Europe see, for example, Carlo Ginzburg, *The Night Battles: Witchcraft and Agrarian Cults in the Sixteenth and Seventeenth Centuries*, trans. John and Anne Tedeschi (Baltimore, 1983).

77. Vansina, *Paths in the Rainforest*, 97.

78. Vansina, *Paths in the Rainforest*, 96.

79. *Transactions*, "Transactions, 1800."

80. See also Kopytoff, ed., *The African Frontier*.

81. See also Steven Feierman, *Peasant Intellectuals: Anthropology and History in Tanzania* (Madison, 1990), esp. 94–119.

82. See, for example, J. V. B. Shrewsbury, *Memorials of Reverend William J. Shrewsbury* (London, 1869), 244.

83. See Peires, *The House of Phalo*, who argues for more political centralization, and Crais, *White Supremacy and Black Resistance*, who suggests rather less.

84. See Vansina, *Paths in the Rainforest*; Kopytoff, ed., *The African Frontier*; McKittrick, "To Dwell Secure." These patters were similar to what one historian has described, in a very different context, as districts, in which a number of homesteads (in Central Africa villages) relied on one another for common defense, ritual, and, in this case, recognized a chief and his residence. And, as in Central Africa, these political domains "were the first victims of the colonial order": Vansina, *Paths in the Rainforest*, 81.

85. (SAM) Sir Andrew Smith, "Kaffir Notes". See also Crais, *White Supremacy and Black Resistance*; Peires, *The House of Phalo*.

86. (SAM) Smith, 3.

87. Alberti, *Account*, 80–1. See also "Journal of a Tour to the North-Eastern Boundary. . . . in 1809," in Donald Moodie, *The Record* (Amsterdam and Cape Town, 1960), part 5, 1–60.

88. On principalities see Vansina, *Paths in the Rainforest*.

89. Alberti, *Account*, 81. See also (SAM) Smith 2. More generally on Ngqika see John Barrow, *Travels into the Interior of South Africa*, 2 vols., 2nd ed. (London, 1806), I, 146–53; Lichtenstein, *Travels*, I, 347, *passim*.

90. *Transactions*, "An Account," 436.

91. (SAM) Smith, 3.

92. (SAM) Smith, "Kaffir Notes."

93. Cf. Peires, *The House of Phalo*.

94. See above, and Lichtenstein, *Travels*, I, 352.

95. See also Kopytoff, ed., *The African Frontier*; Vansina, *Paths in the Rainforest*.

96. For an important archival source see ACC 793, letter book of Major Gawler. See also Peires, *Dead*. On drought see below and also Charles Ballard, "Drought and Economic Distress: South Africa in the 1880s," *Journal of Interdisciplinary History*,

17, 2 (1986): 359–78. More generally see Mike Davis, *Late Victorian Holocausts: El Nino Famines and the Making of the Third World* (New York, 2001).

97. (UCT) BC 293, D10, manuscript of Rev. E. J. Warner containing the history of his father, Rev. Joseph Cox Warner, n.d., t.s.

98. (UCT) BC 293, B2631, Edmonstone, Judge and Grant to secretary for NA, 30 Dec. 1872.

99. Ibid.

100. CO 4521, Graham, Unannexed Tembuland, 16 Aug. 1881.

101. CO 1156, Leonard, Opinion, 23 Apr. 1881.

102. CO 4521, quoted in Graham, Unannexed Tembuland, 16 Aug. 1881.

103. CO 4521, Graham, Unannexed Tembuland, 16 Aug. 1881.

104. By this time the Cape had annexed the entire Transkei with the exception of Pondoland, a region of over 20,000 square miles. See also Brownlee, *The Transkeian Native Territories*.

105. CMT 1/147, Rules and Regulations for the Government of the Transkeian Districts, 16 June 1879.

106. Ibid.

107. CMT 1/27, list.

108. CO 4521, office of resident with Gangelizwe, 28 Oct. 1875.

109. NA 20, minutes of meeting between Major Elliot and the Chief Ngangelizwe, document damaged, n.d. [1880].

110. Ibid. See also CMT 1/146, Genealogy of the Tembu Chiefs, n.d; (UCT) BC 293, B2631, Edmonstone, Judge and Grant to secretary for NA, 30 Dec. 1972.

111. NA 158, Shaw, report, Jan. 1878.

112. Ibid.

113. Ibid.

114. Anthony Atmore, "Moorosi's Rebellion: Lesotho, 1879," in Robert Rotberg and Ali Mazrui, eds., *Protest and Power* (New York, 1970).

115. See Atmore, "Moorosi's Rebellion"; Judy Kimble, "Labour Migration in Basutoland, c. 1870–1885," in Shula Marks and Richard Rathbone, eds., *Industrialisation and Social Change in South Africa* (London, 1982), 119–41.

116. Hope to ?, 23 Apr. 1878, in "Historical Record."

117. This and the above quotations are from NA 158, minutes of meeting of 22 Aug. 1878.

118. Ibid.

119. NA 158, Hope to secretary for NA, 26 Nov. 1878.

120. Ibid.

121. CMK 1/94, Hope to CM, Kokstad, 17 Jan. 1879.

122. See below and CMK 1/94, Hope to Brownlee (CM, Kokstad), 4 Sept. 1879; NA 18, Grant to Elliot, 5 Mar. 1880.

123. CMK 1/94, Hope to Brownlee (CM, Kokstad), 21 Feb. 1879; CMK 1/94, Hope to CM, Kokstad, 5 Apr. 1879; CMK 1/94, meeting of 3 May 1879.

124. CMK 1/94, meeting of 3 May 1879.

125. Ibid.

126. Ibid.

127. CMK 1/94, Hope to CM, Kokstad, 21 May 1879.

128. CMK 1/94, Hope to CM, Kokstad, 19 Sept. 1879.

129. Ibid.
130. See, for example, NA 18, Cumming to CM, Thembuland, 10 Jan. 1880.
131. CMK 1/94, Hope to CM, Kokstad, 25 Aug. 1880.
132. Ibid.
133. CMK 1/94, Hope to CM, Kokstad, 13 Mar. 1880.
134. Ibid.
135. Ibid.
136. Ibid.
137. CMK 1/94, meeting of 23 Mar. 1880.
138. See Keith Thomas, *Religion and the Decline of Magic* (London, 1971).
139. CMK 1/152, Hope to CM, Kokstad, 14 Oct. 1880.
140. CMK 1/152, Hope to CM, Kokstad, 19 Oct. 1880.
141. CMK 1/152, RM, Maclear to CM, Kokstad, 22 Oct. 1880.
142. CMK 1/152, Hope to CM, Kokstad, 19 Oct. 1880.
143. A215, letter to Thomson, 19 Oct. 1880. In the letter "Umhlonhlo is delighted 'maar wagt an bietje' [but wait a bit]." Thomson was magistrate at Maclear.
144. CMK 1/94, Hope to CM, Kokstad, 19 Sept. 1879.
145. (UCT) BC 293, B116.39, Leary to Stanford, 29 June 1922. This also occurred in the Bhambata Rebellion of 1906–08 in Natal, where a European's body was mutilated to strengthen the warriors (see Benedict Carton, *Blood from your Children: The Colonial Origins of Generational Conflict in South Africa* (Charlottesville, 2000), 134) and, earlier and in the Eastern Cape, in the war of 1850. See Peires, *Dead*, 11.
146. CMK 1/94, Leary to officer commanding, 2 May 1881.
147. (UCT) BC 293, B116.39, Leary to Stanford, 29 June 1922; Brownlee, *Reminiscences of a Transkeian*, 112, 84.
148. Report of Commandant Jenner, Dec. 1880, in "Historical Record."
149. With Commandant Jenner's column, Dec. 1880, in "Historical Record."
150. *Graham's Town Journal*, 19 May 1904.
151. Beinart and Bundy, *Hidden Struggles*, 121.
152. *Daily Dispatch*, 7 Nov. 1998. See also 7 Jan. 1999.
153. *Daily Dispatch*, 25 Aug. 2000.
154. Ashforth, *Madumo*; Niehaus, "Witchcraft"; Peires, *Dead*. See also Geschiere, *Modernity of Witchcraft*.
155. CMK 1/94, Hope to CM, Kokstad, 19 Sept. 1879.
156. *Cape Times*, 25 Oct. 1880, in "Historical Record."
157. *The Frontier Guardian and Dordrecht Advocate*, 18 Dec. 1880, in "Historical Record."
158. See Ginzburg, *History, Rhetoric, and Proof*.

2 ETHNOGRAPHIES OF STATE

1. Foucault, "Governmentality," 99.
2. CMK 1/94, minutes of meeting, 23 Dec. 1879. The study of knowledge and colonialism has been of particular importance to scholars of Asian history. See, for example, Arjun Appadurai, "Number in the Colonial Imagination," in Carol A. Breckenridge and Peter van der Veer, eds., *Orientalism and the Postcolonial Predicament: Perspectives on South Asia* (Philadelphia, 1993). See also C. A. Bayly, *Empire and*

Information: Intelligence Gathering and Social Communication in India, 1780–1870 (Cambridge, 1996); Bernard S. Cohn, *Colonialism and its Forms of Knowledge: The British in India* (Princeton, 1996); and, of course, Said, *Orientalism*.

3. *Webster's Dictionary, Second College Edition* (Cleveland, OH, 1986). See also the *Oxford English Dictionary* for a more detailed etymology.

4. *Black's Law Dictionary*, 7th ed. (St. Paul, 1999).

5. The story recounted in this and in the previous chapter bears similarity to the relationship between Theophilus Shepstone and the Zulu king Cetshwayo, at the king's coronation in 1872. See Carolyn Hamilton, *Terrific Majesty: The Powers of Shaka Zulu and the Limits of Historical Invention* (Cambridge, Mass., 1998), 98. Elsewhere (pp. 72–129) Hamilton argues that Shepstone assumed the "mantle" of Shaka Zulu during the coronation ceremonies, and indeed in many respects became Shaka.

6. Quoted in Atmore, "Moorosi's Rebellion," 9.

7. *The Frontier Guardian and Dordrecht Advocate*, 18 Dec. 1880, in "Historical Record." See also White, *Speaking with Vampires*; Harriet Ngubane, *Body and Mind in Zulu Medicine* (London, 1977); Jean Comaroff, *Body of Power, Spirit of Resistance: The Culture and History of a South African People* (Chicago, 1985).

8. See Silk, *A Shanty Town in South Africa*, 12; Hunter, *Reaction to Conquest*, 489; Redding, "Government Witchcraft"; Mbeki, *South Africa*, 108; Niehaus, "Witchcraft"; Lane, "'Jele Tšhelete'"; Ashforth, *Madumo*.

9. Quoted in Jeff Guy, *The Destruction of the Zulu Kingdom: The Civil War in Zululand, 1879–1884* (Johannesburg, 1979), 49.

10. Jordan, *Wrath of the Ancestors*, 9.

11. Evidence of Stanford, G. 4-'83.

12. See Said, *Orientalism*; Dirks, *Colonialism and Culture*.

13. CMK 1/94, minutes of meeting, 23 Dec. 1879.

14. Secular bureaucracy was itself a ritual order. Meeting with colonial subjects, writing memos, issuing passes, and so on constituted so many "commonplace rituals": Herzfeld, *The Social Production of Indifference*, 37. "Ritual," Tambiah has argued, "is constituted of patterned and ordered sequences of words and acts . . . whose content and arrangement are characterized in varying degree by formality (conventionality), stereotypy (rigidity), condensation (fusion), and redundancy (repetition)" (quoted in Herzfeld, *The Social Production of Indifference*, 8). "Almost without modification," Herzfeld argues, "this definition would also fit the popular view of bureaucracy because it describes some familiar aspects of bureaucratic practice: stereotype and practice meet on the common ground of convention."

15. See Said, *Orientalism*; Cohn, *Colonialism*; Dirks, *Colonialism and Culture*; Stoler, *Race*.

16. Harvey, *The Condition of Postmodernity*, 245. See also Martin Jay, *Downcast Eyes: The Denigration of Vision in Twentieth-Century French Thought* (Berkeley and Los Angeles, 1993), 1–82.

17. Jeremy Black, *Maps and Politics* (Chicago, 1997). See also Mary Poovey, "The Production of Abstract Space," in Susan Hardy Aiken et al., *Making Worlds: Gender, Metaphor, Materiality* (Tucson, 1998). On the earlier period see Patricia Seed, *Ceremonies of Possession in Europe's Conquest of the New World, 1492–1640* (New York, 1995), esp. 16–40.

18. Isobel Hofmeyr, *"We Spend Our Years as a Tale That is Told:" Oral Historical Narrative in a South African Chiefdom* (Portsmouth, 1993), 73.

19. Thongchai Winichakul, *Siam Mapped: A History of the Geo-Body of Nation* (Honolulu, 1994), 129–30. See also Seed, *Ceremonies of Possession.*

20. CCP 4/19/11, *Report on the Trigonometrical Survey of a Portion of the Colony and British Kaffraria,* by Captain W. Bailey, R. E. (Cape Town, 1863), 3. See also Yvonne Garson, comp., *Versatile Genius: The Royal Engineers and their Maps* (Johannesburg, 1992), 3, on the 1812 creation of the Royal Engineer Establishment and the 1856 founding of the Corps of Royal Engineers.

21. J. M. Orpen, for example, arrived in South Africa in 1846, and was subsequently appointed as land surveyor of the Cape Colony, Orange River Sovereignty, and later Rhodesia. As we have seen, Orpen also served as the first magistrate to the Mpondomise. See ACC 302, Orpen Papers.

22. See below. See also G. 30-'76, *Report of the Surveyor-General on the Tenure of Land, on the Land Laws and their Results, and on the Topography of the Colony* (1876), which marked the state's increasing concern with space.

23. G. 4-'83.

24. GH 8/37, Maclean, circular, 9 Feb. 1859.

25. (PTA) NTS 10275, secretary for NA to secretary to the treasury, 25 Sept. 1947: "the fact that the Native people viewed the establishment of Closer Settlement Schemes with suspicion, being of the opinion that the Government is introducing this system as a means of obtaining cheap Native Labour for Industrial requirements."

26. Anderson, *Imagined Communities,* 163.

27. Winichakul, *Siam Mapped,* 106.

28. NA 225, RM, Glen Grey, to secretary to the prime minister, June 1896.

29. G. 42-'22, *Report on Native Locations Surveys,* 10. See also A.3-'92, *Report of the Commission Appointed to Inquire into the Tenure of Land &c., in the Glen Grey District,* June 1892, located in NA 215.

30. NA 225, RM, Glen Grey, to secretary to the prime minister, June 1896.

31. See the once seminal, now reductionist, article by Shula Marks and Stanley Trapido, "Lord Milner and the South African State," *History Workshop* (1979): 50–80. See also Richard Muir, *Modern Political Geography* (New York, 1975); Michael Hurst, *States, Countries, Provinces* (Frome and London, 1986); Anderson, *Imagined Communities,* 163–86.

32. In addition to specific acts see, for example, 1/PDE 6/2, RM to secretary of the Native Land Commission, 14 Oct. 1913; CCK 17, NC to chief native commissioner (CNC), 28 Dec. 1935; (CL) uncatalogued, minutes of meeting, 19 Sept. 1923.

33. Silvana Patriarca, *Numbers and Nationhood: Writing Statistics in Nineteenth-Century Italy* (Cambridge, 1996), 50.

34. Appadurai, "Number in the Colonial Imagination," 315.

35. Appadurai, "Number in the Colonial Imagination," 333–4.

36. See below and Mary Poovey, *Making a Social Body: British Cultural Formation, 1830–1864* (Chicago, 1995); Mary Poovey, *History of the Modern Fact: Problems of Knowledge in the Sciences of Wealth and Society* (Chicago, 1998).

37. Patriarca, *Numbers and Nationhood,* 11.

38. Quoted in Ian Hacking, "How Should we do the History of Statistics," in Burchell et al., eds., *The Foucault Effect,* 186.

39. Hacking, "How Should We;" Patriarca, *Numbers and Nationhood*.
40. Anderson, *Imagined Communities*, 166.
41. Appadurai, "Number in the Colonial Imagination," 318.
42. Patriarca, *Numbers and Nationhood*, 35.
43. For example see NA 231, King, annual report, 8 Jan. 1895.
44. See Evans, *Bureaucracy and Race*.
45. Act No. 38 of 1914, "To provide for the collection of statistics relating to agricultural and to industrial, commercial, shipping, fishing and other business undertakings and other matters in the Union."
46. On infant mortality, for example, see CCK 11, n.d. [1930s], which sampled mortality rates from forty-six different Ciskei locations. On malnutrition see, for example, 1/ALC 10/64, "Admissions . . . suffering from diseases due solely to malnutrition," n.d. [1930]. See also Evans, *Bureaucracy and Race*, for the twentieth century.
47. Pasquale Pasquino, "Theatrum Politicum: The Genealogy of Capital – Police and the State of Prosperity," in Burchell et al., eds., *The Foucault Effect*, 113.
48. See Crais, *White Supremacy and Black Resistance*, 216, 194–6.
49. CMT 1/147, Rules and Regulations for the Government of the Transkeian Districts, 16 June 1879. See also NA 190, Steward to Chalmers, 31 Dec. 1881; NA 189, Shaw to secretary for NA, report for 1881, 10 Jan. 1882: "The pass system has been strictly carried out."
50. See, for example, Evans, *Bureaucracy and Race*, 113 and *passim*.
51. For the most recent discussion of this legislation see Evans, *Bureaucracy and Race*. See also Beinart and Bundy, *Hidden Struggles*; Hendricks, *The Pillars of Apartheid*.
52. Appadurai, "Number in the Colonial Imagination," 317.
53. Scott, *Seeing Like a State*, 87.
54. Ibid.
55. Scott, *Seeing Like a State*, 11.
56. LiPuma, *Encompassing Others*, 20.
57. See also Dirks, *Colonialism and Culture*, 3; Stoler, *Race*, 16, on the importance of culture and the creation of colonial orders.
58. *Black's Law Dictionary*.
59. Alberti, *Account*, 98.
60. See, for one example, W. D. Hammond-Tooke, *The Tribes of King William's Town District* (Pretoria, 1958).
61. John Maclean, *Compendium of Kaffir Law and Custom* (London, 1858).
62. See Martin Chanock, *Law, Custom, and Social Order: The Colonial Experience in Malawi and Zambia* (Cambridge, 1985); Kristin Mann and Richard Roberts, eds., *Law in Colonial Africa* (Portsmouth, 1991).
63. "The Reverend H. H. Dugmore's Papers," in Maclean, *Compendium*, 37, 38. See also Alberti, *Account*, 85–6.
64. See also LiPuma, *Encompassing Others*; Sally Engle Merry, *Colonizing Hawai'i: The Cultural Power of Law* (Princeton, 2000). In early trials the accused rarely defended themselves, for example by not taking advantage of their right of cross-examination. It is unclear in such instances whether the accused simply felt intimidated or simply could not quite fathom the colonial legal liturgy based on individual rights and culpability. For some examples see, for instance, ACC 793, letter book of Major Gawler.

65. Max Weber, *The Protestant Ethic and the Spirit of Capitalism*, trans. Talcott Parsons, intro. Anthony Giddens (New York, 1976), 181.
66. See also Brookes, *History of Native Policy*, 109–111.
67. See Comaroff and Comaroff, *Of Revelation and Revolution*, II: *The Dialectics of Modernity on a South African Frontier* (Chicago, 1997), 396, more generally 365–404.
68. Customary law became a central part of the definition of Africans as members of easily discernible tribes, what the Comaroffs have described as the "register of *primal sovereignty*": Comaroff and Comaroff, *Of Revelation and Revolution*, II, 370.
69. 1/ALC 10/11, Hammond-Tooke to Muir, 28 Aug. 1965.
70. 1/ALC 10/11, Hammond-Tooke to Bantu affairs commissioner (BAC), 28 Aug. 1965.
71. CMT 1/143, minutes of meeting, 10 Mar. 1885.
72. In an important sense the erection of telegraph posts and the laying of wire formed an additional physical mapping of colonial space.
73. IDW ADD 1/1/2, journal book, Warner, special magistrate, 4 Nov. 1864.
74. CMT 1/143, minutes of meeting of CM with Dalindyebo and others, 10 Mar. 1885.
75. CMT 1/143, minutes of meeting of CM and Chief Holomisa, 24 June 1884.
76. Ibid.
77. 1/IDW ADD 1/1/1, Colley to CC, 15 Oct. 1858.
78. CMT 1/143, minutes of meeting of CM and Chief Holomisa, 24 June 1884.
79. NA 158, Shaw, report for the year ending 30 Dec. 1877.
80. CMT 1/27, Stanford to Scott, 25 July 1878.
81. NA 158, Shaw, report for the year ending 30 Dec. 1877.
82. NA 158, minutes of meeting, 6 and 7 Aug. 1878. See also NA 158, Welsh to secretary for NA, 1 July 1878.
83. CMK 1/94, minutes of meeting, 23 Dec. 1879. See also CMK 1/94, Hope to CM, 6 Sept. 1879.
84. CMK 1/94, minutes of meeting, 23 Dec. 1879.
85. For example the Pondo chief Valelo. See Beinart, *The Political Economy of Pondoland*, 127–8.
86. CMK 1/94, Hope to Brownlie, 4 Sept. 1879. See also CMT 1/53, Hope to Davis, 6 Aug. 1879; Davis to Hope, 7 Aug. 1879.
87. CMK 1/94, Hope to Brownlie, 4 Sept. 1879. See also CMT 1/53, Hope to Davis, 6 Aug. 1879; Davis to Hope, 7 Aug. 1879; CMT 1/53, Hope to Elliot, 24 July 1879; NA 18, Grant to Elliot, 5 Mar. 1880.
88. See below and CMT 1/143, minutes of meeting, 24 Sept. 1884 and minutes of meeting, 10 Mar. 1885.
89. CMT 1/143, minutes of meeting, 24 Sept. 1884.
90. Ibid.
91. (UCT) BC 293, B2631, Edmonstone, Judge and Grant to secretary for NA, 30 Dec. 1872. See also BC 293, B263.17, statement of Xelo, 8 Feb. 1882; NA 20, minutes of meeting between Major Elliot and Chief Ngangelizwe, document damaged, n.d., 1880; NA 19, Elliot to secretary for NA, 6 May 1880: "Nothing of any moment took place at this meeting beyond a representation from the Chiefs that they are the only Chiefs of any territory taken over by Government who do not receive allowances.

I think it desirable that the Bomvana Chiefs should be placed upon the same footing as others."

92. NA 20, minutes of meeting, n.d., 1880. As the Thembu paramount said: "I know all that you have said. You also desired me not to decide any matters from Bomvana-land."

93. While maps might appear clear, real boundaries seldom were: "surveying could be charmingly vague," and "the possibility of determining boundaries with any degree of precision was remote." There was, as Hofmeyr has argued, an "unholy confusion" of natural markers and land beacons that "were variously shifted, pinched, destroyed, ploughed over, stolen ... and used for target practice": Hofmeyr, *"We Spend our Years as a Tale that is Told,"* 74. True enough, but these vague demarcations were absolutely central to the creation of magisterial districts and the organization of political space on the basis of ethnicity. Colonial demarcations were as powerful as they were perplexing; thousands of people were displaced in their name. Boundaries defined the rule of chiefs, headmen, and resident magistrates. They helped determine access to natural resources such as forests. And they had an important impact on ecology by circumscribing migration and the pasturing of cattle in times of drought.

94. CMT 1/143, minutes of 10 Mar. 1885. Chiefs could forfeit territory on the basis of what the British defined as "disuse," thereby invoking an old English legal practice that has come to be known as adverse possession; (UCT) BC 293 B2631, Edmonstone, Judge and Grant to secretary for NA, 30 Dec. 1872.

95. CO 1156, Frere, proclamation, 15 Sept. 1879.

96. CMT 1/27, Stanford to CM, 11 Sept. 1879.

97. (UCT) BC 293, A70, Stanford to Elliot, 11 Aug. 1879, Stanford to Elliot, 25 Aug. 1879.

98. (UCT) BC 293, A70, Stanford to CM, 27 Aug. 1879.

99. (UCT) BC 293, A70, Stanford to Elliot, 27 Aug. 1879.

100. Lewis, for example, based his critique of the Bundy thesis on the 1848 census of British Kaffraria (Ciskei), "an extensive census" that "is an invaluable tool for historical analysis because it was based on a physical count": Jack Lewis, "The Rise and Fall of the South African Peasantry: A Critique and Reassessment," *Journal of Southern African Studies*, 11, 1 (1984): 1–24. See also Colin Bundy, *The Rise and Fall of the South African Peasantry*, 2nd ed. (Cape Town, 1988). The Transkei, however, was a far larger region.

101. CMT 1/27, Stanford to CM, 11 Sept. 1879.

102. This practice had, and has, a long, ignominious history. As early as the late 1850s officials regularly burned people out of locations for not being registered to live there or for failing to pay their taxes. See, for example, BK 87, Miller to Maclean, 3 Aug. 1859; BK 73, Brownlee, half-yearly-return, 30 June 1865.

103. CO 4521, Graham, Unannexed Tembuland, n.d. [1881–2]. The Cape Colony annexed Thembuland in 1885.

104. CO 4521, Graham, Unannexed Tembuland, n.d. [1881–2].

105. CO 4521, office of resident with Gangelizwe, 28 Oct. 1875. NA 20, minutes of meeting, damaged, 1880. In the 1880 war the paramount wavered, but ultimately did not join the rebels.

106. See, for example, GGR 1, commandant to Merriman, 30 Sept. 1877; (UCT) BC 293; and Brownlee, *The Transkeian Native Territories.*

107. NA 158, Welsh to secretary for NA, 1 July 1878. Welsh equally prosecuted cases of witchcraft. See Welsh to secretary for NA, 26 Nov. 1878.
108. NA 158, minutes of meeting, 6 and 7 Aug. 1878.
109. CMT 3/520, minutes of meeting between the CM and the inhabitants of Elliotdale district, 4 Feb. 1903.
110. CMK 1/94, minutes of meeting, 23 Dec. 1879.
111. NA 18, Elliot to secretary for NA, 18 Feb. 1880.
112. (UCT) BC 293, Stanford to Walker, 12 Feb. 1879.
113. (UCT) BC 293, Stanford to Walker, n.d., 1879.
114. (UCT) BC 293, Stanford to Elliot, 9 July 1879.
115. (UCT) BC 293, Stanford to CM, 27 Aug. 1879.
116. John Ayliff, "Minority Report," G. 4-'83.
117. NA 19, Elliot to secretary for NA, 11 May 1880.
118. NA 19, minutes of meeting, 28 Apr. 1880.
119. NA 19, minutes of meeting, 29 June 1880.
120. NA 20, CM to secretary for NA, 28 July 1880.
121. Ibid.
122. CMT 1/27, Stanford to secretary for NA, 23 Nov. 1880.
123. Ibid.
124. NA 20, Cumming to secretary for NA, 2 Dec. 1880.
125. Ibid.
126. See, for example, 1/CMT 1/28, Stanford, report, 1881.
127. Ibid.

3 RATIONALITIES AND RULE

1. Quoted in Marian Lacey, *Working for Boroko: The Origins of a Coercive Labour System in South Africa* (Johannesburg, 1981), 95.
2. The very language of rule became increasingly mechanistic. See Ashforth, *The Politics of Official Discourse*. "It is as managers of life and survival, of bodies and the race," Foucault has written, "that so many regimes have been able to wage so many wars, causing so many men to be killed": Foucault, *History of Sexuality*, 137. See also Burchell et al., eds., *The Foucault Effect*; Mitchell, *Colonising Egypt*.
3. Indeed, at the highest levels of government considerable disagreement existed as to the proper course of native policy in the Cape. Ultimately this centered on the advantages and disadvantages of direct and indirect models of colonial rule. See Mamdani, *Citizen and Subject*, 16–18. See also Evans, *Bureaucracy and Race*; Rogers, *Native Administration*.
4. See Stanley Trapido, "'The Friends of the Natives': Merchants, Peasants and the Political and Ideological Structure of Liberalism in the Cape, 1854–1910," in Shula Marks and Stanley Trapido, *Economy and Society in Pre-industrial South Africa* (London, 1980), 247–74. Both segregation and apartheid were the subject of considerable debate. See Dubow, *Racial Segregation and the Origins of Apartheid*; John Cell, *The Highest Stage of White Supremacy: The Origins of Segregation in South Africa and the American South* (Cambridge, 1982); Posel, *The Making of Apartheid*; Ashforth, *The Politics of Official Discourse*. Evans, *Bureaucracy and Race*, 25, has pointed out that despite and perhaps because of the "ideological

consensus among whites … a palpable degree of confusion and inconsistency in matters of practical administration [was promoted]."

5. ACC 793, letter of 29 Oct. 1856.
6. See Herzfeld, *The Social Production of Indifference*.
7. Sahlins, *How "Natives" Think*, 153.
8. Sahlins, *How "Natives" Think*, 187.
9. See Warner's note in Maclean, *Compendium*; G. 4-'83.
10. Mamdani, *Citizen and Subject*, 17 and *passim*.
11. This is adapted from Frantz Fanon, *Black Skin, White Masks* (New York, 1967).
12. Hamilton, *Terrific Majesty*, 74.
13. Hamilton, *Terrific Majesty*, 98.
14. Hamilton, *Terrific Majesty*, 82.
15. Hamilton, *Terrific Majesty*, 75.
16. Stanford, *Reminiscences*, 18.
17. Stanford, *Reminiscences*, 55.
18. Stanford, *Reminiscences*, 56.
19. Hamilton, *Terrific Majesty*, 73.
20. Evans, *Bureaucracy and Race*, 180.
21. G. 4-'83, 43. In many areas the position of magistrate became *de facto* hereditary: the job passed from father to son or circulated within the colonizer's extended family. Because the DNA remained relatively small throughout the nineteenth century, a few families (for example the Stanfords, Warners, and Brownlees) dominated the Eastern Cape's colonial system.
22. Beinart and Bundy, *Hidden Struggles*.
23. This can be gleaned from archival material located in the BK series, Cape Archives. See also ACC 793, letter book of Major Gawler, the magistrate ruling over Chief Mhala in the 1850s. For the later period see Beinart and Bundy, *Hidden Struggles*.
24. Quoted in Ashforth, *The Politics of Official Discourse*, 69, 116.
25. NA 554, Erskine to Strange, 9 Mar. 1899.
26. Ibid.
27. 1/ALC 5/1/1/2, comparative statement, 1910.
28. Roger Southall, *South Africa's Transkei: The Political Economy of an "Independent" Bantustan* (London, 1982), 78.
29. Quoted in Southall, *South Africa's Transkei*, 77.
30. See, for example, CCK 25, RM, Alexandria to secretary for NA, 24 Sept. 1926; CMT 3/679, compilation of materials, n.d. [1910–11]; 1/NKE 7/1/60, report, 28 Sept. 1926.
31. 1/AXA 7/17 , Smit to NC, 16 June 1936.
32. Max Weber, *Economy and Society*, ed. Guenther Roth and Claus Wittich, 2 vols. (Berkeley and Los Angeles, 1978, I, 225.
33. See Ashforth, *The Politics of Official Discourse*, and Evans, *Bureaucracy and Race*, on changes in state thinking and policy in this period.
34. "There is," Adorno and Horkheimer wrote, "no form of being in the world that science could not penetrate." In such a world "factuality wins the day; cognition is restricted to its repetition": Adorno and Horkheimer, *Dialectic of Enlightenment*, 26–7.
35. Harvey, *The Condition of Postmodernity*, 13.
36. Scott, *Seeing Like a State*, 5.

37. (UCT) BC 293 D10, "Manuscript of the Rev. E. J. Warner containing the History of his Father, Rev. Joseph Cox Warner," n.d., t.s.

38. G. 42-'22, 5.

39. Ibid.

40. Foucault, *History of Sexuality*, 143.

41. Scott, *Seeing Like a State*, esp. 88–9.

42. 1/ALC 10/14, headman and twelve others to CNC, 2 Jan. 1948. See also Scott, *Seeing Like a State*.

43. NA 723, O'Connell to secretary for NA, 28 Jan., 1908.

44. See, for example, 1/ELN 61, Native Wages, 1 Sept. 1930.

45. See, for example, CCK 11, quinquennal census, 29 Jan. 1934; CCK 26, tables "A" through "E"; CCK 62, figures for 1921, 1930, and 1931. See also (CL), uncatalogued material, "Descriptive Return . . . ," conducted in the 1940s, which included information on whether, and if so where, the male household head was laboring outside the location.

46. See, for example, (CL), uncatalogued minutes of meeting of residents of Gwili Gwili, 19 Sept. 1923.

47. Compare, for example, (PTA) NTS 10275, "Return Showing Manner in Which the District is Occupied, with Population (estimated), large and Small Stock as at June 1945" and (PTA) K 114(3), "Return of Native Labourers and Native Owned Stock," 14 July 1914.

48. See, for example, 1/ALC 10/33, report, 25 Mar. 1938.

49. Ibid.

50. CMT 3/1451, report of the CM for the year ending 31 Dec. 1955.

51. (PTA) NTS 10275, secretary for NA to secretary to the treasury, 25 Sept. 1947.

52. CMT 3/1451, "Livestock Reduction–Culling," n.d. [1961].

53. CMT 3/1451, report for 1955. See also reports for 1957 and 1960.

54. For a now classic, if at times overly mechanistic study, see Harold Wolpe, "Capitalism and Cheap Labour Power," in William Beinart and Saul Dubow, eds., *Segregation and Apartheid in Twentieth-Century South Africa* (London and New York, 1995). See also Trouillot, "Anthropology of the State."

55. (PTA) NTS 7693, NC to CNC, 15 Jan. 1956. See also CMT 3/1480, warrant officer to magistrate, 22 May 1962.

56. (PTA) NTS 2536, magistrate to CNC, 21 Aug. 1929.

57. CCK 120, meeting of 6 April 1933.

58. (CL), uncatalogued material, magistrate to CNC, 4 Sept. 1924.

59. Lacey, *Working for Boroko*, 107. See also Evans, *Bureaucracy and Race*.

60. NA 708, [illeg.] to secretary for NA, 3 Sept. 1908.

61. See Rogers, *Native Administration*, esp. 52–84. See also 1/ALC 10/11, lecture on Bantu Authorities, c. 1963.

62. (PTA) NTS 7664, quarterly meeting, 15 Sept. 1926.

63. CCK 120, assistant NC to NC, 25 Nov. 1933.

64. Lacey, *Working for Boroko*, 95. The second quotation is in reference to the pass system: G. 41-'22, *Report of the Inter-Departmental Committee on the Native Pass Laws, 1922*, 11.

65. Dubow, *Racial Segregation and the Origins of Apartheid*, 177; Wolpe, "Capitalist and Cheap Labour Power."

66. Bantu Authorities Act, Act No. 68 of 1951.
67. 1/ALC 10/11, "Bantu Authorities: Their Aim and Object and the Place of the Chief or Headman in these Authorities," n.d. [1963], emphasis in original. For one case study of the state's manufacture of tradition see Clifton Crais, "Representation and the Politics of Identity in South Africa: An Eastern Cape Example," *International Journal of African Historical Studies*, 25, 1 (1992): 99–126.
68. 1/ALC 10/11, "Bantu Authorities: Their Aim and Object and the Place of the Chief or Headman in these Authorities," n.d. [1963], emphasis in original. See also 1/ALC 10/11, "Lecture on Bantu Authorities," n.d. [1963].
69. 1/ALC 10/11, "Time Table for Native Chiefs' Educational Conference," 25 Jan. 1952.
70. 1/ALC 10/11, "Installation Ceremony," 25 Apr. 1959.
71. Miliband, quoted in Trouillot, "Anthropology of the State."
72. John Lonsdale and Bruce Berman, *Unhappy Valley: Conflict in Kenya and Africa* (Athens, OH, 1992).
73. Weber, *Economy and Society*, II, 1006; see also 956–8, 1112–17.
74. In this sense apartheid was not unlike the grand and disastrous plans of rural collectivization in the Soviet Union or in Tanzania under the policies of *ujaama*. See Scott, *Seeing Like a State*.
75. Evans, *Bureaucracy and Race*, 174.
76. (UCT) BC 293, A 70, Stanford to Innes, 11 July 1889.
77. Cf. Comaroff and Comaroff, *Of Revelation and Revolution*, I.

4 PROPHECIES OF NATION

1. Walter Benjamin, *Illuminations*, ed. and intro. Hannah Arendt, trans. Harry Zohn (New York, 1969).
2. Quoted in Antjie Krog, *Country of my Skull: Guilt, Sorrow, and the Limits of Forgiveness in the New South Africa* (New York, 1998) 247.
3. Krog, *Country of my Skull*, 40.
4. Krog, *Country of my Skull*, 178–9.
5. Ibid. Nationally, between 1984 and 1989 the Eastern Cape accounted for over 30 percent of the total deaths by necklacing and burning. *Truth and Reconciliation Commission of South Africa Report*, 5 vols. (London, 1999), III, 108.
6. *Truth and Reconciliation Commission of South Africa Report*, III, 110–12.
7. Quoted in "Mothers and Fathers of the Nation: The Forgotten People," *Report of the Ministerial Committee on Abuse, Neglect and Ill-Treatment of Older Persons*, 26 February 2001.
8. Truth and Reconciliation Commission, Media Advisory, 4 May 2000.
9. See Platzky and Walker, *The Surplus People*; Les Switzer, *Power and Resistance in an African Society: The Ciskei Xhosa and the Making of South Africa* (Madison, 1993), esp. 313–50; Desmond, *The Discarded People*.
10. Platzky and Walker, *The Surplus People*, 340.
11. NA 195, Fielding to CC, KWT, 20 Dec. 1882. See also NA 193, Roberts, report, 30 Dec. 1882.
12. G. 8-'75, *Report on Immigration and Labour Supply for the Year*, 2.
13. NA 189, Fleischer, report for 1881.

14. This is, admittedly, inferred. See C. 2A-'92, *Appendix to the Report of the Select Committee on the Labour Question*, 54; Keletso Atkins, *The Moon is Dead! Give us our Money: The Cultural Origins of an African Work Ethic, Natal, South Africa, 1843–1900* (Portsmouth, 1993).
15. See NA 556, Erskine to secretary of the NAD, 28 Dec. 1904; NA 555, Roberts to secretary of the NAD, 17 Dec. 1904; NA 554, RM, Dordrecht to secretary of the NAD, 18 Sept. 1902; (BR) 455, 385, Davies to Steil, 4 Nov. 1908; (BR) 455, 385, Martienssen to secretary of central administration, 6 July 1908.
16. Quoted in Robert Edgar, "The Fifth Seal: Enoch Mgijima, the Israelites, and the Bullhoek Massacre" (Ph.D. thesis, University of California, 1977), 24.
17. (PTA) NTS 7204, Mochochoko, Agenda of the Ninth Annual Congress of the South African Native National Congress, 24 May 1920; NTS 7204, inspector, CID, to SAP, 28 May 1920.
18. Quoted in Robert Edgar and Hilary Sapire, *African Apocalypse: The Story of Nontetha Nkwenke, a Twentieth-Century South African Prophet* (Athens, OH, 2000), 7.
19. See, for example, (PM) 1/CNC 312, Rumbelow to magistrate, 2 Oct. 1918; (PTA) SAP 36, du Toit to secretary, South African Police (SAP), 29 Aug. 1918; (PTA) SAP 36, statement of Mekeni, 26 Aug. 1918.
20. Quoted in Edgar, "The Fifth Seal," 24.
21. (PTA) JUS 287, acting deputy commissioner of police to secretary of SAP, 25 April 1921.
22. (PTA) JUS 287, copy of telegram, deputy commissioner of police to commissioner of police, 9 Dec. 1920.
23. Preparatory examination in the trial of the Israelites (June–August 1921) and *Rex v. Israelites* (October–November 1921), evidence of Nightingale, 12.
24. Ibid.
25. Preparatory examination in the trial of the Israelites (June–August 1921) and *Rex v. Israelites* (October–November 1921), evidence of Nightingale, 11. See also 20: "In 1918 at the Kamastone Passover there were about 1000 persons present."
26. CMT 3/781, Roberts et al. to minister of NA, 21 April 1921, *Interim and Final Reports of the Native Affairs Commission...Relative to "Israelites" at Bulhoek and Occurrences in May, 1921.*
27. (PTA) JUS 287, acting deputy commissioner of police, Eastern Cape division, to secretary of SAP, 25 April 1921.
28. *The Bullhoek Tragedy. Illustrated. The Full Story of the Israelite Settlement at Ntabelanga, near Queenstown* (East London Daily Dispatch, Ltd., 1924), 13.
29. Preparatory examination in the trial of the Israelites (June–August 1921) and *Rex v. Israelites* (October–November 1921), 99–101. This mimicry of the state and the military was not unusual. For example the Isitshozi gang on the gold mines, whose members came from the Transkei, particularly Pondoland, had the following ranks: magistrate, chief justice, colonel, captain, sergeant major, corporal, soldier, and doctor. See 1/TAD 6/1/60, Thompson to RM, Mqanduli, 3 Feb. 1930.
30. (PTA) JUS 287, Mgijima to Truter, 22 May 1921.
31. Preparatory examination in the trial of the Israelites (June–August 1921) and *Rex v. Israelites* (October–November 1921), 99–101.

32. Preparatory examination in the trial of the Israelites (June–August 1921) and *Rex v. Israelites* (October–November 1921), 125.
33. *The Bullhoek Tragedy*, 29.
34. Translation of Xhosa text held by the Church of the Prophetess Nonthetha, taken during field research, 1992.
35. Weber, *Economy and Society*, I, 519.
36. Liah Greenfeld, *Nationalism: Five Roads to Modernity* (Cambridge, Mass., 1992), 14.
37. Greenfeld, *Nationalism*, 14–15.
38. Pratt, *Imperial Eyes*, 7.
39. Pratt, *Imperial Eyes*, 7–9.
40. Florencia E. Mallon, *Peasant and Nation: The Making of Postcolonial Mexico and Peru* (Berkeley and Los Angeles, 1995), 1–20.
41. See Mallon, *Peasant and Nation*.
42. Mallon, *Peasant and Nation*, 89.
43. E. J. Hobsbawm, *Nations and Nationalism since 1870* (Cambridge, 1990), 12.
44. See, for example, Brian Willan, *Sol Plaatje: South African Nationalist, 1876–1932* (London, 1984). It was not inevitable that the national identity born out of the literate middle classes would triumph or that the postcolonial world would in the end borrow the "modular forms" of Europe and America. The political question becomes why they did so.
45. Anderson, *Imagined Communities*, 115, 114.
46. As argued in Karl Marx, *The Eighteenth Brumaire of Louis Bonaparte* (Moscow, 1972).
47. Eric R. Wolf, *Peasant Wars of the Twentieth Century* (New York, 1973); George Rudé, *Ideology and Popular Protest* (New York, 1980).
48. Shula Marks, *The Ambiguities of Dependence in South Africa: Class, Nationalism and the State in Twentieth-Century Natal* (Johannesburg, 1986), 91. With relatively little modification this basic schema has informed much of the writing on populist politics in the first part of the twentieth century. See, for example, Helen Bradford, *A Taste of Freedom: The ICU in Rural South Africa, 1924–1930* (New Haven, 1987).
49. Anderson, *Imagined Communities*, 24.
50. Scott, "The Evidence of Experience."
51. See Evans, *Bureaucracy and Race*. See also Frederick Cooper, *On the African Waterfront: Urban Disorder and the Transformation of Work in Colonial Mombasa* (New Haven, 1987).
52. NA 707, Tainton to managing director (MD) 8 Nov. 1906.
53. See also James C. Scott, *Domination and the Arts of Resistance: Hidden Transcripts* (New Haven, 1990); Patrick Joyce, *Visions of the People: Industrial England and the Question of Class: 1848–1914* (Cambridge, 1991), 15.
54. Herzfeld, *The Social Production of Indifference*, 6.
55. (SOAS) LMS 10 (3) C, Brownlee, report for 1827.
56. (SOAS) LMS 11 (1) B, extracts from letters received from the Reverend J. Brownlee, 26 Dec. 1827. See also (SOAS) LMS 20 (3) C, Calderwood to Tidman, 22 Dec. 1844; (SOAS) MMS 305, Kay to secretary of Wesleyan Missionary Society, 23 Aug. 1830.
57. (SOAS) LMS 11 (1) B, extracts from letters received from the Reverend J. Brownlee, 28 Feb. 1828. See also (SOAS) LMS 6 (3) D, journal of Joseph Williams, 15 June 1816 – 7 Aug. 1817.

58. (SOAS) LMS 11 (1) B, extracts from letters received from the Reverend J. Brownlee, 28 Feb. 1828.
59. (SOAS) LMS 11 (1) B, extracts from letters received from the Reverend J. Brownlee, 28 Feb. 1828.
60. (SOAS) LMS 6 (3) D, journal of Joseph Williams, 15 June 1816 – 7 Aug. 1817. See also (SOAS) LMS 13 (3) C, Kayser to directors of the London Missionary Society, 12 July 1833; (SOAS) LMS 13 (1) B, Kayser to Arundel, 15 July 1832.
61. (SOAS) LMS 6 (3) D, journal of Joseph Williams, 15 June 1816 – 7 Aug. 1817.
62. See H. L. Pretorius, *Sound the Trumpet of Zion: Aspects of a Movement in Transkei* (Pretoria, 1985); Meyer, *Translating the Devil*.
63. (SAM) Smith 4.
64. Janet Hodgson, "A Battle for Sacred Power: Christian Beginnings among the Xhosa," in Richard Elphick and Rodney Davenport, eds., *Christianity in South Africa: A Political, Social, and Cultural History* (Berkeley and Los Angeles, 1997), 69.
65. (SOAS) LMS 11 (1) B, extracts from letters received from the Reverend J. Brownlee, 26 Dec. 1827, 12 Feb. 1828, 11 Apr. 1828. See also Brownlee, *Reminiscences*, 227.
66. 1/UTA 2/1/1/1, statement of Umtandayi, 10 July 1879. See also NA 173, statement of Jiba, who used a healer in his attempt to entice back his estranged wife, but was subsequently accused of having made her ill.
67. BK 74, Maclean to Mackinnon, 26 Sept. 1850.
68. GSC 1/2/1/612, 199 of 1952, statement of accused, 28 Mar. 1952.
69. (PTA) JUS 188, RM to CM, 30 Oct. 1922.
70. (SOAS) LMS 11 (1) B, extracts from letters received from the Reverend J. Brownlee, 12 Feb. 1828. See also (PRO) WO 1/445, proceedings of a general court martial, 19 Nov. 1849; ACC 793, letter of 29 Oct. 1856.
71. See GSC 1/2/1/613, 427 of 1952, *Regina v. Mceketi and Mbobi*, and 418 of 1952, *Regina v. Witvoet and Witvoet*. On incendiarism see below and, for example, (UMT) CMT 164, *Rex v. Tonjeni*, 13 Nov. 1913; CMT 3/1481, RM to CM, Transkei, 19 Sept. 1950; GSC 1/2/1/612, 199 of 1952, *Regina v. Nontlevu*, statement of Nontlevu, 28 Mar. 1952. See also W. D. Hammond-Tooke, *Patrolling the Herms: Social Structure, Cosmology and Pollution Concepts in Southern Africa* (Johannesburg, 1981).
72. I owe this point to Neil Parsons.
73. *Truth and Reconciliation Commission of South Africa Report*, III, 110–11.
74. Quoted in Opland, *Xhosa Oral Poetry*, 187. See also (SAM) Smith, 3; Smith, 4.
75. Fischer, quoted in Robin Horton, "On the Rationality of Conversion (Part I)," *Africa*, 45, 3 (1975): 219–35, at 223.
76. Quoted in Opland, *Xhosa Oral Poetry*, 187; See also (SAM) Smith, 3; Smith, 4.
77. See Robin Horton, "African Traditional Thought and Western Science," *Africa*, 37, 1 (1967): 50–71, 155–87.
78. Weber, *Economy and Society*, I, 519.
79. Ibid.
80. Horton, "Rationality", 234.
81. (CL) MS 15,024, Holford, report, 1859.
82. Wallace Mills, "The Role of the African Clergy in the Reorientation of Xhosa Society to the Plural Society in the Cape Colony, 1850–1915'" (Ph.D. thesis, University of California, 1975), 27.

83. Mills, "The Role," 25.

84. (CL) MS 8470, Makiwane to Ross, 18 May 1890; MS 8471, Makiwane, "The Macfarlane contribution . . . ," n.d. [1890s].

85. James Campbell, "Our Fathers, our Children: The African Methodist Episcopal Church in the United States and South Africa" (Ph.D. thesis, Stanford University, 1989), 90. A pamphlet entitled the *Constitution of the Ethiopian Church* can be found in NA 754.

86. NA 498, Bell to secretary for NA, 1 Sept. 1902.

87. See for example NA 754, Mzimba to Jameson, 14 Dec. 1906. Mzimba enclosed statistical information in support of his church. Congregations were spread throughout all of South Africa as well as in Rhodesia (Zimbabwe) and Bechuanaland (Botswana). See also NA 754, Mzimba, *Presbyterian Church of African: Ekutiwa ukubizwa le Bandla lama Afrika*, n.d.

88. NA 498, Woodfield to secretary for NA, 3 Sept. 1902; NA 497, Dovey to RM, Herschel, 29 Sept. 1902.

89. See NA 497, "table showing particulars in regard to the Ethiopian Church in Certain Districts," n.d.

90. NA 497, Rein to CM, Umtata, 27 Aug. 1902.

91. Translation of Xhosa text held by the Church of the Prophetess Nonthetha, taken during field research, 1992. With the 1918 influenza pandemic evil seemed especially triumphant. That disease struck down, often very quickly, otherwise healthy people.

92. (SAM) Smith, 4.

93. Comaroff, *Body of Power*, 201. See also the discussion of water in chapter 1 above.

94. Michael Taussig, "The Sun Gives without Receiving: An Old Story," *Comparative Studies in Society and History*, 37, 2 (April 1995): 368–98, at 381.

95. Horton, "African Traditional Thought," 157, also quoted in Comaroff and Comaroff, *Of Revelation and Revolution*, I, 227.

96. 1/ELN 87, 1542 of 1925, statement of Rubusana.

97. 1/ELN 87, 1542 of 1925, statement of Jacob Tyali.

98. From Acts 14:8–18.

99. From Revelations 21:22–22:5.

100. Quoted in Pretorius, *Sound the Trumpet*, 147.

101. Pretorius, *Sound the Trumpet*, 151.

102. Meyer, *Translating the Devil*, 109.

103. Comaroff, *Body of Power*, 200.

104. Taussig, *Mimesis and Alterity*, 21, paraphrasing Benjamin: "Every day the urge grows stronger to get hold of an object at very close range by way of its likeness, its reproduction."

105. Joseph and Nugent, "Popular Culture," 13.

106. Preparatory examination in the trial of the Israelites (June–August 1921) and *Rex v. Israelites* (October–November 1921).

107. (PTA) JUS 918, statement of Marolong, 16 Aug. 1927; JUS 918, RM, Tabankulu to CM, Umtata, 13 Sept. 1927. The issuing of receipts and writing was also important to Wellington Buthelezi's movement. See, for example, JUS 919, statement of Maqunau, 4 Apr. 1928. Why pigs especially came to be singled out is not clear. Later evidence associates collaborators and officials with pigs. For example, "Fingo

Chiefs work for their own benefit to fill up their stomachs like pigs": 1/BUT 88, Colbert to Gili Bam, n.d., [1963]. It may be because pigs eat virtually anything they came to be associated with illegitimate forms of appropriation and consumption.

108. (PTA) JUS 918, statement of 16 Aug. 1927.
109. Taussig, *Mimesis and Alterity*, 21.
110. Taussig, *Mimesis and Alterity*, 2.
111. See Redding, "Government Witchcraft."
112. (PTA) NTS 7204, inspector to deputy commissioner (DC), 23 Aug. 1923.
113. Redding, "Government Witchcraft."
114. (PTA) JUS 188, statement of Plaatje, 12 April 1921. See also JUS 188, RM, Kentani, to CNC, n.d. 1921. More generally incendiarism was a dominant feature of rural conflict. The 1924 disturbances in Tsolo, presented in the archival record as an ethnic dispute between Mpondomise and Mfengu peoples, involved the considerable destruction of Mfengu huts by fire. Such also was a case a few months earlier in Pondoland, near the Natal border, which involved over a thousand people. See JUS 188, Taylor to DC, 8 April 1924; JUS 188, Hale to DC, 14 Nov. 1923.
115. (PTA) JUS 188, RM, Nqamakwe, to CM, 30 Oct. 1922.
116. (PTA) JUS 922, notes from ICU meeting, Korsten, 9 December 1928. For later references to whites as Satan see GSC 1/2/1/627, case 79 of 1953, statement of Wild re: ANC meeting at Emllotini Square, 16 June 1952. One "extremely enthusiastic convert to the ICU" in the Transvaal, for example, would "'come home with ICU documents, although he could not read." He would also give to other illiterate people "the Union pamphlets to read": quoted in C. Van Onselen, *The Seed is Mine: The Life of Kas Maine, a South African Sharecropper, 1894–1985* (Cape Town, 1996), 148.
117. White, *Speaking with Vampires*, 18.
118. See Taussig, *Mimesis and Alterity*; P. Stoller, *Embodying Colonial Memories: Spirit Possession, Power, and the Hauka of West Africa* (New York, 1995).
119. Beinart and Bundy, *Hidden Struggles*, 252.
120. Quoted in (PTA) JUS 269, commissioner of police to secretary for justice, 14 Aug. 1922.
121. (PTA) JUS 921, notes of meeting, 3 Aug. 1928.
122. Ibid.
123. Ibid.
124. Quoted in Bradford, *A Taste of Freedom*, 216.
125. (PTA) NTS 7660, ? to DC, 12 June 1930.
126. (PTA) JUS 916, Roon to commissioner, 25 Feb. 1927.
127. He attempted to reenter Herschel in the 1930s. See 2/SPT 16, Myburgh to CNC, 9 Sept. 1936.
128. (PTA) JUS 916, statement of Ghu, 21 Mar. 1927; 1/KNT 124, report of Mazwai, 13 Jan. 1929; 1/NKE 7/1/58, statement of Shosha, 12 June 1928.
129. (PTA) JUS 915, statement of Mbebe, 16 May 1926.
130. Bradford, *A Taste of Freedom*, 217.
131. (PTA) JUS 921, notes of meeting, 3 August 1928.
132. 1/MFE 8/14, Pike to RM, 26 Aug. 1927.
133. (PTA) JUS 918, copy of record, 130 of 1927, *Rex v. Maqolo*.
134. (PTA) NTS 7660, ? to DC, 12 June 1930.

135. Comaroff and Comaroff, *Of Revelation and Revolution*, I, 189, 188.
136. Quoted in Jay, *Downcast Eyes*, 69. See also Paul Rabinow, *French Modern: Norms and Forms of the Social Environment* (Cambridge, Mass., 1989).
137. Harvey, *The Condition of Postmodernity*, 245.
138. See chapter 2.
139. (PTA) JUS 916, Roon to secretary of SAP, 31 Jan. 1927.
140. See Bradford, *A Taste of Freedom*; Beinart and Bundy, *Hidden Struggles*.
141. CCK 19, Speech by Mbeki, 30 Oct. 1927.
142. (PTA) NTS 7660, ? to DC, 12 June 1930.
143. See, for example, André Odendaal, *Vukani Bantu! The Beginnings of Black Protest Politics in South Africa to 1912* (Cape Town, 1984); Peter Walshe, *The Rise of African Nationalism in South Africa: The African National Congress, 1912–52* (London, 1970).
144. NA 554, translation of advertisement in *Izwe Labantu*, 16 June 1903. Rules of the SANNC.
145. NA 554, SANNC to prime minister, 2 July 1903; NA 554, Rubusana to Howe, 4 May 1906.
146. (PTA) SAP 39, "The Ninth Annual Conference of the South African Native National Congress, 24 May 1920."
147. (PTA) SAP 39, Ligge to DC, 16 June 1920; SAP 39, inspector to DC, 2 June 1920.
148. (PTA) NTS 7204, inspector in charge to secretary, 28 May 1920. See also NTS 7204, Whitaker to DC, 2 June 1920.
149. 1/ELN 86, statement of Veldtman, 7 Sept. 1923.
150. 2/SPT 16, Herbst to CNC, 17 Mar. 1926; 2/SPT 16, magistrate to CNC, 27 Mar. 1926.
151. 2/SPT 16, Herbst to CNC, 17 Mar. 1926.
152. 2/SPT 16, Nel, notes of speeches, 17 Nov. 1928; (PTA) NTS 2536, Ntlotsueu et al. to prime minister, 20 July 1929.
153. (PTA) NTS 2536, notes of enquiry, 23 Aug. 1929.
154. 2/SPT 16, deputation to under secretary for NA, 5 Jan. 1928.
155. (PTA) NTS 2536, Ntlotsueu et al. to prime minister, 20 July 1929.
156. (PTA) JUS 915, Mundell to district commandant, 20 Apr. 1928.
157. See, for example, (PTA) NTS 7204, Tshiwula to RM, Nqamakwe, 18 July 1921.
158. (PTA) NTS 7204, Whitehead to CNC, 23 Feb. 1925.
159. 2/SPT 16, Nel, notes of meeting, 27 Apr. 1929.
160. (PTA) JUS 924, Gumede, "A Fighting Policy for S. Africa," address delivered 21 Apr. 1930; JUS 269, Beer to commissioner of police, 6 Feb. 1929.
161. Marx, *Eighteenth Brumaire*, 10.
162. Comaroff and Comaroff, *Of Revelation and Revolution*, I, 369. See also chapter 2 above, pp. 68–112.
163. See Lodge, *Black Politics*.
164. Both adhered to a notion of primitivism.
165. See Bradford, *A Taste of Freedom*; Bundy and Beinart, *Hidden Struggles*.

5 GOVERNMENT ACTS

1. (WITS) AD 1912, SAIRR press clippings, *Daily Dispatch*, 26 July 1949.
2. Posel, *The Making of Apartheid*, 91.

3. Posel, *The Making of Apartheid*, 105.
4. See Platzky and Walker, *The Surplus People*; Desmond, *The Discarded People*.
5. Evans, *Bureaucracy and Race*, 280.
6. Evans, *Bureaucracy and Race* 233.
7. (UMT) CMT 66/1177, Secretary for NA to CMT, notes on back of letter written by CMT, 9 Mar. 1953 [1956?].
8. A detailed examination of the apartheid state, however, is beyond the scope of this book. Apartheid's rise has been examined by a number of scholars. See Evans, *Bureaucracy and Race*; Posel, *The Making of Apartheid*; Southall, *South Africa's Transkei*; Hendricks, *The Pillars of Apartheid*.
9. Quoted in Wolpe, "Capitalism and Cheap Labour Power."
10. CMT 3/1451, report of the CM and CNC of the Transkeian territories for the year ending 31 Dec. 1956. On global climate history see Davis, *Late Victorian Holocausts*.
11. See Ashforth, *Madumo*; Hunter, *Reaction to Conquest*, esp. 272–319; (SOAS) LMS 11 (1) B, extracts from letters received from the Reverend J. Brownlee; LMS 6 (3) D, journal of Joseph Williams, 15 June 1816 – 7 Aug. 1817; LMS 13 (3) C, Kayser to directors of London Missionary Society, 12 July 1833.
12. (UMT) CMT 66/1177, C. B. to Ramsay, 16 Nov. 1955.
13. CMT 3/1479, Fenwick, untitled narrative of the Pondoland Revolt, 1 June 1960.
14. Evans, *Bureaucracy and Race*, 232–3.
15. 1/COF 9/1/44, Bantu assistant information officers, report, 20 October 1959.
16. 1/ALC 10/11, "Bantu Authorities: Their Aim and Object and the Place of the Chief or Headmen in these Authorities," n.d. [1963].
17. For a history of the Transkei see Southall, *South Africa's Transkei*.
18. Evans, *Bureaucracy and Race*, 251.
19. (PTA) K 185, "A Guide to the Working of Tribal Authorities in the Lusikisiki District," n.d. [1956–7].
20. CMT 3/1479, Fenwick, untitled narrative of the Pondoland Revolt, 1 June 1960.
21. (PTA) K 185, "A Guide to the Working of Tribal Authorities in the Lusikisiki District," n.d. [1956–7].
22. Ibid.
23. 1/COF 9/1/44, Bantu assistant information officers, report, 20 October 1959.
24. 1/QBU 7/1/70, RM, Qumbu to CM, 2 Oct. 1962; CMT 3/1470, BAC Qumbu to chief BAC, 5 Dec. 1962.
25. Mamdani, *Citizen and Subject*.
26. Southall, *South Africa's Transkei*, 93.
27. Weber, *Economy and Society*, I, 232.
28. See also Mamdani, *Citizen and Subject*; Doyle, *Empires*, 141–372.
29. 1/ALC 10/11, "Bantu Authorities: Their Aim and Object and the Place of the Chief or Headmen in these Authorities," n.d. [1963].
30. CMT 3/1479, Fenwick, untitled narrative of the Pondoland Revolt, 1 June 1960.
31. (UMT) CMT 66/1177, C. B. to Ramsay, 16 Nov. 1955.
32. See, for example, Tom Lodge, "Poqo and Rural Resistance in the Transkei, 1960–1965," *ICS, Collected Seminar Papers on the Societies of Southern Africa in the 19th and 20th Centuries*, 9 (1977–8): 137–47.
33. 1/COF 9/1/44, Jordaan, BAC, to chief BAC, 29 May 1961.

34. Ivan Evans, "The Native Affairs Department and the Reserves in the 1940s and 1950s," in Robin Cohen et al., *Repression and Resistance: Insider Accounts of Apartheid* (London, 1990), 17–51, 43. See also Dubow, *Racial Segregation and the Origins of Apartheid.*

35. Hammond-Tooke, *Tribes of King William's Town District*, 127–9. See also Crais, "Representation and the Politics of Identity." See also 1/ALC 10/11, Hammond-Tooke to BAC, 28 Aug. 1965. The state was involved in the minutiae of fabricating tribalism, for example collecting funds for bride-wealth among "royals": 1/ALC 10/11, Coertze to Chief BAC, 12 Dec. 1959.

36. 1/COF 9/1/44, Jordaan, BAC, to chief BAC, 3 May 1962.

37. CMT 3/1482, Mzoliswa to ?, trans., September 1963.

38. See chapter 5 and CMT 3/1479, Pearce to secretary for Bantu administration and development and annexures, 20 June 1960.

39. 1/BIZ 6/47, Ramsay to secretary for Bantu Administration and Development, 21 Nov. 1958.

40. (PTA) K 185, testimony of Macingwane.

41. Evans, *Bureaucracy and Race*, 89.

42. 1/BIZ 6/47, Ramsay to secretary for Bantu Administration and Development, 21 Nov. 1958.

43. Ibid.

44. 1/BIZ 6/47, Fenwick, "Disaffection in the Lusikisiki District."

45. (PM) 1/KOK Add. 1/1/1/1, 20/61, statement of Myekwa. More generally see (PTA) K 185.

46. (PTA) K 185, statement of chairman.

47. CMT 3/1472, Warren to CM of the Transkeian Territories, 4 July 1960.

48. CMT 3/1472, Harvey to?, 30 Sept. 1960.

49. 1/BIZ 6/47, Ramsay to secretary for Bantu Administration and Development, 21 Nov. 1958.

50. Ibid.

51. 1/BIZ 6/47, Fenwick, "Disaffection in the Lusikisiki District," 1 June 1960

52. Ibid.

53. (PTA) K 185, testimony of Nene.

54. Ibid.

55. CMT 3/1472, "Report of the Departmental Committee of Enquiry into the Unrest in Eastern Pondoland," 9 Aug. 1960.

56. Ibid.

57. Ibid.

58. Leibbrandt, quoted in CMT 3/1470, Leibbrandt to secretary for Bantu Administration and Development, 5 Dec. 1960.

59. CMT 3/1472, "Report of the Departmental Committee of Enquiry into the Unrest in Eastern Pondoland," 9 Aug. 1960.

60. (CL) uncatalogued, notes of meeting, 18 Nov. 1955.

61. (PTA) K 185, statement of Jali.

62. (PTA) K 185, first speaker (refused to give name).

63. (PTA) K 185, statement of Siko.

64. (PTA) K 185, statement of Madikize.

65. Matanzima, in CMT 3/1470, report of meeting, 11 Nov. 1960.

66. Ibid.

67. (PTA) K 185, statement of Lehmkuhl.

68. Posel, *The Making of Apartheid*, 104; Evans, *Bureaucracy and Race*, 88–90.

69. Posel, *The Making of Apartheid*, 104.

70. Evans, *Bureaucracy and Race*, 89. Even censuses became more closely tied to the pass system and the state's control of labor; and they were conducted in a way in which many people believed made no pretense to consultation. See, for example, CMT 3/1478, minutes of meeting held on 10 September 1960. At the local level the two structures – the Bantu Authorities system and the labour bureaux system – blurred. The state had long sought to involve chiefs in organizing the labor supply, but the level of cooperation and the institutional structures that organized it far differed from any other period in South Africa's history. Not surprisingly, soon after the promulgation of the Bantu Laws Amendment Act "chiefs in the Bunga found themselves in support of the labor bureaux system." Indeed, in the early 1960s the local bureaux were renamed "tribal labour bureaux." See Evans, *Bureaucracy and Race*, 257.

71. Wolpe, "Capitalism and Cheap Labour Power."

72. Southall, *South Africa's Transkei*, 36.

73. CMT 3/1593, secretary for Bantu Administration to CM, 4 April 1959; Southall, *South Africa's Transkei*, 37; Evans, *Bureaucracy and Race*, 239–45.

74. CMT 3/1470, Leibbrandt to secretary for Bantu Administration and Development, 5 Dec. 1960.

75. (WITS) SAIRR AD 843, Jokl, *Labour and Manpower Survey*, 21.

76. (CL) MS/PR, uncatalogued material from magistrate's office, Keiskammahoek, "Report of Tour," J. W. Rowland, 9–29 July [1948].

77. Ibid.

78. Quotations in this paragraph are taken from Jokl, *Labour and Manpower Survey*.

79. See (UMT) CMT 164, statement of Maxalanga, 27 Apr. 1925; GSC 1/2/1/792, 285 of 1957, *Regina v. Mtakati and Sixteen Others*, statement of Morris. On sexuality and socialization see Philip and Iona Mayer, "Report on Research on Self-Organisation by Youth among Xhosa-Speaking Peoples of the Ciskei and Transkei," 2 vols. unpub. typescript, Institute of Social and Economic Research, Rhodes University, 1972. Infant mortality rates of 50 percent or more for children two and under have not been uncommon. Childhood malnutrition has been chronic and endemic. Tuberculosis has long plagued the health of people, especially migrant laborers. Men often returned to their homes sick, injured, and dying. Since 1900 the mines have accounted for 60,000 direct deaths and over a million injuries. See David B. Coplan, *In the Time of Cannibals: The Word Music of South Africa's Basotho Migrants* (Chicago, 1994), 130. See also Fox and Back, "Preliminary Survey," 40.

80. (PTA) K 185, statement of Midgley.

81. Ibid.

82. As Leibbrandt, CM of the Transkeian Territories, wrote to the secretary for Bantu Administration and Development in 1960, "it was decided to speed up the development of the Transkei": CMT 3/1470, Leibbrandt to secretary for Bantu Administration and Development, 5 Dec. 1960.

83. See chapter 5 and, for example, CMT 3/1480, Bottoman and others to BAC, 7 November 1960.

84. 1/BIZ 6/47, Midgley to CM, 8 Oct. 1958.
85. (CL) uncatalogued material, minutes of meeting, 19 Sept. 1923.
86. Ibid.
87. GSC 1/2/1/483, statement of Naude, 10 December 1947.
88. CMT 3/1480, Mate to magistrate, 16 July 1947. See also CMT 3/1480, acting CM to secretary for NA, 20 Sept. 1938: "In the Old location, where the only control was that of the headman, these people could encroach on the commonage and acquire lands to the detriment of others. They resent the control which is exercised by the Agricultural Officials." See also 1/ALC 10/12, NC to CNC, 10 July 1936.
89. GSC1/2/1/483, case 261/1948, statement of Mate, 18 Dec., CMT 3/1480, Supreme Court, *Rex v. Fombeza and Ten Others*, 17 May 1948.
90. GSC 1/2/1/483, case 261/1948, statement of Mate, 18 Dec.
91. (WITS) AD 1912, SAIRR, press clippings, *Mercury*, 2 Oct. 1945.
92. GSC 1/21/483, statement of Geel, 10 Dec. 1947; (WITS) AD 1912 SAIRR, press clippings, *Natal Witness*, 17 Apr. 1946. See also CMT 3/1480, *Rex v. Fombeza and Ten Others*, 18 May 1948.
93. CMT 3/1480, Mate to minister of justice, 15 May 1948.
94. CMT 3/1480, Mate to provincial secretary's office, 5 Apr. 1950.
95. CMT 3/1480, Green to magistrate, 3 Apr. 1951.
96. Ibid. This last incident culminated the following month in a gunfight and the death of a young boy. See CMT 3/1480, precis, *Rex v. Sontangane*, 6 June 1951.
97. 1/ALC 1/1/1/42, 339/1950, *Rex vs. Nojoz and Sixteen Others*, 16 Nov. 1950; 1/ALC 10/12, Cordingley to chief NA, 2 Dec. 1950.
98. 1/ALC 10/12, Mgijima to NC, 14 July 1939; 1/ALC 10/12, Liefeldt to CNC, 15 Mar. 1940.
99. See, for example, CMT 3/1480, statement of Bosman, 21 Oct. 1952.
100. GSC 1/2/1/629, 413 of 1953.
101. Ibid.
102. See for example GSC 1/2/1/610, 380 of 1951.
103. CMT 3/1482, CM to secretary for NA, 8 Oct. 1957.
104. (PTA) K 185, statement of Siko.
105. Ibid.
106. (PTA) K 185, testimony of Nene
107. Ibid.
108. CMT 3/1451, report of the CM . . . ending 31 December 1956.

6 CONFLICT IN QUMBU

I shamelessly borrow this subtitle from William Beinart and his now classic study of rural resistance in Qumbu: William Beinart, "Conflict in Qumbu: Rural Consciousness, Ethnicity and Violence in the Colonial Transkei," in Beinart and Bundy, *Hidden Struggles*.

1. Quoted in Hammond-Tooke, *Command or Consensus*, 47. In the first half of the nineteenth century, the region formed part of a wider tableau of conflict, political centralization, and destruction typically referred to as the *mfecane*. Zulu attacks reached well into this area of the Transkei. People anxiously observed the politics of an expansionist Zulu state to the northeast, but also political centralization and

expansion closer to home. By the 1830s two polities adjoined the Tsolo/Qumbu area; in many respects the region comprises a kind borderland or frontier. To the south-east people observed the rise of the Mpondo polity under Faku. To the north, as the hills of Tsolo/Qumbu became the mountains of Basutoland, Moshoeshoe founded a Sotho kingdom. See Beinart, *The Political Economy of Pondoland*; Eldredge, *A South African Kingdom.*

2. The evidence suggests that while chiefly genealogies stress linkages with the Mpondo especially, but also with the Bomvana and Xesibe polities, Mpondomise culture and society is distinctive for the ways it has borrowed cultural practices from its neighbors. In other words there has been a kind of precolonial bricolage that has affirmed, and continues to affirm, Mpondomise distinctiveness and their marginal position relative to the larger polities that surround them and threaten their sense of independence. The history of this area is discussed in Beinart, "Conflict in Qumbu" and W. D. Hammond-Tooke, *Command or Consensus: The Development of Transkeian Government* (Cape Town, 1975). For material on kinship see W. D. Hammond-Tooke, "Descent Groups Scatter in a Mpondomise Ward," *African Studies*, 27, 2 (1968): 83–94; W. D. Hammond-Tooke, "The Morphology of Mpondomise Descent Groups," *Africa*, 38, 1 (Jan. 1968): 26–46. See also Heinz Kuckertz, *Creating Order: The Image of the Homestead in Mpondo Social Life* (Johannesburg, 1990).

3. NA 497, Rein to CM, Transkei, 27 Aug. 1902.

4. See Beinart, "Conflict in Qumbu"; 1/QBU 7/1/8–9, RM to CM, 4 Aug. 1928; 1/QBU 7/1/70, Burg to district commandant, 7 Dec. 1952. One man described in some detail the activities of the Garveyite leader Wellington Buthelezi who "collected a lot of money from the people" in the area around Qumbu: interview with R. T., 23 June 1993.

5. Interview with R. T., 23 June 1993.

6. See chapter 3 above. See also (UMT) CMT 164, Nqwili and others to RM, Qumbu, 7 Dec. 1924; (UMT) CMT 164, RM to [?], 23 May 1923; (UMT) CMT 164, statement of Maxalanga, 27 Apr. 1925; 1/QBU 7/1/8–9, Maraule to RM, 18 Jan. 1938.

7. Elderly men depict a situation in which a very high percentage of men spent time on the mines. R. T. described to me how he walked through the hills to the railhead at Maclear. He worked on the mines for "very many years." R. T. first went to the mines in 1929 on an eight-month contract. Three years later he eloped with a woman. He continued migrating north for the next sixteen years, returning home for a short time each year. After 1945 he managed to gain access to sufficient land and stock to withdraw himself from the migrant-labor system: interview with R. T., 23 June 1993. Another man labored on the mines for about thirteen years before he married and headed to Langa, in Cape Town, where he worked for only a year: interview with M. Z., 24 June 1993.

8. Six-month contracts were typical during the late nineteenth century. From the 1920s, however, migrants might stay away for more than a decade with only the yearly week or two off to visit their kith and kin in the countryside.

9. There was, for example, considerable tension between people living in the older locations at Upper Tyira and Balasi and the inhabitants and newer locations of Lower Tyira and Kwa-Nkese: (UMT) CMT 164, Nqwili and others to RM, Qumbu, 7 Dec. 1924; (UMT) CMT 164, RM to [?], 23 May 1923; interview with E. K., 23 June 1993. The valorization of cattle became even more charged precisely because of their

increasingly fragile existence. For a similar story see Ferguson, *The Anti-Politics Machine*, esp. 135–66.

10. For one useful archival source see CMT 3/679, typewritten papers primarily on public health. n.d. [c. 1910–11].

11. For a recent example see Ashforth, *Madumo*.

12. CMT 3/679, typewritten papers primarily on public health, n.d. [c. 1910–11].

13. From GSC 1/2/1/917, 113/61, preparatory examination. See also below and GSC 1/2/1/917, 113/61, *Regina v. Lehana and Others*, 1 May 1961.

14. See below and GSC 1/2/1/797, 337 of 1957, *Regina v. Memani and Fifteen Others*, 16 Sept. 1957, statement of Scheepers.

15. CMT 3/1481, Ramsay to secretary for NA, 14 Mar. 1957; interview with E. K., 23 June 1993. A number of locations in the area have earned a reputation for being historic centers of stock thieving.

16. 1/QBU 7/1/70, secretary for Makulu Span and others to RM, 17 July 1959 (emphasis mine). In an important respect these written communications to the state constituted the "public declaration" of "hidden transcripts." See Scott, *Domination and the Arts of Resistance*, esp. 202–27.

17. Interview with M. Z., 24 June 1993; interview with E. K., 23 June 1993; GSC 1/2/1/798, 329 of 1957, *Regina v. Nontso and Others*, statement of Kondlo; GSC 1/2/1/736, 328 of 1957, *Regina v. Hlutiya and Eight Others*, statements of Mti and Mamaza; GSC 1/2/1/792, 285 of 1957, statement of Morris; CMT 3/1471, minutes of meetings, 22 Mar. 1957. See also Redding, "Government Witchcraft."

18. CMT 3/1481, Ramsay to secretary for NA, 14 Mar. 1957. See also Hunter, *Reaction to Conquest*, 133, 311.

19. CMT 3/1481, Ramsay to secretary for NA, 14 Mar. 1957.

20. CMT 3/1481, CM to secretary for NA, 26 Aug. 1957 (emphasis mine).

21. (PTA) K 185, testimony of Makizwana. See also QBU 7/1/70, minutes of meeting, 22 Mar.1957.

22. Hammond-Tooke, *Command or Consensus*, 106. Everyone I interviewed used the word "Nephews".

23. Interview with R. T., 23 June 1993. On nephew relations see the now dated work by A. R. Radcliffe-Brown, *Structure and Function in Primitive Society* (New York, 1965), 15–31. Males who remained uncircumcised, even if they were in their thirties, were still in many respects youths who stood outside conventional society.

24. Hammond-Tooke, *Command or Consensus*, 106.

25. The Mayers' description of *indlavini* matches quite closely the world of the Nephews: "It claims the completest autonomy, has the most rigidly endogenous structure and 'laws', gives the most prominence to the male core group, demands the most total loyalty, secrecy and discipline, and punishes its members the most severely. It also has the worst name in its own community": Mayer and Mayer, "Report," 171. It was these older forms of male association in which young males learned of sexuality, respect, and the other important values of the community within which they lived. Circumcision was only one of a number of social practices of male socialization in rural areas of the Eastern Cape. In these other sites of conversation and conversion, males learned of the ways of the world by attending parties with women, engaging in intercrural sex, and through stick fighting and other forms of "battle." The rituals of labor migration and the adoption of new clothes also signified their ascension

to manhood and entrance into the community of senior men. While young boys might go to work on the sugar plantations of Natal, men went to the mines. *Igoli aligoli amakhwenkew, ligoli amadoda*, so a common saying goes ("Johannesburg does not catch boys, it catches men"): Mayer and Mayer, "Report," 128. See also William Beinart, "The Origins of the Indlavini: Male Associations and Migrant Labour in the Transkei," and P. A. McAllister, "Using Ritual to Resist Domination in the Transkei," both in A. D. Spiegel and P. A. McAllister, eds., *Tradition and Transition in Southern Africa* (Johannesburg, 1991).

26. Interview with R. T., 23 June 1993. See also (UMT) CMT 164, statement of Maxalanga, 27 Apr. 1925; GSC 1/2/1/792, 285 of 1957, statement of Morris. The evidence suggests a close relationship between landlessness and violent male associations. This is not to suggest that the Nephews were simply an organization of the displaced proletariat, especially since a number of the thieves were in fact quite well off and a few leaders were headmen. What is clear is that disputes over land and other forms of property informed the emergence and conduct of groups such as the *indlavini* and the Nephews. Unfortunately it is not possible to trace the precise movement of the thieves. Evidence suggests that during the 1950s a substantial number of men who had been working and living in urban areas returned to their rural homes. Three points are especially salient. First there was the onset of the economic downswing in South Africa during the second half of the decade. Second, the decade saw a far more aggressive pursuit of "influx control," that is the conviction of people for illegally living in urban areas. Third, following the 1952 Defiance Campaign, which was strongest in the Eastern Cape, over five thousand people left cities such as Port Elizabeth and East London and returned to rural locations. See Philip and Iona Mayer, *Townsmen or Tribesmen* (Cape Town, 1961), 82–3. On influx control see Posel, *The Making of Apartheid*.

27. Interview with T. N., 24 June 1993, who told me that "people started stealing so they could be well presented at these parties."

28. For contemporary material on witches and zombies see Ashforth, *Madumo*, eg. 74–82. The best material on this period and area is located in GSC 1/2/1/792 and GSC 1/2/1/797.

29. An "illegal" court also emerged in the Northern Transvaal among the Baphurutse, in which four men were sentenced to be buried alive. The sentence was not carried out. By 16 April 1957, the police had arrested 120 people: *Daily Dispatch*, 16 Apr. 1957. There is also evidence of considerable violence between rival gangs. For example, the "Russians" (*amaRashiya*) occasionally fought bloody battles with the "Nephews" and the "Japanese" (*amaJapani*) thieves throughout the Tsolo and Qumbu area. In one incident the Russians murdered eight thieves. In part this violence was in retaliation for the Nephews' stock thieving. Unfortunately, the archival record does not document these early anti-thieving activities, though there is substantial discussion of Russians and other male associations in material surrounding the 1960 Pondoland Revolt. This is especially unfortunate because, like the attire of the thieves, the Russians were also associated with youth gang and migrant culture. This would mean that, at least initially, rural struggles around stock theft involved substantial intra-youth relations within impoverished communities that had long depended on migrant labor. But it is important to recall that "youth" referred less to physical age than to people outside the boundaries of the civic and moral community,

people whose conduct operated according to their own laws. Uninitiated men in their thirties were still in profound ways "youths."

30. A number of thieves burned out in Tsolo, for example, congregated in Ntshigo location, just a few miles from the agricultural school that had suffered greatly from theft. The headman of Ntshigo, Mpiyonke Quvile, was known "to be one of the ring leaders of the stock thieves." In July 1958, two people were murdered in the location: one victim was a Makhulu Span member killed by the thieves, the other was a thief killed by Makhulu Span. I discuss Quvile below. See CMT 3/1482, RM to CM, Umtata, 24 July 1958; GSC 1/2/1/797, 337 of 1957, Jennet, remarks on passing sentence, 20 Sept. 1957.

31. Interview with T. N., 24 June 1993. Mayer and Mayer, *Townsmen or Tribesmen*, 83, report that in 1958 there was a movement to combat gangs in the urban locations of East London.

32. See below and 1/QBU 7/1/70, anon. letter to Chief Majeke, n.d.; GSC 1/2/1/797, 337 of 1957, exhibits "A", "B", "J", and "K".

33. The arsonists divided themselves into two groups. One group of men were armed with guns and served as guards for those who physically set the fires. See CMT 3/1481, statement of Scheepers, 2 May 1957; GSC 1/2/1/796, 328 of 1957; GSC 1/2/1/797, 337 of 1957, exhibit "A".

34. GSC 1/2/1/797, 337 of 1957 (emphasis mine) statement of Nontso.

35. GSC 1/2/1/797, 337 of 1957, statement of Sejossing.

36. Cf. Jeff Peires, "Unsocial Bandits: The Stock Thieves of Qumbu and their Enemies," paper presented to the Conference on Democracy: Popular Precedents, Practice, Culture," University of the Witwatersrand, 13–15 July 1994.

37. GSC 1/2/1/796, 328 of 1957, statement of Gwazilitye. The charges of stock theft in the magistrate's court were withdrawn. Both the victim and those accused in the case of public violence were all from the same location, Tyira, in Qumbu.

38. Interview with M. Z., 24 June 1993.

39. GSC 1/2/1/797, 337 of 1957, statement of Sitemela.

40. GSC 1/2/1/797, 337 of 1957, statement of Gxunayo.

41. A. Cekiso, for example, was "ordered to appear before the committee. I had been charged with having failed to attend meetings. I was then assaulted. I had to appear a second time before the committee as I had lodged a complaint to it. I wanted to know from the committee why some stock thieves were being punished and others allowed to be set free. This question was objected to by the committee and I was told to cover myself to receive cuts...I was [on another occasion] charged with failing to carry an assegai": GSC 1/2/1/797, 337 of 1957, statement of Cekiso.

42. Land was an important issue behind the Makhulu Span trials. In Tsolo, for example, one man was seriously assaulted and his homestead burned down not "on account of his thieving" but because he "was restricting their movements in their lands." Another victim of Makhulu Span noted that her husband and one of the alleged Makhulu Span members were both sub-headmen. There was "a dispute between them over Bokolo's land. My husband was convicted of ploughing this land without authority": GSC 1/2/1/792, 285 of 1957, statements of Yolwa and Mpapama.

43. In many cases, for example, just as thieves had occasionally informed their victims by delivering written notes, so also did Makhulu Span inform suspected thieves that

they were to be attacked. In another instance a chief thief used his guns to drive Makhulu Span away, though his place was burned to the ground. Interview with M. Z., 24 June 1993.

44. Homi Bhabha, "Of Mimicry and Man: The Ambivalence of Colonial Discourse," in Homi Bhabha, *The Location of Culture* (New York, 1994); Mbembe, "The Banality of Power."

45. See chapter 1 below.

46. 1/QBU, 7/1/70, BAC to CM, Umtata, 4 Mar. 1961; (PTA) NTS Native Affairs 10275, Lancaster to CM, 15 Feb. 1947. See also Hammond-Tooke, *Command or Consensus*; Peires, "Unsocial Bandits"; Redding, "Government Witchcraft."

47. CMT 3/1482, RM to CM, Umtata, 24 July 1958; 1/TSO 5/1/52, statement of Sandlana, 17 Apr. 1961. If he did not "he would sooner or later have been killed." See also CMT 3/1471, minutes of meeting, 22 Mar. 1957, statement of Chief Majeke: "Certain Headmen are responsible for state of affairs[,] having connived at Stock Theft." It is unclear just how many headmen were in cahoots with stock thieves. Undoubtedly some were, though a number of headmen and, it seems, especially sub-headmen, participated in Makhulu Span. See, for example, GSC 1/2/1/799, 354 of 1957, *Regina v. Siyotula and Ten Others*, statement of Siyotula; GSC 1/2/1/798, 350 of 1957, *Regina v. Noranga and Twenty-five Others*, statement of James; GSC 1/2/1/797, 331 of 1957, statement of Mgqotsa; GSC 1/2/1/797, 337 of 1957, statement of Bente. See also Redding, "Government Witchcraft."

48. 1/QBU 7/1/70, "Complaints of the Mahlubi's against Headman Valelo Mgobozi," 3 Aug. 1958; statement of Mgobozi, 1 Aug. 1958; CMT 3/1481, statement of Mgobozi, 18 June 1958; GSC 1/2/1/798, 329 of 1957, statement of Dotyeni. Men told me that rangers were deeply implicated in the theft of stock. Informants also noted that the introduction of paddocks made it far easier for thieves to steal stock: interview with T. N., 24 June 1993; interview with R. T., 23 June 1993.

49. 1/QBU 7/1/70, Collen to chief BAC, Umtata, 18 May 1962.

50. 1/TSO 5/1/52, Leibrandt to secretary for Bantu administration and development, 8 May 1960.

51. 1/TSO 5/1/52, statement of Mditshwa, 6 May 1960. See also 1/QBU 7/1/70, Sergeant, monthly report, Qumbu, 22 Mar. 1961. In early 1961, with some alarm Matiwane wrote to the Bantu affairs commissioner that "I find it difficult, somewhat, to distinguish between the lines of the element who first started forming up the so called MAKHULUSPAN and the subsequent cruel ALL OUT REBELLIOUS minded TREASON minded Bantu gangs whose SECRET weapon has been discovered to be 'AWAY WITH THE GOVERNMENT APPOINTED CHIEFS AND AWAY WITH ALL PROGRESSIVE LAWS' ": 1/QBU 7/1/70, Matiwane to BAC, Qumbu, 3 Mar. 1961. Threats to collaborationist chiefs and headmen also invoked historical memory. One letter, with only the title "Wind of Change," warned against complicity with Bantu Authorities. The letter pointed out that "only chiefs like Hintsa, Dingaan, Moshesh and Cetywayo will survive and enjoy the fruits of freedom. There is not the slightest possibility of the oppressors stopping us from achieving our freedom. So on the first leg of our destiny we are now mobilising the entire nation by getting rid of the traitors who will be a nuisance." The letter concluded by declaring that "Not in a distant time, the Blackman is going to be a master of his own country": 1/QBU 7/1/70, "The Wind of Change," to Majeke, 16 Feb. 1961.

59. Ibid.
60. See also Evans, *Bureaucracy and Race*, esp. 224–75.
61. See below and (PTA) K 185, statement of Mkwane; CMT 3/1472, statement of Jase, 5 Oct. 1960.
62. CMT 3/1472, statement of Jase, 5 Oct. 1960; (PTA) K 185, statement of Mkwane; (PTA) NTS 7735, Midgley to CM, Transkeian Territories, 2 Oct. 1957. It is clear from the evidence that the state was anxious to introduce its new policies "as soon as possible." See (UMT) CMT 66/1177, UTTGC min., no. 21/56: Transfer of Trust Land to Bantu Authorities, 4/7/56.
63. CMT 3/1472, statement of Jase, 5 Oct. 1960.
64. Ibid.; (PTA) K 185, statement of Mkwane; (PTA) NTS 7735, Midgley to CM, Transkeian Territories, 2 Oct. 1957.
65. (PTA) K 185, testimony of Nene.
66. 1/BIZ 6/47, "Disturbances in the District of Bizana, 1960," 8.
67. 1/BIZ 6/47, "Disturbances in the District of Bizana, 1960," 13–14, 9.
68. CMT 3/1479, Fenwick, untitled report, 1 June 1960.
69. (PTA) K 185, testimony of Pinyana.
70. Ibid.
71. (PTA) K 185, testimony of Madikizela.
72. (PTA) K 185, testimony of Nkwankwe. See also testimony of Mpahla.
73. 1/BIZ 6/47, Fenwick, "Disaffection in the Lusikisiki District," 1 June 1960.
74. 1/BIZ 6/47, Warner to CM, Transkei, 26 Mar. 1960.
75. CMT 3/1479, Leibbrandt to secretary for Bantu administration and development, 20 June 1960.
76. (PTA) K 185, statement of chairman.
77. (PTA) K 185, annexure, 28, 31; also see 38.
78. (PTA) K 185, 28–9.
79. (PTA) K 185, testimony of Somdizela.
80. (PM) 1/KOK Add. 1/1/1/1, p. 20/61, statement of Majavu.
81. (PM) 1/KOK Add. 1/1/1/1, p. 20/61, statement of Sigwinta.
82. (BSC) 212/61, *State vs. Magawana and Twenty-Nine Others*, judgment on appeal.
83. GSC 1/2/1/942, 377/61, prep. exam.
84. GSC 1/2/1/942, 377/61, prep. exam., statement of Warren. Nomagqwatekana, according to Warren, asked the council to appoint Stanford.
85. GSC 1/2/1/942, 377/61, prep. exam.
86. (BSC) 212/61, *State vs. Magawana and Twenty-Nine Others*, judgment on appeal.
87. Quoted in Hunter, *Reaction to Conquest*, 397.
88. Wilson, *Reaction*, 297, 289.
89. (BSC) 212/61, *State vs. Magawana and Twenty-Nine Others*, judgment on appeal.
90. From GSC 1/2/1/942, 377/61, from testimony of Patekile, though not his words.
91. GSC, 1/2/1/942, 377/61, judgment.
92. From GSC 1/2/1/942, 377/61, testimony of Patekile; testimony of Magadule.
93. GSC /2/1/942, 377/61, testimony of Magadule.
94. GSC 1/2/1/942, 377/61, prep. exam.
95. (BSC) 212/61, *State vs. Magawana and Twenty-Nine Others*, judgment on appeal; GSC 1/2/1/942, 377/61, judgment of van Winsen, 6 Mar. 1962, testimony of Qwebane; testimony of Warren; statement of Qwebane from prep. exam.

96. GSC 1/2/1/942, 377/61, from statement of Yalwa.
97. GSC 1/2/1/942, 377/61, statement of Qwebane from prep. exam.
98. GSC 1/2/1/942, 377/61, testimony of Warren.
99. According to one testimony, Stanford had instructed eight men to travel to Ndlovu hill to inform the Congo that Bantu Authorities had not been accepted by him. Certainly, books had been returned to the magistrate. If this evidence is correct, Stanford clearly had shifted his position – too late. See GSC 1/2/1/942, 377/61, statement of Maxayi, prep. exam.
100. GSC 1/2/1/942, 377/61, minute book, Imizi tribal authority, 21 Jan. 1960. Evangelist were quite involved in the revolt. See also (PM) 1/KOK Add. 1/1/1/1, case p. 10/61.
101. GSC 1/2/1/942, 377/61, testimony of Qwebane; statement of Mxuma, from prep. exam.
102. GSC 1/2/1/942, 377/61, testimony of Joja.
103. 1/BIZ 6/47, Fenwick, "Disaffection in the Lusikisiki District," 1 June 1960; Beinart, *The Political Economy of Pondoland.*
104. (PTA) K 185, testimony of Somadlangati.
105. (PTA) K 185, statement of Dr. Buchan.
106. Joseph Conrad, *The Heart of Darkness* (New York, 1985), 108, 110.
107. (PTA) K 185, statement of Dr. Buchan.
108. 1/BIZ 6/47, Fenwick, "Disaffection in the Lusikisiki District," 1 June 1960; also located in CMT 3/1479.
109. (PTA) K 185, statement of Dr. Buchan.
110. (PTA) K 185, testimony of Macingwane.
111. Beinart, *The Political Economy of Pondoland,* 116.
112. 1/BIZ 6/47, Fenwick, "Disaffection in the Lusikisiki District," 1 June 1960.
113. Beinart, *The Political Economy of Pondoland,* 14.
114. 1/BIZ 6/47, Fenwick, "Disaffection in the Lusikisiki District," 1 June 1960.
115. Ibid.
116. (PTA) K 185, testimonies of Nene, Lehmkuhl, and Somadlangati, and "second speaker." See also chapter 5, pp. 000–00.
117. (PTA) K 185, testimony of Somadlangati.
118. (PTA) K 185, testimony of Goldwana, Dweba.
119. (PTA) K 185, testimony of Siko.
120. Ibid.
121. (UMT) CMT 164, meeting of 27 Nov. 1957.
122. (BSC) 27/61, *State vs. Sitwayi and Twenty-Five Others,* testimony of Swartz.
123. (PTA) K 185, testimony of Somadlangati.
124. (PTA) K 185, statement of Lehmkuhl; statement of Somadlangati.
125. (PTA) K 185, testimony of Somadlangati.
126. Ibid.
127. (PTA) K 185, testimony of Lehmkuhl.
128. (PTA) K 185, testimony of Dweba.
129. (PTA) K 185, testimony of Somadlangati.
130. Indeed, Mhlanga invited people from Bizana "to join the movement": (PTA) K 185, testimony of Goldwana. See also testimony Of Golhach.
131. (PTA) K 185, testimony of Somadlangati.

132. (PTA) K 185, testimony of Dweba; 1/BIZ 6/47, Fenwick, "Disaffection in the Lusikisiki District," 1 June 1960.
133. Leibbrandt, quoted in CMT 3/1470, Leibbrandt to secretary for Bantu administration and development, 5 Dec. 1960.
134. CMT 3/1478, statement of Kave, 3 Nov. 1960.
135. 1/ECO 6/1/98, du Plessis to CM, 18 Feb. 1961.
136. Leibbrandt, quoted in CMT 3/1470, Leibbrandt to secretary for Bantu administration and development, 5 Dec. 1960. See also CMT 3/1470, Leibbrandt to secretary of NA, 31 Oct. 1960.
137. In 1960 Mvalelwa Mzenzi was the Secretary of the Congo. He was suspected of leading the efforts against headman N. Jojo and his supporters, destroying fencing and inciting people "to refuse going for the census," among other things: CMT 3/1480, Bottoman and others to BAC, 7 Nov. 1960. See also CMT 3/1478, minutes of meeting, 10 Sept. 1960.
138. 1/BIZ 6/47, Warren, "Disturbances in the District of Bizana, 1960," 11 July 1960.
139. 1/BIZ 6/47, "Constitution of the Congo," 19 Nov. 1960.
140. CMT 3/1472, chief BAC to secretary for Bantu administration and development, 25 Jan. 1961.
141. (PM) 1/KOK Add. 1/1/1/1, p. 10/61, *Regina vs. Marulumba and Nine Others*, statement of Zanazo.
142. 1/BIZ 6/47, Warren, "Disturbances in the District of Bizana, 1960," 11 July 1960.
143. Ibid.
144. (BSC) 212/61, *State vs. Sitwayi and Twenty-Five Others*, testimony of Sakayedwa.
145. (BSC) 212/61, *State vs. Sitwayi and Twenty-Five Others*, testimony of Ndodana.
146. (PTA) K 185, testimony of Xakatile.
147. 1/BIZ 6/61, statement of Gangata, 15 Nov. 1960.
148. Ibid.
149. GSC 1/2/1/935, 365/61, statement of Coba.
150. See, for example, (BSC) 27/61, *State v. Sitwayi and Twenty-Six Others*, testimony of Card.
151. CMT 3/1472, statement of Madikizela, 31 Dec. 1960.
152. 1/BIZ 6/47, Warren, "Disturbances in the District of Bizana, 1960," 11 July 1960.
153. CMT 3/1472, statement of Jase, 5 Oct. 1960.
154. Ibid.
155. (BSC) 210/61, *State v. Mnconco and Eleven Others*, testimony of Sinkiyakiya.
156. 1/BIZ 6/47, Fenwick, "Disaffection in the Lusikisiki District," 1 June 1960. The district surgeon maintained that the chief's "position is untenable – I don't think he has a hope, and also he is not physically fit. If he is not killed, he will die of a stroke": (PTA) K 185, statement of Dr. Buchan.
157. (PM) 1/KOK Add. 1/1/1/1, 372 of 1961, *State v. Maquatswana and Nineteen Others*, statements of Mgxulwa and Galaka. See also the Mount Fletcher case in GSC 1/2/917, 115 of 1961, *Regina vs. Lehana and Others*.
158. 1/BIZ 6/64, statement of chief Baleni, 27 Feb. 1962. See also 1/BIZ 6/64, statement of Nonkwashu, 3 Mar. 1962. In Flagstaff a Congo leader died from being struck by lightning. Such an event must have affirmed people's belief in the role of magic in political conflict. See (PM) 1/KOK Add. 1/1/1/1, p. 10/61, *Regina vs. Marulumba and Nine Others*.

159. 1/BIZ 6/47, Warren, "Disturbances in the District of Bizana, 1960," 11 July 1960.
160. Ibid.
161. (PTA) K 185, p. 32.; also in 1/BIZ 6/47, Warren, "Disturbances in the District of Bizana, 1960," 11 July 1960.
162. Leibbrandt, quoted in CMT 3/1470, Leibbrandt to secretary for Bantu administration and development, 5 Dec. 1960.
163. (PTA) K 185, p. 21, "second speaker."
164. (PTA) K 185, testimony of Somdizela. See also that of "second speaker."
165. Leibbrandt, quoted in CMT 3/1470, Leibbrandt to secretary for Bantu administration and development, 5 Dec. 1960.
166. 1/BIZ 6/64, statement of Dokolwana, n.d. [1962].
167. (WITS) AD 1646, enclosure of House of Assembly questions, 15 May 1962, in Scott to Nye, 29 May 1962.
168. CMT 3/1472, CBAC to secretary for Bantu administration and development, 25 Jan. 1961.
169. (PTA) K 185, testimony of Somadlangati.
170. CMT 3/1472, Scholtz, magistrate's court, 3 Nov. 1961. See also CMT 3/1472, Schedule of Criminal Cases Arising out of Unrest, 1/3/1960-31/10/61, for statistics on Flagstaff district. In Kokstad the circuit court charged: no less than 139 people with murder, 50 of whom were convicted: CMT 3/1472, n.d. [1961].
171. CMT 3/1472, CBAC to secretary for Bantu administration and development, 25 Jan. 1961.
172. Ibid.
173. Ibid.
174. (PTA) K 185, chairman, 303.
175. See, for example, 1/BIZ, 6/47, Warren, "Disturbances in the District of Bizana, 1960," 11 July 1960, 24.
176. (PTA) K 185, chairman, 303.
177. Lodge, *Black Politics*, 234–5.
178. CMT 3/1480, statement of Skotoyi, 27 Oct. 1961.
179. CMT 3/1480, statement of Ntasi, 3 Nov. 1961.
180. (PTA) K 185, 18.
181. (PTA) K 185, 21.
182. (PTA) K 185, 20.
183. (PTA) K 185, statement of chairman.
184. 1/BIZ 6/47, HQ Battle Group Alpha, to army HQ, 9 Jan. 1961 and 11 Jan. 1961.
185. 1/BIZ 6/47, Matham to chief BAC, 17 Sept. 1962.
186. 1/BIZ 6/64, statement of Mabhena, 8 Apr. 1963.
187. 1/BIZ 6/64, statement of Nncunukelwa, 8 Apr. 1963.
188. *Truth and Reconciliation Commission of South Africa Report*, II, 430.
189. GSC 1/2/1/927, 270/61, *Regina v. Madiki and Five Others*.

8 FLIGHTS OF THE LIGHTNING BIRD

1. 1/QBU 7/1/70, "The Wind of Change," to Majeke, 16 Feb. 1961.
2. GSC, G 116/63, *State v. Shweni and Others*, 1963, confession of Mpoyi.
3. GSC, G 116/63, *State v. Shweni and Others*, 1963, confession of Tyulu.

4. See Lodge, *Black Politics*, 247–55.
5. Quoted in Lodge, *Black Politics*, 216.
6. See GSC, G 116/63, *State v. Shweni and Others*, 1963, confession of Mlamli; GSC, G 9/63, *State v. Ngcongolo and Others*, testimony of Kamteni.
7. GSC, G 116/63, *State v. Shweni and Others*, 1963, confession of Mpoyi. See also confession of Shweni and CMT 3/1481, confession of Miso, 17 Dec. 1962.
8. GSC, G 116/63, *State v. Shweni and Others*, 1963, confession of Ngqebisa.
9. GSC, G 116/63, *State v. Shweni and Others*, 1963, confession of Shweni.
10. GSC, G 116/63, *State v. Shweni and Others*, 1963, confession of Funani.
11. GSC, G 116/63, *State v. Shweni and Others*, 1963, confession of Shweni.
12. *The Star* 15 Dec. 1963, in (WITS) AD 1912, box 856.
13. Ibid.
14. GSC, G 116/63, *State v. Shweni and Others*, 1963, confession of Makwetana.
15. GSC, G 9/63, *State v. Ngcongolo and Others*, 1963, testimony of Hoft, one of the injured police officers.
16. *The Star*, 14 Dec. 1963, in (WITS) AD 1912, box 856.
17. CMT 3/1470, *State v. Gxabagxaba and Others*, 1963, testimony of Dwayi. There were plans to destroy the power station, railroad bridge, the industrial school, and the Bantu Affairs commissioner's office in Kingwilliamstown. Poqo planned to attack the police station in Kingwilliamstown and to release the prisoners from their cells. See GSC, G, 347/63, *State v. Nyobo and Others*, 1963.
18. See *Rand Daily Mail*, 1 August 1963, 21 June 1963, and *Cape Times*, 19 June 1963, both in (WITS) AD 1912, box 856; GSC, G 3/63, *State v. Simon and Others*, 1963; GSC, G 326/63, *State v. Manisi and Others*, 1963; GSC, G 347/63, *State v. Nyobo and others* 1963.
19. (WITS) AD 1912, SAAIR press clippings: *Race Relations News*, June 1963.
20. Ibid.
21. See below and Lodge, *Black Politics*, 233–8.
22. See, for example, GSC, G 1/64, *State v. Mtwalo*, 1964; Lodge, *Black Politics*, 233–8. See also GSC, G 3/64, *State v. Mpongoshe, Gqirana and Mtwalo*, 1964.
23. See CMT 3/1482, statement of Ngceza, 17 Nov. 1959; CMT 3/1484, Nel to magistrate, 16 Dec. 1958; (UMT) CMT 66/1177, CM, Transkei, to secretary for NA, 19 Dec. 1957; 1/COF 9/1/44, Bantu assistant information officers, report, 19 Oct. 1959.
24. Quoted in Bundy, "Land and Liberation," 276.
25. CMT 3/1484, major in charge to CM, 14 Apr. 1958.
26. CMT 3/1472, letter handed in on 8 Nov. 1960.
27. CMT 3/1482, undated letter.
28. On the Congo meeting see 1/BIZ 6/64, statement of Mabhena.
29. Gail Gerhart, *Black Power in South Africa* (Berkeley and Los Angeles), 194. See also Lodge, *Black Power*, esp. 84–6.
30. GSC, G 9/63, *State v. Ngcongolo and Others*, 1963, question to Mlowana.
31. GSC, G 9/63, *State v. Ngcongolo and Others*, 1963, testimony of Kamteni.
32. Ibid.
33. Ibid.
34. GSC, G 9/63, *State v. Ngcongolo and Others*, 1963, testimony of Kula.
35. GSC, G 9/63, *State v. Ngcongolo and Others*, 1963, testimony of Mlolwana.

36. 1/COF 9/1/44, anon. letter to Mantanzima [*sic*], n.d. [1963].
37. 1/COF 9/1/44, anon. letter to Mfebe, 16 Oct. 1963.
38. CMT 3/1481, confession of Miso, 17 Dec. 1962.
39. GSC, G 116/63, *State v. Shweni and Others*, 1963, testimony of Funani.
40. GSC, G 116/63, *State v. Shweni and Others*, 1963, confession of Tonga.
41. 1/COF 9/1/44, statement of Matanzima, n.d., 1953.
42. Ibid.
43. 1/COF 9/1/44, magistrate, Cofimvaba, to CM, 30 July 1953. The confidential correspondence was titled "Status and Position of Chief Kaizer Matanzima, St. Marks District."
44. 1/COF 9/1/44, statement of Matanzima, n.d., 1953.
45. 1/COF 9/1/44, Songca to CM, 25 Sept. 1954.
46. 1/COF 9/1/44, recollection of 8 Dec. 1955.
47. 1/COF 9/1/44, meeting of 23 Dec. 1955.
48. See, for example, 1/COF 9/1/44, minutes of 21 Oct. 1953.
49. (UMT) CMT 66/1177, Ramsay to secretary for NA, 14 Mar. 1956. See also 1/COF 9/1/44, petition of 8 Dec. 1955 of supporters of Matanzima.
50. 1/COF 9/1/44, Thorpe to CM, 7 Feb. 1956.
51. 1/COF 9/1/44, Jordaan to CM, 29 May 1961.
52. 1/COF 9/1/44, Jordaan to CM, 3 May 1962.
53. CMT 3/1474, BAC, Matatiele, to chief BAC, 7 Sept. 1963.
54. 1/COF 9/1/44, Jordaan to CM, 3 May 1962.
55. Southall, *South Africa's Transkei*, 116.
56. Southall, *South Africa's Transkei*, 117.
57. Ibid.
58. See Southall, *South Africa's Transkei*.
59. CMT 3/1474, BAC, Engcobo, to chief BAC, 16 July 1963. See also CMT 3/1474, BAC, Willowvale, to chief BAC, 24 June 1963.
60. 1/NQL 3/107, Blakeway to principal information officer, 25 June 1963.
61. Southall, *South Africa's Transkei*, 116.
62. Quoted in Southall, *South Africa's Transkei*, 122.
63. 1/EDL 6/1/35, chief BAC to all BACs, confidential, 25 Mar. 1963.
64. *The Star*, 5 June 1963 in (WITS) AD 1912, box 856.
65. 1/NQL 3/107, Blakeway to principal information officer, 25 June 1963.

CONCLUSION

1. Nelson Mandela, "Address to the People of Cape Town, Grand Parade, on the Occasion of his Inauguration as State President, 9th May 1994," http://www.anc.org.za/ancdocs/speeches/inaugct.html.
2. *Daily Dispatch*, 15 Dec. 1999.
3. See Mamdani, *Citizen and Subject*.
4. *Daily Dispatch*, 6 May 2000.
5. Reconstruction and Development Programme White Paper. Discussion Document, September 1994, chap. 8, "Conclusion: A National Consensus," 54. See www.polity.org.za/govdocs/rdp.
6. Mamdani, *Citizen and Subject*, 294.

7. Ibid.
8. Constitution of the Republic of South Africa, December 1996, chapter 12, "Traditional Leaders."
9. Department of Provincial and Local Government, 11 April 2000, 43.
10. Department of Provincial and Local Government, 11 April 2000.
11. *Daily Dispatch*, 1 Aug. 2000.
12. *Daily Dispatch*, 6 May 2000.
13. *Daily Dispatch*, 5 Sept. 2000.
14. *Daily Dispatch*, 7 Aug. 2000.
15. See Henry Rousso, *The Vichy Syndrome: History and Memory in France since 1944*, trans. Aruthur Goldhammer (Cambridge, Mass., 1991), 10; David W. Cohen, *The Combing of History* (Chicago, 1994).
16. See, for example, Krog, *Country of my Skull*; Edgar and Sapire, *African Apocalypse*. My thanks to the organizers of the Migrant Labour Museum, Lwandle, and especially Bongani Mgijima, who kindly shared their thoughts about history and memory in contemporary South Africa.
17. *Daily Dispatch*, 2 June 2000.
18. *Daily Dispatch*, 7 Nov. 1998; 7 Jan. 1999.
19. *Daily Dispatch*, 24 Dec. 1999.
20. Marx, *Eighteenth Brumaire*, 10, 13.
21. See André du Toit, "Perpetrator Findings as Artificial Even-handedness? The TRC's Contested Judgements of Moral and Political Accountability for Gross Human Rights Violations," unpub. MS.
22. See Lungisile Ntsebeza, "Democratization and Traditional Authorities in the New South Africa," *Comparative Studies of South Asia, Africa and the Middle East*, 19, 1 (1999): 83–94.
23. Ernest Renan, "Qu'est-ce qu'une nation?" in Ernest Renan, *Oeuvres Complete* (Paris, 1947–61), I.
24. Joseph and Nugent, "Popular Culture," 19.
25. Abrams, "Some Notes on the Difficulty of Studying the State," 59.
26. Mamdani, *Citizen and Subject*.
27. Harvey, *The Condition of Postmodernity*, 13. See also Adorno and Horkheimer, *Dialectic of Enlightenment*.
28. Corrigan and Sayer, *The Great Arch*, 2.
29. See, for example, Joseph and Nugent, *Everyday Forms of State Formation*.
30. President George Bush, State of the Union Address, 29 January 2002 (see http://www.whitehouse.gov/news/releases/2002/01/20020129-11.html).

Select Bibliography

I. MANUSCRIPT SOURCES

A. PUBLIC RECORDS OFFICE (PRO)

1. WO   War Office 1/445

B. SCHOOL OF ORIENTAL AND AFRICAN STUDIES (SOAS)

1. LMS   London Missionary Society 6 (3) B; 6 (3) D; 10 (3) C; 11 (1) B; 13 (1) B; 13 (3) C; 18 (2) D; 20 (3) C; 21 (3) B
2. MMS   Methodist Missionary Society 305; 309 (9)

C. CAPE ARCHIVES (CA)

1. ACC   Accessions
    a. ACC 793 letter book of Major Gawler
    b. ACC 302 Orpen Papers
    c. A215   Craister Papers
2. 1/ALC   Alice 5/1/1/2; 10/11; 10/12; 10/14; 10/33; 10/64; 1/1/1/42
3. 1/AXA   Alexandria 7/17
4. 1/BIZ   Bizana 6/47; 6/61; 6/64
5. BK   British Kaffraria 28; 72; 73; 74; 86; 87
6. 1/BUT   Butterworth 88
7. CCK   chief commissioner, Eastern Cape 11; 17; 19; 25; 26; 62; 105; 120
8. CMK   chief magistrate, Griqualand East 1/94; 1/152
9. CMT   chief magistriate, Transkei 1/27; 1/28; 1/143; 1/146; 1/147; 1/53; 3/520; 3/679; 3/781; 3/1451; 3/1470; 3/1471; 3/1472; 3/1474; 3/1478; 3/1479; 3/1480; 3/1481; 3/1482; 3/1484; 3/1593
10. CO   Colonial Office 1156; 4521
11. 1/COF   Cofimvaba 9/1/44
12. 1/ECO   Engcobo 4/1/1; 6/1/98
13. 1/EDL   Elliotdale 6/1/35
14. 1/ELN   East London 61; 67; 86; 87
15. GGR   Gaika-Galeka Rebellion 1
16. GH   Government House 8/27; 8/34; 8/36; 8/37
17. GSC   Grahamstown Supreme Court 1/2/1/483; 1/2/1/610; 1/2/1/612; 1/2/1/613; 1/2/1/627; 1/2/1/629; 1/2/1/736; 1/2/1/792; 1/2/1/796;

	1/2/1/797; 1/2/1/798; 1/2/1/799; 1/2/1/917; 1/2/1/927; 1/2/1/935; 1/2/1/938; 1/2/1/939; 1/2/1/942
18. 1/KNT	Kentani 124
19. 1/IDW	Idutywa ADD 1/1/1; 1/1/2
20. 1/MFE	Mount Frere 8/1; 8/14
21. NA	Native Affairs 18; 19; 20; 158; 173; 189; 190; 193; 195; 196; 225; 229; 231; 464; 497; 498; 531; 541; 554; 555; 556; 657; 658; 687; 707; 708; 723; 724; 725; 734; 754
22. 1/NKE	Nqamakwe 7/1/58; 7/1/60
23. 1/NQL	Ngqeleni 3/107
24. 1/PDE	Peddie 6/2
25. 1/QBU	Qumbu 7/1/8; 7/1/9; 7/1/70
26. 2/SPT	Sterkspruit 16
27. 1/TAD	Tarkastad 6/1/60
28. 1/TSO	Tsolo 5/1/52
29. 1/UTA	Umtata 2/1/1/1

D. AFRICAN STUDIES LIBRARY, UNIVERSITY OF CAPE TOWN (UCT)

1. BC 293   Sir W. E. M. Stanford Papers

E. SOUTH AFRICAN MUSEUM (SAM)

1. Smith   Andrew Smith Papers 2; 3; 4

F. CORY LIBRARY (CL)

1. MS/PR   manuscripts/printed papers 8470; 8471; 8496; 15,024
2. Uncatalogued material from magistrate's office, Keiskammahoek

G. PIETERMARITZBURG ARCHIVES (PM)

1. 1/CNC   chief native commissioner 312
2. 1/KOK   Kokstad ADD 1/1/1/1

H. UMTATA ARCHIVES (UMT)

1. CMT   chief magistrate, Transkei 164; 66/1177

I. CENTRAL ARCHIVES (PTA)

1. NTS   Native Affairs 2536; 7204; 7660; 7664; 7693; 7695; 7735; 10275
2. SAP   South African Police 36; 39
3. K   commissions and committees of inquiry 114 (Native Land, 1913–15); 185 (Pondoland disturbances)
4. JUS   secretary of Justice 188; 269; 287; 915; 916; 918; 919; 921; 922; 924

J. WILLIAM CULLEN LIBRARY, UNIVERSITY OF THE WITWATERSRAND (WITS)

1. AD 843   Dr. E. Jokl, A Labour and Manpower Survey of the Transkeian Territories (SAIRR, 1943)
2. AD 1912   South African Institute of Race Relations, press clippings
3. AD 1643   South African Institute of Race Relations, records of unrest and removals

K. GRAHAMSTOWN SUPREME COURT, GRAHAMSTOWN (GSC, G)

1/64; 3/63; 3/64; 9/63; 116/63; 326/63; 347/63

L. BLOEMFONTEIN SUPREME COURT (BSC)

27/61; 210/61; 212/61

M. BARLOW RAND (BR)

455

N. "HISTORICAL RECORD OF THE MURDER OF HAMILTON HOPE," TYPESCRIPT ORIGINALLY COMPILED BY W. C. HENMAN

II. ORAL INTERVIEWS (NAMES ABBREVIATED TO MAINTAIN ANONYMITY REQUESTED BY INTERVIEWEES)

E. K., 23 June 1993
J. M., 22 June 1993
M. Z., 24 June 1993
R. T., 23 June 1993
T. N., 24 June 1993

III. OFFICIAL GOVERNMENT PAPERS

A. PUBLISHED REPORTS

G. 4-'83, *Report and Proceedings of the Commission on Native Laws and Customs*
G. 42-'22, *Report on Native Locations Surveys*
G. 30-'76, *Report of the Surveyor-General on the Tenure of Land, on the Land Laws and their Results, and on the Topography of the Colony*
CCP 4/19/11, *Report on the Trigonometrical Survey of a Portion of the Colony and British Kaffraria*, by Captain W. Bailey, R. E. (Cape Town, 1863)
G. 41-'22, *Report of the Inter-Departmental Committee on the Native Pass Laws*
C. 2A-'92, *Appendix to the Report of the Select Committee on the Labour Question*
A. 3-'92, *Report of the Commission Appointed to Inquire into the Tenure of Land & c., in the Glen Grey District*

J. May, *Poverty and Inequality in South Africa: Summary Report prepared for the Office of the Executive Deputy President and the Inter-Ministerial Committee for Poverty and Inequality* (Pretoria, 1998)

"Mothers and Fathers of the Nation: The Forgotten People," *Report of the Ministerial Committee on Abuse, Neglect and Ill-Treatment of Older Persons*, 26 February 2001.

Reconstruction and Development Programme White Paper. Discussion Document, September 1994, chap. 8, "Conclusion: A National Consensus," 54. See www.polity.org.za/govdocs/rdp.

B. UNPUBLISHED REPORTS AND OTHER DOCUMENTS

Department of Provincial and Local Government, "A Draft Discussion Document towards a White Paper on Traditional Leadership and Institutions," 11 April 2000

Truth and Reconciliation Commission, Media Advisory, 4 May 2000

F. William Fox and Douglas Back, "A Preliminary Survey of the Agricultural and Nutritional Problems of the Ciskei and Transkeian Territories with Special Reference to their Bearing on the Recruiting of Labourers for the Gold Mining Industry," 1943

IV. ARTICLES, BOOKS, AND UNPUBLISHED DISSERTATIONS AND PAPERS

Abrams, Philip, "Some Notes on the Difficulty of Studying the State," *Journal of Historical Sociology*, 1, 1 (March 1988): 58–89

Adorno, Theodor and Max Horkheimer, *Dialectic of Enlightenment*, trans. John Cumming (New York, 1979)

Aiken, Susan Hardy et al., *Making Worlds: Gender, Metaphor, Materiality* (Tucson, 1998).

Alberti, Ludwig, *Alberti's Account of the Xhosa in 1807*, trans. W. Fehr (Cape Town, 1968)

Anderson, Benedict, *Imagined Communities: Reflections on the Origin and Spread of Nationalism* (London, 1983, 1991)

Anon., "Kafir Belief in the Existance of a Deity," *Cape Monthly Magazine*, 3 (Oct. 1880): 253

Appadurai, Arjun, "Number in the Colonial Imagination," in Carol A. Breckenridge and Peter van der Veer, eds., *Orientalism and the Postcolonial Predicament: Perspectives on South Asia* (Philadelphia, 1993)

Arendt, Hannah, Eichmann in Jerusalem: A Report on the Banality of Evil (Gloucester, Mass., 1964)

Asad, Talal, Genealogies of Religion: Discipline and Reasons of Power in Christianity and Islam (Baltimore, 1993)

Ashforth, Adam, *Madumo: A Man Bewitched* (Chicago, 2000)

   The Politics of Official Discourse in Twentieth Century South Africa (Oxford, 1992)

Atkins, Keletso, *The Moon is Dead! Give us our Money: The Cultural Origins of an African Work Ethic, Natal, South Africa, 1843–1900* (Portsmouth, 1993)

Atmore, Anthony, "Moorosi's Rebellion: Lesotho, 1879," in Robert Rotberg and Ali Mazrui, eds., *Protest and Power* (New York, 1970)

Ayliff, John, *The Journal of John Ayliff*, ed. Peter Hinchliff (Grahamstown, 1971)

Ballard, Charles, "Drought and Economic Distress: South Africa in the 1880s," *Journal of Interdisciplinary History*, 17, 2 (1986): 359–78

Barrow, John, *Travels into the Interior of South Africa*, 2 vols., 2nd ed. (London, 1806)

Bayart, Jean-Francois, *The State in Africa: The Politics of the Belly* (London, 1993)

Bayly, C. A., *Empire and Information: Intelligence Gathering and Social Communication in India, 1780–1870* (Cambridge, 1996)

Beidelman, T. O., *Colonial Evangelism: A Socio-historical Study of an East African Mission at the Grassroots* (Bloomington, 1982)

Beinart,William, "Conflict in Qumbu: Rural Consciousness, Ethnicity and Violence in the Colonial Transkei," in Beinart and Bundy, *Hidden Struggles*
    "The Origins of the *Indlavini*: Male Associations and Migrant Labour in the Transkei," in Spiegel and McAllister, eds., *Tradition and Transition in Southern Africa*
    The Political Economy of Pondoland, 1860–1930 (Cambridge, 1982)

Beinart, William and Colin Bundy, *Hidden Struggles in Rural South Africa: Politics and Popular Movements in the Transkei and Eastern Cape, 1890–1930* (Berkeley and Los Angeles, 1987)

Benjamin, Walter, *Illuminations*, ed. and intro. Hannah Arendt, trans. Harry Zohn (New York, 1969)

Bernstein, Richard, ed., *Habermas and Modernity* (Oxford, 1985)

Berry, Sara, *No Condition is Permanent: The Social Dynamics of Agrarian Change in Sub-Saharan Africa* (Madison, 1993)

Bhabha, Homi, "Of Mimicry and Man: The Ambivalence of Colonial Discourse," in Homi Bhabha, *The Location of Culture* (New York, 1994)

Black, Jeremy, *Maps and Politics* (Chicago, 1997)

Black's Law Dictionary, 7th ed. (St. Paul, 1999)

Bonnell, Victoria E. and Lynn Hunt, eds., *Beyond the Cultural Turn: New Directions in the Study of Society and Culture* (Berkeley and Los Angeles, 1999)

Borofsky, Robert, "Cook, Lono, Obeyesekere, and Sahlins," in Robert Borofsky, ed., *Remembrance of Pacific Pasts*
    Remembrance of Pacific Pasts: An Invitation to Remake History (Honolulu, 2000)

Bozzoli, Belinda, *The Political Nature of a Ruling Class: Capital and Ideology in South Africa, 1890–1933* (London, 1981)

Bradford, Helen, *A Taste of Freedom: The ICU in Rural South Africa, 1924–1930* (New Haven, 1987)

Brookes, E. H., *A History of Native Policy in South Africa from 1830 to the Present Day* (Cape Town, 1924)

Brownlee, Frank, *The Transkeian Native Territories: Historical Records. Compiled by Frank Brownlee, Resident Magistrate, Mount Ayliff* (Lovedale, 1923; repr. Westport, Conn., 1970)

Brownlee, W. T., *Reminiscences of a Transkeian* (Pietermaritzburg, 1975)

The Bullhoek Tragedy. Illustrated. The Full Story of the Israelite Settlement at Ntabelanga, near Queenstown (East London Daily Dispatch, Ltd., 1921)

Bundy, Colin, "Land and Liberation: Popular Rural Protest and the National Liberation Movements in South Africa, 1920–1960," in Shula Marks and Stanley Trapido, eds., *The Politics of Race, Class and Nationalism in Twentieth Century South Africa* (Burnt Hill, 1987)
    The Rise and Fall of the South African Peasantry, 2nd ed. (Cape Town,1988)

Burchell, Graham, Colin Gordon, and Peter Miller, eds., *The Foucault Effect: Studies in Governmentality* (Chicago, 1991)

Campbell, James, "Our Fathers, our Children: The African Methodist Episcopal Church in the United States and South Africa" (Ph.D. thesis, Stanford University, 1989)

Carton, Benedict, *Blood from your Children: The Colonial Origins of Generational Conflict in South Africa* (Charlottesville, 2000)

Cell, John, *The Highest Stage of White Supremacy: The Origins of Segregation in South Africa and the American South* (Cambridge, 1982)

Chanock, Martin, *Law, Custom, and Social Order: The Colonial Experience in Malawi and Zambia* (Cambridge, 1985)

Cohen, David W., *The Combing of History* (Chicago, 1994)

Womunafu's Bunafu: A Study of Authority in a Nineteenth-Century African Community (Princeton, 1977)

Cohn, Bernard S., *Colonialism and its Forms of Knowledge: The British in India* (Princeton, 1996)

Comaroff, Jean, *Body of Power, Spirit of Resistance: The Culture and History of a South African People* (Chicago, 1985)

Comaroff, John L., "Reflections on the Colonial State, in South Africa and Elsewhere: Factions, Fragments, Facts and Fictions," *Social Identities*, 4, 3 (October 1998): 321–62

Comaroff, John and Jean Comaroff, eds., *Modernity and its Malcontents: Ritual and Power in Postcolonial Africa* (Chicago, 1993)

Of Revelation and Revolution: vol. I, *Christianity, Colonialism, and Consciousness in South Africa* (Chicago, 1991); vol. II, *The Dialectics of Modernity on a South African Frontier* (Chicago, 1997)

Conrad, Joseph, *The Heart of Darkness* (New York, 1985)

Cooper, Frederick, *On the African Waterfront: Urban Disorder and the Transformation of Work in Colonial Mombasa* (New Haven, 1987)

Cooper, Frederick and Ann Stoler, eds., *Tensions of Empire: Colonial Cultures in a Bourgeois World* (Berkeley and Los Angeles, 1997)

Coplan, David B., *In the Time of Cannibals: The Word Music of South Africa's Basotho Migrants* (Chicago, 1994)

Coronil, Fernando, "Smelling Like a State," *American Historical Review*, 106, 1 (February 2001): 119–29

Corrigan, Philip, "State Formation," in Joseph and Nugent, eds., *Everyday Forms of State Formation*

Corrigan, Philip and Derek Sayer, *The Great Arch: English State Formation as Cultural Revolution*, foreword G. E. Aylmer (Oxford, 1985)

Crais, Clifton, *A Century of Sadness: Poverty and Power in Rural South Africa* (Portsmouth, forthcoming)

"Representation and the Politics of Identity in South Africa: An Eastern Cape Example," *International Journal of African Historical Studies*, 25, 1 (1992): 99–126

White Supremacy and Black Resistance: The Making of the Colonial Order in the Eastern Cape, 1770–1865 (Cambridge, 1992)

Crais, Clifton ed., *The Culture of Power in Southern Africa: Essays on State Formation and the Political Imagination* (Portsmouth, 2002)

Dasgupta, Partha, *An Inquiry into Well-Being and Destitution* (Oxford, 1993)

Davis, Mike, *Late Victorian Holocausts: El Nino Famines and the Making of the Third World* (New York, 2001)

Dening, Greg, *Islands and Beaches* (Honolulu, 1980)

Desmond, Cosmos, *The Discarded People: An Account of African Resettlement in South Africa* (Harmondsworth, 1971)

Dirks, Nicholas B., ed., *Colonialism and Culture* (Ann Arbor, 1992)

Doyle, Michael W., *Empires* (Ithaca, 1986)

Dubow, Saul, "The Elaboration of Segregationist Ideology," in William Beinart and Saul Dubow, eds., *Segregation and Apartheid in Twentieth-Century South Africa* (London and New York, 1995)

    Racial Segregation and the Origins of Apartheid in South Africa, 1919–1936 (Oxford, 1989)

Du Toit, André, "Perpetrator Findings as Artificial Even-handedness? The TRC's Contested Judgements of Moral and Political Accountability for Gross Human Rights Violations," unpub. MS

Edgar, Robert, "The Fifth Seal: Enoch Mgijima, the Israelites, and the Bullhoek Massacre" (Ph.D. thesis, University of California, 1977)

Edgar, Robert and Hilary Sapire, *African Apocalypse: The Story of Nontetha Nkwenkwe, A Twentieth Century South African Prophet* (Athens, OH, 2000)

Ehret, Christopher, *An African Classical Age: Eastern and Southern Africa in World History, 1000 BC to AD 400* (Charlottesville, 1998)

Ehret, Christopher and Merrick Posnansky, eds., *The Archaeological and Linguistic Reconstruction of African History* (Berkeley and Los Angeles, 1982)

Eldredge, Elizabeth, *A South African Kingdom: The Pursuit of Security in Nineteenth-Century Lesotho* (Cambridge, 1993)

Evans, Ivan, *Bureaucracy and Race: Native Administration in South Africa* (Berkeley and Los Angeles, 1997)

    "The Native Affairs Department and the Reserves in the 1940s and 1950s," in Robin Cohen et al., *Repression and Resistance: Insider Accounts of Apartheid* (London, 1990)

Fanon, Frantz, *Black Skin, White Masks* (New York, 1967)

Feierman, Steven, *Peasant Intellectuals: Anthropology and History in Tanzania* (Madison, 1990)

Ferguson, James, *The Anti-Politics Machine: "Development," Depoliticization, and Bureaucratic Power in Lesotho* (Cambridge, 1990)

Foucault, Michel, "Governmentality." In Burchell et al., eds., *The Foucault Effect History of Sexuality: An Introduction* (New York, 1990)

Galbraith, John, *Reluctant Empire: British Policy on the South African Frontier, 1834–54* (Berkeley and Los Angeles, 1963)

Garson, Yvonne, comp., *Versatile Genius: The Royal Engineers and their Maps* (Johannesburg, 1992)

Gerhart, Gail, *Black Power in South Africa* (Berkeley and Los Angeles, 1978)

Geschiere, Peter, *The Modernity of Witchcraft: Politics and the Occult in Postcolonial Africa* (Charlottesville, 1997)

Giddens, Anthony, *The Consequences of Modernity* (Stanford, 1990)

Ginzburg, Carlo, *History, Rhetoric, and Proof* (Hanover and London, 1999)

    The Night Battles: Witchcraft and Agrarian Cults in the Sixteenth and Seventeenth Centuries, trans. John and Anne Tedeschi (Baltimore, 1983)

Gluckman, Max, *Rituals of Rebellion in South-East Africa* (Manchester, 1952)

Gramsci, Antonio, *Selections from the Prison Notebooks of Antonio Gramsci*, ed. Q. Hoare and G. N. Smith (New York, 1971)

Greenfeld, Liah, *Nationalism: Five Roads to Modernity* (Cambridge, Mass., 1992)

Guha, Ranajit, "On Some Aspects of the Historiography of Colonial India," in Ranajit Guha, ed., *Subaltern Studies I: Writings on South Asian History and Society* (Delhi, 1982)

Guthrie, Malcolm, *Comparative Bantu*, 4 vols. (Amersham, 1970)

Guy, Jeff, The Destruction of the Zulu Kingdom: The Civil War in Zululand, 1879–1884 (Johannesburg, 1979)

Hacking, Ian, "How Should we do the History of Statistics," in Burchell et al., eds., *The Foucault Effect*

Hamilton, Carolyn, *Terrific Majesty: The Powers of Shaka Zulu and the Limits of Historical Invention* (Cambridge, Mass., 1998)

Hammond-Tooke, W. D., *Bhaca Society: A People of the Transkeian Uplands, South Africa* (Cape Town, 1962)

  Command or Consensus: The Development of Transkeian Government (Cape Town, 1975)

  "Descent Groups Scatter in a Mpondomise Ward," *African Studies*, 27, 2 (1968): 83–94

  "The Morphology of Mpondomise Descent Groups," *Africa*, 38, 1 (Jan. 1968): 26–46

  Patrolling the Herms: Social Structure, Cosmology and Pollution Concepts in Southern Africa (Johannesburg, 1981)

  The Tribes of King William's Town District (Pretoria, 1958)

Harms, Robert, *River of Wealth, River of Sorrow: The Central Zaire Basin in the Era of the Slave and Ivory Trade, 1500–1891* (New Haven, 1981)

Harvey, David, *The Condition of Postmodernity* (Oxford, 1990)

Headrick, Daniel R., *The Tentacles of Progress: Technology Transfer in the Age of Imperialism, 1850–1940* (New York, 1988)

  The Tools of Empire: Technology and European Imperialism in the Nineteenth Century (New York, 1981)

Hendricks, F., *The Pillars of Apartheid: Land Tenure, Rural Planning and the Chieftaincy* (Uppsala, 1990).

Herzfeld, Michael, *The Social Production of Indifference: Exploring the Symbolic Roots of Western Bureaucracy* (New York, 1992)

Heywood, Linda, "Towards an Understanding of Modern Political Ideology in Africa: The Case of the Ovimbundu of Angola," *Journal of Modern African Studies*, 36 (1998):139–67

Hobsbawm, E. J., *Nations and Nationalism since 1870* (Cambridge, 1990)

Hodgson, Janet, "A Battle for Sacred Power: Christian Beginnings among the Xhosa," in Richard Elphick and Rodney Davenport, eds., *Christianity in South Africa: A Political, Social, and Cultural History* (Berkeley and Los Angeles, 1997)

Hofmeyr, Isobel, *"We Spend Our Years as a Tale That is Told": Oral Historical Narrative in a South African Chiefdom* (Portsmouth, 1993)

Horton, Robin, "African Traditional Thought and Western Science," *Africa*, 37, 1(1967): 155–87

  "On the Rationality of Conversion (Part I)," *Africa*, 45, 3 (1975): 219–35

Hunter, Monica, *Reaction to Conquest: Effects of Contact with Europeans on the Pondo of South Africa* (London, 1961)

Hurst, Michael, *States, Countries, Provinces* (Frome and London, 1986)

Jay, Martin, *Downcast Eyes: The Denigration of Vision in Twentieth-Century French Thought* (Berkeley and Los Angeles, 1993)

Jordan, A. C., *The Wrath of the Ancestors (a Novel)*, trans. Priscilla P. Jordan (Lovedale, 1980)

Joseph, George, and Daniel Nugent, "Popular Culture and State Formation," in Joseph and Nugent, eds., *Everyday Forms of State Formation*

Joseph, George and Daniel Nugent, eds., *Everyday Forms of State Formation* (Durham, N.C., 1994)

Joyce, Patrick, *Visions of the People: Industrial England and the Question of Class: 1848–1914* (Cambridge, 1991)

Kimble, Judy, "Labour Migration in Basutoland, c. 1870–1885," in Shula Marks and Richard Rathbone, eds., *Industrialisation and Social Change in South Africa* (London, 1982)

Kopytoff, Igor, ed., *The African Frontier: The Reproduction of Traditional African Societies* (Bloomington, 1987)

Krog, Antjie, *Country of my Skull: Guilt, Sorrow, and the Limits of Forgiveness in the New South Africa* (New York, 1998)

Kuckertz, Heinz, *Creating Order: The Image of the Homestead in Mpondo Social Life* (Johannesburg, 1990)

Lacey, Marian, *Working for Boroko: The Origins of a Coercive Labour system in South Africa* (Johannesburg, 1981)

Lan, David, *Guns and Rain: Guerrillas and Spirit Mediums in Zimbabwe* (Berkeley and Los Angeles, 1985)

Landau, Paul, *The Realm of the Word: Language, Gender, and Christianity in a Southern African Kingdom* (Portsmouth, 1995)

Landes, David, *The Wealth and Poverty of Nations: Why Some are so Rich and Some so Poor* (New York, 1998)

Lane, Tim, "Jele Tšhelete': Witchcraft, Chiefs, and the State in the Northern Transvaal, 1900–1930," in Crais, ed., *The Culture of Power in Southern Africa*

Lewis, Jack, "An Economic History of the Ciskei, 1848–1900" (Ph.D. thesis, University of Cape Town, 1984)

   "The Rise and Fall of the South African Peasantry: A Critique and Reassessment," *Journal of Southern African Studies*, 11, 1 (1984): 1–24

   "Rural Contradictions and Class Consciousness: Migrant Labour in Historical Perspective," paper presented to Centre for African Studies, University of Cape Town, 27 Feb. 1985

Lichtenstein, H. *Travels in Southern Africa*, trans. A. Plumptre, 2 vols. (Cape Town, 1928–30)

LiPuma, Edward, *Encompassing Others: The Magic of Modernity in Melanesia* (Ann Arbor, 2000)

Lodge, Tom, *Black Politics in South Africa since 1945* (London, 1983)

   "Poqo and Rural Resistance in the Transkei, 1960–1965," *ICS, Collected Seminar Papers on the Societies of Southern Africa in the 19th and 20th Centuries*, 9 (1977–8): 137–47

Lonsdale, John, "The Conquest State of Kenya, 1895–1920," in Lonsdale and Berman, *Unhappy Valley*

Lonsdale, John and Bruce Berman, *Unhappy Valley: Conflict in Kenya and Africa* (Athens, OH, 1992)

MacDonald, James, "Manners, Customs, and Superstitions and Religions of South African Tribes," *Journal of the Anthropological Institute*, 19 (1889)

Maclean, John, *Compendium of Kaffir Law and Custom* (London, 1858)

Mallon, Florencia E., *Peasant and Nation: The Making of Postcolonial Mexico and Peru* (Berkeley and Los Angeles, 1995)

Mamdani, Mahmood, *Citizen and Subject: Contemporary Africa and the Legacy of Late Colonialism* (Princeton, 1996)

Politics and Class Formation in Uganda (London, 1976)

Mann, Kristin and Richard Roberts, eds., *Law in Colonial Africa* (Portsmouth, 1991)

Marks, Shula, *The Ambiguities of Dependence in South Africa: Class, Nationalism and the State in Twentieth-Century Natal* (Johannesburg, 1986)

Marks, Shula and Stanley Trapido, *Economy and Society in Pre-industrial South Africa* (London, 1980)

"Lord Milner and the South African State," *History Workshop* (1979): 50–80

Marx, Anthony W., *Lessons of Struggle: South African Internal Opposition, 1960–1990* (New York, 1992)

Marx, Karl, *The Eighteenth Brumaire of Louis Bonaparte* (Moscow, 1972)

Mayer Philip and Iona, "Report on Research on Self-Organisation by Youth among Xhosa-speaking Peoples of the Ciskei and Transkei," 2 vols., unpub. typescript, Institute of Social and Economic Research, Rhodes University, 1972)

Townsmen or Tribesmen (Cape Town, 1961)

Mbeki, Govan, *South Africa: The Peasants' Revolt* (Baltimore, 1964)

Mbembe, Achille, "The Banality of Power and the Aesthetics of Vulgarity in the Post-colony," *Public Culture*, 4, 2 (Spring 1992): 1–30

McAllister, P. A., "Conservatism and Resistance to 'Betterment' in the Transkei – a Case Study from Willowvale District," University Seminar 2, Institute of Social and Economic Research, Rhodes University, 6 August 1985

"Using Ritual to Resist Domination in the Transkei," in Spiegel and McAllister, eds., *Tradition and Transition in Southern Africa*

McKittrick, Meredith, "To Dwell Secure: Gender, Generation and Christianity in Northern Namibia," unpub. MS

Memmi, Albert, *The Colonizer and the Colonized* (New York, 1965)

Merry, Sally Engle, *Colonizing Hawai'i: The Cultural Power of Law* (Princeton, 2000)

Meyer, Birgit, *Translating the Devil: Religion and Modernity among the Ewe in Ghana* (Trenton, 1999)

Mills, Wallace, "The Role of the African Clergy in the Reorientation of Xhosa Society to the Plural Society in the Cape Colony, 1850–1915'" (Ph.D. thesis, University of California, 1975)

Minogue, Kenneth, "State," in J. Kuper, ed., *Political Science and Political Theory* (London, 1987)

Mitchell, Timothy, *Colonising Egypt* (Berkeley and Los Angeles, 1991)

Moodie, Donald, *The Record* (Amsterdam and Cape Town, 1960)

Moore, Barrington Jr., *The Social Origins of Dictatorship and Democracy: Landlord and Peasant in the Making of the Modern World* (Boston, 1967)

Muir, Richard, *Modern Political Geography* (New York, 1975)

Murray, Martin, *The Revolution Deferred: The Painful Birth of Post-Apartheid South Africa* (London, 1994)

Ngubane, Harriet, *Body and Mind in Zulu Medicine* (London, 1977)

Niehaus, Isak, "Witchcraft, Whites, and the 1994 South African Elections," unpub. seminar paper, Institute for Advanced Social Research, University of the Witwatersrand, 1995

Ntsebeza, Lungisile, "Democratization and Traditional Authorities in the New South Africa," *Comparative Studies of South Asia, Africa and the Middle East*, 19, 1 (1999): 83–94

Obeyesekere, Gananath, *The Apotheosis of Captain Cook: European Mythmaking in the Pacific* (Princeton, 1997)

Odendaal, André, *Vukani Bantu! The Beginnings of Black Protest Politics in South Africa to 1912* (Cape Town, 1984)

Opland, Jeff, *Xhosa Oral Poetry: Aspects of a Black South African Tradition* (Cambridge, 1983)

Packard, Randall, *Chiefship and Cosmology: An Historical Study of Political Competition* (Bloomington, 1981)

Pasquino, Pasquale, "Theatrum Politicum: The Genealogy of Capital – Police and the State of Prosperity," in Burchell et al., eds., *The Foucault Effect*

Patriarca, Silvana, *Numbers and Nationhood: Writing Statistics in Nineteenth-Century Italy* (Cambridge, 1996)

Peires, J. B., *The Dead Will Arise: Nongqawuse and the Great Cattle-Killing Movement of 1856–7* (Johannesburg, 1989)

  The House of Phalo: A History of the Xhosa People in the Days of their Independence (Berkeley and Los Angeles, 1981)

  "Unsocial Bandits: The Stock Thieves of Qumbu and their Enemies," paper presented to the Conference on Democracy: Popular Precedents, Practice, Culture, University of the Witwatersrand, 13–15 July 1994

Pirie, Gordon, "Railways and Labour Migration to the Rand Mines: Constraints and Significance," *Journal of Southern African Studies*, 19, 4 (December 1993): 713–30

Platzky, Laurine and Cherryl Walker, *The Surplus People: Forced Removals in South Africa* (Johannesburg, 1985)

Poovey, Mary, *History of the Modern Fact: Problems of Knowledge in the Sciences of Wealth and Society* (Chicago, 1998)

  Making a Social Body: British Cultural Formation, 1830–1864 (Chicago, 1995)

  "The Production of Abstract Space," in Aiken et al., *Making Worlds*

Posel, Deborah, *The Making of Apartheid* (Oxford, 1991)

Pratt, Mary Louise, *Imperial Eyes: Travel Writing and Transculturation* (London and New York, 1992)

Pretorius, H. L., *Sound the Trumpet of Zion: Aspects of a Movement in Transkei* (Pretoria, 1985)

Rabinow, Paul, *French Modern: Norms and Forms of the Social Environment* (Cambridge, Mass., 1989)

Race Relations Survey (Johannesburg, 1984–94)

Radcliffe-Brown, A. R., *Structure and Function in Primitive Society* (New York, 1965)

Ranger, Terence, "Africa in the Age of Extremes: The Irrelevance of African History,"
    in Simon McGrath, Charles Jedrej, Kenneth King, and Jack Thompson, eds.,
    Rethinking African History (Edinburgh, 1997)
Redding, Sean, "Government Witchcraft: Taxation, the Supernatural, and the Mpondo
    Revolt in the Transkei, South Africa, 1955–63," *African Affairs*, 95 (1996): 555–79
Renan, Ernest, "Qu'est-ce qu'une nation?" In Ernest Renan, *Oeuvres Complete* (Paris,
    1947–61), I
Robey, T. S., "The Ecology of the Iron Age in the Transkei," report on archeological
    research in the Mbashe River catchment, University of Cape Town, February, 1985
Rogers, Howard, *Native Administration in the Union of South Africa* (Johannesburg,
    1933)
Rousso, Henry, *The Vichy Syndrome: History and Memory in France since 1944*, trans.
    Arthur Goldhammer (Cambridge, Mass., 1991)
Rudé, George, *Ideology and Popular Protest* (New York, 1980)
Sahlins, Marshal, *How "Natives" Think, about Captain Cook, for Example* (Chicago,
    1995)
Said, Edward, *Orientalism* (New York, 1979)
Scheub, Harold, *The Tongue is Fire: South African Storytellers and Apartheid* (Madison,
    1996)
Scott, James C., *Domination and the Arts of Resistance: Hidden Transcripts* (New
    Haven, 1990)
    *Seeing Like a State: How Certain Schemes to Improve the Human Condition have
    Failed* (New Haven, 1998)
Scott, Joan, "The Evidence of Experience," *Critical Inquiry*, 17 (Summer 1991): 773–97
Seed, Patricia, *Ceremonies of Possession in Europe's Conquest of the New World, 1492–
    1640* (New York, 1995)
Sewell, William, "The Concept(s) of Culture," in Bonnell and Hunt, eds., *Beyond the
    Cultural Turn*
Shaw, William, *The Journal of William Shaw*, ed. W. D. Hammond-Tooke (Cape Town,
    1972)
Shrewsbury, J. V. B., *Memorials of the Reverend William J. Shrewsbury* (London, 1869)
Silk, Andrew, *A Shanty Town in South Africa: The Story of Modderdam* (Johannesburg,
    1981)
Southall, Roger, *South Africa's Transkei: The Political Economy of an "Independent"
    Bantustan* (London, 1982)
Sparks, Allister, *Tomorrow is a Different Country* (Chicago, 1995)
Spiegel, A. D. and P. A. McAllister, eds., *Tradition and Transition in Southern Africa*
    (Johannesburg, 1991)
Stanford, Sir Walter, *The Reminiscences of Sir Walter Stanford*, ed. J. W. McQuarrie,
    2 vols.: vol. 1, *1850–1885* (Cape Town, 1958)
Stapleton, Timothy, *Maqoma: Xhosa Resistance to Colonial Advance* (Johannesburg,
    1994)
Steedman, Andrew, *Wanderings and Adventures in the Interior of Southern Africa*,
    2 vols. (London, 1835)
Stoler, Ann Laura, *Race and the Education of Desire: Foucault's History of Sexuality
    and the Colonial Order of Things* (Durham, N.C., 1997)
    "Rethinking Colonial Categories: European Communities and the Boundaries of
    Rule," in Dirks, ed., *Colonialism and Culture*

Stoller, P., *Embodying Colonial Memories: Spirit Possession, Power, and the Hauka of West Africa* (New York, 1995)

Switzer, Les, *Power and Resistance in an African Society: The Ciskei Xhosa and the Making of South Africa* (Madison, 1993)

Taussig, Michael, *The Magic of the State* (New York, 1997)

   Mimesis and Alterity: A Particular History of the Senses (New York, 1993)

   "The Sun Gives without Receiving: An Old Story," *Comparative Studies in Society and History*, 37, 2 (April 1995): 368–98

Thomas, Keith, *Religion and the Decline of Magic* (London, 1971)

Thompson, Leonard, *A History of South Africa*, rev. ed. (New Haven, 1995)

Todorov, Tzvetan, *The Conquest of America*, trans. Richard Howard (New York, 1982)

Transactions of the London Missionary Society Volume I, From its Institution in the Year 1795, to the End of the Year 1802. The Second Edition; Published for the Benefit of the Society (London, 1804) ("Journey of Caffraria from the Cape of Good Hope in the Year 1799," pp. 372–80; "First Attempt to Enter Caffraria," pp. 380–9; "Second Attempt to Enter Caffraria," pp. 390–411; "Transactions of Dr. Vanderkemp, in the Year 1800," pp. 412–31; "An Account of the Religion, Customs, Population, Government, Language, History, and Natural Productions of Caffraria, by Dr. Vanderkemp," pp. 432–68; "Transactions of Dr. Vanderkemp, in the Year 1801," pp. 469–505)

Trapido, Stanley, "'The Friends of the Natives': Merchants, Peasants and the Political and Ideological Structure of Liberalism in the Cape, 1854–1910," in Marks and Trapido, *Economy and Society in Pre-industrial South Africa*

Trouillot, Michel-Rolph, "The Anthropology of the State in the Age of Globalization: Close Encounters of the Deceptive Kind,"*Current Anthropology*, 42, 1 (February 2001): 125–35

Truax, Alice, "When Cultures Collide: Winning and Losing in Nineteenth-Century Borneo," *New Yorker*, 14 Sept. 1998

Truth and Reconciliation Commission of South Africa Report, 5 vols. (London, 1999)

Turok, Ben, "The Pondo Revolt" (Congress of Democrats, n.d.)

Vail, Leroy and Landeg White, *Power and the Praise Poem: Southern African Voices in History* (Charlottesville, 1991)

van Onselen, C., *The Seed is Mine: The Life of Kas Maine, a South African Sharecropper, 1894–1985* (Cape Town, 1996)

Vansina, Jan, *Paths in the Rainforest: Toward a History of Political Tradition in Equatorial Africa* (Madison, 1990)

Walshe, Peter, *The Rise of African Nationalism in South Africa: The African National Congress, 1912–52* (London, 1970)

Weber, Max, *Economy and Society*, ed. Guenther Roth and Claus Wittich, 2 vols. (Berkeley and Los Angeles, 1978)

   The Protestant Ethic and the Spirit of Capitalism, trans. Talcott Parsons, intro. Anthony Giddens (New York, 1976)

Webster's Dictionary, Second College Edition (Cleveland, OH, 1986)

Wells, Allen and Gilbert Joseph, *Summer of Discontent, Seasons of Upheaval: Elite Politics and Rural Insurgency in Yucatan, 1876–1915* (Stanford, 1996)

White, Luise, *Speaking with Vampires: Rumor and History in Colonial Africa* (Berkeley and Los Angeles, 2000)

Willan, Brian, *Sol Plaatje: South African Nationalist, 1876–1932* (London, 1984)

Wilson, Francis and Mamphela Ramphele, *Uprooting Poverty* (New York, 1989)

Winichakul, Thongchai, *Siam Mapped: A History of the Geo-Body of Nation* (Honolulu, 1994)

Winslow, Thomas J., "Paying the Price: Women and Domestic Conflict in Late 19th Century Thembuland," unpub. paper presented to the History Department, University of Cape Town, n.d., [1989]

Wolf, Eric R., *Peasant Wars of the Twentieth Century* (New York, 1973)

Wolpe, Harold, "Capitalism and Cheap Labour Power," in William Beinart and Saul Dubow, eds., *Segregation and Apartheid in Twentieth-Century South Africa* (London and New York, 1995)

Index

Act of Union (1910), 9, 16, 25, 102
Adorno, Theodor,
  on modernity and rationality, 9
African National Congress (ANC), 1, 2, 9,
  11, 30–1, 141–4, 147, 165, 188–91,
  207, 212–13, 218, 226–7
African Presbyterian Church, 132
agriculture
  chiefship and, 28, 35–67, 130, 197
  colonialism and, 22, 26–7, 104,
    159–60
  drought and, 22, 35–97
  rains and, 5, 44
Alice, 23, 105, 132, 162
All-African Convention (AAC), 187–9,
  212
amakhasmen, 182
Anderson, Benedict, 76
  on nationalism, 123–4
anthropology
  apartheid and, 110
  colonialism and, 87
apartheid, 1, 9, 20–2
  anthropology and, 110
  colonial origins of, 10, 68–87
  legacy of, 2–3, 30–1, 220–330
  policies of, 3, 25–7, 145–64
  torture and, 1, 208
  see also authoritarianism; instrumental
    rationality
authoritarianism, 10, 27
  beginnings of, 28, 87–98
  see also apartheid; instrumental
    rationality; segregation
authority,
  precolonial nature of, 39–57
autochthon, 47
  agriculture and, 47–8
  chiefship and, 47–50
  see also San
Azanian People's Liberation Army (APLA),
  115

Bantu Authorities Act (1951), 9, 27, 87, 109,
  145, 157, 176, 178
Bantu Authorities system, 109, 149–60
Bantu Laws Amendment Act (1952), 87, 109,
  145, 157
Bantu Self-Government Act (1959), 145
Bantustans, 115, 148, 218, 220
  see also apartheid; Bantu Authorities system
baptism, 119, 125, 133–5
Bartle Frere, High Commissioner Sir, 19, 92
Basotho, 118
Basuto Gun War (1880–1), 35–7
Basutoland, 51, 58
betterment, 21, 26, 27, 76, 78, 105, 108, 145,
  146, 152, 159–65, 180
  see also apartheid
Betterment Act (1939), 21, 26, 76, 157
Bhaca, 47, 49, 52
biopower, 9–10
Birth and Death Registration Act (1896), 80,
  103
Bizana, 23, 155, 194–8
black nation, 120
  emergence of, 121–44
  relationship to elite nationalism, 141–4
  social health and, 121–2, 125, 130–1
Bomvana, 55–6, 91–2
boundaries, 8, 17
  apartheid, 150–2
  colonial, 17, 71–8
  post-apartheid, 31, 220
  precolonial, 50–2
British Kaffararia, 14
Bulhoek massacre, 117–21
Bunga, 142, 149, 152
bureaucratic rationality, 9, 86, 228
  see also rationality
bureaucratization, 10
  process of, 68–112
bureaucrats, 8, 13, 26, 68–9, 71, 146
Buthelezi, Wellington, 138–41
  see also Nonthetha

294